Administrative Culture in a Global Context

Administrative Culture in a Global Context

EDITED BY

JOSEPH G. JABBRA
AND
O.P. DWIVEDI

CANADIAN CATALOGUING IN PUBLICATION DATA

Administrative Culture in a Global Context
Joseph G. Jabbra and O.P. Dwivedi

ISBN 1-897160-15-1

© Editorial matter and organization, Joseph G. Jabbra and O.P. Dwivedi, 2005
© The chapters their several authors, 2005.

All rights are reserved. No part of this publication may be reproduced, translated, stored in a retrieval system, or transmitted in any form or by any means, electronic, mechanical, photocopying, recording or otherwise, without prior written permission from the publisher.

Authorization to photocopy items for internal or personal use is granted by the publisher provided that the appropriate fees are paid directly to de Sitter Publications. Fees are subject to change.

Cover design: de Sitter Publications.
Front cover: Image © by Verna Bice.

de Sitter Publications
104 Consumers Dr.
Whitby, ON
L1N 1C4, Canada

www.desitterpublications.com

Contents

ABOUT THE AUTHORS.. vii

INTRODUCTION
THE GLOBALIZATION OF OUR WORLD: CHALLENGES
FOR ADMINISTRATIVE CULTURE
    JOSEPH G. JABBRA AND O. P. DWIVEDI.. 1

CHAPTER 1
ADMINISTRATIVE CULTURE AND VALUES: APPROACHES
    O. P. DWIVEDI.. 19

CHAPTER 2
AMERICAN ADMINISTRATIVE CULTURE: AN
EVOLUTIONARY PERSPECTIVE
    KEITH M. HENDERSON.. 37

CHAPTER 3
TOWARDS A MANAGERIAL CULTURE: THE BRITISH
CIVIL SERVICE EXPERIENCE
    JOHN GREENWOOD AND LYNTON ROBINS................................. 58

CHAPTER 4
THE NEW ADMINISTRATIVE CULTURES AS THEY RELATE
TO THE CITIZEN: COMPARATIVE STUDY OF BELGIUM,
FRANCE, AND THE EUROPEAN INSTITUTIONS
    MARIE-JOSÉ CHIDIAC... 75

CHAPTER 5
ADMINISTRATIVE CULTURE IN A BORDERLESS WORLD: RUSSIA
    ANATOLY ZHUPLEV AND VLADIMIR I. SHEIN............................. 109

CHAPTER 6
ADMINISTRATIVE CULTURE IN THE MIDDLE EAST: THE CASE
OF THE ARAB WORLD
    JOSEPH G. JABBRA AND NANCY W. JABBRA............................... 135

CHAPTER 7
NATIONAL CULTURE, CORRUPTION, AND GOVERNANCE IN PAKISTAN
      NASIR ISLAM 154

CHAPTER 8
WHITHER CHINA'S ADMINISTRATIVE CULTURE IN THE TWENTY-FIRST CENTURY?
      STEPHEN K. MA 174

CHAPTER 9
PUBLIC SERVICE REFORMS AND THE NEW PARTNERSHIP
ON AFRICAN DEVELOPMENT (NEPAD): MOVING FROM
TACTICAL TO STRATEGIC RESPONSES
      BAMIDELE OLOWU AND EJEVIOME ELOHO OTOBO 189

CHAPTER 10
RECONSTRUCTING SOUTH AFRICAN ADMINISTRATIVE CULTURE:
FROM APARTHEID TO UBUNTU ORIENTED ADMINISTRATIVE CULTURE
      LONDOLOZA L. LUVUNO 207

CHAPTER 11
THE CULTURE OF DISTRUST IN LATIN AMERICAN PUBLIC ADMINISTRATION
      JORGE NEF 232

CHAPTER 12
ARE ADMINISTRATIVE CULTURES THAT DIFFERENT?
      GERALD E. CAIDEN 246

CHAPTER 13
GOOD GOVERNANCE IN A MULTICULTURAL WORLD: OCEANS
APART, YET WORLD TOGETHER
      O. P. DWIVEDI 265

INDEX 285

About the Authors

Gerald Caiden, a native of London, England, graduated from the London School of Economics and Political Science, and has served on the faculties of the University of London (1957-1959), Carleton University (1959-1960), The Australian National University (1961-1966), The Hebrew University (1966-1968), University of California, Berkeley (1968-1971), Haifa University (1971-1975), and The University of Southern California (1975 to present). He has published over thirty books and monographs and over two hundred and sixty journal articles, and has acted as editorial consultant to several leading journals in the field of public administration and as a reader for notable publishing houses. He has acted as consultant, researcher, and administrator of a wide variety of public organizations ranging from the World Bank and the United Nations Organization to local authorities and public utilities. He is known best for his research in administrative and public service reform, corruption and administrative ethics, and administrative culture and organizational diagnosis.

Marie-José Chidiac is a Doctor of Law at the University of Liège (Belgium), a senior Lecturer with the Namur Law Faculty and is the First Adviser to the Mediator of the Walloon Region. She has authored a book on constitutional rights, *Notions de droit constitutionnel* (Notions of Constitutional Law), numerous articles of public law, and the academic syllabus. "Les médiateurs, l'action administrative et l' éthique des services publics" (Mediators, Administrative Action and the Ethic of Public Services. She is has been a guest speaker at the Institut des Affaires Publiques in Charleroi. From 1989 to 1995 Dr. Chidiac provided legal council to the Walloon Region. As editor of law proposals and decrees, she helped prepare the law of regional ombudsman that inspired the federal ombudsman law in Belgium. Dr. Chidiac served as regional Ombudsman from 1996 to1997 and has written numerous articles on the role of the Ombudsman. A consultant to political decision-makers on issues of public management, Dr. Chidiac has contributed in particular towards the improvement of dialogue with citizens.

O.P. Dwivedi, Ph.D., LL.D. (Hon), Fellow of the Royal Society (Canada), is Professor Emeritus, Department of Political Science, University of Guelph, Guelph, Canada where he taught since 1967. His specializes in comparative public administration, public service ethics, development administration, and environmental policy/law. A past president of the Canadian Political Science Association (Ottawa), a former president of the Canadian Asian Studies Association (Montreal), and a past Vice President of the International Association of Schools and Institutes of Administration (Brussels, Belgium), he has written, co-authored and edited 31 books and over 100 articles and chapters in scholarly publications. He has been consultant with the World Bank, UNESCO, WHO, UNO, UNESCAP,

CIDA, and IDRC; and served as a member of environmental tribunal with the Government of Ontario, Toronto, Canada.

Keith M. Henderson is Professor of Political Science at the State University of New York at Buffalo and a former Department Chair. He previously was Associate Professor of Public Administration at the Wagner School for Public Service, New York University (the Graduate School of Public Administration at the time). He has also taught overseas, most recently on a Senior Fulbright grant at the School of Law, University of Rijeka, Croatia. He has published widely in the area of Comparative Public Administration and has worked in local government administration for the City of Los Angeles.

Nasir Islam is an Adjunct Professor of Public Policy & Management at the University of Ottawa. He took his Master's degree in Political Science at the Punjab University, standing first and winning the Sir Tej Bahadur Supro Gold Medal. He took his MPA and a Doctorate in Public Administration at the University of Southern California. His Doctoral thesis focused on a comparative analysis of administrative systems in Ghana, Nigeria, India and Pakistan and was published by the International Public Administration Center. In his early career, he worked for International Labor Office at Geneva and the Citibank of New York. He taught Public Administration at Université Laval and served as Chair at the Department of Political Science. He served as Assistant Dean (Graduate Programs) and Director (MBA program) at the Faculty of Administration at University of Ottawa, where he also served as the Chairman of the Department of Public Administration. He was promoted to the rank of a Full Professor in 1991. Occasionally, he has worked as a consultant to IDRC, CIDA, the UNDP, the Commonwealth Secretariat, the Canadian Foreign Service Institute and the Government of Pakistan. He has been a Visiting Professor at Cornell University's International Study Center, University of Sri Jaywardenepura in Sri Lanka and l'Institut National de Gestion et Affaires Internationales of Haiti's National University. His work has been published in major international and national journals, including *International Review of Administrative Sciences, Canadian Public Administration, Public Administration & Development, International Journal of Middle Eastern Studies, Canadian Journal of Development Studies, International Journal, Canadian Review of Studies in Nationalism, Etudes Internationales, Gestion: La Revue Internationale and International Perspectives*. Recently his work has been focused on governance, institutional development, inter-cultural management. In 2003, the International Association of Schools and Institutes of Public Administration conferred on him their prestigious Pierre de Celles Award for Excellence.

Professor Islam occasionally provides cross cultural briefing sessions to the Canadian experts going to Pakistan and other South Asian countries for working on CIDA projects. He has been involved in major mid career training programs for middle and top level public managers from developing countries. He was Co-ordinator of the prestigious Pearson Fellowship Program of the IDRC and the Top Management Training Program of the Commonwealth Secretariat in cooperation with the Indian Institute of Management at Ahmedabad. For several years he taught a course at the Canadian Foreign Service Institute on Ottawa Policy Arena. He is often called upon by various TV and Radio programs to comment on Indo –Pak Relations and South Asian Politics.

Following politics in South Asia, particularly Pakistan is his passionate hobby. Another hobby he enjoys is traveling to Italy and France, exploring renaissance art and architecture.

Joseph G. Jabbra received his Licence en droit from the Université St. Joseph and his Ph.D. in political science from the Catholic University of America. He is President of the Lebanese American University in Beirut and Byblos, Lebanon. Previous to that he served as Academic Vice President of Loyola Marymount University in Los Angeles, California, and as Vice President, Academic and Research, at St. Mary's University in Halifax, Nova Scotia.

He is the author or co-author of ten books. He has also published thirty scholarly articles and book chapters, more than twenty-six book reviews in both English and French, and delivered numerous conference papers and keynote addresses. Dr. Jabbra belongs to fifteen professional societies.

Nancy W. Jabbra is an anthropologist, and Professor and Chair of Women's Studies at Loyola Marymount University in Los Angeles, California. Before coming to Loyola Marymount, she was Associate Professor of Social Anthropology in the Department of Sociology and Social Anthropology at Dalhousie University in Halifax, Nova Scotia. She also served as Director of the International Development Studies Programme and the Interdisciplinary Centre at Dalhousie University, and as President of the Canadian Ethnic Studies Association.

She is the author or co-author of numerous publications on gender roles in Lebanon and other Middle Eastern countries, gender and development, ethnic groups in Canada and the United States, politics and government in Lebanon, and environmental issues in Lebanon.

Londoloza L. Luvuno is a Senior Lecturer in the Department of Public Management at the University of the Free State, South Africa. He was born in Cumakala, a rural area near Stutterheim in the Eastern Cape Province. He obtained his junior degree from the University of the Western Cape and completed his Masters and Ph.D. studies in Public Management at the University of the Free State. He was a fellow of the much sought after Andrew W. Mellon scholarship. He tutored and lectured in Public Administration/Management for 11 years and presented international papers in Athens, Greece; Istanbul, Turkey; Miami, USA; and Seoul, South Korea.

Prof. Luvuno specializes in Public Sector Management Techniques, such as Information Technologies (IT), System Analysis (SA), Management by Results (MBR), Strategic Public Management (SPM), Social Benefit Analysis (SBA), Service Quality Management (TQM), Public Project Management (PPM), Programme Budgeting Systems (PBS), Cost Performance Improvement (CPI),

Workload Analysis (WA), Time Management (TM) and Performance Management Systems (PMS); Executive Public Management (both State and Municipal Management); Organizational Analysis and Development; Public Policy Management; Administrative Culture; Research Methodology; and Training of the Trainers.

Stephen K. Ma, Professor of Political Science, is Director of the Institute for Executive Leadership at California State University, Los Angeles. He is the author of *Administrative Reform in Post-Mao China: Efficiency or Ethics?* (University Press of America 1996) and *US Civil Service and Ethical Codes* (in Chinese) (Tsinghua University Press 1999). His research articles have appeared in *Pacific Affairs, Asian Survey, Journal of Contemporary China, Chinese Public Administration, Asian Journal of Political Science, International Journal of Public Administration, Policy Studies Review*. He has contributed to *Handbook of Economic Development* (1998), *Administrative Reform and National Economic Development* (2000), and *Where Corruption Lives* (2001).

Jorge Nef is Professor of Latin American, Caribbean and Latino Studies, and Political Science at the University of South Florida (USF) in Tampa and has been Professor of Politics, International Development and Rural Extension Studies at the University of Guelph. A graduate of the University of Chile and a Ph.D. in Political Science (UCSB), he has been a Visiting Professor in many Canadian and foreign universities and institutes. He has done work in a wide array of subjects —development, democratization, administrative reform, international relations, technology, food security, ethics, violence, and human rights. He has been Vice President of the Chilean College of Public Administrators and President of the Canadian Association of Latin American and Caribbean Studies (CALACS), and the recipient of numerous teaching awards.

He has written over a dozen books and monographs, and edited collections, while contributing over one hundred articles to refereed journals, edited books and to other national and international publications. His book *Human Security and Mutual Vulnerability* appeared in 1999. He has worked with national and international development agencies in Latin America and the Pacific. He has been the Director of the School of Government, Public Administration and Political Science at the University of Chile and is currently the Director of Latin American, Caribbean and Latino Studies at USF.

Bamidele Olowu was educated at the Universities of Ibadan and Ile-Ife in Nigeria (1971-79); University of Birmingham, England (1978); and received a post-doctorate at Indiana University, Indiana, USA (1985-87).

He was Professor and Head of Local Government and Public Administration at Obafemi Awolowo University, Ile-Ife, Nigeria (1991-1996); Director of Research at the National Commission on Intergovernmental Relations; Presidency, Federal Government, Nigeria (1992-3); Adviser on Governance and Capacity Building, United Nations Economic Commission for Africa, Addis

Ababa, Ethiopia (1995-8); Convenor, Governance, Democratisation & Public Policy Programme at Institute of Social Studies, The Hague, Netherlands (2001-4); Member of the Board of European Centre for Development Policy & Management, Maastricht, Netherlands (1999-Present);
Member of Evaluation Commission, African Studies Center, Leiden University, Netherlands (2004); and Advisory Board member for journals such as *African Administrative Studies* (Tangier, Morocco).

Previous Publications include the following books: *The Failure of the Centralized State* (Westview Press 1990, with J.Wunsch), *Indigenous Governance Systems in Nigeria* (edited with John Erero, 1997); *African Perspectives on Governance* (with G. Hyden, W. Okoth-Ogendo, Trenton Press 2000); *Better Governance and Public Policy* (edited with S. Sako, Kumarian Press 2002) and *Local Governance in Africa: The Challenges of Democratic Decentralization* (Lynne Rienner Publishers 2004, also with J. Wunsch).

Dr. Olowu has published over 100 articles in refereed journals and books. He has served as editor for *Quarterly Journal of Administration* (Ile-Ife, Nigeria, 1988-92); Guest Editor for *Planning and Administration* (1987)—Special issue on "African Local Governments"; *International Political Science Review* (with O.P. Dwivedi, 1988)—special issue on "Ethics in Public Service," *Public Administration and Development* (with Paul Smoke, 1992) –"Successes in African Local Governments" and *African Development* (2002) –special issue on "New Public Management in Africa."

Ejeviome Eloho Otobo is Chief of Policy Analysis and Monitoring Unit in the Office of the Special Adviser on Africa at the United Nations headquarters in New York. His areas of research interest are business-government relations, public management, institutional reforms, economic governance and corporate governance. Some of his most recent book chapters have appeared in *African Development and Governance Strategies in the 21st Century* (Zed Publishers London 2003); *Better Governance and Public Policy: Capacity Building and Democratic Renewal in Africa* (Kumarian Press 2002); and *Public Administration in Africa: Main Issues and Selected Country Studies* (Westview Press 1999). His articles have been published in a number of scholarly journals and policy bulletins. He was a contributor to the 2001 African Development Bank's Report devoted to the theme of *Fostering Good Governance in Africa*.

Lynton Robins is Coordinator for Public Policy at De Montfort University, UK, and a Fellow of the Politics Association. He was a Fairbridge Scholar and completed doctoral research at the University of Southampton, UK. He is a former editor of *Talking Politics*, the journal of the Politics Association. His books include *Contemporary British Politics* (Palgrave Macmillan), *British Politics Since the War* (Macmillan), *Debates in British Politics Today* (Manchester University Press), *United Kingdom Governance* (Macmillan), *Britain's Changing Party System* (Leicester University Press), *Public Policy Under Thatcher* (Macmillan), *Introducing Political Science* (Longman), *The American Way*

(Longman) and *Political Institutions in Britain* (Longman). Together with Professor John Greenwood, he is a project director of an IASIA working group which has published findings on global public administration education.

Vladimir I. Shein serves as Director at the Center for Leadership Training, the Academy of National Economy under the Government of the Russian Federation (Moscow, Russia). Throughout his career he held affiliated and independent positions as a research fellow, a management consultant, an educator, and an administrator in institutions and government agencies in Russia and abroad. His publications include more than 60 articles, eight books and brochures on corporate governance, privatization, management, market reforms, and personnel. He earned his Ph.D. in 1967 from the Institute of Precise Mechanics and Computers in Moscow, and his B.S. in 1959 from the Bashkirsky State University in Ufa.

Anatoly Zhuplev is a Professor of International Business at Loyola Marymount University (Los Angeles, California). He taught for ten years at the Moscow Management Institute, and subsequently at the Advanced Training Institute of the State Committee for Printing and Publishing in Moscow; in Bonn, Germany; and at Northeastern University in Boston. His books and articles on International Management, International Entrepreneurship, International Business, and Corporate Governance have been published in the U.S., Western Europe, Russia, and the former USSR. He received his Ph.D. from the Moscow Management Institute, Russia, in 1981, and his B.S. from the Moscow Engineer-Economics Institute in 1974.

Introduction

THE GLOBALIZATION OF OUR WORLD: CHALLENGES FOR ADMINISTRATIVE CULTURE

Joseph G. Jabbra and O. P. Dwivedi

I. Globalization: An Introduction

Globalization reflects an interdependent state of the world and points to how events, issues, and challenges in one part of the globe affect other parts. Contrary to popular perception, globalization is not new. The first globalization wave took place under the Roman Empire and spread to what is now known as the Middle East. The second globalization wave began in 1870 under the British Empire and ended with the independence of India in 1947, although some historians think that it ended around World War I (Baldwin and Martin 1999). The third globalization wave may have begun after World War II, and certainly gained momentum in the late 1980s with the collapse of the Soviet Union, the end of the Cold War era, and the emergence of the United States as a hegemonic power. Since the 1990s, the world has been living in the unique polar phase of the third globalization wave (Milanovic 1999).

A number of important and common features characterized globalization under the Roman and British empires: communities speaking different languages, consisting of many ethnicities and races, professing a variety of faiths, exhibiting numerous cultural and economic systems, free trade and exchange of goods and services, all inextricably tied to and guided by a powerful hegemon, at least for a significant period of time. These common features of globalization have been pointedly accentuated under the hegemonic power of the United States, particularly since the 1990s, and with special emphasis on technology, trade and investment, new and lucrative markets, and aggressive and innovative American strategic managerial expertise. However, the phenomenon of globalization has sharply divided its advocates and detractors. While globalization means different things to different people, the debate about its significance continues to be emotionally charged and intellectually vigorous. In this introductory chapter, we propose to provide a functional definition of globalization, a brief description of the positions adopted by its proponents and opponents, a summary of the Chapters included in the book, and a conclusion summarizing our findings and pointing to new, important, and challenging research areas.

Definition

No definition can do justice to globalization (for a variety of definitions see Kiggundu 2002:3-6). However, to help us understand the forces unleashed by globalization and their impact on administrative cultures, we propose to define it as an integrative process pushing the world toward greater interdependence and setting free in its wake colliding administrative, socioeconomic, cultural, political, ideological, and technological changes. Both scholars and practitioners of public administration in the countries of the North as well as in those of the South have interpreted these changes differently.

Advocates of Globalization

In his book, *The Lexus and the Olive Tree: Understanding Globalization*, Thomas Friedman (2000) believes that globalization is inevitable and it is here to stay. In his view, it enables "individuals, corporations and nation-states to reach around the world farther, faster, deeper and cheaper than ever before," and, in a way, it empowers "the world to reach into individuals, corporations and nation-states, farther, faster, deeper, cheaper than ever before" (pp.145-46). Most advocates of globalization firmly believe that globalization, whether it is a new, old, or familiar phenomenon, is creating positive advantages for all those who are willing to engage and accept it. In *Understanding Globalization* Robert K. Schaeffer (2003:2-3), reflecting an emerging consensus among advocates of globalization, points to five advantageous developments caused by globalization: the growth and spread of investment, capital, and financial services; the expansion of free trade and production, with businesses moving their production centers around the globe where new locations might give them a competitive advantage; the technological revolution, which continues to draw the different parts of the world ever closer together and give globalization unstoppable momentum; and an inexorable democratizing process that has contributed dramatically to the collapse of communist and other dictatorships the world over.

It is clear that advocates of globalization believe that both countries of the South and of the North welcome globalization because they see in it a solution to some of their most pressing problems, ranging from more jobs to better standards of living, from a divided to a collaborative world, and from a poor to a prosperous world (Gilpin 2000:170). They also argue that while in the beginning globalization may cause some disruptions and dislocations, ultimately, it will pay off handsomely (Schaeffer 2003:7). Further, they claim that United Nations officials are convinced that globalization has begun to open doors of opportunity for the inhabitants of the global village (United Nations Development Program Report 1999:341).

Opponents of Globalization

Despite its actual benefits and its potential for improving the human condition, globalization has many articulate and vociferous opponents. Some prominent world leaders have, at times, expressed doubt about both the actual and potential benefits of globalization. In his *Search for Global Order: The Problems of Survival* (1992), Hans d'Orville lists a number of prominent people such as Pope John Paul II, Nelson Mandela, and Mikhail Gorbachev, whose questioning of the ethical and moral foundations of globalization strengthened the protesters' opposition in Seattle, Gothenberg, Washington, and Genoa. Furthermore, unskilled workers and trade unionists in the countries of the North are also opposed to globalization, because technology, globalization's main driving engine, has made jobs for unskilled workers difficult to obtain, especially in times of economic downturns. Moreover, because of the advances in technology and in the means of communication and transportation, trade unions in the industrialized countries also fear that their members might lose jobs to emerging economies where there is a surplus of cheap and available labor and to where multinational corporations can easily move their factories and other means of production and services. Further, trade unions are concerned that as globalization creates liberalized trade and relaxed immigration laws, their membership will be at a distinct disadvantage competing with foreign cheap labor moving with ease from the South into the industrialized countries of the North; and both cheap labor and international competition may lead to layoffs and/or rolling back of the salaries of their membership (Kiggundu 2002:13-14).

For the same reasons, farmers in the industrialized countries are opposed to globalization. Governments in the United States, Canada, Western Europe, and Japan subsidize their farmers at the rate of one billion dollars a day. The World Trade Organization requires that subsidies be abolished and import of agricultural staples be allowed into the industrialized countries from the third and fourth worlds. Moreover, countries of the South argue that the enormous government subsidies that farmers in the industrialized world receive are eliminating any competitive advantage their farmers might have and contributing to the abject poverty of their citizens. According to Kiggundu (2002:14), farmers in the industrialized countries are using their powerful lobbying practices to stop their governments from abolishing the subsidies they receive because they give them a significant competitive advantage in world markets.

Environmentalists have attacked globalization because in their judgment it will ultimately threaten the planet's ecosystems. They argue that the world is already grappling with such important environmental challenges (global warming, water and air pollution, acid rain, and social inequality), which are causing serious international concerns about the viability of the planet and the human species (Arrighi 2000:129). Other critics maintain that globalization is not inevitable, as advanced by Friedman (2000) and Greider (1997), because the socioeconomic, political, cultural, economic, and financial forces it unleashes can create chaos in the international system and cause national systems to fail. The influential international financier, George Soros, has already warned us against the excesses of uncontrolled globalization, and the major economic collapse of the economies of Thailand, Russia, Indonesia and Mexico, in the 1990s, seriously threatened the viability of the international economic system (Schaeffer 2003:12).

A significant number of countries in the third and fourth worlds are opposed to globalization as well. They are poor; they have a weak infrastructure and weak financial institutions; they don't have capital, and they feel vulnerable and unable to be active participants in the process of globalization. Because of these handicaps, they feel that globalization will add to their marginalization on the world stage and increase their poverty. Moreover, citizens in these countries also fear that the traditions and practices that keep them connected and together will be laid bare and eventually eroded by globalization and its relentless pressure for standardization and homogeneity. In fact, globalization's harshest critics attack the negative consequences of homogeneity arguing that globalization and its instruments are disrupting the lives of families and tribes, local traditions and communities, linguistic practices, and cultural life, eliminating choice and diversity, and setting up, in their place, greedy monopolies (Schaeffer 2003:11). Their worst fear is that a large number of people in the poor countries may not benefit from globalization and, at the same time, because of globalization, lose their primordial ties and cultural traditions that give them strength and solace in their dire poverty. Further, the opponents of globalization fear that whatever natural resources poor countries might have, those resources will ultimately be exploited by outside economic and corporate forces, enriching only a small number of local elites who will deposit their profits in Suisse bank accounts with no benefits accruing to the indigenous citizenry.

Robert K. Schaeffer (2003:3-4) adds three more criticisms of globalization: first, feminists argue that globalization through the rise of manufacturing pockets, the tourist industry and other service industries, and the movement of labor and soldiers across the globe have contributed significantly to the sexual and labor (the rise of sweatshops) exploitation of women; second, the international and regional agreements produced by globalization have seriously limited the sovereignty of the nation state and affected the poor countries of the South negatively; finally, the forces of globalization continue to create tribal, national, regional, religious, and international dislocations, producing, in their wake, inexcusable violence and unnecessary hunger and deprivation.

Middle of the Road Approach

On the basis of our readings about globalization, we have concluded that a middle of the road approach to understanding its multifaceted impact is more productive than either of the two opposite positions advocated by its proponents and opponents. While John F. Helliwell (2002:77) acknowledges that some actual and significant benefits can derive from globalization, he warns us against the exaggerated hype that surrounds its potential advantages. And, while Don Kalb recognizes that globalization may benefit some people, he cautions against turning it into *globalism*, an ideology of free market neoliberalism that "preaches the absolute truth and desirability of unregulated global capitalism" (Kalb 2000:4). That is why Kiggundu (2002:18-23) and Soros (1998:96-97) speak so cogently about the necessity to strive toward a joint effort between the rich centers of the North and the poor periphery of the South to balance the availability of resources needed to promote globalization and the benefits that ensue from it, without destroying wholesale the indigenous and valuable traditions that bind communities together. Only with a genuine effort to reach that balance will globalization be legitimized and begin to pay handsome dividends to both the center and the periphery. Without that balance, globalization will be doomed to failure, further complicating the already tenuous and strained relationship between the have and have not countries.

Globalization and Governance

The forces of globalization and their consequences stem from, and collide with, international and national systems of governments. Moreover, a country is likely to benefit more from globalization if it has an effective governance system in place. Although governance, like globalization, is difficult to define, we can, however, point to a number of constituent elements that concretize the concept of governance and determine its effectiveness, such as values, institutions, laws, and policies, which are used by a society to govern itself and manage its relationship with NGOs (civil society), the private sector, and with other societies. It is "the framework of rules, institutions and practices that set limits and provide incentives for individuals, organizations and businesses" (Cheema 2000:6-7). And so, in this context,

"…globalization needs good governance. Only the state can provide the necessary leadership for good governance. Therefore, globalization, good governance, and the state are inextricably connected" (Kiggundu 2002:29). It is in this sense that globalization can be a positive force in nation building and in making sure that efficiency, effectiveness, and accountability in the governmental and administrative processes are paramount. Moreover, globalization can contribute significantly to good governance by applying pressure on national governments to revisit, assess, and rectify the dysfunctional forces that threaten the very foundation of their systems of governance, or their abilities to build effective systems. According to Kiggundu (2002:32), if managed well, the interplay between globalization and good governance can become a transformative process providing the countries of the world with stabilization through effective public security, economic management, and public administration; a shared system of values through core public and private sector institutions; and a capacity to develop, within an indigenous framework, a civil society governed by democratic institutions and practices.

II. Challenges for the Globalization of our World

Globalization during the twenty-first century is somewhat different than Britannia ruling the waves and boasting that their empire was the best thing that ever happened to world safety and security. Essentially, what makes a world-class globalization stronger is its political power supported by technology, economic wealth, and a solid demographic base. Drawing upon the previous arguments, we will now consider the challenges that the third wave of globalization has created.

Americanization as a Dominant World Culture

Though there has emerged a dominant culture sometimes called the Americanization of our global village through food-chains such as McDonald's and Burger King, Hollywood films, music, Levi jeans, the corporate America, information technology, and dominant scientific research and discoveries, all eliciting from, and by, the United States. Despite such overwhelming acculturation, people are trying to preserve and strengthen their diversity of ideas and cultures, the languages and customs, different values and beliefs, and the style of doing things differently. It should be noted that, cultural homogeneity, unlike economic integration, is not good because when people lose their culture, they lose their identity and heritage. It is important that Americans, as world leaders, encourage unity in cultural diversity. Moreover, a crucial test in being a socially just global power is how to help in the eradication of poverty worldwide. Historically, we already know that the Second Globalization (because of the British Empire during the nineteenth century and the earlier part of the twentieth century) produced a massive increase in world inequality. For example, during the nineteenth century, the increased wealth of Western Europe coincided with growing poverty and deprivation in the non-white colonies, Asia in particular. Poverty and concomitant famines in British India were the result of imperial taxation policies. Thus, the challenge for the United States and for the Third Globalization is the expectation, all over the world, that wealth will be shared by all and that destitute will be taken care of beyond the immediate borders of the United States.

The NPM as a Globalizing Paradigm

It was in the early 1980s that a New Public Management (NPM) movement was launched in the West to solve the financial problems that beset those governments. The various versions of the welfare state seemed too expensive. The Keynesian economics on which they were based were discredited because politicians had taken to running systematic deficits in order to finance government programs. There were also reactions to public sector unions, strikes, and the rigid bureaucracy that came from combining big government with collective agreements. Finally, the 1980s were a time when conservative ideologies experienced a revival. The election of Margaret Thatcher in Britain and Ronald Reagan in the United States gave powerful support to the New Public Management movement with its accent on results, greater attention to cost, and the use of private sector approaches to motivate employees (Dwivedi and Gow 1999:130). This paradigm is based on the premise that by reducing the opportunities for incompetence and corruption through the narrowing of the scope of government activities, efficient, transparent, effective, and accountable governance would appear. The rationale is that with less bureaucratic structures there would be fewer bureaucratic problems. Once more, heavy emphasis was placed on the objective criteria of responsibility and accountability with a blind faith on structures, processes, and procedures, but with total disregard for the moral (or subjective) dimension. Developing nations are being urged to have market-friendly governance and administration. Because the field of development administration is posited more as a problem than a solution, New Public Management, in the garb of "development management," is recommended as a "cure-all." International aid is being made conditional upon accepting this prescription. It includes shrinking the bureaucracy, eliminating subsidies and protectionism, accepting currency devaluation, and other changes in monetary and fiscal policy (Dwivedi 1994).

NPM as a movement still survives, at least in developing nations. Some Asian nations are still trying hard to implement the NPM philosophy although the movement in the West has already become a spent force. For example, in China, down-sizing was one of the main aims of the 1998 public sector reforms with a number of positions of administrative heads being cut, retraining programs introduced for a number of cadres, and regrouping of some ministries and state corporations. Nevertheless, according to Drewry and Chan (2001): "no one has been left unemployed…So, there is no real 'lay-off' of staff. Sooner or later, cadres affected by the restructuring find themselves once more in government-funded positions" (p.466). Take another example from India: while the federal and state governments have initiated a number of privatization plans of their public sector industrial units, labor unrest and the use of public interest litigation have forced governments to take a step backwards. Thus, privatization is not moving as fast as the government wants. Another example is the report of India's Fifth Pay Commission in the late 1990s, which recommended a streamlining of pay scale, increasing it many fold but suggesting that such a pay increase should be accompanied by a reduction in the number of positions and employees, and a revamped system of accountability. While the pay increase (including the two-year increase in the age of retirement) was immediately implemented (retroactively), no downsizing has taken place. It seems that the dismantling of structures and reducing bureaucracy is still a most difficult challenge, although the positives associated with NPM reforms are easily accepted.

Impact of Globalization on the Public Administration of the South

Development administration as an academic field has been the handmaiden of Western comparative public administration. It has not yet succeeded in breaking loose from its old moorings because it still presses for Northern, universalistic designs tied to a single, competitive and capitalistic world economy. For example, details of administrative structure; procedural and financial accountability; human-resources management; central-local relationships; organization of ministries or departments; the role of parastatals; linkages with civil society and grassroots groups for purposes of licensing; permitting and regulation; and recruitment/ socialization mechanisms; all these are based on a system perfected in the North. Sometimes, lonely voices in the development community call for realizable change from the bottom up, and suggest that it would be desirable if the North could use many ideas from different sources in the South to enrich its own disciplines of public administration and development administration by including sensitivity to the local customs, indigenous culture, as well as spirituality; thereby bridging the gap between North and South by drawing a new course more holistic and multicultural.

It is now acknowledged even in the West that such an imitative system has not worked well. What could be the reason? O.P. Dwivedi (2003) offers the following explanations:

(A) For years, the Western scholars have been unable to include the alternatives in the form of non-Western contributions to developmental studies. They ought to appreciate the importance of indigenous culture, traditions, and style of governance, and administrative cultures that reflect the distinctiveness and complexity of various national identities, realities, and cultural diversities. These factors must be taken into consideration when public service reforms and aid-related conditionalities are being imposed. For example, we do know that in Asian and other developing nations, the nature of public expectations from their governments is basically different from that prevailing in the West, despite the fact that demands on the public sector to provide more services are growing while the state apparatus in these nations is being forced to shrink and retreat. Thus, it is counterproductive to force debureaucratization and privatization in the South, especially to compel these nations to follow the costly fads prevailing in the industrialized nations.

(B) We also know that the outer layer of these nations' style of governance is directly affected by current circumstances and global challenges. Any profound administrative reform entails significant attitudinal and value changes that are based on local culture and traditions. Thus, efforts at administrative restructuring, "modernization," and bringing other types of reforms in the South must address first, either directly or indirectly, the question of the indigenous style, values, and culture of governance.

(C) If we take the premise that a country's culture and style of governance are the key to the understanding of what makes a country function, it is imperative that any public sector reform forced upon on developing nations draws on the local customs, culture, and traditions, especially with respect to Asian countries that can draw on their centuries of administrative and cultural heritage. Because, when the local culture and traditions are discarded in the favor of Western-style management practices, and when there is not enough time given to these nations to see if such a transplantation has already taken root in the body politic, a hodge-podge of two value systems start operating simultaneously with no one specific standard left against which the effectiveness of the existing administrative system as well as the conduct of public officials can be measured. Instead, there is a need to develop an inclusive and multicultural mixture of alternate medicine rather than always depending on the purely mono-cultural indicators of performance measurement coming from the North.

Disrupting Indigenous Administrative Culture

The time has also come to examine the disruptive impacts of frequent public service reorganizations and reforms, as well as periodic paradigm shifts brought on by the West. We already know that it is tougher to implement reforms than to design them; and we also know that the work is not finished with implementation alone, because the danger of backsliding is always present. Without ongoing nurturing, reforms generally fade away. Thus, there is a need to get out of the apparent frenzy for many reforms so that public service institutions are able to have a breathing space to solidify gains made, and to strengthen their organizational culture. Could we not pause for some time to see what gains have been made thus far, and whether such gains are effective enough? Only thereafter, should further reforms and changes be tried. It is equally important that when international development agencies and their advisors contemplate new reforms, they consider alternatives available at the local level so that improvements are based on local circumstances, history, and culture. In addition, developing nations should undertake regular (periodic) assessments of progress made; indeed, introducing measures does not mean that these measure will adhered to or that they will, over time, remain in place. Progress ought to be regularly and consistently assessed.

A Theory of Inclusive and Multicultural Comparative Public Administration

During the past century, scholars and practitioners of public administration carried out their work as if all public administration and governance values emanating from the West were akin to general scientific principles and, thus, universally applicable; in such an equation, local context or culture did not matter. The vestiges of a one-dimensional rationalism is now slowly giving way to a fuller recognition and understanding of the impact and consequences of people's values. It is also clear that through globalization, certain dependence and continued reliance on the theory and methodology of the Western-style administration is being emphasized. Would it not be a sad situation if everywhere on the globe, not only the governing system but also the style of doing things became the mirror image of Western values and practices? Developing countries must overcome many challenges, but so, too, must the West. One thing is clear: the current crisis of development and administration is precisely a consequence of the inability of the West to incorporate the substance of other non-Western developmental experiences into the prevailing conceptual mold. It is also worth acknowledging that alternatives to Western-led reforms might have value for other nations, just as alternative medicine has finally received acceptance in the West. The success of these alternatives requires new approaches to North-South relations. The essence of this plea is the identification of the "unity in diversity principle," so that alternatives (based in the South) do not get discarded simply because they are not well argued or because they are not presented in an academic fashion. At the same time, the author is not advocating a non-involvement or a total detachment of development administration from public (and comparative) administration. Because, there *are* some core values (such as the rule of law and due process, efficiency, economy, accountability, impartiality, integrity, fairness, protecting and serving the common good, etc.) of public administration that are universal in nature and are applicable everywhere irrespective of local traditions, culture, and context. Thus, there is a need to consider a holistic approach to public administration inclusive of available alternatives.

An Outlook for the Twenty-First Century

The twentieth century has left with us some paradoxical images of our global village, especially with respect to the developing world: abject poverty amid clusters of affluence; immense unsanitary conditions versus modest, but competently clean and healthy areas; and shanty-towns set against palaces and five-star hotels. There is no doubt that these images will continue to affect many people, and those that do experience positive change in their lifetime are among the fortunate. For the poor of the Third World, however, the second millennium (which has just passed into history) is a sad reminder of many failings: the dream of a perfect society did not materialize; the concept of a just society advocated by some Western political leaders has never been realized; the promises made to the poor of third world by the West, as well as by their own leaders, were never fulfilled; the dream that opportunities were unlimited and the future was unbounded did not materialize; and the entire world benefiting from an open-ended economic liberalization and the eradication of poverty has not happened thus far. Instead, these nations had a sense of profound loss: loss of the opportunity to create a perfect world; loss of the opportunity to have lasting peace on earth; and loss of the opportunity to effect a worldwide *sarvodaya* (universal human development, progress of all people and nations together). What has continued, instead, is a series of ills such as destitution, social inequality, environmental diseases, and ecological disasters that are happening on an unprecedented scale. In our global village, peace, prosperity, and social justice are still illusions. What we need is some kind of hope for achieving the ideal of a mutually sustaining and ecologically balanced global society that supports diversity (of want, culture, religion, and lifestyle), the sharing of knowledge and technology, controlling further ecological damage, and encouraging a system of moral governance throughout the world (Dwivedi 2003).

III. About the Book

This book is comprised of thirteen chapters. Here, a brief summary of each one is provided. In his chapter, *Administrative Culture and Values: Approaches,* O. P. Dwivedi states administrative culture can best be understood as the patterns of beliefs, dispositions, values, and attitudes that identify and characterize any public or private administrative system. He adds that as nations differ in their administrative cultures, there should not be one common criterion by which these are measured, since each is unique and differs significantly from the other. For Dwivedi, culture is defined as a society's way of life "through which it views the world around it, attributes meanings and attaches significance to it, and organizes itself to preserve and eventually pass it on as its legacy to future generations". The author concludes that the diversity displayed by the administrative cultures of different nations should be protected; that what works for one country might not work for another; and that deeply valued indigenous elements should be taken into consideration if external inducements (for administrative reforms which eventually modify administrative cultures) are to be successful in improving governance.

Keith M. Henderson has written, in Chapter 2, about the U.S. administrative culture, which he defines as a set of beliefs, attitudes, and values that should characterize the behavior of appointed public servants. He adds that the United States is a unique example of how administrative culture can also reflect a nation's history and ideals. Further, Henderson claims government is meant not only as a means of carrying out political ideals, but also, and most importantly, the administrative culture of the government itself serves as a physical manifestation and example of these ideals in action. Looking back at the history of the U.S. government, patrician and patronage administrative culture have given way to a more merit-based administrative culture. Now, American values lie more in the quality of one's work and ability to do the job with the greatest effectiveness and efficiency; of course, this is done within the parameters of representing the will of the people.

In Chapter 3, which deals with managerial British culture, John Greenwood and Lynton Robins tell us that there still exist today many traces of past inefficiencies in the English system but, nonetheless, it has made significant improvement in terms of its organization, accountability, and efficiency. Of course, these improvements in Whitehall have come at a price. Many feel that the English system lacks the unity it once had. Undeniably, it is advantageous that the government has become more diversified with the benefit of better management, which has led to greater efficiency and accountability. However, this effective management of smaller agencies has eliminated the ability of a central source to effectively manage the entire government. In addition, Britain's involvement and continued integration with the European Union has also led to further challenges in central British control over its administrative system.

In analyzing the administrative culture of Belgium, France, and other European nations, Marie-José Chidiac argues in Chapter 4 that the most significant administrative changes involved becoming more accountable to the citizenry. These governments became obligated to provide formal and adequate justification for their acts. The public was empowered with the right to review, to receive an explanation, and the right to discovery: "It is public authority that draws expectations from its citizens". This quote is representative of the new spirit in which Belgian, French, and other European governments function. There is a theme of transparency that resonates with the new systems. Essentially, the above-mentioned European models successfully modernized themselves so that they would more closely resemble the efficiency, accountability, and transparency of the private sector.

In Chapter 5, *Administrative Culture in a Borderless World: Russia*, Anatoly Zhuplev and Vladimir Shein mention that Russia's distinct cultural profile, geography, history, and the mentality of its citizens and government cannot be understood by making direct comparisons with the administrative cultures of other countries. The explain that some unique features have created a series of critical factors that have had a significant impact on Russian culture and administration: Russia's sheer geographic size, centralization and authoritarian leadership, a "top-down" approach to administrative changes and reforms, and blurry and feeble mechanisms for the transfer and delegation of administrative power. Although present-day Russia displays signs of improvement in its governmental and bureaucratic structure, it is still plagued with problems.

Joseph G. Jabbra and Nancy W. Jabbra, in Chapter 6, have examined the prevailing system of administrative behavior and culture in the Arab world. For them, the puzzling factor is the inability of Arab governments to reform bureaucracy to control the poor performance of their administrative apparatus by tightening the formal control mechanisms designed to insure accountability and integrity. They reason that there are two sets of sources that are pervasive enough to influence the prevailing situation. The inherent structural and administrative sources are: over-centralization, outmoded systems, administrative expansion, overstaffing, the rigidity and complexity of rules, and salary structure; while the other sources are behavioral and social: nepotism and favoritism, patron-client relationship, corruption, laxity and avoidance of responsibility, and inadequate training of public servants. They note that these sources of administrative behavior and structural issues impose a heavy financial burden on Arab countries and hinder their economic, social, and political development. However, they hope that a coordinated implementation of suggested reforms will enable Arab governments to modify and gradually replace their current administrative culture with a more effective one that would combine the best from both the traditional and the modern systems of effective governance.

In his study on Pakistan, Nasir Islam states in Chapter 7 that although Pakistan's administrative culture has undergone progressive change since its independence, it is still plagued by many of the same problems it faced under the older system. The old system was based on rank classification, and can be understood in the same manner as the Hindu caste system. There was little opportunity for upward mobility and many positions were gained based on social status, family connections, or financial incentives. Although reforms began to take place in 1973 under Prime Minister Bhutto, Pakistan continued to experience a great deal of corruption. Sycophancy, or the institutionalized exchange of favors and flattery for rewards, the culture of Sifarish, which refers to connections or recommendations that stop just short of straight bribery, and a heightened concern for one's extended family, continue to be inherent features of the Pakistani system.

In *Whither China's Administrative Culture in the Twenty-First Century*, Chapter 8, Stephen K. Ma states that the Chinese administrative culture has inherent problems and weaknesses, which contribute to the high level of corruption within it. In recent years, high-ranking civil servants have been convicted of corruption crimes. Because of bribery and corruption, the Chinese government devised a new ethos guiding acceptable bureaucratic behavior and stressing accountability among civil servants. In addition, measures to make the government's operations more efficient were made to instill greater confidence in the general Chinese population. Although measures have been taken to curb the corruption and improve the Chinese administrative culture, it seems as though the news media has been the most effective force in challenging the government and catalyzing change.

Bamidele Olowu and Ejeviome E. Otobo, in Chapter 9, *The Objectives of The New Partnership for African Development (NEPAD)*, review and highlight the implications of the reform of African public services. They acknowledge that if African leaders want to achieve the greatest success for their respective countries and the continent as a whole, they must utilize the advantages of globalization while limiting its negative impact. They add that reforms must take place in terms of African public services and address the following challenges: a large number of low-wage civil servants, the relatively small size of African public services compared to those of other countries, coordination between and among departments, and recruitment of more motivated, talented, dedicated, and loyal public servants.

In chapter 10, *Reconstructing South African Administrative Culture: From Apartheid to Ubuntu Oriented Administrative Culture*, Londolozo Luvuno argues that prior to 1994, the apartheid system of South Africa was characterized by inefficiency and corruption. With the advent of South Africa's new administrative culture, called "Ubuntu-oriented administrative culture," positive changes have been increasing the government's overall productivity and accountability. This new approach in South Africa's government has created an atmosphere of awareness. Government managers and workers alike have developed a heightened consciousness and responsibility to the community and State, as well as their fellow workers. Several sources account for the changes in South Africa's public service: a written constitution guaranteeing that government power will not be abused, valuation of human dignity and supremacy of the rule of law, accountability, and transparency.

According to Jorge Nef, there exists a great degree of diversity among the administrative cultures of Latin American countries. Yet, they all share commonalities that make it possible to analyze their governments and public services. In Chapter 11, Nef claims that despite a shift to republican political systems modeled after French and American governmental structures, in Latin America there evolved a sharp discrepancy between the theoretical nature of the systems in place and the practices of government officials. The old practices of nepotism, patronage, particularism, and sinecures still exist despite the explicit calls for fair and representative government. The administrative systems remain highly aristocratic. The author concludes that if improvement is to be made, changes must occur not only in the political structure of government, but also in the ideologies and social consciousness with which the Latin American ruling class approach economic and social concerns.

In Chapter 12, Gerald Caiden argues that despite the unmistakable influences of globalization, administrative cultures nonetheless differ from one another in specific ways and for specific reasons. Entitled *Are Administrative Cultures that Different?* Caiden's article highlights the distinguishing features among the administrative cultures of countries like Canada, the U.K., Australia, and Israel. He adds that the perceived character of a country's administrative culture is shaped by how one has been bred, where one stands, with whom one comes into contact, and what position one holds. However, Professor Caiden also explains that the influences of globalization on the distinct cultural identities of different administrative cultures cannot be ignored. Unless "regional variations are exaggerated...and deliberately widened as international alliances shift," the contrasting distinctions of different administrative cultures will be diminished in the future. Just as the distinct differences between public and private organizations have weakened over the last fifty years, the same fate will apply to the differences among different administrative cultures if the present trend continues.

Finally, in the concluding Chapter of this book, O.P. Dwivedi writes about *Good Governance in a Multicultural World: Oceans Apart, Yet World Together.* He states that the word governance replaced government in the 1980s to suggest a greater scope in responsibility, accountability, efficiency, citizens' needs, and the ability to protect citizens' basic rights. He argues that it is impossible to apply a single framework or model for judging whether or not a government is displaying good administration. Good governance displays public participation, rule of law, transparency, responsiveness, consensus, equity, effective and efficient responsibility and accountability, strategic vision, transparency, and stewardship. Furthermore, good governance is possible in the Third World, but the same standards must apply to public officials in the Third World as they do to those in the technological world. Public officials in the Third World must accept their responsibility to the state and the people, and be accountable for their actions. Dwivedi further contends that the basic needs of the people of developing countries must first be met, which he considers to be "the most basic and fundamental requisite," before good governance should become a concern.

An Overview

The book as a whole provides a broad overview of administrative challenges facing a variety of nations. The foregoing review of various essays commissioned for this book reveal that although bureaucratic structures among nations appear similar, their style of conducting government business still varies from nation to nation, or from one geographic region to another. But one thing is clear: the process of globalization has brought the operationalization of all administrative systems closer, with the result that even practices are being changed to comply with international requirements due to liberalization, WTO, and the pressure brought to bear upon governments by multinational corporations. Is it possible that the twenty-first century could create one universally understood administrative culture, a seemingly unfeasible objective during the past 50 years of development? Would this be an imitative and replicative system of public management, as more and more Western values and practices get instituted everywhere? However, the editors believe that for a just and sustainable world, diversity in thought and action is more desirable than the self-proclaimed universal paradigms always originating in the West. We do know that globalization is here to stay and, thus, the major challenge before the non-Western nations will be how to maximize the positive effects of globalization, and yet keep their identity and indigenous system alive but with proper accountability and transparency in governance. Administrative culture will be the key to achieve that goal.

REFERENCES

Arrighi, Giovanni. 2000. "Globalization, State Sovereignty, and the 'Endless' Accumulation of Capital." In *The Ends of Globalization: Bringing Society Back In,* edited by Don Kalb, Marco Van der Land, Richard Staring, Bart Van Steen Bergen, and Nico Wilterdink. Lanam, Maryland: Rowman and Littlefield.

Baldwin, Richard and Philip Martin. 1999. "Two Waves of Globalization: Superficial Similarities, Fundamental Differences." Working Paper No. 6904, National Bureau of Economic Research, Washington DC.

Cheema, Shabbir. 2000. "Good Governance: A Path to Poverty Eradication." *Choices: The Human Development Magazine* 9(1):6-7.

D'Orville, Hans. 1992. "The Search for Global Order: The Problems of Survival." The Tenth Session of the Interaction Council, May 28-31, Queretaro, Mexico.

Drewry, Gavin and Che-po Chan. 2001. "Civil Service Reform in the People's Republic of China: Another Mirage of the New Global Paradigm of Public Administration?" *International Review of Administrative Sciences* 67(3):461-478.

Dwivedi, O. P. 1994. *Development Administration: From Underdevelopment to Sustainable Development.* London, UK: Macmillan Press.

———. 2003. "The Globalization of Our World: A Cross-Cultural Perspective." Public Lecture delivered April 14, University of South Florida, Tampa.

Dwivedi, O. P. and James Iain Gow. 1999. *From Bureaucracy to Public Management: The Administrative Culture of the Government of Canada.* Peterborough, Canada: Broadview Press.

Friedman, Thomas L. 2000. *The Lexus and the Olive Tree: Understanding Globalization.* New York: Anchor Books.

Gilpin, Robert. 2000. *The Challenge of Global Capitalism: The World Economy in the 21st Century.* Princeton, New Jersey: Princeton University Press.

Greider, William. 1997. *One World, Ready or Not: The Manic Logic of Global Capitalism.* New York: Simon and Schuster.

Helliwell, John F. 2002. *Globalization and Well- Being* Vancouver, Canada: UBC Press.

Kalb, Don. 2000. "Localizing Flows: Power, Paths, Institutions, and Networks". In *The*

Ends of Globalization: Bringing Society Back In, edited by Don Kalb, Marco Van der Land, Richard Staring, Bart Van Steen Bergen, and Nico Wilterdink. Lanam, Maryland: Rowman and Littlefield.

Kiggundu, Moses N. 2002. *Managing Globalization in Developing Countries and Transition Economies.* Westport, Connecticut: Praeger.

Milanovic, Branco. 1999. "On the Threshold of the Third Globalization: Why Liberal Capitalism Might Fail?" World Bank Research Department. Unpublished Manuscript. Available at (www.worldbank.org/research/inequality/).

Schaeffer, Robert K. 2003. *Understanding Globalization: The Social Consequences of Political, Economic, and Environmental Change.* New York: Rowman and Littlefield Publishers.

Soros, George. 1998. *The Crisis of Global Capitalism.* New York: Public Affairs.

United Nations Development Programme (UNDP). 1999. *Human Development Report.* New York: UNDP & Oxford University Press.

Chapter 1

ADMINISTRATIVE CULTURE AND VALUES: APPROACHES

O. P. Dwivedi

Introduction: Administrative Culture and Values

The profession and the academic discipline of Public Administration all over the world is going through a period of turmoil, both in practice and in theory. After a period of unprecedented growth from the end of World War II until the mid-1970s the industrialized world experienced increasing financial difficulties for which it blames, among other things, its large bureaucracies and the welfare state that had been created. This led to strong challenges, mostly from politicians and people in business. Consequently, the management practices used in the business sector were seen as great cure-alls for the ills facing public sector management anywhere. This resulted in the creation of a new Public Management movement, and the remedies proffered by the movement are lionized in and by the West as the panacea for public management problems facing the world.

In recent years, this subject has received worldwide attention, especially as people wonder if the concept and operation of administrative processes are universally common or if there is a difference between the administrative cultures of nations. Thus, the main purpose of this essay is to raise the fundamental question: Do administrative cultures really differ? Gerald Caiden, in 1998, alerted us to this issue. However, he also said that despite the lure of Americanization (read "globalization"), people are interested in retaining their distinctive identity and culture (Caiden 1998:388). This appears to be true. For example, French people are keen to preserve not only their culture and language but also their administrative system. Similarly, other European nations have their distinctive administrative cultures, though they do share some core administrative values. In this essay, we are interested in developing a general framework for understanding administrative culture, as well as examining what approaches can be utilized to study and compare different administrative cultures.

The most important challenge to conventional views of administration is the process of globalization. Irrespective of the definition used for "globality," the context, the structure, the processes, and the effects of administration are decisively influenced by it. The circumstances of administration are increasingly defined by parameters outside the confines of the nation-state. So are goals, resources (human, material, and "semiotic"), communications, and performance. The same is the case with the impact of policy decisions, non-decisions, actions, and inactions upon the context of administration. For the latter encompasses interwoven domestic and extraterritorial dimensions. In an era of growing interdependence, but also of mutual vulnerability, domestic and international micro and macro security is interconnected. At the centre of this global-local interface, there is an emerging global consciousness (Dwivedi and Nef 1998:6).

This essay focuses on the debate regarding administrative culture, understood here in its broadest sense as the modal pattern of values, beliefs, attitudes, and predispositions that characterize and identify any given administrative system. In this inclusive definition we are covering both the private and public spheres of the managerial ethos, for societies in general possess certain specific ways of "getting things done," which transcend the official sphere. We recognize that the construction of an administrative mind-set presents significant difficulties. Yet, we also recognize that it is possible to configure clusters of cultural matrices that have important heuristic value in understanding the relationship among contexts, structures, behaviors, and effects. This modal outline, though tentative, may also endow the analyst with ways to hypothesize upon the sources and effects of such culture upon the larger social and political order. Dwivedi and Nef have suggested eight general propositions that researchers may explore, in their specific ways, because we believe that administrative cultures, like all cultures, do differ (Dwivedi and Nef 1998:6-7):

(1) The administrative culture of any part of the globe reflects the distinctiveness and complexity of the various regional, national, and local realities; their unique historical experiences; their forms of insertion (subordination or domination) into the system of regional and global relations; and their levels of development and fragmentation.
(2) Such cultures are historical products, where past experiences, myths, and traditions have shaped modal psychological orientations.
(3) Any administrative culture is also conditioned by existing structural and conjunctural circumstances and challenges. Even perceptions of the past are mediated by current experience.
(4) The administrative culture is part of a larger attitudinal matrix, containing values, practices, and orientations toward the physical environment, the

economy, the social system, the polity, and culture itself.
(5) Administrative cultures, like all cultures, are dynamic and subject to change. Syncretism, continuities, and discontinuities are part and parcel of their fabric and texture.
(6) An administrative culture is the result of a process of immersion, acculturation, and socialization, whose structural drivers are both implicit as well as induced and explicit.
(7) Most attempts at administrative reform and "modernization" address, either directly or indirectly, the question of administrative culture. Any profound administrative reform entails significant attitudinal and value changes.
(8) Administrative cultures are influenced by global and regional trends. In the lesser-developed regions of the world, they are particularly derivative, reflecting a center-periphery mode of international political economy.

In addition, a researcher should ask the following questions: what is culture and where does it come from? What are the sources of such culture, and to what extent have these sources influenced the prevailing norms and values of administration? How might administrative culture, and particularly its values, be studied in a reasonably objective way? What are organizational culture, corporate culture, and administrative culture? And, finally, what do we mean by the term "culture"?

What is Culture?

Anthropologists tend to define culture in broad terms. According to Singer, the anthropological concept of culture covers all facets of humans in society: knowledge, behavior, beliefs, art, morals, law, customs, etc. (Singer 1968). Culture should also be seen not only as a material possession but also consisting of institutions, people, behaviors or emotions, a style of accomplishing things, and, specifically, how people perceive, relate, and interpret events both from within and without. Essentially, culture in this sense refers to the shared values and representations of the members of an organization, such as a governmental bureaucracy.

Despite some differences of emphasis, anthropologists agree that a culture is the way of life of a given society. However, this concept has some implications: (a) the concept is holistic because it involves the entire society; (b) it implies a certain coherence among the elements of a culture; and (c) it reveals the fundamental values of a society, including its attributes, patterns (both explicit and implicit), and acquired behavior transmitted by symbols (Singer 1968:528). The author suggests the following definition of culture: a way of life of a group of people or a society through which it views the world around it, attributes meanings, attaches significance to it, and organizes itself to accomplish, preserve, and eventually pass on its legacy to future generations. The study of culture attracts our attention to the world of symbols and meanings, the values and patterns of organizations, and their behavior, which constitute particular ways of seeing, interpreting, and judging the world. However, when it comes to the transmission of culture from one place to another, several actors participate (both consciously and unconsciously) in the process, such as the state apparatus, socioeconomic and political factors as well as religious institutions.

Administrative Culture

We should note that like most other concepts used in the social sciences, the term "administrative culture" does not always mean the same thing for all people. Different perspectives may be offered, and a variety of conclusions can be drawn by people (from different places or geographic regions) studying the administrative culture. But, the most important question that we should ask is why should anyone study administrative culture? Will such study lead to new perspectives on the administrative history of a nation? Is it because by studying it, we are able to study the learning experiences by which an administrative culture is passed on from generation to generation? Is it because by studying it, one can explain how the administrative system of the nation operates the way it does? In this essay, an attempt will be made to answer these questions.

Two main perspectives may assist us in understanding the administrative culture of a nation. First, the government administration in all nations happens to be larger and more complex than any single organization, being composed of many departments, agencies, corporations, and so on. Of course, there are some multinational corporations with larger administrations than some small countries, but for our purpose, we are talking about the state which is, in reality, "an organization of organizations" (Bergeron 1990:181). Second, policies and administrative decisions get implemented through the state apparatus, state financial and other resources are distributed, and the entire society is affected in many ways by the attending administrative culture. The behavior of the state apparatus depends on the kind of administrative culture that prevails in a country. Lack of transparency and professionalism, as we have seen in several countries, are symptoms of malaise prevailing in the administrative culture (as well as in the political culture) of certain nations. We should also note that no administrative culture is monolithic; instead, it is a part of the wider culture of a society including its constituent parts such as political, economic, social, religious, corporate, and civil society cultures. Nevertheless, it is the political culture that influences the administrative culture most because it brings its political values to modulate the behavior of state employees. Finally, the culture of the administration is sometimes supported, sometimes challenged, by two important subcultures: first, the culture of each department or agency of government, with its own mandate, interests, client groups, and major professional and occupational components; second, professional subcultures, such as those of accountants, lawyers, economists, engineers, diplomats, and scientists, that cut across organizational boundaries. A composite administrative culture then reflects the values of all its constituent parts.

The Place of Value in Administration

A value can be defined as a principle or a quality from which may be inferred a norm or standard conducive to ordering or ranking, by preference, objects, activities, results, or people. Values may be either personal or collective (Dwivedi and Gow 1999:23). Obviously, culture deals with collective values, but an important source of conflict may come when individual members' personal values are at a variance with the collective values of an organization. Values are, generally, of two kinds: the desired and desirable. The "desired" value is observable (for example, an audit of an account can tell us if the funds have been spent appropriately). But what is "desirable" need not be grounded or evident in behavior. Hofstede notes two possible contradictions coming from this: (1) the contradiction between behavior and what is desired (we act so as to achieve what we desire); (2) between what is desired and what is desirable (this involves someone else's judgment about what we desire) (Hofstede 1981:21). However, when it comes to the place of values in public administration, the subject, in the past, was untouchable.

The Values and Facts Dichotomy

In the past century, two major events occurred which shaped the future of public administration as a discipline and profession. First was the emphasis that Woodrow Wilson and Frank W. Goodnow placed on the separation of administration from politics as the single most essential reform in achieving efficiency and removing the objectionable and unethical practices of spoils and patronage besetting the democratic system of governing. For Woodrow Wilson, administration as a field was outside the sphere of politics because administrative questions were not political questions. After Wilson, other scholars in the United States, the United Kingdom, and Germany joined a steady stream of advocates who viewed the politics-administration dichotomy both as a self-evident truth and as a desirable goal. Public administration was perceived as a self-contained world of its own, with its own rules and methods. Politics, then, came to be viewed as the domain of values, whereas administration was considered the universe of fact, enshrined in a value-free environment. Thus, the stage was set in the education and training courses of public administration for the exclusion of ethical issues and value questions.

The second event that further strengthened the deliberate neglect of ethics and values from public administration programs was the rise of European-led scienticism in the discipline with the two core elements: rational objectivity and quantification. The main purpose of these scientific elements was, and still is, to remove the biases and fallacies of human thought by searching for "hard data," which can be measured, quantified, and then presented in an objective and rational manner. In this context, academics and practitioners of public administration were considered applied scientists who were to stay dispassionately aloof from that subjective (and therefore irrational) realm of values and ethical issues. The European ideal of detached "scientific" administration (or administrative science) meant that policies were to be implemented without much thoughtful reflection. The impact of scienticism supplemented by the American-led public service reforms was most visible in the form of several administrative reforms introduced as "performance budgeting," "Planning Programming Budgeting System" (PPBS), "Zero Based Budgeting" (ZBB), "Policy and Expenditure Management System" (PEMS), New Public Management (NPM), and now New Public Expectations (NPE). These efforts in the West were made in the name of increasing efficiency while relying on quantification. The more complex the governing process became, the stronger was the insistence on the use of scientific methodology. One specific result by the use of this methodology was that the system became too obsessed with quantification, thereby bringing such dysfunctions into the public service system as social inequity, institutionalized biases, and the minimization of the human element. Perhaps the greatest fallacy of this approach was to imply that public servants were akin to "robots," blindly implementing policies. Experts failed to realize that government managers were also supposed to exercise thoughtful action while implementing policies and programs. Development administration, as a subfield of public administration, could not escape from the above excessive emphasis on formal aspects of organization while the effectiveness of institutions suffered.

It would not be wrong to say that the entire twentieth century either relegated the question of values and ethics to the periphery, or dismissed it altogether. The dichotomy between politics and administration has continued and it still appears to dominate the formulation, implementation, and evaluation of public policy issues without due regard to ethical implications and moral reasoning. Finally, the dichotomy is basically false that the field of public administration (or its subfield, development administration), is value-neutral and ought to be performed in a dispassionate, scientific, and almost mechanical manner.

Efforts to separate politics and administration, accompanied by the simultaneous movement to make a science out of the art of administration, account for an early and persistent neglect of ethics and values not only in the teaching of public policy and administration courses, but also in the public service training programs. The baneful influence of these two major factors has contributed to the rise of amoralism in the public sector (more insidious in the developing nations) as well as to the weakening of such underlying ideals as: (a) government is a public trust and the public service is a profession for those who should know how to behave morally; (b) public servants should perform their duties impartially, efficiently, and ethically; and (c) serving the state is the highest calling, which is intricately connected to serving democratic ideals (Dwivedi 1987).

The above set of ethical ideals have come into conflict with the narrow outlook characteristic of organizations that are influenced by business practices, including some precepts advocated by the New Public Management Movement (factors such as: budget restraint, downsizing bureaucracy, accent on results at any cost, treating the public as customers, decentralization and devolution, contracting out, and accountability), and essentially market-driven rhetoric. The rationale was that with fewer bureaucratic structures there would be fewer bureaucratic problems. Once more, heavy emphasis was placed on quantification in the name of applying objective criteria for securing accountability with a blind faith on structures, processes, and procedures while showing a total disregard for the moral or ethical dimension (called a subjective matter by NPM people).

Studying Administrative Culture: Approaches

The author suggests three main approaches to studying the administrative culture of a nation: (1) deontological approach, (2) teleological approach, and (3) spiritual approach. It should be noted that these three approaches are based on some common values such as fundamental rights and freedoms, efficiency, accountability, fairness, etc. These values can be considered the core values of any nation. The three approaches are discussed briefly below.

The Deontological Approach

Deontology is the study of duty and ethical/moral obligations of human beings as well as of the organizations they represent. By using this approach in the study of administrative culture, one focuses on the ethics and morality of the administrator.

This approach is based on the search for the cardinal virtues of the nation as reflected in the nation's constitution and other legal treaties. It seeks to emphasize a person's duty regardless of the circumstances. Deontological judgments take place in the realm of the desirable, or ethics. Thinking about ends and means has always been at the heart of public administration as a discipline. It has long been recognized that there are two great paths to improving the performance of an administration: you can either try to improve the people by leadership, motivation, and training, or tinker with institutions and systems in order to create an atmosphere of desired accountability among officials. The deontological approach also seeks its sources in either religion or philosophy. This author has for some years been an exponent of an "administrative theology" based on a synthesis of world cultures, religions, and their leaders (Dwivedi 1987). Such an attempt follows upon the invitation of Dwight Waldo to survey religion to see "what instruments of navigation it can provide" (Waldo 1980:109). Dwivedi sees a secular administrative theology as providing guidelines for administrative ethics and the idea of a vocation in the service of the public good. This is tricky ground, for the modern secular state has had difficulty disengaging itself from the embrace of established religion, which often has had the effect of placing the spiritual beliefs of some over those of others.

Morality and spirituality, which have been guiding forces in the history of human civilization, are often seen as closely associated with religion. But, the moment one raises the issue of religion in relation to governmental affairs, the forces of secularism feel threatened. The result is not only the weakening of morality in state affairs, but also the emergence of "amorality" or "ethical relativism" in the individual's conduct and behavior, and the rise of unethical activities in the public sphere all over the world. If justice, equality, equity, and freedom are to be maintained, proximate political and administrative acts must draw on some ethical foundations, such as public service as a vocation (Dwivedi 1995). It is a concept based on the ideal of service to the community. That ideal draws upon the concept of sacrifice—a concept that rises above individualism and materialism in order to create a shared feeling or spirit of public duty among government officials. Of course, the concept of sacrifice, in the context of modern times, does not mean that public servants must take a vow of poverty. Rather, it means adhering to the principle of serving others by setting a high standard of moral conduct and by considering a job a vocation, a calling, with conviction and duty. By considering public service a vocation, emphasis is placed on the service dimension of public service, an ideal to be acknowledged by public servants as higher than other economic and material considerations. Public service, then, approaches the status of a secular religion, similar to medical practice or nursing, rather than a mere occupation. Public servants ought to derive inner satisfaction from rendering service unto others rather than from material gains. For them, the symbols and myths of public service are equally, if not more, valued than other employment related benefits.

In this traditional or classical role, there are correct ways of doing things by adhering to what Hennessy calls "a genetic code of conduct," which includes the following values: probity, care for the evidence, respect for reason, willingness to speak the truth to Ministers, a readiness to carry out instructions to the contrary if overridden, an appreciation of the wider public interest, equity, and a constant concern for democratic ideals (Hennessy 1989:5). To them, any movement toward greater symbiosis with their political masters, as is the case in many countries, is to be avoided.

The Teleological Approach

The teleological approach is based on analyzing the success of a decision in producing a desired effect. While still in the realm of the desirable, this approach pays much more attention to intervening realities on the path to realizing goals or respecting values. The teleological approach also concerns the causal relationship between means and desired ends. Teleology is the doctrine of final causes. As an approach to the study of administrative culture, the doctrine would assert that processes and procedures in government administration ought to be determined by their ultimate purposes/ends. Thus, the emphasis is on the effects observed, results achieved, and ends met.

The Spiritual Approach

When we refer to spirituality, we generally mean a kind of energy source that (a) is beyond ourselves and transcendent; (b) impels us to search for the purpose of life here and after, as well as why are we here on earth; (c) has an overarching influence on our sense of right and wrong; (d) empowers us to care for others; and (e) inspires us to act for the common good. Willa Bruce and John Novinson, in an article dealing with spirituality in public service, suggested that an effort ought to be made to operationalize the concept (Bruce and Novinson 1999). A few years ago, the present author suggested a similar approach about the place of morality and spirituality in managing statecraft by stating "the moral dimension of governance represents a concern for an improvement in the quality of public service and the conduct of statecraft" (Dwivedi 1987:707). Although spirituality is supposed to be an integral part of our religious traditions and beliefs, its secular dimension (which is yet to be particularly acknowledged by secular institutions) is crucial in governance, especially with respect to public service ethics and values. That energy source, mentioned earlier in this paragraph, can be converted into a moral force to be used for good governance. How can this be possible? Through understanding the relevance of spirituality in the management of statecraft, a common strategy for good governance can be developed. Such a strategy depends upon how public officials (a) perceive a common future for their society; (b) act both individually and collectively toward protecting the common good; and (c) realize that they as individuals have a moral obligation to support their society's goals since their acts will have repercussions on the future of their society. In addition, it is important to note that the demonstration of social conscience and caring behavior by public officials is intertwined with the general concept of a common good. It is an obligation that human beings owe not only to each other within a society but also to others living elsewhere. It is most important for public officials to know how they can better serve the common good. In a liberal democratic system of governance, there is the no higher public service value than the mission of demonstrating social conscience and caring behavior by doing one's respective duties toward the common good and good governance.

There is a general misconception in the field of public policy and administration that the development of public policy and its application is purely an objective and secular endeavor, where moral, subjective, and spiritual factors have no specific role to play at all. However, values and morality are not limited to personal matters only. A democratic society is founded on the principle of the dignity and worth of all people; and that moral principles emanate from basic religious values that hold human life both sacred and social. Furthermore, every constitution is generally the embodiment of moral values that guarantee us fundamental freedoms, justice, rule of law, and the like. These are the moral foundations upon which public policy and its management must be based. We live in a world of interdependence, in which morality and secularism share and balance each other in the protection and development of human values. There is no need to fence out morality and spirituality in the name of secularism, public service objectivity, and neutrality, lest the moral vision that has shaped and guided humanity thus far may well be compromised by immorality, expediency, and corruption.

By insisting on morality in public policy and governmental decision making, we may be able to strengthen the ethical and moral obligations of the people as well as of the organizations they represent. The focus must be on the ethics and morality of the administrator. What sense of duty should the public servant have, toward whom, and how can this sense be operationalized? The spiritual approach assumes there are correct ways of doing things, that there are standards and rules that should be adhered to. Public servants in this mold believe that administrative responsibility is primarily a moral question (Bernard 1948). They are moved by a higher cause, believing they have been entrusted with the stewardship of the state, and therefore owe special obligations, have specific expectations, and reside in a fiduciary world. Here, the spiritual approach or spiritual dimension (discussed later) acquires a holistic tone. Ultimately, our public servants exist for the public they are employed to serve. This approach needs to be revitalized in our public service. The commitment to a collective vision is one of the cardinal virtues of public servants; it is derived from the concept of public service as vocation. For, if the profession of public service is not a calling, then it is merely a job. In that case, loyalty to that job will depend largely on the material benefits and satisfaction that job provides. Under these circumstances, no one can expect public servants to exhibit the virtues of service to society, prudence in the use of taxpayers' money, and commitment to the common good and collective welfare of the people.

We are also aware that morality can lead to mastery over our baser impulses such as greed, exploitation, abuse of power, and mistreatment of people. Spirituality requires self-discipline, humility, and, above all, the absence of arrogance in holding public office. Morality enables people to center their values on the notion that there is a cosmic ordinance and divine law that must be maintained. Spirituality serves as a model, and as an operative strategy, for the transformation of human character by strengthening the genuine, substantive will to serve the common people. If our goal is to serve and protect the common good, then spirituality can provide the incentive for public officials to serve the public with dignity and respect.

A comprehensive account of the use of power and authority by public officials would be incomplete without these approaches (deontological, teleological, and spiritual). By using these approaches to good governance, we may be able to create a holistic vision for human governance. In their absence, no number of laws, codes of conduct, external or internal control mechanisms, or threats of punishment can force public officials to behave ethically and morally. Indeed, all the nations that are deemed the most corrupt, according to Transparency International, do have various laws and mechanisms to control corruption, and yet it continues. Unless public officials are guided also by a sense of a vocation, service to others, and inner spirituality, we cannot expect good governance. This sense of vocation holds that "government is a public trust and public service is a vocation for persons who should know how to behave morally. Behavior emanating from ideals associated with service as the highest calling includes possessing and exhibiting such virtues as honesty, impartiality, sincerity, and justice. Further, it is equally desirable that the conduct of public administrators should be beyond reproach; and that they should perform their duties loyally, efficiently, and economically" (Dwivedi 1995:297).

The author believes that confidence and trust in democracy can be safeguarded only when the governing process exhibits a higher, credible, and ethical stand, based on the trinity of justice, equity, and morality. Only by bringing together the domains of moral and procedural accountability, can we wage a strong fight against corruption, mismanagement, and bad governance. For no nation or society, irrespective of its political and religious orientation, can survive in a spiritual or moral vacuum. Furthermore, the author believes that there must be articles of faith (drawn from societal values, cultural traditions, and moral ideals) that govern our lives and that these should be encouraged, reinforced, resurrected, and strengthened, because good governance is essentially a moral enterprise. From a holistic viewpoint, a comprehensive study of administrative culture cannot be complete unless these approaches are utilized. That is why a study of administrative culture should employ all three approaches, although the author realizes that one treads difficult ground by venturing into the realm of spirituality.

New Public Management and Administrative Culture

Although public service reformers keep hoping (or claim to *know*) that their new institution, method, or device will deliver change in government policy and programs in order to bring efficiency, accountability and transparency, there are some propositions that are so well established they seem axiomatic. The first is that the choice of objectives depends in part on the means available. That is, in public policy and administration, most choices are not moral absolutes, but depend on calculations of costs and benefits, not only to the public, but also to politicians and public servants. Second, administrative reforms have both intended and unintended consequences.

When applied to Public Management, this approach offers the following observations: (1) there is symmetry, for the managerial revolution is part of the worldwide triumph of democratic capitalist values; (2) the metaphorical language of management seems easily adapted to the public sector, as in "corporate culture," "corporate management," "management by results," etc.; (3) there is much ambiguity in expressions like "value for money" or "excellence"; (4) it requires the suspension of disbelief, corresponding to what Dunsire says of doctrine: "it makes plain, but in the manner of 'revealed truth' rather than the tentative hypothesizing of theory: it shows what must be done but as if it were from necessity rather than the mere instrumentalism of policy" (Dunsire 1973:39); (5) selectivity in argument is found in the recourse to examples, to "best practices" and to anecdotal evidence without considering contrary evidence; (6) a doctrine based on private interest, it is said to meet the requirements of the public good (Dwivedi and Gow 1999:171).

The trouble with New Public Management, then, is that it is all technique. If politics is about the art of the possible, or what is acceptable in a society, and if it is also about the major value choices of that society—"authenticity" and "justice" values—then management has forgotten politics (Manzer 1984:27).

Public management also appears to neglect the importance of law in public administration. This can be seen at two levels. At the top, in introducing notions like corporate management, corporate culture, and even that of management itself, it tends to obscure how relations between senior officials and ministers are constitutional in nature. As we have seen, when Canadian officials answer questions from members of parliament, they do so in the name of their minister. Faced with the complexities of day-to-day administration and the conflicting values that the system has thrust upon them, they need some fundamental reference point to which they may turn in case of doubt. As John Rohr states, the constitution must serve as a source of regime values for administrators (Rohr 1978:67). That is why at lower levels of administration, the law is a guarantor of democratic government. In this respect, a public manager differs from a private one, because while the latter may regard the law as a constraint, something he must obey, the public manager must also uphold the rule of law.

To us, the greatest charge against managerialism is its reductionism and its lack of imagination. It tries to reduce a complex phenomenon to a single model drawn from business. We argued above that the appropriate image for the public administrator is the steward, not the entrepreneur. What remains to be pointed out is another curious paradox of management. Astley and Van de Ven have observed that there are two versions of organization theory, one which is basically deterministic and the other which is proactive in its outlook (Astley and Van de Ven 1983). The deterministic school sees management as a kind of fine tuning; adapting organizations to changes occurring in the environment. The proactive outlook takes a strategic view of that environment. It is there to be acted upon.

The paradox of the New Public Management is that while its language is full of references to a proactive stance, where strategic planning, innovation, change, and growth are promoted, in its basic thrust the NPM is profoundly deterministic. Its message is that there really are no choices; that deficits, structural economic change, and world trade competition are forcing governments of all developed countries to adopt the same policies. This obscures the fact that these same governments do things very differently, with European countries accepting a more corporatist form of national bargaining with business and labor, while

Britain, the United States, and Canada have more liberal societies, where individualism reigns supreme. It also masks the fact that there are other models of the new state different from the market model. In sum, if the New Public Management movement (which is essentially based on the teleological model of administrative analysis) is carried to the extreme, technique drives out the desirable. What is feasible informs what is desirable, but if feasibility is the only criterion for the desirable, then our vision has become too limited. It is here where the deontological and spiritual approaches become relevant. Against this context, these two approaches acquire a holistic tone. In the end, our public servants exist for the public they are employed to serve. It is this aspect that needs to be revitalized in our public services. Even with the current emphasis on downsizing public services, one should not abdicate its belief in serving the collective interests of its society. Rather, it should express more of a concern for the collective welfare of its people. This commitment to a collective vision is one of the cardinal virtues of our public servants. Abandonment of the commitment for public service as a vocation that would follow from the adoption of market-based practices would be highly undesirable. Any predisposition to reject duty and commitment to vocation among public servants is not going to serve a country well. Of course, duty-based deontological approaches have disadvantages apart from the fact that not all agree on their contents. In public administration, difficulties often arise because two or more values are in conflict, such as the sense of patriotism and the obligation to do one's legal and constitutional duty.

Diversity in Theory and Practice of Administration Ought to be Protected

The trilogy of approaches employed in the study of administrative culture and administration should not be seen as contradictory; each is incomplete without the other. No amount of factual analysis can allow one to escape certain moral and spiritual judgements, fundamental choices about both the public service and public life of a country. On the other hand, the kind of all-embracing ethical and spiritual dimensions do provide us with a deeper perspective but not the whole picture. That is why all three approaches should be used to study administrative cultures. The three approaches discussed ought to be considered a package deal when one wishes to examine the administrative culture of any nation. Among these three, the deontological approach has its basis both in philosophy and policy analysis. The most relevant school of philosophy, utilitarianism, took as its slogan "the greatest good for the greatest number." However, such an approach offers little help in deciding when the rights of the larger number may be invoked to limit those of the few, nor does it give consideration to the means to achieve a desired end. On the other hand, the teleological approach is blamed for being all method and no result. Complementing the above two approaches is the spiritual approach that, while accentuating the positive elements of public service vocation, emphasizes the relationship between the desirable and the feasible. While the study of administrative culture may be done in a detached, relatively objective way, it raises the problem of the best way to treat values. Finally, without the presence of individual spirituality and a sense of duty, laws and codes of conduct would not create the environment for good government.

It is also clear that in the name of globalization, a certain dependence and continued reliance on the theory and methodology of Western-style administration is being fostered in the developing nations, with an emphasis on transplanting and replicating the ideas and institutions of the West. As more and more Western values and practices prevail everywhere, with standards of performance based on the indicators developed in the West, an imitative and replicative system of public management is emerging in the rest of the world, and public servants everywhere mirror the bureaucratic structures and mores in Washington DC, London, Paris, Bonn, and Ottawa. We should be ever vigilant in the field of public administration so that the diversity in administrative culture does not face the same fate as is happening with the declining of bio-diversity in the world. With this perspective, let us also worry about what is happening in the world around us (Nef 1998):

(1) For years, Western scholars have been unable to include alternatives in the form of non-Western contributions to administrative studies. Instead, it was expected that institutional imitation would easily produce similar results to those obtained in the West.
(2) Ethnocentrism and ignorance in the West have continued to overshadow the need to appreciate the importance of local culture, traditions, and style of governance. It is their style of governance and the administrative culture that reflect the distinctiveness and complexity of various national identities, realities, and cultural diversities. These factors should be taken into consideration when imposing public service reforms and other conditionalities.
(3) The public sector reform imposed by Western ideology has created, in its wake, skewed management styles and structures that are unrelated to the prevailing cultural norms, needs, and realities; these styles and structures reproduce the symbolism, but not the substance, of Western administration. It is also not surprising that the culture of governance in the Third World has tended to follow, or has been forced to replicate, the costly fads in the industrialized nations. Thus, efforts at administrative restructuring, "modernization," and other types of reforms must address first, either

directly or indirectly, the question of the indigenous style, values, and culture of governance.

As culture and style of governance are the keys to understanding what makes a country function, it is imperative that any public sector reform imposed on developing nations draws from the local customs, culture, and traditions. When the local culture and traditions are discarded in the favor of Western-style management practices, and when not enough time is given to these nations to see if such a transplantation has germinated, a hodge-podge of two value systems start operating simultaneously with no one specific standard against which the conduct of public officials can be measured. For the West as well as for the Third World, a key to a just and sustainable world requires diversity in thought and action rather than the self-proclaimed universal relevance of Western originated paradigms and administrative culture. Finally, true globalization means the ability to decide with an open mind, to understand and to incorporate different and alternative cultural traditions into a common matrix, and to respect diversity all around. That ability to incorporate these new strains and challenges in the governing system of a nation will determine, to a large extent, the quality of life that ours and future generations will enjoy, or suffer.

NOTE

This essay draws from Dwivedi, O. P. and James Iain Gow. 1999. *From Bureaucracy to Public Management: The Administrative Culture of the Government of Canada.* Peterborough, Canada: Broadview Press. Chapters 1 and 6.

REFERENCES

Astley, W. Graham and Andrew Van de Ven. 1983. "Central Perspectives and Debates in Organization Theory." *Administrative Science Quarterly* 28:245-273.

Bergeron, G. 1990. *Petit traite de l'Etate* (A Minor Treatise on the State). Paris: Presses universitaires de France.

Bernard, Chester I. 1948. *The Functions of the Executive.* Cambridge, MA: Harvard University Press.

Caiden, Gerald E. 1998. "Are Administrative Cultures that Different?" Pp. 377-393 in *Governing India: Issues Concerning Public Policy, Institutions and Administration,* edited by O. P. Dwivedi, R. B. Jain, K. Dhirendra and K. Vajpeyi. Delhi: B. R. Publishing.

Dunsire, Andrew. 1973. "Administrative Doctrine and Administrative Change" *Public*

Administration Bulletin (UK) 13:39-56.

Dwivedi, O. P. 1985. "Ethics and Values of Public Responsibility and Accountability." *International Review of Administrative Sciences* 51:61-66.

———. 1987. "Moral Dimensions of Statecraft: A Plea for Administrative Theology." *Canadian Journal of Political Science* 20(4):699-706.

———. 1995. "Reflections on Moral Government and Public Service as a Vocation." *Indian Journal of Public Administration* 41(3):296-306.

———. 2002. "On Common Good and Good Governance: An Alternative Approach." Pp. 35-51 in *Better Governance and Public Policy: Capacity Building and Democratic Renewal in Africa,* edited by Dele Olowu and Soumana Sako. Bloomfield, CT: Kumarian Press.

Dwivedi, O. P. and E. A. Engelbert. 1981. "Education and Training for Values and Ethics in the Public Service: An International Perspective." *Public Personnel Management* 10(1):140-145.

Dwivedi, O. P. and James Iain Gow. 1999. *From Bureaucracy to Public Management: The Administrative Culture of the Government of Canada.* Peterborough, Canada: Broadview Press. A joint publication with the Institute of Public Administration of Canada, Toronto.

Dwivedi, O. P. and J. Nef. 1998. "Administrative Culture: A Global Perspective." *Africanus* 28(2):5-7.

Guillen, Mauro F. 1994. *Models of Management, Work, Authority and Organization in a Comparative Perspective.* Chicago. IL: Chicago University Press.

Hennessy, P. 1989. "Genetic Code of Conduct Inherited by Mandarines." *The Independent* (UK), 5 June.

Hofstede, Geert. 1981. "Culture and Organizations." *International Studies on Man and Organizations*, 10(4):15-41.

Manzer, R. 1984. "Policy Rationality and Policy Analysis: The Problem of the Choice of Criteria for Decision-Making." Pp. 27-40 in *Policy and Administrative Studies,* edited by O. P. Dwivedi. Guelph, Canada: University of Guelph.

Mosher, Frederick C. 1968. *Democracy and the Public Service.* New York, NY: Oxford University Press.

Nef, Jorge. 1998. "Administrative Culture in Latin America: Historical and Structural Outline." *Africanus* 28(2):19-32.

Nevitte, Neil. 1996. *The Decline of Deference: Canadian Value Change in Cross-National Perspective.* Peterborough, Canada: Broadview Press.

Rohr, John A. 1978. *Ethics for Bureaucrats: An Essay on Law and Values.* New York: Marcel Decker.

Sayre, W. 1958. "Premises of Public Administration: Past and Emerging." Pp. 103-106 in *Administrative Questions and Political Answers,* edited by C. E. Hawley and Ruth G. Weintraub. Princeton, New Jersey: Van Nostrand.

Singer, Milton. 1968. "The Concept of Culture." In *International Encyclopedia of the Social Sciences*. New York: Macmillan Press.

Waldo, Dwight. 1980. *The Enterprise of Public Administration*. Nuvato, CA: Chandler and Sharp.

Willa, Bruce and John Novinson. 1999. "Spirituality in Public Service: A Dialogue." *Public Administration Review* 59(2):163-169.

Wilson, Woodrow. [1887] 1992. "The Study of Administration." In *Classics of Public Administration,* edited by Jay M. Shafritz and Albert C. Hyde. Pacific Grove, CA: Brooks/Cole Publishing.

Chapter 2

AMERICAN ADMINISTRATIVE CULTURE: AN EVOLUTIONARY PERSPECTIVE

Keith M. Henderson

Definition and Classification

This chapter will contrast administrative culture with the related concepts of organizational culture and political culture and develop a case study of American public administration—in its public personnel aspect—based on the important concept of administrative culture. The sources and foundations of administrative culture will be indicated along with an evolutionary perspective from the earliest days of the republic to the present. Subcultures will also be discussed. Finally, the globalization of American administrative values will be discussed.

Administrative culture is not a new concept but neither is it one in common usage in the United States. Book length treatments have been developed for Canada (Dwivedi and Gow 1999), Israel (Caiden 1970), Korea (Paik 1990), India (Sharma 2000), and elsewhere, but none for the United States. In various ways, it has been the organizing concept for journal articles (e.g., Anechiarico 1998; Keraudren 1996) and academic colloquia, but it has been largely eclipsed by other cultural interpretations, particularly organizational culture and political culture.

The term culture, of course, was originally used in Anthropology to indicate clusters or patterns of common behavior, knowledge, custom, etc., and has since been adapted and expanded in numerous ways in other fields of inquiry. Academic interpretations of "American culture" along with widespread journalistic and popular usage of that term make it familiar. In the U.S. context, administrative culture allows us to focus on the values, beliefs, and attitudes held by administrators, recognizing change over time from a patrician notion of "administration by gentlemen" in colonial times, through endemic spoils as the reward for winning political office, to the merit system for government employment, modified in the last half-century by the introduction of values relating to equal employment opportunity and affirmative action. Comparative features and evolutionary changes in public administration—reflected in numerous reorganizations and reforms as well as subtle changes in morale within the government workforce—can be well understood through the concept of administrative culture.

Organizational Culture

There is a vast literature on organizational culture in the field of organization theory, most of it centered on the "culture" within an organization. Edgar Schein was one of the pioneers with his detailed listing of dimensions of workplace analysis associated with culture (Schein 1985). He, along with other pioneers such as Pettigrew (1979) and Hofstede (1980, 1991), helped to define the concept. Earlier studies of organizational climate by social psychologists informed the later formulations by Schein and others. Schein elaborated a number of categories of organizational analysis which include:

1. Observed behavioral regularities when people interact (language, customs, traditions, rituals);
2. Espoused values (e.g., "product quality," or "price leadership");
3. Formal philosophy (guiding a group's actions toward stockholders, employees, customers, and others);
4. Rules of the game (implicit rules for getting along in the organization, the "ropes" that a new employee must learn);
5. Climate (the feeling conveyed in a group);
6. Embedded skills (e.g., special competencies);
7. Habits of thinking, mental models, linguistic paradigms (Schein 1985:8-9).

The seven categories are *artifacts* and *patterns of behavior* of organizational culture and are the most visible aspect of it. There are also underlying basic assumptions deriving from the culture at large (Schein 1985).

The concept of climate is included in the categories and represents a departure from the original field theory approaches and the quantitative study of attitudes within organizations by social psychologists. In a more recent discussion, Schein seeks to clarify the difference between climate and culture (Schein 2001).

The concept of organizational culture has developed to encompass a vast number of studies of business organizations and a few public agencies. Bozeman, for example, has recently researched the Internal Revenue Service in terms of its "risk culture" (Bozeman 2003). Organizational culture remains a useful concept and one that should be borne in mind as we move to a higher level of abstraction and a public focus. A good overview of the field is available in Joanne Martin's *Organizational Culture: Mapping the Terrain* (2002). Martin, a leading figure in current organization theory, includes the latest research and an insightful three-perspective model. Disputes in the field are highlighted and her own approach elaborated. A good compendium to supplement Martin is the *Handbook of Organizational Culture and Climate* (Ashkanasy, Wilderom, and Peterson 2000).

Insights from organizational culture studies inform public administration researchers by highlighting specific cases and developing theoretical approaches to understanding organizational behavior. Taken together, they contribute to the larger overview of patterns of orientation by public officials and their shared values, attitudes, and beliefs.

Political Culture

Political culture—on the other hand—takes the entire political system as the unit of analysis rather than discrete organizations. It derives from the well-known work of Almond and Verba (1965) on civic cultures. It is the structuring framework for many introductory texts and is familiar, in its various guises, to all students in the field. Although it has been criticized and is sometimes regarded as a concept associated with earlier development and modernization theories, it remains in widespread use.

The political culture reflects distinguishing values, attitudes, and beliefs characterizing a political community. In nearly all the U.S. formulations, democratic-constitutional values are at the core, typically including liberty, freedom, majority rule, minority protection, equality, self-government, unity, representation, rule of law, judicial review, separation of powers, secularism, tolerance, individualism, participation, transparency, civil rights, and similar concerns. The political culture in the United States is participatory—based on indirect representation—and emphasizes values that many Americans regard as universally valid.

Monroe Eagles and Larry Johnston indicate that every society possesses a political culture (and, often, subcultures) that encompasses beliefs, attitudes, and values people have about politics (Eagles and Johnston 1999:137). They regard political culture as the "collective political consciousness of a polity"(138); it is an important comparative concept.

Similar constructions are legion in introductory texts and interpretations of American democracy.

In public administration interpretations, the administrative side of American government reflects the ebb and flow of political trends and movements along with the basic values of the broader political culture. Political scientists have sought to characterize administration and administrative personnel in the U.S. context with themes such as growth and power, trade-offs between democracy and efficiency, proper oversight and control, policy development and implementation, and bureaucratic politics. The link between civil service systems and elected officials is an important administrative theme (see Ingraham 1995).

Administrative Culture

In this chapter, administrative culture will be thought of as a mid-point between orientation analyses of personnel in individual agencies (organizations), which can be studied as organizational culture, and the broader political science concern with the entire polity and its features, which has been labeled political culture. At its most basic, administrative culture may be thought of as the general characteristics of public officials (i.e., shared values, attitudes, beliefs), at the federal, state, and local levels. Administrative culture is related to the broader political culture, from which it derives, and can be further discussed in terms of subcultures. Therefore, American administrative culture will be defined as that set of commonly held values, attitudes, and beliefs to which public servants (appointed, not elected, "public officials," or "bureaucrats") subscribe and are expected to follow, and which provide an "ideal-type" of actual and official behavior. Because of the enormous variation in administrative contexts in the United States, as well as the changes over time, additional constructs for proper understanding and cross-national comparison are required. These will be identified as "subcultures" and are three in number: traditional, self-protective, and entrepreneurial. Students of political science will remember that political culture in the United States has been similarly analyzed, such as Daniel Elazar's three cultures: traditional, moralistic, and individualistic, corresponding to regions of the country and early historical experience (Elazar 1984:114-122).

The administrative culture in the United States has reflected the struggle over how political values would be realized and who would have the responsibility for managing government service delivery. From the "era of the gentleman," to the Jacksonian "era of the common man," to the belief that objectively determined skills and abilities (merit) should be paramount, the United States has evinced differing interpretations of how political values can be translated into administrative values. Differences and challenges are found throughout American history, recently in the emphasis upon New Public Management (NPM) and the "reinvention" movement (inspired by Vice President Gore's National Performance Review of the 1990s). As a new paradigm—reflected here in the "entrepreneurial" subculture—NPM values innovation, customer service, and adaptability over rule-application and constitutional responsiveness. A lively debate argued the virtues of the more conventional approach—properly rooted in constitutional law and service to the public—in opposition to the business-world values of flexibility, consumer satisfaction, and entrepreneurial skills (for a good review see Kettl, Ingraham, Sanders, and Horner 1996).

Sources of Administrative Culture in the United States

Many argue that the American experience is unique. As the "first new nation," we have been fortunate in our geography both in its richness and plentitude, and our isolation by two oceans from the conflicts of Europe and elsewhere. The "spirit of the frontier" gave rise to an independence of character, an equality in interpersonal relations, and a chance to physically move to better circumstances or the prospects, if not the reality, of all these. An optimism and hopefulness in society, coupled with sharp regional differences served as sources for the development of administrative culture. Some have argued that there is a mode of thought embodying the value of "individual distinctiveness" or "independence" that forms a contrast with Eastern modes of thought embodying the values of "harmonious social relations" or "interdependence" (see Nisbett 2003).

Even when contrasted with other parts of the world, it is clear that American administrative culture—as with American Political Culture—is a product of indigenous experience. Dwight Waldo long ago showed its uniqueness (Waldo 1948) and its "culture-exclusiveness." Armed struggle to separate from English rule, expansion to the West, a devastating Civil War, and world-involvement help to define the American style.

The United States experienced economic prosperity, propelled by an industrial as well as agricultural sector in the nineteenth century, which was coupled with relative isolation until the early twentieth century and, then, continued prosperity interrupted by a major depression and both mild and severe recessions. Involvement in the world's affairs and leadership thereof commenced on a large scale with the First World War, although the failure of the United States to support the League of Nations doomed it to failure and contributed to worldwide instability. The Second World War reordered the international landscape and propelled the United States, and its allies, into a "cold war" with the Communist block of nations. The subsequent collapse of Communism again reordered the relationships of nation-states and left the United States as the sole super-power, politically and economically.

Throughout this process, American corporate behavior has influenced U.S. administrative culture, first by its excessive influence through financial power, pressure groups, and political parties; later by its dominant value systems, information technology, and techniques for improved productivity. Recent emphasis upon the New Public Management derives from the suggested superiority of the business model over the allegedly inefficient and ineffective public sector. Similar quests for improved performance and productivity have inspired numerous other reform efforts.

Many point out that Civil Society developed early and rapidly in the United States with distrust of the government prominent in the nineteenth century and consequent efforts to severely limit the powers of officials. Elected officials in particular were held to short terms and long ballots, and administrative officials to patrician standards (to the 1820s), then spoils standards (from the 1820s to the 1880s) and—from the end of the century—merit.

The Progressive Era brought reform of abuses, extension of the merit principle to state and local officials, and a watchful and participatory Civil Society assisted by a vigilant group of journalists. War and Depression made their marks and left a legacy of "big government," which prevailed up to the Reagan era, when public administration became not the solver of problems but—in conservative, Republican terms—"part of the problem." Big Government, of course, continued but the rate of growth was reduced. Some functional areas were deregulated, privatized, contracted-out, or shifted to the state level; and considerable talk of downsizing, as found in the private sector, impacted government bureaucracy.

The current administrative culture, it might be argued, reflects some defensiveness on the part of non-elected American officialdom to attacks from both the political right and left, including elected officials at all levels, as well as journalists and pundits. This "bureaucrat bashing" is widespread and is not limited to the United States.

Since the September 11 terrorist attack on the World Trade Center and the Pentagon, the public workforce has been affected by the realization that only government can lead the War on Terror. The prominent protective role of public-sector unions has been tempered by successful efforts to achieve more Presidential control—in the case of the Homeland Security Department—and by further attempts to undercut traditional union power among civilian workers in the Department of Defense. An article in the Washington Post characterized the latter and its extension to other Departments as "An Overhaul, Not a Tune-Up" (*Washington Post* 2003).

Foundations of American Administrative Culture

The United States has the world's oldest continuously accepted written constitution, a constitution that is short, flexible for changing times, and amendable as necessary. However, in its entire history, the U.S. Constitution has been amended only 27 times. Judicial interpretation, custom, legislative and executive action, and uncontested historical changes have accomplished what in other nations has required constant modifications or replacements.

The foundations of American administrative culture are found in ideals rooted in constitutionalism and the rule of law. There are provisions for protection of minorities against a tyranny of the majority; for dividing power into three branches so that no one branch can dominate; and an agreed role for the judiciary in resolving legal issues. In the institutions of the executive branch, non-partisan neutrality and exclusion from partisan politics remain prized values for those who execute policy. The most basic doctrine of separation of powers specified distinct arenas for the three branches, with Congress designated for law making and the Executive Branch for execution. Federalism, as a form of government, avoided the concentration of power of England's unitary system and, at the other extreme, the lack of central coordination and control of the earlier Articles of Confederation, under which the Revolutionary War had been conducted. The two-tiered structure of Federalism (with an effective third tier for local government) allows for a dispersion of power to different levels of sovereignty, both national and state.

Accountability for administrative actions is also a foundation of American administrative culture. Various formal mechanisms are provided, which check and oversee administrative actions. A continuing effort to reconcile the demands of efficiency with those of democratic government is part of the underpinnings of administration. In addition, a basic moral quality was identified many years ago by scholars such as Paul Appleby and Stephen Bailey (Appleby 1952; Bailey 1964). Along with the influence of religious values, administrators are expected to heed inner voices even in the absence of external checks.

The evolution of the ideal of democracy from ancient origins through the Renaissance, English and Continental development, and the American experiment continues a liberal tradition that has been widely emulated elsewhere.

Patrician (Guardian) Administrative Culture

Van Riper's definitive study of the U.S. public (civil) service describes the administrative environment of the early years of the Republic. Government officials were selected based on their social and economic background with high valuation placed on birth, educational attainment, and ownership of property (Van Riper 1958). Their orientation was one of guardianship, with the widespread belief that "men of character" (of course, only white men and no women) should lead the nation and staff its incipient government agencies. The Platonic logic reflects the understanding of the founding fathers on proper governance that would, without question, be best pursued by those with the highest social standing. In addition, prior to 1800, the staffing was largely confined to philosophical federalists, that political grouping which supported a strong central government as opposed to the decentralized, state and rural preference of the anti-federalists. Once in power, after the presidential election of 1800, the anti-federalists continued elitist staffing until Andrew Jackson's presidency.

George Washington and his "men of character" (Dresang 2002) staffed the early public administration apparatus with a dedicated group united by military service and social status. Washington looked for loyalty, family background, and formal education. There were letters of recommendation from prominent politicians attesting to reputational traits and these were usually enough to make the case, along with the additional advantage of military service (Dresang 2002:19).

As might be expected, Washington's successors found their men of character on their home turfs. Both Adams sought appointees among New England merchants and professionals and Jefferson, Madison, and Monroe (from Virginia) found many of theirs in the ranks of southern landholders (Riley 2002:7).

The importance of the patrician administrative culture is more than merely historical. Through the years, and even at present, a few agencies, jurisdictions, and departments at various levels of government (local, state, and federal) have evinced a strong elitism combined with parochial selection of a particular ethnic, religious, and/or social grouping.

The patrician orientation is one of "father knows what is good for you" and "trust us to do what is best." In many ways, it is anti-democratic and it is now an isolated phenomenon.

Patronage (Spoils) Administrative Culture

Begun under earlier Presidencies but usually ascribed to the Presidency of Andrew Jackson, the notion of the election winner taking the spoils of the election (like the spoils of war) was an alternative administrative culture to the patrician version. Although often combined in early years, it is the dominant set of attitudes with which we are concerned. A different orientation is associated with the uneducated (even illiterate) "Spoilsmen" who were appointed in the Jackson years and thereafter. They contrast sharply with the elitist patricians who were highly educated and socially prominent. Less believers in service and stewardship than in a narrow self-advancement and promotion of a political position, the Spoilsmen (again, nearly always white men) were a different breed. Jackson, in a well-known quote, stated that the duties of government were sufficiently simple that any able-bodied man could perform them. Indeed, the scope of public administration was limited and little expertise was required. Nevertheless, public administration scholars for many years decried the Spoilsmen and pointed to numerous evidences of their petty corruption and misuse of position. The contrasting revisionist view is that this was an instance of true democracy that moved the public service from the hands of the elite to a more representative bureaucracy. The era of the common man is the way it is now often described, with emphasis upon the inclusiveness of political and administrative action rather than its quality. At least it expanded the base for recruitment.

The historical record is clear that a reform movement developed after the Civil War (Lincoln was a great indulger in patronage) and sought encouragement in Europe, first in Germany and then in Britain. The Northcote-Trevelyan Act of 1854 in Britain was understood and admired by the reformers who sought a similar type of legislation in the United States without the British notion of the generalist/well-rounded official. It was not until the assassination of President Garfield by a disaffected office-seeker that the precipitating impetus for reform was realized. Senator Pendleton gave his name to the Civil Service Act of 1883 that gradually delineated the dominant administrative orientation since that time.

As with the patrician administrative culture still found in some elitist organizations, so is it possible to find instances of spoils as the paramount value system in some jurisdictions. Of note, some highly-politicized town and city governments in the northeast and county governments in the south, which exist in partisan political areas, can evidence spoils in their appointments to bureaucratic positions and in their overall orientation. This is in spite of nominal merit systems in the jurisdictions, required for federal grants and by various laws.

Merit Administrative Culture

The dominant value of administrative culture in the United States for the last 120 years can be labeled "merit." The values, attitudes, and beliefs of civil servants are expected to reflect this orientation in both professional and technical manners, although there have been numerous deviances and a number of challenges. The essential idea, of course, is that spoils or patronage concepts should be rejected in favor of those related to skills and abilities as measured by some objective test or, more recently, by tests *and* considerations of diversity and representativeness (EEO/Affirmative Action).

As is well known, the Pendleton Act (Civil Service Act) of 1883 provided for tests of fitness administered by a bi-partisan Civil Service Commission (only 2 of the 3 members could be from the same party) and elimination of particularistic criteria related to partisan politics and, additionally, race, religion, or sex. Recent extensions of the concept have included the elimination of age discrimination, disabilities discrimination (Americans with Disabilities Act of 1990), and sexual preference. The latter is in contrast to the milieu of the 1950s when President Eisenhower issued an executive order banning homosexuals as security risks in the public service.

Originally, only 10.5 percent of the federal workforce was covered by the Civil Service Act and the number of positions was only 132,800 (Key Communications Group 2003:13). Subsequently, the coverage expanded and state and local jurisdictions developed their own systems. Today, well over 80 percent of all employees in federal service are covered and many of the others are in specialized personnel systems similar to the general one. This would be true of the Foreign Service, the Armed Services, the CIA and FBI, the Public Health Service, the Forest Service, the Postal Service, the Tennessee Valley Authority (TVA), and others. All of these have their own merit-type systems. State and local government officials also operate under merit systems.

The 1883 Act has been supplemented by other legislative enactments including (Key Communications Group 2003):

- The Retirement Act of 1920, which established a Civil Service Retirement Plan
- The Classification Act of 1923, which created classes and series of positions
- The Hatch Act of 1939, which prohibited partisan political activity
- The Veteran's Preference Act of 1944, which provided for a number of changes in the Civil Service as well as bonus points for veterans, including an appeals process for unfavorably perceived personnel actions
- The Classification Act of 1949, which amended the 1923 Act by introducing, among other things, higher pay grades associated with the top administrative positions.
- The Sick Leave Act of 1951
- The Incentive Awards Act of 1954
- The Group Life Insurance Act of 1954
- The Training Act of 1958
- The Health Benefits Act of 1959
- The Federal Salary Reform Act of 1962
- The Pay Comparability Acts of 1970 and 1990

Other Acts as well as Executive Orders related, importantly, to Equal Employment Opportunity and, beginning with President Kennedy, Affirmative Action. Collective bargaining in the federal workforce was also the subject of legislative enactments. It is important to emphasize that the philosophy of EEO/Affirmative Action argues for a representative work force as well as one based on merit. The notion of a "meritocracy," in which people skilled at test taking dominate the public service, has been replaced with a modified merit concept, which stresses the "public" nature of public service. The public service should reflect, in gender and race, the composition of the broader society that it serves. Numerous court cases have eschewed quotas as a selection and promotion standard but have emphasized the significance of targets and representation objectives. The courts have said that race may be a selection factor but not the only factor. On the other hand, courts have required jurisdictions to bring the classified service into conformity with the broader community that it serves; i.e., if the jurisdiction is 18 percent Hispanic, then the government work force should approximate 18 percent and, until it does, personnel decisions should favor Hispanics.

Civil Rights, whistleblower protection (Act of 1989), retirement and pay provisions, and other matters have been dealt with formally over the years. All are part of the values, belief, and attitude pattern of federal civil servants and most have been applied in state and local jurisdictions with a resulting reinforcement of the Merit culture, as modified for Equal Employment Opportunity/Affirmative Action.

If one legislative authorization needs to be identified as the most important in the last 30 years, it would arguably be the Civil Service Reform Act of 1978, aggressively pursued by President Carter and finally enacted by Congress. This act abolished the Civil Service Commission (but not its purpose) and allocated its functions to two new agencies, the Merit System Protection Board and the Office of Personnel Management (OPM). Thus, appellate functions were included in a separate agency from personnel standard setting and oversight. The 1978 Act also provided for merit pay, a generalist Senior Civil Service (long sought by reformers), and other changes.

While the early years of the OPM were clouded by what the public administration establishment regarded as politicizing, there was no successful demand for additional structural change until the Homeland Security Department was created in 2003 as a response to terrorist threats. Republican congressional efforts in the mid-1990s, following the 1994 election, were ambitious in their attempt to change the civil service by eliminating departments and traditions, but were unrealized. President Bush, however, in the wake of 9/11, was able to quickly get the Patriot Act through Congress, create an Office of Homeland Security in the Executive Office of the President, and finally—against the opposition of Civil Service unions and their Democratic allies—to obtain a 15th Federal Government Department (Homeland Security) that would eliminate certain existing civil service protections.

As suggested above, beginning in the 1960s with the Civil Rights movement—but promoted earlier (for a good analysis see Krislov 1974)—a shift occurred in the merit orientation toward a more representative bureaucracy. This is reflected in the attitudes, values, and beliefs of much of the civil service. The trend for many years had been to recruit, hire, and promote white males who had military service. The latter became a key consideration with the introduction of "veterans' preference" following World War II and the consequent exclusion of those who had not served in the military. Five to ten point bonuses on civil service entrance exams were typical. Clearly, this increased the proportion of males since few women qualified as veterans. Women had assumed a variety of government jobs during the Second World War—while men were away—and many continued in the public service, helping to gender-balance the new male hires in an expanding public service. Over time, however, as women retired, the disparity increased, particularly at the higher levels.

Additionally, the Civil Rights movement called attention to the lack of minority representation in government and attempts to remedy the imbalances commenced at all levels.

Under Title VII of the Civil Rights Act of 1964, as amended, the Equal Employment Opportunity Commission assumed the leadership and enforcement of civil rights legislation affecting both the public and private sectors. Its mandate included hearing and resolving discrimination complaints.

Finding that merely not discriminating was insufficient to remedy past abuses, political demands were made to affirmatively bring about a more representative public work force without sacrificing the merit concept. Affirmative action became the theme of the day.

Various empirical surveys have been done on the social backgrounds of public officials and their values, attitudes, and beliefs. Generally speaking, it has been found that as a group they are somewhat more liberal, tolerant, and better educated than the population at large. Both the Merit System Protection Board and the Office of Personnel Management have conducted broad-based empirical surveys of federal employees. The former, in 1997, released the results of a survey of federal views of the merit principle (Merit System Protection Board 1997) and the latter conducted attitude surveys in 1983, 1991/1992, and 2002. In 1991/1992, questionnaires for the primary sample of federal employees, randomly selected, were mailed to approximately 57,000 employees and nearly 32,000 were returned (OPM 1992). In the 2002 "Human Capital Survey," the OPM questioned over 100,000 Federal employees, also randomly selected, and found that 91 percent believe they do important work. Other findings were that 68 percent are satisfied with their jobs compared to 67 percent in a private industry survey. There were reservations, however, on the part of many federal employees about rewards for good performance with only 30 percent agreeing that the awards programs give them an incentive to do their best. Also, it was discovered that a substantial proportion of federal employees are considering leaving their current jobs.

The OPM indicates that the survey was "the largest survey of federal employees ever undertaken to assess the presence and extent of conditions that characterize high performance organizations" (OPM 2002:1).

Academic research in public personnel administration/human resources administration has also addressed the question of government employees' attitudes, values, and beliefs. Results have not always been consistent, contributing to a debate over the "bureaucratic mind" as opposed to the "dedicated official."

Considerable speculation surrounds the true mentality of the American "bureaucrat." At one extreme is the exposition of Ralph Hummel who finds endemic pathologies and a bureaucratic mind-set, which not only determines workplace behavior but behavior in their private lives. His bureaucrat is a narrow minded, rule-bound tender of the government store who has few redeeming values. That his widely read book has gone into five editions bespeaks its influence. The fifth edition has added critiques of postmodern theories of organization and evidence that it is still "business as usual" for bureaucracies in spite of nearly a decade of "reinvention" (Hummel 2000).

At the other end of the spectrum is the extolling of virtues, dedication, commitment, and contribution of "public officials" (a better sounding term than "bureaucrats"). Ceremonies, honors, traditions, public employee interest groups, yearly awards for excellence, commissions (e.g., the Volker Commissions), and other factors promote a positive view of public officials.

Academically, Charles Goodsell's answer to theories of Hummel exemplifies this more positive view and is closer to the position held by most public administrationists, who find Hummel's thinking a stereotype pandering to popular denigrating of government. Goodsell presents considerable evidence that public officials are ordinary people who approximate the larger society in their values, attitudes, and beliefs (Goodsell 1994).

The Core Values

It is appropriate at this point to summarize the core values of the merit administrative culture as it has evolved over time and as it has been "exported" to other nations. The latter stretch from civil service reforms in Latin America in the 1920s, through numerous missions to Third World countries in Asia, Africa, and the Middle East, as well as Latin America in the heyday of Comparative Public Administration (1950s, 1960s, and 1970s), to installation of merit ideas in Afghanistan and Iraq following replacement of oppressive regimes by the United States and its allies in the twenty-first century.

Based on the broader political culture, which in turn reflects "American culture," and recognizing both the enormous variation in separate organizational cultures as well as the three subcultures discussed below, the following are broadly held values, beliefs, and attitudes, which characterize an "ideal-type" American administrative culture. Civil Servants in the United States acknowledge these norms and they symbolize the operation of the administrative system.

Neutrality and Objectivity

Although recognized to be "political" in the generic, behavioral sense, the public service reflects neutrality in relation to political parties and factions. It is not selected, promoted, reduced in size, disciplined, or otherwise acted upon in a partisan political fashion when it comes to individual personnel decisions. It also serves its public objectively—in accordance with laws and rules—without partiality toward those of any particular creed, area, gender, race, ethnicity, age, or other such variables.

Professionalism and Expertise

Public servants are competent to do their work as measured by tests of fitness and by professional standards: firefighters know how to put out fires; regulatory administrators know their regulated organizations; foreign service officials know diplomacy. Pay and benefits accord with skill requirements (as well as the marketplace and negotiated union agreements) and advancement is also by tests of fitness. Frequently, professional organizations maintain standards: for librarians, the American Library Association defines professionalism and expertise; teachers' organizations promote certification requirements; doctors, lawyers, engineers, and others are covered by the standards of the American Medical Association, American Bar Association, etc. The American Society for Public Administration has established general criteria to advance the science, processes, and art of public administration. It lists five basic principles supplemented by 32 sub-principles: (1) Serve the Public Interest, (2) Respect the Constitution and the Law, (3) Demonstrate Personal Integrity, (4) Promote Ethical Organizations, and (5) Strive for Professional Excellence (ASPA 1994).

Transparency and Accountability

As also recognized in the ASPA Mission Statement and Code of Ethics, neutrality, objectivity, professionalism, and expertise are not sufficient for public administrators. They must also avoid both impropriety and the appearance of impropriety by being open to scrutiny, responsive to the public, and accountable for their actions. The latter, of course, is somewhat different in the American context than the parliamentary context, which emphasizes Ministerial and collective responsibility for all actions. The American standard, in general, is one of open reporting, public records, and access to public agents, including their formal decision-making meetings. The legislative body oversees executive action, and reporting occurs routinely up the hierarchy, and outside it, to legislators and the public. This may consist of only a yearly budget hearing and quarterly or annual reports or may involve constant and pervasive oversight and hundreds of reports. Since the passage of the Freedom of Information Act, fewer documents qualify as sufficiently confidential to warrant exclusion from the public eye, although the Patriot Act of 1991 has introduced new security restrictions. In the information age, the availability of data and its accessibility increased dramatically, creating a host of new possibilities for bringing services to citizens, while, at the same time, questions of security, privacy, confidentiality, and the misuse of data are consistently raised. In addition, investigative reporters keep a watchful eye on public officials, always interested in ferreting out wrongdoing or unusual action that will make news.

Administrative Subcultures

Arguably, no one characterization fits all officials. Sub-types are necessary to help differentiate the sets of values, beliefs, and attitudes in American public administration and to avoid static characterizations. At one level, it is possible to talk of the American administrative culture but to distinguish variation over time (e.g., demoralization in the Reagan era; reorientation for "homeland security" in the post-9/11 era) and by place, hierarchical level, even age, requires "subculture" analysis. Three types are suggested here.

Traditional

This subculture defines a large group of officials (probably the largest) in federal, state, and local government who appreciate the security and benefits provided but at the same time are oriented to serving the public following laws and rules. They are at the heart of Goodsell's analysis and they do their jobs faithfully and with some degree of efficiency and effectiveness. As Norma Riccucci (1995) points out, many officials labor in relative obscurity yet make significant contributions beyond the normal duties and responsibilities of their positions. They should be celebrated, Riccucci tells us, but usually escape public attention.

The range of federal, state, and local officialdom is enormous, with "street-level bureaucrats" (e.g., police, case workers, educators) composing a large group who are in direct touch with the public. Others are less visible and may become known only in the breach (or alleged breach) of some rule or norm while the vast majority of officials continue to work outside the scope of media scrutiny.

A large body of empirical and theoretical literature exists which characterizes groups of U.S. officials (e.g., elites), compares officials in different nations, contrasts public and private sector employees, and assesses areas such as risk-aversion. The best "traditionalists" reflect an ethos that emphasizes virtuous, moral behavior and eschews the temptations of corruption and/or favoritism.

Self-Protective

At certain times and in certain places, public officials have perceived themselves under attack from chief executives, legislators, and the public. The response, short of paranoia, has often been to redirect their behavior toward careful and cautious calculation of ways to survive downsizing, rightsizing, threats of privatization, or just widespread "bureaucrat bashing." M. M. Golden (2000) provides a good description of this process during the Reagan years. Strategies of exit, voice, and loyalty (A. O. Hirschman's well-known trilogy) are supplemented by "neglect." Officials hunker down for a difficult time during which they feel under-appreciated and over-scrutinized by legislators, political appointees, the general public, and (often most importantly) the media. However, they continue cooperating, at least in a passive sense: "In essence, neglect is cooperative behavior motivated by reasons other than loyalty" (Golden 2000:19).

Entrepreneurial

One of the goals of the New Public Management, evidenced clearly in the Reinvention movement of the 1990s, was to change the culture "away from complacency and entitlement and toward initiative and empowerment" (Clinton 1993). Achieving such an entrepreneurial culture would be a major objective of the Clinton White House, the guidelines for which were first defined by Osbourne and Gaebler (1992) in their celebrated work. The official end of "Reinventing Government" and the National Performance Review (renamed the National Partnership for Reinventing Government in its second phase) preceded slightly the end of the Clinton administration but its directives and initial experiments were not overturned by the George W. Bush administration. Rather, Bush and his policy advisors, prior to 9/11, talked mildly of Civil Service Reform, greater flexibility in the merit system and in pay schedules, and new accountability and performance measures. The congressionally mandated Government Performance and Results Act remained in force.

After 9/11, "entrepreneurial" took on new significance as government officials were called upon to answer the challenge of Homeland Security through rapid, flexible, coordinated responses to internal and external threats. Agencies were realigned—most notably in the new Federal Department of Homeland Security—and new cooperative mechanisms instituted that would involve state and local officials along with federal. Funding was adjusted accordingly with high priority to defense and security functions and lower priority to standard programs less involved in defense and security.

Following the removal of Saddam Hussein, the United States government took on the task of recreating the government of Iraq, even as it continued to build institutions and reorient behaviors in Afghanistan. Administrative globalization assumed a new meaning, arguably requiring "entrepreneurial," or at least innovative, actions by U.S. officials in a variety of agencies from USAID (Agency for International Development) and State generally, to the Defense Department, Agriculture, Energy, and other departments involved in the reconstruction efforts.

The Merit Culture in a Borderless World

Unlike most nation-states, the United States has been a net exporter of administrative ideas and institutions, including the values and attitudes of the administrative culture. Convergence of nation-based administrative cultures in developing countries with that of the United States and other Northern countries seems to be occurring. CNN, the World Wide Web, international commerce, increased travel, and other factors facilitate mutual awareness and contribute to what Marshall McLuhan famously identified as the global village. The global administrative village breaks barriers to understanding and increases the impetus toward homogenization at the same time as it marginalizes the indigenous quality of national administration. This, of course, is not without considerable controversy including that related to the relative prospects for self-direction as opposed to "internationalization" (Henderson 2001)

Many years ago, beginning in Latin America, the United States introduced its understanding of the merit culture to others through a variety of civil service reform efforts. As far back as the 1920s, these were supplemented by incipient civil service training academies and education programs for the public service designed to modernize administration. Attempts were made—at the invitation of the host governments—to instill values of integrity and service in public workforces more usually hidebound to rule enforcement and corruption norms.

Although the Chinese are usually given credit for inventing the notion of merit for officialdom and the British (and Germans) for perfecting it in the industrializing world, it is the United States that made the greatest effort to universalize the norm of a competent, honest, non-political group of officials (excepting, of course, such doubtful claims for colonialism). Following the Second World War, the Marshall Plan helped with the reconstruction of Europe and the restoration of government services. In the Comparative Public Administration movement of the 1950s, 1960s, and 1970s, numerous attempts (often dramatically unsuccessful) were made to instill public service values around the globe. With the advent of New Public Management in the 1980s and 1990s, a shift occurred towards business-like flexibility and customer responsiveness values, along with downsizing. This was promoted by the World Bank, International Monetary Fund, United States Agency for International Development (USAID), and other multilateral and bilateral donors, often as a condition for financial assistance. Public administration reform as such received less emphasis than overall requirements for downsizing, lowering costs, reducing subsidies, privatizing, and changing macroeconomic policies.

Interestingly, the rebuilding of Afghanistan and Iraq at the beginning of the twenty-first century reflects some of the earlier thinking and less of the rhetoric of the New Public Management or even "structural adjustment."

In Afghanistan, following defeat of the Taliban, the United States and its coalition partners, including an important public administration program by the European Union, sought to restore and develop rudimentary public services. As in Iraq, beginning in 2003, the question of who should assume the public servant roles arose and the obvious answer, applied before in post-Communist administrative reforms, was to remove regime-tainted top officials (called Lustration in the Communist examples) but retain most others. A new public service ethos, however, was expected from officials and this could be characterized as similar to the merit administrative culture described in this chapter.

Toward a Globalization of American Administrative Culture

It is, perhaps, ironic that the widely extended American administrative culture is commonly regarded by people outside the United States as parochial (Huddleston 2000). In order to overcome perceived parochialism, Huddleston and others suggest rediscovering comparative administration; replacing outdated ideas on hierarchy and other obsolete concepts with "flat, networked, and responsive global styles" (Huddleston 2000); embracing diversity, and building bridges to partners abroad by sharing ideas and best practices. Information technology, international competitiveness, and avoidance of parochialism would be the key elements of the American public service in the twenty-first century.

For better or worse, the rapid spread of interest in the New Public Management and its applications in the United States, Britain, Australia, New Zealand, and elsewhere has encouraged a globalization of the basic public service values associated with it. As suggested here in the entrepreneurial subculture, these values are focused on the processes of entrepreneurial, customer oriented behavior more than the end values of constitutionalism (see Rosenbloom 2000). Many have suggested a preferred alternative to the New Public Management—or at least its modification—as the administrative world becomes uni-polar and administrative change is urged on all nation-states. The dominance of one administrative culture may be foreseen and that culture would be rooted in Western traditions, particularly American. A value ethics (Caiden, Dwivedi, and Jabbra 2001) or "new public service" (Denhardt and Denhardt 2003) would shift the focus from entrepreneurial, job satisfaction measures, which require process values back to values associated with ends rather than means. Universal values long prized in public administration (see Appleby 1952; Bailey 1964) would be restored and augmented by requirements for proficiency in information technology and avoidance of parochialism.

Accordingly, a "new administrative culture" (in the words of Rosenbloom and Kravchuk) would be required, which "will be at ease with complexity, law, and flexibility. They [the public officials] will be performance oriented, have a strong service ethic, span boundaries, and be adroit at conflict avoidance and resolution" (Rosenbloom and Kravchuk 2002).

Such a new administrative culture would extend the core values of the merit system to embrace twenty-first century needs without sacrificing neutrality, professionalism, and transparency.

REFERENCES

Almond, G. and S. Verba. 1965. *The Civic Culture*. Boston: Little Brown.

Anechiarico, F. 1998. "Administrative Culture and Civil Society." *Administration and Society* 30(1):13-24.

Appleby, P. 1952. *Morality and Administration*. Baton Rouge, LA: LSU Press.

Ashkanasy, N., C. Wilderom, and M. Peterson, eds. 2000. *Handbook of Organizational Culture and Climate*. Thousand Oaks, CA: Sage.

ASPA. 1994. "Mission Statement and Code of Ethics." Washington, DC: ASPA.

Bailey, S. 1964. "Ethics and the Public Service." *Public Administration Review* 24(4):234-43.

Bozeman, B. 2003. "Risk, Reform and Organizational Culture: The Case of IRS Tax Systems Modernization." *International Public Management Journal* 6(2):117-143.

Caiden, G. 1970. *Israel's Administrative Culture*. Berkeley, CA: Institute of Governmental Studies.

Caiden, G., O. P. Dwivedi, and J. Jabbra, eds. 2001. *Where Corruption Lies*. Bloomfield, CT: Kumarian Press.

Clinton, W. 1993. "Remarks Announcing the National Performance Review." *Public Papers of the Presidents* March 1993. Washington, DC: Government Printing Office.

Denhardt, R. and A. Denhardt. 2003. *The New Public Service, Serving not Steering.* Armonk, NY: M. E. Sharpe.

Dresang, D. 2002. *Public Personnel Management and Public Policy*, 4th edition. New York, NY: Longman.

Dwivedi, O. P., and J. I. Gow, eds. 1999. *From Bureaucracy to Public Management.* Peterborough, Ontario: Broadview Press for Institute of Public Administration of Canada.

Eagles, Monroe and Larry Johnston. 1999. *Politics: An Introduction to Democratic Politics*. Peterborough, Ontario: Broadview Press.

Elazar, D. 1984. *American Federalism, A View from the States*, 3rd ed. New York, NY: Harper and Row.

Golden, M. M. 2000. *What Motivates Bureaucrats?* New York, NY: Columbia University Press.

Goodsell, Charles. 1994. *The Case for Bureaucracy, A Public Administration Polemic*, 3d ed. Chatham, NJ: Chatham House.

Henderson, K. 2001. "Indigenization versus Internationalization." In *Handbook of Comparative and Development Public Administration*, 2d ed, edited by A. Farazmand. New York, NY: Marcel Dekker.

Hofstede, G. 1991. *Cultures and Organizations.* London: McGraw Hill.

———. 1980. *Culture's Consequences, International Differences in Work-Related Values.* Beverly Hills, CA: Sage.

Huddleston, M. W. 2000. *Onto the Darkling Plain: Globalization and the American Public Service in the Twenty-first Century* Pp.177-191 in *The Future of Merit*, edited by James P. Pfiffner and Douglas Brook. Baltimore, Md: Johns Hopkins.

Hummel, R. 2000. *The Bureaucratic Experience.* New York, NY: St. Martins.

Ingraham, P. W. 1995. *The Foundations of Merit: Public Service in American Democracy.* Baltimore, MD: Johns Hopkins.

Keraudren, P. 1996. "Administrative Culture and Civil Society." *Administration and Society* 30(1):13-24.

Kettl, Donald, Patricia Ingraham, Ronald Sanders, and Constance Horner. 1996. *Civil Service Reform: Building a Government that Works.* Washington, DC: Brookings.

Key Communications Group. 2003. *Federal Personnel Guide, 2003.* Washington, DC: Key Communications Group.

Krislov, S. 1974. *Representative Bureaucracy.* Englewood Cliffs, NJ: Prentice-Hall.

Martin, Joanne. 2002. *Organizational Culture: Mapping the Terrain.* Thousand Oaks, CA:

Sage Publications.

Merit System Protection Board. 1997. "Adherence to the Merit Principle in the Workplace: Federal Employees' Views." Washington, DC: The Board.

Nisbett, Richard E. 2003. *The Geography of Thought: How Asians and Westerns Think Differently...and Why.* New York, NY: The Free Press.

Office of Personnel Management. 1992. "Personnel Research Highlights, Special Report on the Survey of Federal Employees (SOFE)." Washington, DC: OPM.

Office of Personnel Management. 2002. "What Do Federal Employees Say? Results from the 2002 Federal Human Capital Survey." Washington, DC: OPM.

Osbourne, D. and Ted Gaebler. 1992. *Reinventing Government.* Reading, MA: Addison-Wesley.

Paik, Wanki. 1990. *Korean Administrative Culture.* Seoul, Korea: Korea University Press.

Pettigrew, Andrew. 1979. "On Studying Organizational Culture." *Administrative Science Quarterly* 24(4):570-581.

Riccucci, Norma. 1995. *Unsung Heroes: Federal Executives Making a Difference.* Washington, DC: Georgetown University Press.

Riley, R. 2002. *Public Personnel Administration.* New York, NY: Longman.

Rosenbloom, D. 2000. "Retrofitting the Administrative State to the Constitution." *Public Administration Review* 60(1):39-46.

Rosenbloom, D. and Robert Kravchuk. 2002. *Public Administration*, 5th ed. New York, NY: McGraw Hill.

Schein, Edgar. 2000. "Sense and Nonsense About Culture and Climate." Pp. xiii-xv in *Handbook of Organizational Culture and Climate,* edited by Ashkanasy, Wilderom, and Peterson. Thousand Oaks, CA: Sage.

———. 1985. *Organizational Culture and Leadership.* San Francisco, CA: Jossey-Bass

Sharma, R. D. 2000. *Administrative Culture in India.* New Delhi: Anamika Publishers.

Van Riper, P. 1958. *History of the United States Civil Service.* New York, NY: Harper and Row.

Waldo, Dwight. 1948. *The Administrative State.* New York, NY: Ronald.

Washington Post. 2003. "An Overhaul, Not a Tune-Up." June 16-22, p.30.

Chapter 3

TOWARDS A MANAGERIAL CULTURE: THE BRITISH CIVIL SERVICE EXPERIENCE

John Greenwood and Lynton Robins

Changes in the British civil service during the last few decades of the twentieth century have made it a very different organization from what it used to be. In keeping with the gradual development that has characterized many British institutions, the civil service had previously evolved slowly and until the last quarter of the twentieth century it still bore many of the features of past ages. During the late twentieth century, however, the British civil service underwent profound changes. Most of these changes were motivated by a desire to achieve greater managerial efficiency and better "value for money." In the process, however, many of the traditional features that characterized the British Civil Service also changed, creating not only a profoundly different culture but also changes in technique, ethos, and structure

The Traditional Civil Service Culture

To understand the traditional administrative culture within the British civil service it is important to recognize the significance of historical influences. Until the nineteenth century there was often no clear distinction between political and administrative roles. Recruitment was usually through ministerial patronage and promotion by seniority. Ministers were directly responsible to the monarch, while civil servants owed their responsibility to their immediate superior and ultimately to the minister himself. From the late eighteenth century onwards, however, demands for reform appeared and these gained momentum during the early nineteenth century as, with the industrial revolution, the state acquired new functions and the cost of administration rose. The main reforms at this time flowed from the Northcote-Trevelyan Report (1854) which made four basic recommendations: (1) recruitment by open competitive examination; (2) promotion by merit; (3) unification of the service, and (4) a division between "intellectual" work performed by graduates and routine "mechanical" work to be performed by those with lesser ability. These radical proposals met some contemporary opposition—mostly from politicians who valued their powers of patronage—and they were implemented only gradually. Nevertheless, all were eventually put in place and they thus came to form the basis of Britain's civil service during much of the twentieth century.

The administrative culture that flowed from Northcote-Trevelyan was that of a constitutional bureaucracy recruited and promoted by merit. Unlike the "spoils system," which developed under different conditions in the United States and many other countries, British civil servants owed their appointment, and their promotion, to the application of meritocratic principles. One inevitable consequence of this was that the British civil service became a career service; hence, civil servants were permanent career officials who served different governments irrespective of their political complexion. This, in turn, required them to be politically neutral. Their primary allegiance, in fact, was not to politicians, not even to politicians forming the government of the day, but to the Crown in whose name government was conducted. In fact, the generally agreed upon definition of civil servants used by the Tomlin Report (1931) was "Servants of the Crown, other than holders of political or judicial offices, who are employed in a civil capacity and whose remuneration is paid wholly and directly out of monies voted by Parliament." These servants of the Crown, in order to manifest political neutrality, were prohibited from engaging in partisan political activity or allowing personal views to intrude upon official duties. They were to provide impartial advice to ministers but, once the minister's decision was known, implement it faithfully irrespective of whatever personal political views they themselves might hold. A further feature that flowed from the application of the Northcote-Trevelyan principles was that because too close an identification with particular politicians on polices might compromise neutrality, civil servants should be anonymous. Permanence, political neutrality, and anonymity thus became bedrock features upon which the administrative culture of the twentieth century British civil service was built.

Northcote-Trevelyan also influenced the administrative culture in other ways. The recommended division between "intellectuals" and "mechanicals," for example, influenced the creation of hierarchical class divisions that have survived in some respects through to the present time. It also entrenched the dominance of the "generalist" administrator. In the mid-nineteenth century, the performance of efficient administration was within the compass of any intelligent man; specialist skills were largely unnecessary because there was little need for them. Consequently, there developed what the Fulton Report (1968) described as the tradition of the "all-rounder" or "amateur"; a tradition that continued to manifest itself in the upper echelons of the civil service during the twentieth century when the complexity of government—and the increasing need to develop public policy in fields requiring specialist knowledge—placed a premium on not only high administrative skills, but also technical expertise and managerial competence. Unlike many other political systems such as the United States, France, and Germany, where top level civil servants usually have expertise in fields relevant to their work, specialists in Britain have traditionally been excluded from the highest posts. The effect of this was heightened by the fact that a high proportion of graduate recruits throughout the twentieth century came from exclusive educational backgrounds—typically prestigious public schools (which in Britain are private schools outside the state system) and the ancient universities at Oxford and Cambridge —and many also had degrees in arts subjects such as history and classics. As a result, the service was traditionally dominated by a graduate elite drawn largely from arts disciplines and exclusive social and educational backgrounds. This "generalist" dominance—interestingly not replicated in the other major tier of governance in Britain, local government, where specialist professionals tended to predominate—was, and to a large extent still is, a dominant feature of the civil service administrative culture. Needless to say, most of those at the very top were also male as well as middle aged and middle class (not, of course, at all unlike the political elite that they usually happened to serve).

Another important influence upon civil service administrative culture was Northcote-Trevelyan's recommendation that the civil service should be unified. Until the nineteenth century, there had been no attempt to coordinate the work of the civil service. The service was contained within largely autonomous departments and agencies for which each minister was directly responsible to the monarch. No department, and no individual, had general supervisory responsibility for the service as a whole. Indeed, many posts were actually sinecures and many procedures obsolete. Northcote-Trevelyan's recommendation for a unified service was a direct response to the inefficiency that such arrangements inevitably created and led eventually to the creation of a single integrated civil service, recruited and managed as a whole. Recruitment to the service became the responsibility of an independent Civil Service Commission established in 1855 and gradually the Treasury came to be regarded as the department primarily responsible for civil service pay and management. Over time, as many common grades, pay scales, pension arrangements, appointment and promotion procedures were introduced, the civil service became increasingly unified; a process that helped to unify a workforce still structured around hierarchical grades and functional departments. Civil servants were not seen as employees of a particular department—indeed many moved between departments several times during their careers—but as servants of the crown collectively loyal to the government of the day. Indeed, during the second half of the twentieth century, several steps were taken to try to unify the service still further. In 1968, for example, the Fulton Report recommended that a single, unified grading structure should be created throughout the service; and that a civil service department be created with responsibility for pay, management, and administrative efficiency throughout the service. While the single unified grading structure was never fully implemented—and the Civil Service Department in the form it was established following Fulton was abolished by Mrs Thatcher in 1981—these key recommendations clearly illustrate the belief in a unified civil service that characterized the pre-Thatcher era. Even after Thatcher, there were still several manifestations of this. Subsequent Prime Ministers, for example, maintained primary responsibility for civil service management within a lead department, and the Blair government in 1999 retained the concept of a unified civil service serving not only the UK government in London, but also the devolved executives established in Scotland and Wales. As one authoritative observer put it, "its sense of unity"—characterized by centralized recruitment, common pay, grading and conditions, and service-wide promotion opportunities—was traditionally regarded as "the most important characteristic of the British civil service" (Chapman 1992: 2).

Of course, changes within the civil service do not take place within a vacuum. During the nineteenth and twentieth centuries, democratic advances occurred, the effect of which was to massively reduce the role of the monarch and increase that of Parliament, and, in particular, the House of Commons. As a result, ministers, who in the eighteenth century had been responsible to the monarch had, by the twentieth century, become responsible to Parliament. By the convention of ministerial responsibility, ministers were assumed to be responsible for not only their own actions and decisions, but also those of their departmental civil servants. Civil servants were thus accountable through ministers to Parliament. While there were occasional instances of civil servants being "named and blamed" when things went wrong, this was not the normal pattern. Ministers generally accepted both the praise and the blame for the actions and decisions of their officials thus maintaining and reinforcing the anonymity and political neutrality of civil servants themselves.

As a result of these developments, by the last quarter of the twentieth century, the administrative culture of the civil service was built around five main features. These were (1) Accountability through ministers to Parliament; (2) Permanence: in contrast to the "spoils system" in the United States, British civil servants were permanent. Many spent their entire career within the service; (3) Political Neutrality: Permanence was reinforced by political neutrality; (4) Anonymity: Permanence and neutrality were further reinforced by anonymity. Civil servants did not engage in public debate about their official duties, and their advice to ministers remained confidential; (5) Unity: The civil service was a unified service with many common features, such as pay scales, grades, and pension arrangements, which applied throughout the service.

Changing the Culture: The Impact of Mrs Thatcher

Several factors underlie Mrs. Thatcher's concern to reform the civil service. One was that, unlike predecessors such as Wilson and Heath, Thatcher had not previously been a civil servant and her experience as a cabinet minister consisted of a single spell as Minister of Education. She was thus something of a Whitehall outsider, less steeped in the traditional administrative culture of the civil service and more prepared to adopt fresh approaches. Another was that, while the 1979 Conservative election manifesto said little about the civil service, it did stress the need to control public spending and reduce waste. A third was that Thatcher's premiership coincided with a period when changes were occurring in public bureaucracies in many advanced countries. Under the influence of the "New Public Management," hierarchic Weberian bureaucracies were being systematically dismantled and replaced with new structures and techniques based around private sector models which stressed market-based forms of public management. Such developments naturally appealed to a politician such as Thatcher from the New Right and were reinforced in her case by the belief that the civil service inherited from previous Labour governments had been bloated through the culture of "big government" and state intervention. Central to Thatcher's approach was a drive to change civil service culture by drawing on expertise and techniques associated with the private sector. Senior civil servants were to be re-cast more as managers, rather than formerly as policy makers and administrators, in order deliver to tax payers greater "value for money." As Margaret Thatcher herself explained, "there was even a problem at the very top. Some Permanent Secretaries had come to think of themselves mainly as policy advisers, forgetting that they were also responsible for the efficient management of their departments" (Thatcher 1993:4).

Thatcher's main reforms were applied incrementally through a series of measures, which, collectively, were to result in a fundamental shift toward a more managerial culture within the service. Under Thatcher, three measures were particularly important: (1) The Rayner Scrutiny Programme; (2) The Financial Management Initiative; and (3) The Next Steps Report.

Rayner Scrutiny Programme

One of Thatcher's first acts as Prime Minister was to appoint Sir (later Lord) Derek Rayner (formerly head of a major UK retail chain) as an advisor on administrative efficiency. Leading a small "efficiency unit" and reporting directly to Thatcher, his main approach was developed through a series of "efficiency scrutinies" of departmental activities. By the 1990s, savings totalling £1.5 billion had been claimed.

Perhaps more significant were two early scrutinies that led to more lasting reforms which were encompassed within the Financial Management Initiative launched in 1982.

The Financial Management Initiative (FMI)

Less a discrete initiative than a rolling program under which a new management philosophy was developed, the FMI launched in 1982 was designed to improve managerial efficiency within Whitehall. It had several key elements, all of which were intended to develop more of a management culture among top civil servants.

The Development of Managerial Information Systems within Government Departments

Managerial information systems were designed to enable top management to review departmental aims, examine its "business" and "customers," to set objectives, and establish priorities. This was important both in terms of providing a new management tool within Whitehall and for requiring top civil servants to think increasingly about their departments' "businesses" and "customers."

Decentralization and Delegation

The post-war British civil service, reflecting the emergence of a welfare state and increased state economic intervention, had grown inexorably in size. Government departments had also grown in both size and complexity and, in 1970, several of these merged together into what came to be known as "Giant" departments. The outcome of one early Rayner scrutiny was to divide one of these "Giant" departments, the Department of the Environment, into 120 cost centers, and this subsequently became the basis for restructuring all Whitehall departments. Thereafter, civil servants were required to show greater concern for efficient financial management within departments through structures that directly related the activities for which they were responsible to the cost of carrying them out.

Performance Measurement

Performance Measurement—the measurement of economy, efficiency, and effectiveness (the three Es) of both administrative functions and programs—was a central feature of the FMI and came to be widely used as a tool for measuring "value for money" (VFM) within Whitehall.

Although implementation of the FMI was somewhat patchy, it promised to bring about a gradual transformation within the civil service and, crucially, laid the foundations for the third plank of Thatcher's reforms.

The Next Steps Report

Originating partly from frustration that the scrutiny program was not generating more radical change, the Efficiency Unit, now under Sir Robin Ibbs (who, like Rayner also had a private sector background), in 1988 produced what came to be popularly known as "The Next Steps Report." The report, entitled *Improving Management in Government: The Next Steps*, identified five key findings (Efficiency Unit 1988):

1. 95 percent of civil servants were concerned with service delivery
2. Senior civil servants lacked skill in service delivery
3. Ministers were overloaded
4. There was insufficient emphasis on results and performance
5. The Civil Service was too big and too diverse to be managed as a single service

The remedy proposed for addressing these problems was radical, flying as it did in the face of the traditional wisdom, inherited from Northcote-Trevelyan, that the civil service should function as a single unified entity. The key proposals were the following: (1) Executive Agencies (which quickly became known as "Next Steps Agencies") should be created to deliver the executive services of government; (2) Ministers should determine the policy and budget of Agencies, set performance targets, and monitor performance; (3) Agencies should be headed by a ministerially appointed chief executive responsible for management of the agency and performance.

On this analysis lay a realization that Whitehall departments were overwhelmingly concerned with service delivery rather than policy and that the traditional, largely uniform, design of departments—with common grading, pay, and organization—was no longer appropriate. Policy work should thus be separated from service delivery, with the latter becoming the responsibility of "agencies" headed by chief executives enjoying substantial managerial autonomy. Conventional departments would not disappear, but their role and size would be considerably reduced. Henceforth, they would be primarily concerned with policy making, supporting ministers' parliamentary roles, and with setting the strategic framework of agencies and monitoring their work. The agencies would work to targets, budgets, and policy guidelines set by ministers in their "sponsoring department."

The Thatcher government immediately accepted these proposals. A "Next Steps" project team was created within the Cabinet Office and several agencies were quickly established. These included the Vehicle Inspectorate (responsible for testing roadworthiness of heavy goods and public service vehicles); the

Employment Service (responsible for job placement services); and Companies House (responsible for corporate sector company information). The government also committed itself to having 75 percent of civil servants working in agencies within ten years. When Thatcher herself left office in 1990, twenty-five agencies had been established and numerous other activities had been identified for agency status.

Thatcher was succeeded as Prime Minister by John Major. Under the Major government, the creation of Next Steps agencies accelerated. By 1997, one hundred and thirty agencies containing 387,000 civil servants (approximately 74 percent) had been established, thereby meeting Thatcher's target announced in 1988. Major also introduced a review program every five years. This program, *Prior Options*, required each agency to examine whether agency status was still appropriate or whether some other arrangement such as privatization or contractorization might be more appropriate. By 1998, eleven agencies had been privatized and three had had all their functions contracted-out. Under Major, it also became normal for chief executives to be appointed on fixed term contracts linked to performance and for their recruitment to be by Open Competition: by 1997, 23 percent had been recruited from outside and 67 percent appointed by open competition.

In 1997, Major was succeeded as Prime Minister by Tony Blair. Under Blair, NSAs were accepted as "an integral part of the government machine" (Butcher 1998:1). However, while some new agencies were formed, the Blair government took the view that agency creation was largely complete and that emphasis should switch to performance improvement. Subsequently, the Next Steps unit in the Cabinet Office was disbanded, although *Prior Options* was reaffirmed, as was recruitment of chief executives through Open Competition. By 2000, 78 percent of civil servants were then working within Next Steps arrangements and there were 133 agencies. Four government departments (Crown Prosecution Service, Customs and Excise, Inland Revenue, and Serious Fraud Office) were also reported to be operating fully on Next Steps lines (Stationery Office 2002).

Today, NSAs are an accepted feature of UK government. The functions they perform vary enormously. These include: inspecting public service vehicles; running conference centers and prisons; and providing services that issue driving licences, passports, and social security benefits. In 2000, the largest NSA, the Social Security Benefits Agency, employed 69,230 people, and the smallest, the Debt Management Office, just 30. The relationships between each NSA and its parent departments is usually contained in a published framework document that typically will include the agency's aims and objectives; its relations with Parliament and ministers; financial responsibilities and any performance measures; and delegated responsibilities for personnel and training. While precise relationships between sponsoring departments and NSAs may vary, and in some cases may be somewhat blurred, the underlying principle is a repositioning of central government executive operations "at arm's length" from departments, allowing a considerable degree of managerial autonomy to chief executives. In 1996, all departments and agencies received delegated responsibility for pay and grading of all except the most senior civil service staff. Thus, while strengthening the culture of management in Whitehall, Next Steps has largely removed the previous near-uniform pay and grading structure that formerly was one of the hallmarks of the unified British civil service.

Inevitably, departmental roles have also been refocused. They are now responsible for policy-making, ministerial support, legislation, finance, personnel, plus performance monitoring and target setting for agencies. Major also required departments to undertake Fundamental Expenditure Reviews and Senior Management Reviews, identifying objectives and better ways of meeting goals, leading to staffing and core budget reductions in most departments. Next Steps has thus impacted more widely upon Whitehall reinforcing the emphasis on performance and managerial efficiency in departments, which has been a feature of successive governments since the late 1970s.

Changing the Culture: The Major and Blair Governments

As we have seen, the governments of John Major and Tony Blair accepted and built on the earlier civil service reforms of Margaret Thatcher, in particular by accelerating, expanding, and further developing the Next Steps program. However, they have also introduced other changes that profoundly affected the service. Two key initiatives introduced by Major in 1991 illustrate his government's commitment to continuing Thatcher's civil service reform agenda. One was Market Testing, following publication of the White Paper *Competing for Quality* in 1991(HM Treasury 1991). Effectively, this required key central government activities to be put out to tender along lines similar to compulsory competitive tendering, which Thatcher had imposed on local government in the 1980s. Presented by Major as a logical further step in the search for value for money, between 1992 and 1996 £3.6 billion of activities were market tested leading to considerable contracting-out of agency and departmental functions. The other significant early initiative launched by Major, also in 1991, was the Citizen's Charter (Prime Minister's Office 1991) designed to promote quality and customer awareness within public services through published performance targets and audited performance. Subsequently continued by Blair, albeit under the new name of "Service First," the Charter initiative (which applied throughout the public sector and not just Whitehall) was specifically intended to reinforce customer focus and performance improvement and, thereby, to build on earlier Thatcherite initiatives.

Major also further developed the Thatcherite search for increased value for money within the civil service. In 1994 and 1995, he issued two White Papers: *The Civil Service: Continuity and Change* (Prime Minister 1994); and *The Civil Service: Taking Forward Continuity and Change* (Prime Minister 1995). These papers contained significant proposals concerning structure, pay and grading, recruitment, and promotion. As a response to the fragmentation that had accompanied the development of NSAs, Major proposed, and subsequently established, a new Senior Civil Service (SCS) comprised of roughly 3500 top level civil servants including NSA chief executives. Formed in 1996, a major objective was strengthening the cohesion of not only the senior management of departments but also the cohesion of the wider Senior Civil Service. However, SCS pay was to be based on individual contracts linked to performance. Below SCS level, pay systems were delegated to individual departments, thus ending the traditional pattern of centralized service-wide pay scales.

Major also largely abandoned the centralized recruitment system, which had been a key feature of the Northcote-Trevelyan structure. In 1991, the Civil Service Commission, responsible for recruitment throughout the service, was abolished and the task of recruitment fragmented among different departments and agencies Also, the largely internal system of promotion to the top posts, which was already being undermined by the steady recruitment of NSA chief executives from outside, was effectively abolished by the recommendation that open competition should apply to posts within the SCS itself. Indeed, in 1995, it was applied to Permanent Secretary level (the top departmental grade) when Michael Bichard was appointed Permanent Secretary at the Department of Employment. Subsequently, when this department merged with another, Bichard was again appointed Permanent Secretary following open competition. Thus, open competition effectively came to cover almost the entire civil service with the inevitable result that thereafter the numbers of "outsiders" brought into top Whitehall positions steadily increased.

Significantly, under Major one prominent civil servant, Sir Peter Kemp, Second Permanent secretary at the Office of Public Service and Science, was dismissed. His minister, William Waldegrave, claimed to need a Permanent Secretary with different skills, and so Kemp was effectively dismissed. While in many ways a logical step in the continued pursuit of greater managerial efficiency, such a development had obvious implications for civil service permanence—one of most hallowed building blocks of the Northcote-Trevelyan system.

Blair's government, although representing a new party in government for the first time since 1979, continued with the civil service managerial reforms inherited from Thatcher and Blair. Indeed, not only were key initiatives such as Next Steps and the Citizen's Charter maintained by the new government, but they were linked with a wider emphasis on public sector reform, which became a key item of Blair's domestic political agenda. In 1999, the government published a key White Paper, *Modernising Government,* which, while dealing with public services generally, proposed "a change of course for the Civil Service for the next 10 years as important as Next Steps 10 years previously." It outlined "seven challenges for the civil service" including a renewed emphasis on improving the quality of public services and the creation of a "more innovative and less-risk averse culture in the civil service." However, conscious that the government's devolution policy, which included the creation of devolved executives in Scotland and Wales, *Modernising Government* significantly moved against further fragmentation by announcing the intention to preserve "a unified civil service" in order to ensure "close working between the UK government and the devolved administrations" (Prime Minister and Minister for the Cabinet Office 1999).

The job of fleshing out the detail necessary to achieve these goals was subsequently given to the then Cabinet Secretary, Sir Richard Wilson. His response, produced after consultation within senior ranks within the service, constituted what came to be known as the "Wilson Report" (Wilson 1999). This contained a number of key themes, notably:

1. Stronger leadership with a clear sense of purpose
2. Better business planning from top to bottom
3. Sharper performance management
4. A dramatic improvement in diversity
5. A service more open to people and ideas, which brings on talent
6. A better deal for staff

Responsibility for implementing these "themes" was given to the Cabinet Office Corporate Management Command section. Departments were to prepare Departmental Action Plans linked to targets. Some of the most far-reaching targets included: an annual 10 percent increase in open competition for five years, 65 percent of SCS to have outside experience by 2005, and 100 key tasks to attract high quality inward secondees during 2000. There were also commitments to recruit more mid-career outsiders; to broaden Fast Stream entry; to expand inter-departmental mobility; and to introduce a new scheme to develop 100 non-Fast Stream managers. It was anticipated that targeted early retirement would create "more space at the top."

The reaction to these proposals was mixed. While some perceived them as an extension of earlier initiatives such as Next Steps, others claimed to "detect sweeping reforms to shake up Whitehall," which could potentially transform the service. These latter views rested on the belief that more staff mobility, private sector experience, fast track promotions, etc., would effectively transform the service "along the lines of a thriving private enterprise" (*The Times,* December 16, 1999; *The Observer,* December 19, 1999). It would also, however, further erode permanence and unity and, arguably, dilute its public sector ethos.

There has been one other important development in Blair's approach to the civil service. From the 1960s, governments had gradually instituted the practice of drawing on the expertise of a small number of special advisers. Their role was essentially to provide ministers with an alternative source of policy advice to that offered by civil servants. When Major left office in 1997, there were just 38 of these in post. Blair, however, considerably increased their numbers and by 2000 there were more than 70. Many of these worked in Blair's much expanded Prime Minister's Office and many were employed not to give advice over policy, but as spin-doctors who controlled media presentation and publicity. While views about their usefulness varied, one thing was clear: Special advisors, unlike professional civil servants, were neither neutral nor permanent, but were appointed, in part, for their political sympathies and left office with their minister. Some, moreover, were far from anonymous. Alistair Campbell, Blair's one-time Press Secretary, and Jonathan Powell, his Chief of Staff, both became high profile figures; the more so because their responsibilities allowed them to give instructions to permanent officials. Taken alongside other developments their increased use by, particularly, the Blair government further challenged traditional features of civil service culture.

The Civil Service Today

Since the late 1970s, successive governments have worked systematically to change the traditional administrative culture to one that is more concerned with value for money and managerial efficiency. To this end, Thatcher, after initial experimentation with Rayner Scrutinies and the Financial Management Initiative, launched Next Steps and with it a comprehensive restructuring of the machinery of government along more "business-like" lines. Major built on this by extending open competition firstly to NSA Chief Executive posts and then more widely within the service. Under Major, centralized systems of recruitment and pay were dismantled; market testing was introduced, and the Citizen's Charter designed to improve quality by focusing managers' attention upon service standards and customer responsiveness. Blair, despite leading a different political party from Thatcher and Major, has accepted and built upon his predecessors' reforms. The Wilson Report, couched in the language of "stronger leadership," "better business planning," and "sharper performance management" envisages much more interchange of personnel between the private sector and the civil service. Today's senior civil servants, especially those in NSAs, are far more likely than their predecessors, a quarter of a century before, to think and act less like bureaucrats and administrators and much more like business managers. They are also much more likely to be budget holders, focused on customers and on contracts linking pay with performance.

What is interesting, however, is that as the civil service has been redefined in more managerialist terms, many of the traditional features upon which the service was built have also changed. While the motivation in the case of Thatcher, Major, and Blair was, essentially, efficient service delivery and "value for money," the point that is emphasized here is that, in the process of managerial change, the features that traditionally characterized Britain's civil service have also changed substantially.

Accountability of Civil Servants through Ministers to Parliament

The accountability of civil servants has inevitably changed with the shift toward a more managerial culture. A key theme of the managerial culture, evident especially with NSAs but also with the Financial Management Initiative and Majorite initiatives such as the Citizen's Charter and performance related pay, has been to make civil servants responsible for their own performance. Thus, the principle underlying NSAs is that, while ministers are responsible for setting policy frameworks and deferring budgets and performance targets, Chief Executives are personally responsible for efficient administration and for meeting targets. One indication of the implications of this for accountability is that where agencies have substantial financial independence, Chief Executives now give evidence direct to the House of Commons Public Accounts Committee. Another is that where administrative (as opposed to policy) matters are concerned, MPs now receive replies to letters and Parliamentary Questions from Chief Executives rather than departmental ministers. More significantly, in at least one notorious case involving the Prison Service Agency, a Chief Executive was dismissed by his minister (in contravention of the traditional constitutional convention of ministerial responsibility) for alleged operational failings. This case was particularly complicated because it was unclear, precisely, where blame lay—with the Chief Executive for managerial shortcomings, or with the minister for imposing unrealistic administrative demands and budgetary constraints. Students of public administration will not be surprised to learn that there is a policy/administration dichotomy, but its practical manifestation in the division of responsibilities between NSA Chief Executives and their sponsoring ministers has, in some cases, blurred rather than clarified accountability.

Permanence

While British civil servants are still overwhelmingly permanent career officials, the shift toward a more managerial culture has clearly had an effect. The practice (initiated by Thatcher) of bringing businessmen such as Rayner into Whitehall, the expansion of open competition and fixed term contracts under Major, and the proposals in the Wilson Report envisaging the recruitment of secondees and mid-career officials from outside, all point to a departure from the traditional concept of a permanent career service. The sacking of Permanant Secretaries such as Kemp by Major, and the Wilson Report's reference to targeted "early retirement" to "create space at the top" are further indicators of the same trend; a trend reinforced by the growing numbers of special advisers employed by Blair. At the time of writing (January 2004), Sir Andrew Turnbull, the Cabinet Secretary, had reportedly "decided that all 3,000 senior civil servants should be given limited posts to encourage greater movement in and out of Whitehall." The policy was described as part of a "plan to stop old-timers from blocking senior posts for younger talented insiders and external recruits" (*The Times,* January 19, 2004). Permanence as a continuing feature of the British Civil Service is clearly under threat.

Political Neutrality

Political neutrality has also been eroded by managerial reform. Mrs Thatcher, for example, was accused of intervening in civil service promotions to secure the appointment of managerial "can-do" types. Major, while taking less interest in civil service promotions, nevertheless dismissed Sir Peter Kemp purportedly because he wanted someone with different skills. His government also saw NSA Chief Executives appointed on fixed term contracts and, in at least two cases, facing dismissal or resignation because ministers claimed that there had been management shortcomings. Such developments have clear implications for neutrality.

Anonymity

The anonymity of civil servants, along with permanence and neutrality, has also been eroded. While other factors have played a part, the shift to a more managerial culture has had an obvious effect. For example, parliamentary questions and letters from MPs are routinely answered by Chief Executives (on the grounds that they, not ministers, are responsible for operational matters). Again, some NSA Chief Executives have found themselves at the center of public controversy. Ros Hepplewhite, Chief Executive of the Child Support Agency, appeared on TV and radio, as well as before parliamentary inquiries, to answer public criticism about her and her agency's operations. Derek Lewis was not only "blamed" by the Home Secretary for alleged operational failures at HM Prison Service Agency, but was "named" in parliamentary and press reports.[1]

Unity

One of the most obvious casualties of the shift to managerialism has been the unity of the civil service, which traditionally was reflected in the common features (pay scales, grades, pension arrangements, etc.) that applied throughout the service. The civil service today is clearly no longer a unified service. Indeed, the diagnosis of the Next Steps Report was that the service had become "too big and too diverse to be managed as a single service" (Efficiency Unit 1988:4), and its recommendations produced a restructuring of Whitehall which devolved to NSAs the "service delivery" functions formerly performed by departments. By 2000, there were some 133 NSAs each with their own framework document, sponsoring department, chief executive, targets, etc. In addition, a small number of agencies had been privatized or had functions wholly contracted-out. Civil service pay has effectively been delegated so as to allow individual departments and NSAs the "flexibility to support" what the Cabinet Office in 2004 described as "their different business requirements" (*The Times*, January 22, 2004). What remained of the core Whitehall departments was headed by the SCS whose remuneration was tied to individual contracts linked to performance.

Of course, other factors have also contributed to the erosion of unity. Britain's membership of the increasingly integrationist European Union, for example, has influenced fragmentary tendencies within Whitehall, with some departments (and the officials working within them) becoming substantially Europeanized in focus while others have retained an essentially domestic policy agenda. Devolution, with officials of the same civil service serving both the UK government and devolved executives, potentially at least, poses a further threat to civil service unity. Nevertheless, the managerialist-inspired developments herein outlined have played a major part. Not only the creation of NSAs and delegated pay and grading, but also other aspects discussed above, such as market testing, have resulted in the further recasting of the Whitehall structure. The British civil service is no longer unified. It has become fragmented or "Balkanized."

Conclusion

Since the Northcote-Trevelyan reforms of the nineteenth century much has changed, especially the role of the state and the demands placed on governments. Indeed, one would expect the civil service to change and develop over time and expect significant reforms. In the late twentieth century, the driving force behind change was the need to improve managerial efficiency through the adoption of techniques, processes, and, in some cases, personnel, drawn from the private sector. As a result, attempts to instill a more managerial culture into the British civil service have been almost relentless over the last quarter of a century. Both Conservative and Labour governments have pursued them with almost equal vigour and it now seems unlikely that they will not continue into the foreseeable future.

Of course, it is possible to exaggerate the change that has occurred. Much of the civil service, for example, is still anonymous, permanent, and neutral, and, as has been shown, some of the weakening of these principles, where it has occurred, has resulted from factors unrelated to managerialism. Nevertheless, it is undeniable that many of the key features upon which the twentieth century British civil service was built have been altered. Until the 1970s, the civil service evolved only slowly, which is why so many of the Northcote-Trevelyan features were still in place. Subsequently, however, it underwent a profound revolution, which, motivated by a desire to achieve greater managerial efficiency and to deliver "value for money," in the process changed many of the features that had traditionally characterized the service. Key principles such as permanence, neutrality, and anonymity eroded, not because they were considered undesirable in principle, but because they stood in the way of managerial reform.

Perhaps the lesson that emerges from this is that changing from an administrative to a managerial culture cannot take place within a vacuum. In the case of Britain, it had far-reaching and, perhaps, unanticipated effects so that, today, the civil service is barely recognizable in key respects from the service that existed only a quarter of a century before.

NOTE

[1] For a brief discussion of these cases and wider implications see Greenwood and Wilson (2002, especially pages 34-37).

REFERENCES

Butcher, Tony. 1998. "The Blair Government and the Civil Service, Continuity and Change." *Teaching Public Administration* 17(1):1-8.

Cabinet Office. 1998. *The 1997 Next Steps Report.* Cm. 3889. London: The Stationery Office.

Chapman, Richard A. 1992. "The End of the Civil Service?" *Teaching Public Administration* 12(2):1-5.

Efficiency Unit. 1988. *Improving Management in Government: The Next Steps, Report to the Prime Minister.* London: HMSO.

Fulton Report. 1961. *Report of the Committee on the Civil Service, 1966-68 Vol.1: Report of the Committee.* Cmnd. 3638. London: HMSO.

Greenwood, John, R. Pyper, and D. Wilson. 2002. *New Public Administration in Britain.* London and New York: Routledge.

HM Treasury. 1991. *Competing for Quality: Buying Better Public Services*, Cm. 1730. London: HMSO.

Northcote-Trevelyan Report. 1854. *Report on the Organisation of the Permanent Civil Service.* C. 1713. London: HMSO.

Prime Minister's Office. 1991. *The Citizen's Charter.* Cm. 1599. London: HMSO.

Prime Minister. 1994. *The Civil Service: Continuity and Change.* Cm. 2627. London: HMSO.

Prime Minister. 1995. *The Civil Service: Taking Forward Continuity and Change.* Cm. 2748. London: HMSO.

Prime Minister and Minister for the Cabinet Office. 1999. *Modernising Government.* Cm. 4310. London: The Stationery Office.

Stationery Office. 2002. *Civil Service Yearbook 2000-2001.* London: The Stationery Office.

Thatcher, Margaret. 1993. *The Downing Street Years.* London: Harper Collins.

Theakston, Kevin. 1995. *The Civil Service Since 1945.* Oxford: Blackwell.

Tomlin Report. 1931. *Report of the Royal Commission on the Civil Service, 1929-31.* Cmd. 3909 London: HMSO.

Wilson, Sir Richard. 1999. *Report to the Prime Minister from Sir Richard Wilson, Head of the Home Civil Service.* (http://www.cabinet-office.gov.uk/civilservice/performanceandreward/documents/cs_reform_report.pdf).

Chapter 4

THE NEW ADMINISTRATIVE CULTURES AS THEY RELATE TO THE CITIZEN: COMPARATIVE STUDY OF BELGIUM, FRANCE, AND THE EUROPEAN INSTITUTIONS

Marie-José Chidiac

"Administrative despotism is the only thing that democracies should fear."
—*Alexis de Tocqueville*

"Citizenship, would it be only political? Citizenship, would it stop at the doors of the Administration? Would the administrative democracy not be just a useless word?"
—*Francis Delpérée*

General Historical Context

In 1914, Professor Maurice Hauriou wrote: "Modern conscience requires that the Administration take action in broad daylight. For a long time, we have tolerated its secret decisions. Now, we want all of its decisions and all of its actions to be public and we feel that what was not done publicly is not valid" (Laveissière 1998:11).

Article 5 of the French Declaration of Human Rights of August 26, 1789, indeed made an implicit reference to the "right to know," by acknowledging a "right to society to hold accountable every government official for his administrative acts." However, between this solemn proclamation and the actual establishment of rights that are at the foundation of administrative democracy, namely the right to obtain information, the right to access administrative documents, the right to obtain a justification of the administrative acts, or the citizen's right to participate in decisions that concern him or her, there remained a long way to go.

In fact, except for Sweden, who adopted in 1766 provisions particularly related to the right to obtain information, most European countries have, until recently, lived "in a kind of democratic profession of faith that was summarized in a very simple equation: there is a parliament; therefore, the public is necessarily informed" (Laveissière 1998:11). However, the citizens were not informed.

The traditional conception of the public administration in France and Belgium—as in every Western democracy, up to a few years after the 1939-1945 war—was of an administration that is subordinate to the Government and in charge of putting into effect the policies set by the Government and approved by Parliament.

In this traditional conception of public function, civil servants or public officials had to scrupulously implement the statutes, faithfully serve the State, and act loyally toward the institutions. This represented an advantage of objectivity and impartiality, and was a guarantee for the public interest. In this context, the administration seemed omnipotent and elevated above a "group of beings" (at the time, individuals were referred to as beings or subjects), to whom the decisions of the Government or the administrative decisions were handed down. It was a strict pre-eminence of administrative law and of the rule of law in the administration and in its relationship with the citizens.

The administrative tradition in European states, at least in the two states under our current analysis, was thus characterized by excessive "secrecy." Secrecy was the result of domination by an administration that was convinced of being the omnipotent public power over the subjects who were considered intruders by the administration.

World War II brought about a new historical context, a context described by Alain Stenmans:

> Victory over the national-socialist totalitarianism as well as the struggle against Soviet totalitarianism inspired Western nations with the vital need to assert the basic rights and the fundamental liberties of human beings. That is the meaning of the *Universal Declaration of Human Rights* promulgated by the United Nations' General Assembly on December 10, 1948, the European Convention for the Protection of Human Rights and Fundamental Freedoms initiated by the European Council on November 4 1950, and the International Pact relative to Civil and Political Rights adopted by the United Nations' General Assembly on December 19 1966. Despite having a different juridical significance, these international instruments particularly acknowledge, in identical or very close terms, the freedom of thought and conscience and the freedom of opinion and expres-

sion, to which the European Convention adds the freedom to assemble peacefully and the freedom of association, including the right to unionize. (Stenmans 1999:119)

The Welfare State that "takes care of everything" and that has an increasing hold over the economic, social, and cultural life (thus leading to the emergence of an administration with a constantly increasing, complex, and impervious power), has become obsolete and the citizen is not willing to rely on it entirely. In fact, the governed have realized that administrative actions have a palpable effect on their being and on their daily life, that they have the right to have an opinion about the administrative decisions that concern them, and to ask the administration to account for its acts, to be less closed, less impervious; they ask civil servants for better explanations, for justifications for their decisions, and for more information.

Thus, the mentalities have changed. In the seventies, in the European states, (including France and Belgium) the public began to demand administrative transparency and better administrative information.

The European Council stressed the significance of "taking into account the importance for the public in a democratic society of adequate information about public life" (EU 1981). It adopted, in a recommendation dated November 25 1981, a concise and specific text that asserts and sets up "the right of every person who is within the jurisdiction of a member state, to obtain within a reasonable period of time, at his request and without having to show a specific interest, information held by government agencies other than the legislative bodies and the judicial authorities. Refusals to provide such information must be justified and may be subject to an appeal. This right to obtain information held by government agencies is equated by the European Council to the basic rights and fundamental liberties it acknowledged since 1950" (Stenmans 1999:120).

The State has gradually lost the right it held through age-old norms "to the confidentiality of what it knows" (Stenmans 1999:121).

The evolution of ideas continues and, with the emphasis on modern communication techniques in the eighties and nineties, the citizen-users become increasingly demanding toward the administration services, just like a consumer of private goods. As for civil servants, they use private sector management techniques and are increasingly monitored by the public who asks for quality services delivered in an efficient manner, and who requires an administration that performs well.

Administrative democracy strengthens its position within the European institutions in France and Belgium where legislative texts are adopted in relation to the justification of the administrative acts and to the access to administrative documents.

Nevertheless, one should note that the progress of these new ideas is made, after all, in difficult circumstances, in that the administration is required to be certainly more efficient and, above all, to be less weighty in state budgets.

Currently, phrases such as "efficiency and quality of service" or "emphasis on the human aspects of a public service," or even "strengthening of the citizens' rights vis-à-vis public power" have an impressive dimension in public administration parlance. Little is heard about "massive bureaucratization" or "bureaucratic power," validated by the public interest pursued by the administration, or about "technocracy" or the "technocratic power" of the administration, validated by specialized techniques and methods based on the rationality of choices and on the growth and development of a country.

Also, currently, the relations between the administration and the citizen-user evolve around two main axes: (1) Democracy or administrative transparency, based mainly[1] on the justification of the administrative acts (or the obligation imposed on the administration to justify its acts) and on the public nature of the administration's actions (or the citizen's right to access administrative documents); (2) The emphasis on "the human aspect of public services," based on the charters of citizens and public services and on the Ombudsmen or Mediators (Stenmans 1999:156).

These key themes constitute, in my opinion, the public services ethic. Therefore, they will be examined in a comparative perspective, i.e., in France, Belgium, and in relation to the European Institutions. Where possible, they will also be analyzed from an intra-Belgian comparative angle; Belgium is a federation composed of three Regions (Walloon, Flemish, and Brussels-Capital) and three Communities (French, Flemish, and German-speaking) and there exists a federal administration, regional administrations, community administrations, and several autonomous rights of the public function, with each of the federated entities having the right to set the rules of its administration with deference to the common general principles and to the laws that are applicable to all of the levels of power.

Democracy or Administrative Transparency

> "The first public service is the law itself."
> —L. Duguit

As mentioned above, democracy, or administrative democracy, is mainly based on the justification of the administrative acts (or the mandate that the administration justify its acts) and on the public nature of the acts of the administration (or the citizen's right to access administrative documents).

Formal Justification of Administrative Acts

The Belgian, French, and European systems, like every democratic system, are essentially based on representation values. These values compel the establishment of a concrete mechanism of accountability and imputability.

The citizens not only expect their representatives in parliament and in government to account for their acts, but also the employees of public agencies to account for their acts by showing the grounds for the administrative decisions. This is transparency, which is a factor of efficiency and credibility of the institutional machinery.

However, failing to explain "the reason for things," and evading the legal and factual reasons that make the basis for a decision, denotes an impervious and non-transparent attitude of the administration. Furthermore, there is a true lack of transparency when the administration, in order to justify a decision or an administrative act, only refers to the legislative provision or regulation and leaves the citizen with no understanding of the measure to which he is subject. And, because the citizen does not understand the decision, he will be unable to contest it before the courts or the administrative commissions.

In Belgium

In Belgium, the Law of July 29, 1991, related to the formal justification of administrative acts (effective January 1, 1992) establishes the obligation to justify the administrative acts. Henceforth, the legal and factual reasons that form the basis for the decisions of public agencies must be indicated in the document that contains the decision:

> From all the rules of the game that the legislature and the government officials strive to define, this appears to be one of the most important: it guarantees to the individual who is subject to a given jurisdiction that the administrative decisions that relate to him, in his particular case, and in his personal or professional life, are made for specific reasons, expressly formulated, which he will be able to clearly contest in accordance with the facts and the applicable law. What has constituted since the beginning of the Belgian independence one of the bases of good justice is also becoming one of the bases of good administration. (Stenmans 1999:133-134)

It is true that the Law of July 29, 1991, although brief (it contains six articles), presents a host of advantages: "the justification of decisions makes the controller's task easier," he only needs to read the decision to appreciate the legality of the explanation provided. It favors the citizen; he can understand the decision by reading it and he is in a better position to contest its terms if that is needed. It is also useful for the administration in that "the hurdles it has to go through lead to the improvement of its decision-making and encourage a show of coherence" (Bouvier 2002:204).

It is interesting to note, here, that not only the Federal State but also the federated entities (i.e., the regions, the communities, and even the local organizations) are subject to the obligation of formally justifying their acts. Thus, this becomes a part of the administrative culture of the entire Belgian State. As Stenmans comments, "actually, the rights and the fundamental liberties are in question, as well as the smooth operation of the justice system" (1999:133). Moreover, the obligation of justification is a formality of substance; if it is absent, the State Council may annul its decision. To maintain the perspective of the comparison among the administrative cultures within the Belgian State, let us note that the Law of July 29, 1991, authorizes the Regions and the Communities to complete, refine, and reinforce the minimal obligations that are stated therein, but certainly not to depart from the general obligation to formally justify their administrative acts (Bouvier 2002:216).

(i) Field of Application of the Law of July 29, 1991

Under the terms of Articles 1 and 2 of this law, a formal justification must be made for each unilateral legal act bearing on the individual, originating from administrative authorities and having legal effects toward one or more citizens or toward another administrative authority.[2]

(ii) *The Justification Must be Formal*

If Article 2 of the Law of July 29, 1991, stipulates that the administrative act must be formally justified, Article 3 specifies the nature of such justification. In combining both Articles, it appears that the justification must refer to the facts; that the justification must refer to legal rules that were applied; and that the justification must indicate how and why these legal rules, based on the enumerated facts, led to such a decision.

The term "formal" means that the justification on which a decision is based must be reiterated in the decision itself. The decision should contain not only its terms, but also the reasons on which the decision is based.

According to the Preparatory Works (of the Law of July 29, 1991), "for a more transparent administration, it is preferable that those reasons expressly appear in the decision. Such is the meaning of the obligation for a formal justification" (Belgium Senate 1998:13).

(iii) *The Formal Justification Must be Adequate*

Pursuant to Article 3, Paragraph 2 of the Law of July 29, 1991, the formal justification must be adequate. This notion was a target for criticism. Today, it is accepted that this word means that the justification should be clear, accurate, concrete, and sufficient. According to Philippe Bouvier, senior member of the Council of the State, with this notion "we leave the field of formal justification and enter into the field of material justification" (2002:213).

(iv) *Exceptions to the Obligation to Justify*

Urgency does not excuse the administration from justifying its acts. No doubt, this is a sign of more administrative transparency because the administration cannot hide behind the "urgency" to excuse itself from justifying its decision.

However, in four instances that are expressly and exclusively enumerated, the administrative authority is not obligated to justify its decision. Those instances are where enumerating the motives behind the act may compromise State security, breach the peace, violate the right to privacy, or breach the provisions related to professional secrecy.

In France

In France, it is Law 79-584 of July 11, 1979, which sets up the obligation to justify the administrative acts and to improve the relations between the administration and the public. This law was amended in 1986 and was followed by a memorandum and by ministry notes in 1982, 1987, and 1988.

This law does not require a general obligation to justify, but it widely expands the situations where mandatory justification is required.

Article 1, Paragraph 1 states: "individuals or legal entities have the right to be informed without delay of the motives of unfavorable individual administrative decisions that concern them." Paragraph 2 enumerates the decisions that are subject to the obligation to justify.

This enumeration shows us that unfavorable individual administrative decisions are significant, such as those that impose a sanction or limit the exercise of public freedoms. Decisions concerning specific obligations, such as the refusal of sick leave, the refusal to acknowledge a work-related accident, or decisions that refuse an authorization are subject to the obligation to justify.

The lack of justification, if a result of the extreme urgency of the decision at hand, does not make such a decision irregular. This exemption is only temporary. If requested, the motives must be communicated to concerned parties within one month. The justification must be in writing, clear and precise, and must include the statements of fact and law upon which the decision is based. Such justification may not be limited to quoting the statute or referring to the case at hand and to laws and regulations in effect. It is not sufficient to state that the conditions specified by statute are not met; the specific issues must be addressed as well as the way in which they do not meet the requirements of the statute. It is not sufficient to copy or paraphrase the applicable rule without indicating how and why this rule leads, in a particular case, to the ultimate decision. Finally, in order to ensure that the rules related to the justification of the administrative acts are followed, the administrative law judge has jurisdiction.[3]

At the European Level

Community law, that is the law of the European Union, had provided for the justification of all of the acts of the institutions of the Union (Articles 190 CEE, 15 CECA) and had imposed pertinent obligations at the level of the national authorities of member-States.

Thus, for example, the October 15, 1987, ruling of the European Community Court, which stated the principle that every time a national authority refuses to give to a citizen of a member-State the benefit of a fundamental right guaranteed by the Treaty, the relevant national authority has the obligation to communicate to him the motives upon which its refusal is based, either in the decision itself or later in a communication made upon his request (Bribosia 1992).

Resolution No. (177) 31, which was adopted on September 28, 1977, by the Committee of Ministers of the Council of Europe in relation to the protection of the individual vis-à-vis the administration, recommended a minimum level of protection that would be acceptable by all of the member-States, notably by way of the "justification of the administrative acts."

Another European Recommendation, No. (80) 2 of March 11, 1980, stated "when the administrative authority, while exercising a discretionary power, moves away from a general administrative directive by an act that is likely to undermine the rights, liberties or interests of a given person, the latter must be informed of *the motives* [emphasis added] of such decision" (EU 1980).

A close reading of Resolution No. (77) 31 of September 28, 1977, shows that the effect of such resolution is *to ensure that the citizens are informed* of the motives, rather than addressing the justification of administrative acts in a general way. Indeed, the required justification does not forcibly or necessarily consist of showing the reasons in the act itself, a formality of substance without which the act is null and void. Actually, the required justification consists of a right of the citizens, subsequent to the issuance of the administrative act, to receive in writing, within a reasonable amount of time, the reasons behind the act. It is rather the acknowledgment of a right to access information than the acknowledgment of a right to justification. Furthermore, the Belgian law of July 29, 1991, on the justification of administrative acts has been considered the corollary of a fundamental right of the citizen to obtain information in his relationship with the administration. That leads us to the second pillar of the new administrative culture: administrative publicity.[4]

Administrative Publicity

A myriad of factors comprising what might be described as a lack of information may sometimes lead to serious consequences, such as "being barred," i.e., losing the right to appeal. Lack of information could mean anything from ambiguous instructions to incomplete or hastily delivered information, a multiplicity of answering machines, explanations that are not "released," complete uncertainty regarding the steps followed by a file from one administrative service to another or from one administration to another, the silence of the administration following a technical investigation (related to the environment) performed on real property, the refusal to deliver a document that includes technical data or details concerning the method of calculation of subsidies, or insufficient information on appeals and on the periods within which administrative or judicial appeals must be lodged. All of the above would indicate that the citizen is not the main priority for such an administration and, as a result, citizens do not trust the administration.

At the European and International Levels

The right to obtain information is a fundamental right considered part of the freedom of expression and has been established by various international conventions, especially the *Universal Declaration of Human Rights* of 1948,[5] in the international compact related to civil and political rights of 1966 (United Nations) and the European Convention for the preservation of human rights and fundamental liberties (CEDH). These international statutes showed the acknowledgment by the international community that honoring the freedom of expression and opinion implies the right of citizens to be informed and to have the freedom to find information.

Moreover, the Belgian Council of State considers administrative publicity as related to Article 10 of the Convention for the Preservation of Human Rights and Fundamental Liberties.

In addition, the Council of Europe has spent a lot of energy on the question of access to public information held by the public sector. Its Recommendation R (18) 19 of November 25, 1981, contained most of the principles on which the member-States based their legislation related to access to administrative information. According to the recommendation, all of the individual and legal entities have the right to receive, upon request, information held by government agencies, without the need to prove a specific interest. If the administration refuses access to the requested information, it should justify its refusal, which can be for legitimate public interests (such as public safety) or private interests (such as the protection of privacy). This obligation concerns only the executive power, and not the judicial or legislative powers.

The European Union strongly encourages community institutions and the States to respect this right. As stated in the declaration of the Conference during the adoption of the Treaty on the European Union, "the transparency...reinforces the democratic character of the institutions, as well as the trust of the public towards the administration" (EU 1992).[6]

Finally, the European Parliament and the Council adopted, on May 30, 2001, Regulation (CE) No. 1049/2001 relating to public access to the documents of the European Parliament, the Council, and the Committee (EU 2001) allowing citizens, whether they reside within the Union's territory or not, to assert before the European Parliament, the Council, and the Committee the right to access the administrative documents held[7] by any of these institutions.[8]

I would like to add that the citizens' right of inspection started in Sweden in 1766. Only two centuries later have other European States begun to adopt laws related to administrative transparency.

In Belgium

In Belgium, Article 32 of the Constitution of 1993 states "each person has the right to consult each administrative document and to make a copy of it, except in cases determined by law or by regulation." The publicity of administrative acts, upon the request of a constituent, has been addressed by the federal legislator (Law of April 11, 1994) and also by all levels of authority (communities, regions, and even on the local level), which adds up to not less than ten laws.[9] This overthrows the administrative tradition of secrecy that prevailed for centuries!

These legislations contain provisions similar to certain variants that I will emphasize by using the federal Law of April 11, 1994, which is related to administrative publicity. The lack of cohesion in this subject is decried by some, but Belgium has become a federal State and this causes a multiplicity of standards.

(i) *The Administrative Document*

The definition of the notion of the administrative document is the same in all Belgian legislation. According to Article 1 of the Law of April 11, 1994, "the administrative document is each piece of information, under any form, that is at the disposal of the administrative authority."

This definition is broad and supported by the Preliminary Works of the Law, according to which "the term relates to all of the information available, regardless of how its is supported: written documents, audio-visual recordings, including the data repeated in automated information processing, reports, even studies made by the unofficial advisory committees, certain reviews and proceedings, statistics, administrative directives, circulars, contracts, licenses, public inquiry registers, test books, films, photos, etc., which are at the disposal of an authority, are, as a general rule, considered as public records" (Parliament 1992-93). This list is not exhaustive.

(ii) *Passive Publicity or Consultation Right*

Each person, even without a show of interest, may request the review of an administrative document, unless the document relates to a private matter, in which case the person must show interest.

This is a real upheaval in the administrative law, since "the administrative secret has been a part of our administrative heritage" and insofar as "the secret of administrative matters was associated with the prominent exercise of power, it shared in the hallowed character of power" (Bouvier 2002:218). Henceforth, it is the "'show all' that becomes the attribute of power" (Stenmans 199:149).

Thus:

- Each person has the right to review, on location, all administrative documents: this is the right to review.
- Each person has the right to receive explanations related to the document reviewed: this is the right to receive an explanation.
- Each person has the right to discovery by obtaining a copy of the document reviewed: this is the right to discovery.

This set of laws constitutes the passive publicity of the administration. Note the word *right*. It is truly a "right" to review an administrative document that is acknowledged by the federal legislator. This same right is acknowledged by the Walloon legislator. However, the legislator of the French Community provides that each person *may* review a document, without specifying that such is a right, which, in my opinion, is a restriction in comparison with the legislations of the federal State and the Walloon Region.

On the other hand, in the Flanders they go further. The Flemish decree provides not only for the rights to review, to discovery, and to an explanation, but also for the feasibility of borrowing the administrative document.

We note that Article 32 of the Constitution enshrines the rights to review and to discovery, but it is the federal legislations and the legislations of the federated entities that add to these rights the right to receive explanations.

(iii) *Active Publicity or the Spontaneous Process of the Administration*

While Article 32 of the Constitution enshrines the passive publicity of the administration, other legislators of the country go further and acknowledge active publicity: the provision of information at the initiative of the administrative authority itself.

The law of April 11, 1994 (Article 2), for example, imposes on the federal authorities "to-do obligations" such as the following:

- Provision of an information service
- Publication of a guide about the administration in question
- Identification of a contact person
- Information about appeals

This is a spontaneous process of the administration vis-à-vis the user.

(iv) *Exceptions*

Though the right to receive information is a fundamental right that is acknowledged and legitimate, one should not forget that administrative publicity conflicts with the policy of secrecy that has been in place for quite a long time. In this situation, the citizen's interest may sometimes weigh less when balanced against the protection of public interest or the interest of an individual.

The federal Law of April 11, 1994, has contemplated a series of exceptions to the principle of passive publicity. These exceptions are twofold: mandatory exceptions that are applicable to all of the administrations of the country and optional exceptions that are applicable to federal administrations only.

The mandatory exceptions that, again, apply to all of the administrations of the Kingdom are absolute or relative.

With respect to absolute exceptions, the administrations have no choice but to refuse a request to access administrative documents. To do otherwise would lead to a violation of principles or fundamental rights. There are three such exceptions: (a) invasion of privacy, unless the concerned person has given his prior written consent to the review or the discovery; (b) an obligation of secrecy established by law; and (c) the secrecy of deliberations of the federal Government and the relevant government agencies of the federal executive power or the government agencies with a federal mandate.

With respect to relative exceptions, the government agencies, upon each request for access to an administrative document, must compare the opposing interests and decide whether the interest of publicity outweighs the protection of certain other interests. These exceptions or interests are the following: the safety of the people; the freedoms and the fundamental rights of the citizens; the federal international relations of Belgium; law and order; national security or defense; the search for or the prosecution of punishable acts; a federal economic or financial interest; the currency or public finance; the confidential character of industry or manufacturing information that is conveyed to the government; and the secret identity of the individual who conveys, in confidence, a document or information to the government in order to expose a punishable act or an act that is assumed to be punishable.

Four optional exceptions apply only to federal government agencies. The interests they protect are "less fundamental" than those protected by the other exceptions. At any rate, the federal administrative authority has discretionary power to refuse the publishing of a document after evaluating the interests of the concerned, provided there is adequate justification.[10]

(v) *Appeal*

The law of April 11, 1994, establishes a Committee to deal with access to administrative documents, in order to hear appeals of refusals by a federal administrative authority to grant a request for publicity (and also to grant a request for correction). This Committee may also be consulted by a federal administrative authority and can issue an opinion on the general applicability of the law. It may submit to the legislative branch suggestions related to the applicability of the law and its possible revision. In 1997, the jurisdiction of this Committee was extended to include local and provincial authorities.[11]

The Committee publishes, on an annual basis, a Report on its opinions and suggestions. Its jurisprudence is plentiful already, a proof that the law on administrative publicity has started to get recognition from the public. This jurisprudence presents a great interest, especially in the interpretation and the examination of the "exceptions" provided for by the law.

In France

In France, the tradition of secrecy in the administration remained a principle until the 1970s (Laveissière 1988; Le Rendu 2001). Despite a few exceptions, such as the Law of April 22, 1905, which compels the administration to communicate to the civil servant his file before taking any disciplinary action against him or before transferring him, secrecy in the administration remained the rule until the adoption of the Law of July 17, 1978, which reversed the principle of secrecy in favor of administrative transparency.[12]

In fact, the Law of July 17, 1978, which "included various measures to improve the relations between the administration and the public," enshrines in Title One the principle of free access to administrative documents. Title One was first amended on July 6, 1978, and on July 11, 1979; it was then amended by the April 12, 2000, law with the intent to extend its field of application.

The result of this (amended) law is that France adopted a wide concept of the kind of documents that must be communicated: decisions, reports, studies, directives, memoranda, minutes, etc., whether they are in writing, on audio or video recordings, or in the form of automatically processed data that do not includes names. In addition, documents related to computerized files and even opinions of the Council of State and the administrative tribunals must be communicated.

The right to access is open to all (individuals and legal entities); that is, any individual may request the review of a document that does not implicate others. However, when an administrative document implicates another person, only the latter may have access to that document.

One is not required to prove a special interest in order to have access to an administrative document. Documents that can be communicated to persons who request them originate from government agencies, local communities, public entities, and private entities that administer public services.

It is useful to note that government agencies must communicate the administrative documents under their control even if they have not generated them. For example, within his sphere of authority a department administrator must communicate local community instruments to the person who requests them without the need for approval by such local community.

As in Belgium, there are exceptions to the right of access to administrative documents. They are interpreted restrictively and concern the obstruction of public powers, the compromising of the public interest, the compromising of the private interest that is protected by law, or the protection of private secrets such as the secrecy of consanguinity, tax secrecy, industrial and commercial secrecy, or medical confidentiality.

A Committee for the Access to Administrative Documents (CAAD), made of ten members and presided over by the senior member of the Council of State, is in charge of ensuring that the law is followed. It will be stated at a later point that its jurisdiction is mandatory prior to any legal action.

The CAAD may act in any of the following four manners:

- Issue opinions upon request of the persons who have difficulties in obtaining administrative documents
- Advise the relevant authorities on every question relating to the smooth exercise of the right to access
- Suggest amendments to the texts where it deems useful
- Establish a report and make it public.[13]

Partial Conclusion: Important Effects of these Themes on the Administrative Ethic

Before proceeding with this study, we shall briefly consider the impact of these two legislations, namely, the formal justification and the administrative publicity vis-à-vis administrative life. Further, we consider the relationship they may have to ethics.

I would simply state that these legislations could not succeed in the improvement of the rights of citizens vis-à-vis the administration and thus bring about, in a concrete and effective way, the administrative democracy without the help of civil servants and public agents. The era where a civil servant believes his work complete after applying the regulation correctly and completely without regard to explaining it or communicating it in an efficient manner has not fully passed.

Ethics in public service—especially based on these legislations—consists of civil servants recognizing that it is their duty to inform citizens; and this duty of information is within the very nature of public service. It is no longer acceptable for civil servants to consider their duty complete having merely applied a regulation correctly. The citizen must also receive an explanation.

The administrative ethic requires the public agent, of whatever rank and function, to become an "information provider." This is reinforced by the appearance of educational programs directed towards certain civil servants in order to sensitize them to their duties to inform.

Indeed, the Mediators of the French Republic affirmed almost thirty years ago that "the radical solution to the problem of administrative information will be at hand when the duty to provide information and the primacy of transferable information, will be so integrated into the administrative conscience that each public agent…whatever his rank and function, will have become an 'information provider' because, in his own conscience, the citizen is always present" (Pinay 1973:253-4).

Communicating to the user the decisions that relate to him while explaining their motives in terms he understands, and indicating clearly the rights and the recourses that are at his disposal vis-à-vis an administrative decision, these are, in my opinion, the new obligations of a civil servant.

The administrative ethic requires transparency, which includes the respect of the citizens' freedom to access documents that concern them. Therefore, we should henceforth explain, justify, and clarify the administrative decisions to the citizens and also allow the citizens to review those decisions. At any rate, the administrative ethic seeks to prevent the civil servant from treating the citizen as a file or a faceless number. He must personalize his relationship with the user.

In short, the administrative ethic aims at a having civil servant who feels "responsible" because, in reality, administrative transparency and accountability go hand in hand. Personally, I have always pleaded for an autonomous file manager, without the need for constant hierarchical consultations.

The file manager, the front-line individual, is better able to find the actual problem that the citizen has, is able to compensate for an insufficient rule, and, if necessary, adapt the application of such rule to the case at hand. Front-line managers are as important as the head of the organization. Without an intent to undermine the duty of discretion or the professional confidence of those managers, they should be given a maneuvering margin or they should be allowed to express themselves in order to clarify a decision or the progress of a file. This would facilitate the relations between the administration and the citizens and would give the civil servant a sense of responsibility. In addition, the civil servant must have adequate education and training and "the hierarchical superior" must properly assume his "control power" in order to avoid subjectivity or eventual mistakes.

Thus, I have explained what I view as the ethic of the administrative function. As expressed in the words of the former Citizen Protector of Quebec, Daniel Jacoby, "democracy must reach the bureaucracy and ethics must be a catalyst; ethics and accountability go hand in hand" (Jacoby 1995).

Development of the Human Aspects of Public Service

The development of the human aspects of public service seeks to replace the relation of power between the administration and the citizen-user with a relation of service and attention and thus contributes to the establishment of a new administrative culture (Stenmans 1999).

The development of the human aspects of public service is mainly based on the Charters for the users of public services and the Ombudsmen.

The Charters for the Users of Public Services

The Charters for the users of public services, as adopted in Belgium, France, and especially in Great Britain, also known as the Codes of good administrative manners at the European level, constitute guarantees of the administrative ethic. They contribute to the furthering of a new administrative culture by emphasizing improvement in the behavior of public servants in the accomplishment of their tasks that relate to the people. Public servants are not to treat the administration as omnipotent, but as an administration that is more accessible and more in tune with the expectations of the citizens. This is signified through the use of the words "users" and "citizens" to describe the persons under the jurisdiction of the administration, and through the enactment of "to-do obligations" for the civil servants.

Certainly, the Charters and their "equivalents" do not contain measures that sanction their deficiencies, but they constitute a symbol of something greater than themselves and, as such, they become untouchable!

In Belgium

The Initiatives of the Federal State

In Belgium, the *Charter for the Users of Public Services* was adopted on December 4, 1992. It is a type of "formal directive" that aims at prompting the federal administrations to improve the quality of services delivered to the public. It was published in the *Belgian Monitor* and made applicable by Memorandum No. 379 of January 12, 1993, of the Minister of Internal Affairs and Public Service at that time, Mr. Louis Tobback: "The main thrust of this Charter is to provide a public service that is adapted to the needs of every consumer. In fact, nothing, not even the principle of equality, prohibits the public service from endeavoring to give consideration to each consumer, instead of addressing him in an impersonal manner" (Tobback 1993).

This provision of the preamble to the Charter summarizes well what is expected from a public service or an administration: it is to be attentive to the needs of the public. The users do not want to be considered mere numbers any longer. They do not want to be treated like the anonymous objects of administrative action. Rather, they want to be viewed and treated as real people.

The charter consists of a preamble and two parts, one dedicated to "general principles" and the other to the "measures" that put into effect the stated principles.

The Charter addresses the federal public services; a College of Secretaries General is in charge of its application. In fact, ministerial memorandum No. 370 states that "every year, the regulatory legislative initiatives and others, taken within the framework of putting this Charter into effect, will be the object of a summary." The College of Secretaries General assures the drafting of a synthesis on the subject.

The Charter rests on three basic elements, namely, transparency, flexibility, and legal protection. These themes express, in fact, key ideas and, in order to reinforce the content of the Charter, the part entitled "measures" indicates the manner in which these themes can actually be accomplished.

(a) Transparency: It aims at increasing consumers' confidence in public services, which reinforces efficiency. It revolves around two axes, namely, information and review of administrative documents; it is a question of "communicating" and "taking initiatives" to inform the public and to give it access to the information that concerns it. To that end, it is henceforth required of the agents of public services to list their contact information on correspondence with the users. Further, in addition to reviewing administrative documents, the users may also request that inaccurate personal data found in such documents be corrected.

(b) Flexibility: It revolves around two axes, namely, the accessibility of public services and the adaptability of the service. According to the Charter, the public services must be accessible in a broad sense of the term, going beyond the problems of physical accessibility and closeness, both of which remain all-important. It is also a question of clarity of the statutes. Writing administrative documents and statutes in a manner that makes them very difficult to understand by the public must be avoided. Emphasis is placed on quality access and a quality contact, a clear and precise language (precise and understandable memoranda and forms), and clear laws. The adaptability of the service can entail automatically offering users, without them asking for it, the benefit of certain rights that they are entitled to and that derive from the laws and regulations. It is also a matter of immediately transmitting documents that are within the jurisdiction of the relevant government agencies and assuring a quality service.

(c) Legal Protection: The consumer must be able to have his rights respected by others and to assert his interests. To that end, legal protection evolves around six fundamental points:

- the protection of personal data
- adversary proceedings
- treatment of complaints, especially by Mediators
- swiftness of payments
- the contesting of decisions and the respect of the rights of defense
- the suspension of execution of administrative decisions

The Initiatives of Federated Entities

In Flanders, a Deontological Code of the Flemish Deputies exists (since 1999) and relates to the provision of services to the public. It states, on one hand, the services permitted to the Deputies and to their circle (like informing citizens or acting as intermediaries between the citizens and the administration where a mediation service is non-existent) and, on the other hand, the services that are not permitted like taking steps before the administration in order to accelerate a procedure or to obtain a promotion. This Code illustrates what the ethics of political powers could be.

In Walloon, a Charter of Public Services is being worked on by the Minister of Interior Affairs of the Walloon Region.

In France

The *Charte des Services Publics,* published in 1992, is based on four sets of public service principles: transparency and responsibility, simplicity and accessibility, participation and adaptation (of public services to the more diverse needs of users), and confidence and trust (in secure public services and judicial protection of rights) (Clark 2000). Central to the policy intention behind the 1992 charter is the modernization of the republican model of public service action by revitalizing principles of legality and due process in the relationship between the providers and users of public services. Charterism consolidates "de-bureaucratization" initiatives reminiscent of an earlier phase of reform (simplification of procedures; improved dissemination of information about legal rights and entitlements) and anticipates a more equal access to public services on the part of "excluded" citizens by the creation of "one-stop shops" (maisons des services publics) in rural and poor urban areas.

The *Charte des Services Publics* is not a legal document. However, it assumes considerable political significance as a discursive endorsement of changing patterns of legitimation in public management.

There is a significant difference between this Charte and the Citizens Charter of the United Kingdom (of 1991), which served as a model for Anglo-Saxon countries and as a reference inside the United Kingdom for many sectorial and local charters. That difference lies in the manner in which the citizen is treated. The English Citizens Charter makes the citizen a partner whereas in France, although there is a change from the concept of governed citizen to that of citizen-user, the public mission of services, accessibility, equality, and the common good or public interest are strongly upheld and remain principal values.

The citizen in France began to be a partner only at the end of the nineties and the beginning of 2000 with the codification (Law of March 30, 2000) of the options and the orientations embodied in Alain Juppe's memorandum of July 25, 1995.

For that reason, David Clark (2000:169) has rightly stated:

> The *Charte des Services Publics*, the regulation of the relationship between the citizen and the public services in France is a matter for the judicial system rather than executive self-regulation. Charterism à la française is less an exercise in public service consumerism than a reassertion of the republican principle of equal citizenship, which requires that users must be placed on an equal footing, without discrimination or special advantages. This philosophy of charterism may come under increasing strain given the persistence of exclusion as a socio-political phenomenon.

In fact, France is traditionally a strongly centralized state and changes in the rules and practices of administrative regulation are most apparent in business-government relations, with the decline of traditional state dirigisme and in the emerging system of "territorial regulation," where it is possible to discern a shift from local administration to local governance.

In France, to the extent that charterism has developed beyond the broad political and administrative principles contained in the 1992 *Charte*, "quality charters" are used as tools of strategic management in specific ministries and public services. Rather than looking for distinctive charter-type mechanisms for ensuring service standards in public administration, it may be more meaningful to point to a seamless web of quality initiatives and charters spawned by ministerial modernization plans in which the common feature is the "technocratic" assumption that reinforcing the autonomy of public service management, such as the legal status of "maisons des citoyens et des services publics," will lead to a better quality of service delivery for the user (Trosa 1995).

Henceforth, each of the local administrations will endow itself with a "quality charter," published by government agencies and available to the public, setting the commitments of those agencies toward the users and the rights of such users. However, unlike Anglo-Saxons countries, the citizen hardly begins to be a partner. Currently, in some localities, the pilot experiment of the one-stop shop and public service deserves particular attention. Volunteer agents have a mission of easing the access of the public to the administrations. Beyond the initial contact and information, they assure that the users' business is taken care of, help the users prepare and relay their files, and may, if necessary, deliver titles to property or services and make simple decisions (Thibault 1999).

At the European Level

At the level of the European Institutions, the European parliament has adopted, on September 6, 2001, a Resolution that approved *The Code of Good Administrative Behavior* that the institutions and the communal organs, their administrations, and their civil servants ought to respect in their relations with the public.

In fact, the idea of establishing such Code was proposed for the first time by Mr. Roy Perry, the European Deputy who chaired the Committee of Petitions during the parliamentary year 1996-1997. As for the European Mediator, he had initiated his own inquiry on the accessibility of the public to the institutions and the communal organs and has written a statute and submitted it to the European parliament as a special report. *The Resolution of the European Parliament* in relation to the Code is based on the proposal of the European Mediator and the revisions made to it by Mr. Roy Perry.

We also find in this Code a series of principles such as access to administrative documents (Article 23), justification of decisions (Article 8) and their adoption within a reasonable time frame (Article 17), advising of the appeals process (Article 19), and the right to have recourse to the Mediator (Article 26). We also especially find "to-do suggestions" for the civil servants to improve their relations with the European citizens, such as impartiality, independence (Article 8), objectivity (Article 9), to act in an equitable and reasonable manner (Article 11), or to be courteous and proper (Article 12). Such are the behaviors and attitudes required of civil servants, indicating that public services are analyzed and perceived from the point of view of the beneficiary of such services and not from the point of view of the public agent who provides these services.

It is useful to emphasize that the September 6, 2001, *Resolution of the European Parliament* approving the Code, invites the European Commission to also submit a proposed Regulation that includes this Code (based on Article 308 of the treaty that establishes the European Community).

This is of a great importance because casting the Code into a Regulation indicates to the citizens and to the civil servants the mandatory nature of the principles and rules contained in the Code.

Partial Conclusion: The Impact of the Charters

Whether it is for the *Charter of the Users of Public Services* or the *Code of Good Administrative Behavior*, it is important to recognize that, contrary to the situation in the United Kingdom where the Charter of the Citizens or the Charter of the People is popular and has brought competition, the citizens in Belgium, in France, and at the European level are not aware or know very little about them; they are unaware of their very existence.

If these Charters are unrecognized on the public side, it should be noted that on the public agents' side this new role of accessibility, transparency, proximity, and responsibility is increasingly recognized as important.

The political powers, in addition to adopting legislation on administrative publicity or the establishment of the position of Mediator, have pursued institutional efforts in this direction by creating, for example, commissioners for administrative simplification (at the federal level and the Walloon regional level), and by adopting in Flanders a decree on the right of the citizen to complain about the functioning of the administration. Also, the political powers have encouraged the signing of management contracts for public enterprises, which stress quality management or an efficient approach based on the needs of the clientele. The federal government conducted a questionnaire addressed to all of the people and concerning the functioning of the administration before applying new administrative management rules such as quality service, efficient management, or satisfaction of the clientele, as referred to in the Belgian Copernic Plan for public function.

However, despite these inquiries, it is not easy to know the citizens' expectations or to make the administration more responsive to those expectations, especially considering that the citizens' demands are sometimes contradictory and that there is not a typical profile of the citizen just as, incidentally, there is no typical profile of an administration. Yet, there is an institution that, by virtue of its proximity, can contribute to recognizing the citizens' needs and even attempt to meet those needs: the Ombudsman or the Mediator.

The Institution of Ombudsman or Mediator

If it is true that the institution of Ombudsman or Mediator is an old one (nearly two hundred years old), it remains that it is current and constitutes one of the human aspects of the new administrative culture.

A Brief Historical Overview

The Ombudsman, a term that means "the one who speaks on behalf of others," started in Sweden in 1809. A senior and a model Swedish institution, it served as a model to the Scandinavian and Anglo-Saxon states (1918 in Finland, 1954 in Denmark, 1962 in Norway and New Zealand, 1967 in the United Kingdom).

After World War II, the phenomenon expanded throughout the world under various designations, such as Ombudsman, People's Defender in Spain, Specialized Parliamentary Commissioner, Citizen's Protector in Quebec, and Mediator of the Republic in France.

A feature common to all is that the institution is dedicated to defending the citizens' rights in their relations with public administrations. In fact, the common purpose is truly the struggle against "misadministration" and the dysfunction of the administration. In the face of an administration that is considered all too powerful, there was a desire to give the citizens an appeal process that would make their voices heard.

Each state has shaped its own institution in accordance with its own administrative and judicial organization and its parliamentary traditions.

In Belgium, the institution of the Mediator or Ombudsman is still new and, as stated in the introduction to this article, is in a dual evolution process from state to federal state and toward democracy and administrative transparency (just as the other pillars of the new administrative culture).

As in the other states, there was a certain imbalance between an omnipotent administration and the population, leading to the assumption that a Mediator or an Ombudsman, also the instrument of an administrative democracy, should be established in order to give the citizens a means to counterbalance the excesses of the administration and to bring an equilibrium between it and the citizens.

The change from a unitarian state to a federal state has increased the number of administrations, making them more complex in the eyes of the citizen. Faced with a plethora of rules, the citizen often did not know where to turn. Especially, he did not understand the reason why, for example, as an "administered citizen" he had to prove certain acts or formalities that he had already proved to another "administration."

The citizen felt like a victim of a splintered administrative machine, lost in heavy procedural steps or lost before administrations that were far removed from his expectations and which he therefore considered inhuman.

Hence, the theory was that an Ombudsman or a Mediator would establish and improve the dialogue between the users and their administration, clarify the personal situation of the citizen, and humanize the relations between the administration and the citizen.

That is how the Flemish community, the Walloon region, and the federal state acquired, in 1991, 1994, and 1995 respectively, Ombudsmen or Mediators.[14]

The Flemish Ombudsman is competent in cases of conflict between individuals and the administration of the Flemish Community. Considering that, in accordance with Article 1 of the Special Law of August 8, 1980, the Flemish Community has competence over the Flemish region, the Flemish Ombudsman is also competent for regional Flemish matters.

The Walloon regional Mediator intervenes in cases of conflict between individuals and the Walloon regional administration. Thus, contrary to the Flemish Mediator, the regional Walloon Mediator is only competent in the Walloon region and not in the French Community because there was no "fusion," as this term is used in the politico-legal jargon, between the French Community and the Walloon region.

The College of Federal Mediators, comprised of a federal French-speaking Mediator and a federal Dutch-speaking Mediator, is competent in matters arising between citizens and the federal administrations.

There is no hierarchy between these Mediators; they exercise their competences independently of one another. They "work" on an equal footing. By definition, they handle different administrations.

In the 1970s, France instituted the "Mediator of the Republic" function in a legislative movement directed at giving more room and more attention to the citizen vis-à-vis the powerful administration. Hence, the Law of January 3, 1973, has established the Mediator of the Republic and was further expanded in 1976, 1982, 1989, and 2000 in order to increase the competences of the Mediator.

At the European level, the European Mediator was established by Article 138E of the European Union Treaty and was regulated by a May 4, 1994, decision of the European Parliament.

The Institution of Ombudsman is a Pillar of the New Administrative Culture fulfilling the following roles:

(a) *It is a public authority that draws expectations from the citizens.* Many Ombudsmen act at the direct request of the users who bring individual complaints before them. This is the case of the institutions of Ombudsman in Belgium (the federal College of Mediators, the Flemish Mediator, the Walloon Region Mediator) and the European Mediator. The latter may receive referrals from a member of the European parliament. Therefore, they act on a case-by-case basis. Thus, the Ombudsmen care for the daily business of the users and thereby have a good perception of the users' problems. They become the spokespersons of the citizens vis-à-vis their administration and contribute to meeting the citizens' expectations, especially to humanize the dialogue between the administration and the users and to make the administration less anonymous. Finally, by receiving complaints that originate directly at the "base," that is from the user himself, the Ombudsman is the only institution that can conduct a "permanent poll" relating to the needs and aspirations of the user.

In France, the Mediator of the Republic receives indirect referrals from the citizen. The latter files a complaint with a Member of Parliament or a Senator who transmits it to the Ombudsman.

(b) *The Ombudsman is a recourse that benefits the transparency of the administrative authority.* In the exercise of his duties, the Ombudsman has wide powers of inquiry and investigation that allow the uncovering of instances of "misadministration" that would otherwise go unnoticed or remain unknown. These instances may be slowness, bad coordination of services, passivity, silence, or administrative error. The Ombudsman can make observations on the spot, obtain all the documents and information that he deems necessary, and hear all interested individuals. If the Ombudsman is bound by professional confidentiality, the personnel of the administrative authorities are released from such confidentiality within the framework of the inquiry that the Ombudsman is leading. To his inquiry powers are added injunction powers: the Ombudsman may impose mandatory deadlines on the administrative authorities to which he addresses his questions. Therefore, the Ombudsman contributes to showing the least visible side of the administration: "he can bring light to dark corners, despite those who would prefer to close the curtain" (Milvain 1970).

In endeavoring to make the administrative action more transparent, the Ombudsman does not judge the administration or criticize it; he simply calls the attention of the administration to the harmful or prejudicial effects of certain decisions it has adopted. On the other hand, he draws the attention of the political decision-makers to the foreseeable consequences of the legislation.

The European Mediator as well as the federal College of Mediators, the Flemish and Walloon Mediators, and the Mediator of the Republic in France, expose the lack of information from an administration that is under their control and play the role of information providers (in lieu of the administration) before the complainant. The Mediators emphasize in their Annual Reports the opacity of the administration and remind of the importance of formally justifying the administrative acts, in a way such that even a refusal, if formally justified by the administration, is better understood and better accepted by the complainant.

While discussing "information" and "annual report," we should add that it is through the public annual reports that Mediators also inform the political decision-makers and the administration of what changes are appropriate in the statutes or in the behavior of the administration in order to foster a better rapprochement between the citizen, on the one hand, and the administration and even the state on the other hand.

(c) *It is a public authority that fights against "misadministration" and intervenes impartially.* The Ombudsman is a public authority whose role is to defend the citizen against the inadequate functioning of the administrative authority. His mission covers the field of the malfunction and the "misadministration." Frequently, the notion that "you can't fight city hall" suddenly appears in the mind of the citizen who does not know how to address the administration in order to prove that he was the victim of an error, a prolonged silence, or slowness. For every complaint submitted to the Ombudsman and deemed valid by him, he leads an inquiry on the actions or the deficiencies of the administration. He handles disputes related to actions that are not in line with the mission of public service that the administration must follow. The Ombudsman will attempt to reconcile the points of view of the administration and the users, establish relations of understanding between the parties, and attempt to assure a better equilibrium between them.

While establishing balanced relations between the administration and the citizens, and while improving the functioning of the administrative authority, the Ombudsman also corrects instances of injustice, even if committed in the name of the law. He remedies unfair situations; he acts in equity. In fact, sometimes it happens that an administrative decision, while strictly following the law or regulation, leads to unfair consequences that are inequitable to the individual. It is difficult for the individual to show the administration the harmful effects of the administrative decision on his personal situation. Here we see the image of an administration that acknowledges nothing but files and turns a blind eye to humanity. This is when the Ombudsman intervenes in equity. He humanizes the rule of law by asking the administration to adapt it to the particular situation of the citizen.

The European Mediator, the French Mediator of the Republic, the Flemish Mediator, the Mediator of the Walloon Region, and the federal College of Mediators in Belgium have exposed in their annual reports the excessive strictness and legalism of the administration and have acted in equity. They all act in equity, but only as an exception and very prudently.

(d) *The Ombudsman is an independent public authority.* His effectiveness and his credibility rest on his independence vis-à-vis the administration that he controls and on his independence vis-à-vis the power that appoints him—in general, the Parliament. His independence is always established in the organic text that sets up his office. This independence is frequently reinforced by rules of immunity and incompatibility expressly defined in this same organic text. The Ombudsman is thus not subject to any hierarchical control or tutelage.

The Mediator of the Flemish Community, until 1998, was designated by the government of the Flemish community. However, his statute was completely revised by the July 7, 1998, decree. Since then, he has been appointed by the Flemish Parliament for a six-year period, renewable only once.

The Mediator of the Walloon region is appointed by the Parliament of the Walloon region for a six-year period, renewable once, and the federal College of Mediators is appointed by the federal Parliament for a six-year period, renewable indefinitely.

The Mediator of the Republic in France is appointed by the President of the Republic by decree and adopted by the Council of Ministers (a decree in France is an act of the executive branch of government, whereas in Belgium a decree is a legislative act of regional authorities). The Mediator of the Republic is appointed for a six-year period that is renewable.

The European Mediator is appointed after each European parliamentary election for the duration of the legislative period. His mandate is renewable.

The statutes of these Ombudsmen (the conditions for appointment, the incompatibilities and the immunities) are quasi-similar for these institutions.

(e) *The Ombudsman is a simple recourse, free of charge and therefore very accessible for conflict resolution.* For the party who is injured by the administrative authority, there are certainly internal administrative recourses that cause the administration to reconsider its decision and there are recourses before administrative jurisdictions. Nevertheless, the Mediator is an original recourse with a specific character. The Mediator is neither a judge nor an arbitrator. He takes a position regarding the problems that are presented to him by dissatisfied users, but he does not impose a decision, even if he shows tenacity.

This originality can also be found in his interventions that are directed not only at the legality of the decisions of the administration, but also at the good sense, the equity, and the "reasonableness" of such decisions.

The Ombudsman offers to the individual the chance to defend his version or "his argument," without any intermediary and without excessive formalism, up to the highest level. The review of a complaint by the Ombudsman is especially subject to the condition that the preliminary steps must be completed before the relevant administration or that the internal administrative recourses must have been pursued.

(f) *A public authority that suggests reforms. The Ombudsman is an agent of change.* The Ombudsman is not content with drawing the attention of the administration and the political decision-makers to the consequences of their acts, decisions or regulations. Based on individual complaints that are presented to him, the Ombudsman "acts" by way of recommendations and suggestions:

- He formulates recommendations to the administrative authority in order to equitably settle the situation of a claimant;
- He offers suggestions that target the improvement of the functioning of the administrative authority; and
- He suggests revisions to statutes, decrees, or regulations.

The purpose of his recommendations is to bring to a particular case a new answer that is satisfactory. His suggestions are directed beyond a specific case to the satisfaction of a general interest. In this sense, the Ombudsman plays the role of "an agent of change." Furthermore, the European Mediator, the Mediator of the Republic in France, the federal Mediators, the Mediator of the Walloon Region, and the Flemish Mediator all suggest statutory revisions to their respective parliaments.

General Conclusion

In the framework of this study, we progressed from an administered individual or "subject" to a user of the public service, to a consumer of public services, to a citizen, and even to the "individual." We also progressed from the proper and legal application of a statute to the necessity of its explanation, to its justification in fact and in substance, to its publication and its availability to the public. We progressed from a loyal and proper administrative management to an effective and quality administrative management. We progressed from an anonymous and impersonal administration to a humane administration that is closer to the citizen.

What a distance we have covered! This is the result of the transformation of the administrative function and, indeed, the transformation of the administrative law of the public function.

This is a good illustration of the context of the new administrative culture. Does all this make the citizen, who is referred to by some as the "consumer of public services," a real partner of the administration or of the public enterprise in the same manner as he is a "partner" of his interlocutor in the private sector?

It is important to remember that a consumer of private goods has "a choice" among the goods he acquires or uses. If the quality of goods or services does not suit him, he can switch to the competition, freely choose the product that he desires, or become the "client" of another business. However, the consumer of public services does not have this choice. He has only one avenue of access to the public service.

In addition, in the public sector, the authorities make the rules in a unilateral way, and the relationship between the users and the public enterprise is a regulated one.

Let us think of adhesion contracts, such as the purchase of a commuting pass or of water supply: the conditions of these contracts are unilaterally determined by the relevant public authority and the only thing that the citizen can do is to adhere to them. The public administration does not maintain relations of the "equal partnership type" with the user because the administration, in order to effectively fulfill its public interest mission, is obligated to use its prerogatives of public power. In addition, the administration must continue to abide by the laws of public service, that is, the law of change or mutability, the law of regularity or continuity, and the law of equality among users.[15] However, today the law of equality among users does not prevent the differentiation in the modes of action of the public service in accordance with the diversity of the situations of the users.

Today, as Weiner argues, "the administration does not act in a vacuum any longer, but the cultural and social evolution everywhere lead it to be more open to considering the users as interlocutors rather than passive beneficiaries of its action" (Weiner 1991:18).

The citizens-users are not subject to the administration's whim any longer. They have the capability to ask the administration to account for its actions and to make the administration discuss matters and engage in a dialogue.

In this new conception of the public function, the administration is not perceived as an anonymous machine any longer. The civil servants or public agents, while serving the state with loyalty, independence, and competence, have new values and new preoccupations for the benefit of the citizens. The administrative law remains the rule, but it is a more personal one vis-à-vis the citizen. Such is the ethic of the public services. And, such is the new administrative culture, in Belgium, in France, and in the European Institutions, a guarantee of democracy.

NOTES

[1] The administrative democracy is also based on the "administrative injunction," which is a jurisdictional guarantee for the citizen, and on the judicial protection of personal matters.

[2] Chidiac, Marie-José. 1999-2000. "Les médiateurs, l'action administrative et l'éthique des services publics" (Mediators, Administrative Action and the Ethic of Public Services). Syllabus. Namur: Facultés Universitaires Notre-Dame de la Paix.

A legal act targets the modification of a legal situation. Therefore, an act or operation that is purely material, an interior measure or a preparatory act is not subject to the law. An act that causes involuntary damage is not a unilateral act even if it may have legal effects, because in itself it does not target the modification of a legal situation. On the other hand, the promotion of a civil servant is a legal act.

A unilateral act is an act that contrasts a legal bilateral act. Therefore, the law does not apply to contracts. But the acts called "detachable" that precede a contract, in the case of a government contract for example, are legal unilateral acts.

An enforceable decision must have immediate legal effect. Decisions that are not yet defined or preparatory decisions, such as a warning or a formal notice, are not enforceable; consequently, they are outside the field of applicability of the law.

A unilateral legal act impacting an individual refers to a known distinction in administrative law contrasting specific decisions to regulations of general import. The regulations or decisions of general import that do not contain legal rules are outside the field of applicability of the law because they are drafted in a manner that is different from the decisions that apply to individuals and according to procedures that give more guarantees at the level of formal and material justifications.

A legal act issued by an administrative authority where the administrative authority is referred to within the meaning of Article 14 of the joint laws related to the Council of State. One may consider that, according to the jurisprudence of the Council of State, the administrative authority includes:
- the executive power (federal, community, regional);
- the provinces, towns, suburbs;
- the cross-state, the cross-regional and cross-community organisms; and
- the private individuals who are in charge of a public service mission and who have been delegated with the rights of a public authority.
- In any case, they are authorities that are not a part of the legislative or the judicial power.

3   For further background one may refer to the website of the Syndicat National des Enseignements de Second Degré (http://www.snes.edu/memos).

4   Closer to us, the European institutions have acknowledged or put into effect the obligation to justify, such as in the Charter of Fundamental Rights of the European Union, declared at Nice in December 2000, which I address later.

5   Article 19: "Each person has the right to freedom…of expression, that is the right…to look for, receive and spread information and ideas by any means of expression and without regard to borders." United Nations. *Universal Declaration of Human Rights*, 1948.

6   Following this Declaration, the Conference has recommended that the Commission submit to the Council, in 1993 at the latest, a report on the measures aimed at increasing public access to information at the disposal of the institutions.

7   "That is, created or received by the institution and in its possession, in all fields where the European Union operates." E.U. Regulation (CE) Article 2, Section 3. No. 1049/2001. Adopted May 30, 2001.

8   This Regulation allows for several absolute exceptions for reasons of public interest, the protection of privacy and individual integrity, as well as related exceptions, implying a balance of interests. This regulation also allows for a special system for handling sensitive documents, public safety, defense and military matters, international relations, and financial, monetary or economic policies of the Community or of a member-State (Article 4, Section 1 of the Regulation).

9   Thus have been adopted the Flemish decree of October 23, 1991 related to "the publicity of administrative documents in the services and establishments of the Flemish executive branch of government" and the decree of May 18, 1999 related to administrative publicity. In fact, the Flemish legislator, who "preceded" by two years the enactment of Article 32 of the Constitution by adopting the decree of October 23, 1991 has abrogated its first statute and replaced it with the decree of May 18, 1999, the federal law of April 11, 1994 related to administrative publicity, the French Community decree of December 22, 1994, the Walloon Regional Council decree of March 30, 1995, the decree of the German-speaking Community of October 16, 1995, the Brussels-capital Region Ruling of March 30, 1995 and the decree of the Commission of the French community of the Region of Brussels-Capital of July 11,1996 and the Law of November 12, 1997 related to administrative publicity in the Provinces and Towns.

10 The administrative authority may reject a request to access if the request relates to an administrative document the disclosure of which can lead to an erroneous understanding of such document, due to it being unfinished or incomplete, or because it relates to an opinion freely and confidentially communicated to the government, is patently abusive, or is stated in a patently vague manner.

11 The other levels of power, with the exception of the German-speaking Community, have provided for the establishment of an appeals process that is for some a Committee (e.g., the Walloon Region) and for others, like in Flanders, a government official at the Flemish Community ministry appointed by the Government, or the Government itself, depending on the nature of the appeal.

12 In the name of administrative transparency, the following laws were also adopted: the Law of 1973 instituting the Mediator of the Republic (see below), the Law of 1976 related to installations earmarked for the protection of the environment and the Law of January 6, 1978 related to data processing, files and liberties.

13 The special situation of environmental documents and the legislation related to electronic access to administrative documents will not be analyzed here. However, see Marie-José Chidiac, The Pillars of the Administrative Culture, Symposium IISA, June, 2002.

14 In Flanders, the Ombudsman was created by an October 23, 1991 decree of the Flemish Council; its office was regulated by a December 9, 1992 order of the Flemish government. These statutes were repealed and currently, the July 7, 1998 decree of the Flemish Council establishes the service of the Flemish Mediator.
- In the Walloon Region, "the Institution of the Mediator for the Walloon Region" was established by a decree of the Walloon Regional Council dated December 22, 1994.
- The federal College of Mediators was established by the federal Law of March 22, 1995.

15 The law of change or mutability authorizes the public powers to revise at any time the rules of organization and functioning of the public services, as well as the conditions in which the services are provided to the public, in order to quickly adapt the public services to the progress and the evolution of the needs to be satisfied.

The law of regularity or continuity requires the public services to provide their services, which by definition are a public interest and without which the public will suffer great harm, on a daily basis and in a regular and continuous manner.

The law of equality among users and consumers requires that every individual who faces a situation where he is subject to conditions that are set by law or regulation in an impersonal and general manner, may avail himself of the benefits or services of the government agency in question, in exchange for a set fee, without any discrimination.

REFERENCES

Belgian Monitor. 1993 (January 22). 1150.
Belgium. Parliament. Chambre (House of Representatives). Parliamentary document. Session 1992-1993. 1112/1:12.
Belgium Senate. 1998. *Parliamentary Document*. Extraordinary Session. No. 15/3.

Bouvier, Philippe. 2002. *Eléments de droit administratif* (Elements of Administrative Law). Brussels: De Boeck University.

Bribosia, Henri. 1992. "*La motivation formelle des actes administratifs, loi du 29 juillet 1991: Actes de la journée d'études du 8 mai 1992* (The Formal Justification of the administrative acts, Law of July 29, 1991: Acts of the day of study of May 8, 1992). *Declaration Related to the Right to Access to Information*. Brugge: La Charte.

Chidiac, Marie-José. 1999-2000. "Les médiateurs, l'action administrative et l'éthique des services publics" (Mediators, Administrative Action and the Ethic of Public Services). Syllabus. Namur: Facultés Universitaires Notre-Dame de la Paix. (http//www.droit.fundp.ac.be/cours/syllabus%20Chidiac.pdf)

Clark, David. 2000. "Citizens, Charters and Public Service in France and Britain." *Government and Opposition, An International Journal of Comparative Politics*. 35(2):153-169.

European Union. Council. 1980. Recommendation. (March 11) No. 80, 2.

_____. Council. 1981. Recommendation (November 25). Quoted in Alain Stenmans. 1999. "The Transformation of the Administrative Function in Belgium." Public Administration and Society. Brussels: CRISP Edition.

_____. 1992. *Declaration Related to the Right to Access to Information*. Journal officiel No. C 191 (July 29): 0101.

_____. Parliament and the Council. 2001. Regulation (CE) No. 1049/2001. Official Gazette. No. L 145 of May 31, 2001. (in force December 3, 2001): 0043-0048.

Hauriou, Maurice. 1914. "Note sous Conseil d'Etat Français." (March 27). Quoted in Jean Laveissière, "L'accès aux documents administratifs", *Information et transparence administratives*. Amiens: Presses Universitaires de France. 1998.

Jacoby, Daniel. 1995-1996. Protecteur du citoyen du Québec. *26th Annual Report* Assemblée Nationale de Québec.

Laveissière, Jean. 1988. "L'accès aux documents administratifs" (Access to administrative documents). *Information et transparence administratives*. Amiens: Presses Universitaires de France.

Le Rendu, Jean-Patrick. 1998 "L'accès aux documents administratifs en France" (Access to administrative documents in France). Paper presented at symposium: "La Gestion des Archives Courantes et Intermédiaires." International Association of French Archives. 11-18.

_____. 2001. "L'accès aux documents administratifs, loi du 12 avril 2000" (Access to administrative documents, law of April 12, 2000). Option (December 10), 419.

Milvain, James V. 1970. Order re: *Ombudsman, Act*. Quoted by D. Jacoby, Protecteur du citoyen du Quebec. Assemblée Nationale de Québec. *26th Annual Report* (1995-1996):13.

Paquet, Aimé. 1976. "Mediator's Report to The President of Republic of France and to the Parliament". Paris: French Documentation. 112.

Pinay, Antoine. 1973. Annual Report of the Mediator, Paris, French Documentation. 253-254.

Stenmans, Alain. 1999. *"La transformation de la fonction administrative en Belgique"* (The Transformation of the Administrative Function in Belgium). Public Administration and Society. Brussels: CRISP Edition.

Thibault, André. 1999. "Les références administratives et les rôles des citoyens (The Administrative References and the Roles of the Citizens)." *Telescope* (March), vol. 1.

Tobback, Louis. 1993. Memorandum, no. 379 (January 12): 28.

Trosa, Sylvie. 1995. "To Modernize the Administration, How Do the Others Do that?" Paris: Les Editions d'Organisation.

United Nations. 1948. *Universal Declaration of Human Rights*, Article 19.

Wiener, Céline. 1991. *The Evolution of Relations Between the Administration and the Users*. Paris: Economica.

Chapter 5

ADMINISTRATIVE CULTURE IN A BORDERLESS WORLD: RUSSIA

Anatoly Zhuplev and Vladimir I. Shein

Russian Administrative Culture in the Environmental Context[1]

Administrative systems and processes within national boundaries usually occur as *macro*governance or government administration, typically on a federal, regional/state, or municipal level, and *micro*administration representing management in organizations. Geert Hofstede, a reputed scholar, defines societal culture as "a collective mental programming of people who share a similar environment, shaping work-related cultural values and behavior in organizations" (Hofstede 1997). A modern version of an authoritative Russian encyclopedia defines culture as a general state of the populace in its material and spiritual regards. Under this definition, the *material* culture encompasses housing, clothes, forms, means, and outcomes of economic activity, arts, etc.; the *spiritual* culture deals with language, cultural customs, faith, written artifacts of culture, literature, etc.; and the *public* culture covers government and public institutions and agencies, laws, etc. Sometimes, spiritual and public culture is termed as civilization or good citizenship (Brokgauz and Efron 2002).

Administrative culture manifests itself in behavioral norms, adopted and adhered to by participants of the governance process on the macro and micro level. Cultural norms in this process are established, shaped, and institutionalized as the nation develops on the basis of its fundamental, time-tested, societal interrelationships. From this viewpoint, the most crucial for the initial normative stage are the periods of transition when changes brought about by environmental conditions occur in the government and societal fabric in an explosive fashion, while the new order has not yet been institutionalized. Hence, the most critical impact on the contemporary Russian administrative culture occurred in the two latest swings of the Russian historical pendulum: the 1917 Bolshevik Revolution that created the U.S.S.R., and the political-economic transformation in the late twentieth/early twenty-first centuries that re-established Russia from its ashes.

In a country of Russia's magnitude, the uncertainty of post-Soviet outcomes and the political-economic transition have created a government that is often preoccupied with short-term urgencies, thus losing sight of its long-term priorities and goals. Instead of focusing on long-term objectives for the country, the government seeks its own self-serving bureaucratic and personal goals. Inadequate judicial standards, confusing moral criteria and norms, outdated organizational structures, and erratic shifts in the direction and pace of reforms over the past dozen transitional years have not created a sound foundation for a strong and coherent concept of administrative culture in Russia. Under the nation's continuing and seemingly never ending transformation, it has yet to identify its fundamental watersheds from the not-so-distant Soviet past. On the other hand, any attempt to accelerate the formation and development of Russian administrative culture by drawing direct parallels and analogies with foreign countries is likely to be misleading because of Russia's different historical background, cultural profile, and mentality. Figure 1 shows key interrelationships between culture and other structural elements of the environment in which the formation of administrative culture takes place. The lower part of the chart presents historical background as a platform for current occurrences and trends that evolve into a foundation for future developments. Political, legal, government, economic, and socio-cultural systems in the upper part comprise the environment in which culture evolves and realizes itself. The political system is the foundation and driving force for the legal, government, and economic systems.

Within the nation's socio-cultural system (highlighted in bold), culture in general, and administrative culture in particular, result from evolution and a current state of intertwined political, legal, government, and economic systems. In turn, political, legal, government, and economic systems and processes in the nation, as well as their future state, are interrelated with and dependent on cultural developments. Technological variables (not included in the chart) and their impact are of paramount significance for administration and play a crucial role in affecting all other systems by creating access to vital information for decision makers and the public, resulting in efficiency in the generation, gathering, processing, and dissemination of information; the domestic and international exchange of information; and travel, cultural exchanges, and other venues. The Internet, e-mail, television, multimedia, and the other technological means, coupled with the availability of independent information sources, have drastically changed thinking and behavioral patterns in Russia over the last several decades.

At different evolutionary stages, the impact of these variables on the Russian administrative culture has varied under external and internal conditions. In this context, scholars often emphasize the following critical factors of impact on

ADMINISTRATIVE CULTURE IN A BORDERLESS WORLD

Figure 1. Culture in the Environmental Context

Outcomes ← Processes & changes ← Systems & institutions

Political system	Legal system	Government system	Economic system	Socio-cultural system
- Politecon platform (slavery, serfdom, capitalism, communism)	- Constitution (republic, monarchy)	- Politecon platform (central planning, state-controlled, mixed, free market)	- Politecon platform (central planning, state-controlled, mixed, free market)	- Demographics (life expectancy, age distribution, health, birth, fertility)
- Democracy vs. totalitarianism (representative democracy, communism, fascism, totalitarianism)	- Type of law (common, civil, religious)	- Degree of politecon centralization (taxation, control of natural and intellectual resources, planning, resource allocation, regulatory role, administrative control of economic development	- Geographic conditions (climate, terrain, strategic location, economic size, economic conditions)	- Family, education
- Political elections	- Freedoms and rights		- Natural resource endowment and allocation within national boundaries	- Religion
- Political parties	- Sophistication (completeness, coverage) of the legal system	- Balance of power (checks & balances, independence of legislative, judiciary)	- Politecon philosophy (a "cradle to grave" vs. hands-off approach)	- Business and society
- International political doctrine, cooperation and active participation	- Effectiveness of law enforcement	- Social support and control		- Middle class
- Military and its political role in domestic and international affairs		- Power sharing (federal, regions, localities)	- Openness toward international trade and investment	- Entrepreneurship
		- Efficiency (decision making, accountability, transparency, corruption)	- Distribution of wealth among population	- Self-dependency of population
- Police, security, special forces and their impact on political system and population	- Independent media		- Quality of life	- Cultural dimensions (power distance, individualism, masculinity, uncertainty avoidance, long-term orientation, content vs. context in communication)
			- Budgetary system, taxation, fiscal issues	- Law obedience
				- Gender roles
				- Crime and bribery

Historical background ··········· The time flow ··········· Current trends & developments

Future developments

111

culture and administration: (1) Russia's sheer geographic size; (2) high centralization and authoritarian leadership; (3) blurry and feeble mechanisms for transfer of political-administrative power in the upper echelons; (4) a predominantly "top-down" approach to administrative changes and reforms; and (5) geographic, political-economic, and cultural isolation from the world. Sometimes, Russia's observers also include religious impact, arguing that the Orthodox Church, along with the geographic vastness and climate harshness, administrative centralism, authoritarian leadership, and poor roads[2] provide a fertile ground for the nation's self-isolation, reliance on administrative power, and limited access to information (Gratchev, Rogovsky, Rakitski 2001).

Russia's geography (particularly its huge territory, harsh climate, and relative isolation from the world's major centers of political-economic power) plays a fundamental role in shaping Russia's politics, especially in shaping administrative culture in Russian provinces with their immense variety in language, ethnicity, and cultural patterns. Although the Russian character has, to some extent, been determined by unrelenting autocratic rule and governance, the two chief factors in the formation of Russian values and core beliefs were over and above any government control. These prevailing determinants were the incalculable vastness of the Russia land and the unvarying harshness of its climate. The boundless, often indefensible steppes bred a deep sense of vulnerability and remoteness, which caused groups to blend together for survival, and develop hostility to outsiders. This, in turn, elevated the governing and protecting role of local community and central government. The influence of the harsh climate, along with the country's geographic vastness, was particularly hard on Russian peasants,[3] who were traditionally forced to virtually hibernate for long periods, then struggle frantically to till, sow, and harvest in the little time left. The long-suffering Russian peasants, ill-favored by cruel geography and denied (by immense distances, difficult terrain, strict legal and other restrictions on internal migration, international travel) chances of adequate communication and education were easy prey for those with ambitions and power to rule (Lewis 2002).

V. Klyuchevskiy and S. Soloviev, two highly regarded Russian historians of the early twentieth century, portray the Russian national character as one of cautiousness, unpredictability, intensive work and rest, communal work, and a high level of unity and centralization (Lawrence and Vlachoutsicos 1990). A 2001 worldwide, cross-cultural GLOBE survey placed Russia among the lowest ranked countries on future orientation, uncertainty avoidance, and performance orientation, and among the highest ranked on power distance (Gratchev at al. 2001). Vast distances, along with centralization and strong communal impact, add another dimension to the picture. Even after the dissolution of the U.S.S.R. in 1991, Russia still remains the largest territory in the world and is 1.8 times larger than the United States, but the total length of its railways in 2002 was only 41 percent of that in the United States, the paved highways only 13 percent, and airports with paved runways at just 9 percent of that in the United States (CIA 2002).

Commensurate with Russia's gigantic geographic size is the tradition of high centralism and authoritarian rule in administration. From the Kievan Rus' (established in 862 AD) through the current stage of Russian statehood, centralism and authoritarian rule played crucial role in culture and administration. Similarly, dependency on government support, the expectation of strong charismatic leadership, and a popular belief in a "benevolent dictatorship" as a way of delivering justice and problem solving, has always been widespread among the population.

Many Russian contemporary statesmen and business executives, as well as common people, draw inspiration from the autocratic, iron-fisted figures from the past: Ivan IV the Terrible (1533-1584), Peter I the Great (1682-1725), Catherine II the Great, (1762-1796), and Joseph Stalin (1879-1953), among others.[4] Thus, despite Russia's long history, its technological advances, and the recent democratic developments, it is not uncommon for contemporaries to look to the past and resort to authoritarian means in search for answers to the nation's problems.

Ivan IV was the first Russian ruler to be crowned as Tsar and later recognized, at least by the Orthodox Church, as Emperor. He strengthened the power of the Tsar to an unprecedented degree, demonstrating the risks of unbridled power in the hands of a charismatic but mentally unstable leader. Although apparently intelligent and energetic, Ivan IV suffered from bouts of paranoia and depression and his rule was punctuated by acts of extreme violence reaching far beyond his close circles. In the late 1550s, he developed hostility toward his advisers, the government, and the boyars and unleashed the *oprichnina,* a policy of mass terror and repression (that was later reproduced in the 1930s on a much wider scale under Stalin).

Peter I, the Great, another acclaimed Russian leader, had transformed Muscovy from a static, isolated, and traditional state into a more dynamic, partially Westernized and secular Russian Empire. His major contributions to administrative culture included streamlining the government, creating of government ministries, colleges, and the senate to coordinate government policy, enhancement of local tax collection, and maintaining order. As part of his government reform, Peter partially incorporated the Orthodox Church into the country's governmental structure. Perhaps Peter's most prominent achievement was the adoption of a Law of the State Service in the Russian Empire (the Table of Ranks), which determined a person's position and career status according to service to the Tsar, rather than to his/her birth origin or seniority. Peter's Table of Ranks was modeled after similar legislation already existing in Prussia and Denmark and some other western European countries that were culturally very different from Russia. Although the Table of Ranks had ceased to exist, *de facto*, by the end of the eighteenth century, some of its traces are still recognizable in Russia's current government system. Peter's numerous attempts to Westernize Russia collided with Russian traditional nationalism, initiating a debate over Russia's place in the world and its future. His introduction of European customs generated nationalistic resentments in society and spawned the deep division between "Westernizers" and nationalistic "Slavophiles," that remains a key dynamic of current Russian thought in sociopolitical and administrative domains (U.S. Department of State 2002).

Following Peter's course, Catherine II, the Great, strived to organize society into well-structured social groups and issued charters to nobles and townsmen. She also attempted to rationalize government procedures through law by creating the Legislative Commission, drawn from nobles, townsmen, and others.

Despite many accomplishments, the Empire that Peter I and Catherine II had built was beset with fundamental problems that, to some extent, are still present in contemporary Russia. A small Europeanized elite, alienated from the mass of ordinary Russians, raised questions about the very essence of Russia's history, culture, and identity. Russian military preeminence had been achieved by reliance on coercion and a primitive command economy essentially based on serfdom. Although Russia's economic development was almost sufficient for its eighteenth century needs, it was no match for the transformation that the Industrial Revolution was causing in the West. Catherine II's attempts at organizing society into corporate estates was already being challenged by the French Revolution, which emphasized democracy and individual citizenship. Russia's territorial expansion and the incorporation of an increasing number of non-Russians into the empire set the stage for future inter-ethnic problems.

The 1917 Bolshevik Revolution in Russia created a radically new type of communist governance. Russian administrative culture has been increasingly affected by the impact of the Soviet model with its strong emphasis on centralism, universalism, suppression of ethnicity, individual freedoms and democracy, private ownership, and entrepreneurship. Consequently, a "dictatorship of the proletariat,"[5] the dominant role of the party in public and private life, and an increase in bureaucracy, military, secret police, and enforcement have flourished.

Joseph Stalin's accession to power in the second half of the 1920s unleashed unprecedented government control, mobilization, and terrorization of society in Russia that translated into a series of large-scale administrative and sociopolitical experiments. Under Stalin's idea of "revolution from above" in the late 1920s to 1930s, Soviet agriculture and industry underwent forced collectivization and industrialization; cultural activities were restricted and subjugated by ideology; and purges eliminated thousands of individuals deemed dangerous to the Soviet state. Stalin's strict rule and personal authoritarian leadership had a profound impact on generations of Russian business executives and government administrators.

Based on strong, centralized, authoritarian rule with limited individual and democratic freedoms, the Russian administrative apparatus has traditionally been rigid. For centuries, Russia, from a governance standpoint, was either under a legal monarchy or under totalitarian rule. Unopposed to their constituencies by independent interests, media, or democratic checks and balances, Russia's administrators had no urgency for reformation, dooming the nation to chronically lag behind its advanced European counterparts. When reforms occur throughout Russian history, they have usually been contemplated and implemented in a predominantly "top-down" bureaucratic manner, limited to narrow administrative circles. Coping with the tremendous weight of Russia's economic-geographic size, dealing with challenges of immense administrative magnitude, having corrupt checks and balances in its highly centralized and autocratic governance system, and yet very local in its communal culture and spirit (for this matter, resistant towards intervention from above by federal government), Russian rulers have had a tendency to rely on campaigns rather than long-term vision and strategies in reforming the nation.

High centralization and totalitarianism in the Russian administrative culture have often been fraught with volatility and violence in a transfer of political/administrative power. From Rurik, the founder of the Kievan Rus', to Gorbachev, the last Soviet president, many top statesmen were removed from office by force via a coup d'etat, or Byzantine palace intrigue, or died in office without having named a successor or without having established a legal-political mechanism for the transfer of power, thus exposing the nation to crises in power transfer. Over many centuries, this trait has elevated to the top the role of *silovye structury (siloviki)* or the power structures (security services, military, police, etc.) in the Russian governing establishment.

Being the largest territory on earth, with its transportation network limited both domestically and internationally, Russia, in essence, has been geographically land-locked and isolated from both Europe and Asia. Wide strategic northern access to the Arctic Ocean and the Pacific Ocean in the Far East nonetheless gives Russia a very limited political-economic leverage because of the harsh weather and low level of economic activity in those areas.[6] It should be noted, though, that at various stages of Russian history, the nation has experienced differing degrees of German, French, and American political-economic and cultural influence, traces of which can be found in many elements of administration and governance today.

Current Administrative Structure and Culture

The governing structure of the new, post-Soviet Russia differs significantly from that of the Russian Soviet Federated Socialist Republic (RSFSR),[7] a former Soviet republic. Since its establishment in 1991, Russia, or the Russian Federation, has been characterized by a weak judiciary and an ongoing power struggle between the executive and legislative branches, primarily over issues of constitutional authority and the pace and direction of democratic and economic reform. Conflicts came to a head in September 1993 when President Yeltsin dissolved the Russian parliament. Members of the parliament and their allies revolted and were suppressed only through military intervention.

In December 1993, a new constitution proposed by Yeltsin was approved in a nationwide referendum providing the president with significantly increased powers. Under this constitution, the president appoints the prime minister, key judges, as well as cabinet members, and may override and even dissolve the legislature in some cases. There is no vice-president, and the legislative branch is far weaker than the executive branch. The president nominates the highest state officials, including the prime minister, who must be approved by the Duma. He can (and quite often does) pass decrees without consent from the Duma.[8]

The new parliament consists of the Federation Council, a 178-member upper house with equal representation for all of the Russia's 89 territorial-administrative units (republics and regions) and a State Duma, a 450-member lower house elected through proportional representation on a party basis and through single-member constituencies (CIA 2002). The new constitution reduced the status of the regions and made all regions subject to central authorities.

Under Yeltsin's voluntary resignation in December 1999 (a very rare case in Russian political-administrative history), Vladimir Putin was hand picked as a successor and was elected Russia's president in May 2000. In 2000, at the initiative of the Putin Administration, each of the country's 89 provinces and autonomous republics, regions, and districts had been assigned to one of the seven new federal districts to enhance the power of the federal government, to streamline the administrative process, and to reduce regional power. To ensure this, Putin nominated seven presidential plenipotentiaries in the regions, most of them with strong security and military service backgrounds and connections, and/or personal loyalty to Putin.

Although Russia is a federation, the precise distribution of power between the central government and the regional and local authorities is still very much evolving. The Russian Federation consists of 89 subjects, including two federal cities, Moscow and St. Petersburg. The constitution explicitly defines the federal government's exclusive powers, but it also describes most key regional issues as the joint responsibility of the federal government and the Federation components. The young age of the Russian legislation, the hectic pace of the legislative process, and the plentiful legislative voids and gray areas in a division of power between the executive and legislative branches create a multitude of overlaps, discrepancies, and discretionary applications of federal, regional, and municipal legislation.

Russia's judiciary and justice systems remain weak and are expected to be in a state of flux for years to come. Numerous matters that are normally dealt with by administrative authorities in European countries often remain subject to political influence in Russia. Yeltsin reconvened the Constitutional Court in 1995 following its suspension in October 1993. The 1993 constitution empowers the court to arbitrate disputes between the executive and legislative branches, and between Moscow and the regional and local governments. The court is also authorized to rule on violations of constitutional rights, to examine appeals from various bodies, and to participate in impeachment proceedings against the president. The July 1994 Law prohibits the Constitutional Court from examining cases on its own initiative and limits the scope of issues the court can hear.

In the past few years, the Russian Government has begun to reform the criminal justice system and judicial institutions. Despite these efforts, judges are only beginning to assert their constitutionally mandated independence from other branches of power, and remain highly dependent on federal, regional, and local government concerning budgetary allocations, logistics, and other vital organizational matters, with the judges' personal careers frequently at stake.

The judiciary is often subject to manipulation by political authorities and is plagued by large case backlogs and trial delays. Lengthy pre-trial detention remains a serious problem and is often used by law enforcement agencies, with the blessing of the political leadership and administrative organs, to intimidate those in opposition. Meanwhile, there are some attempts to replace "law and order" with the opposite "order and law" formula in bringing Russian transitional affairs under the basic array after seven decades of communism and the anarchy unleashed during the Yeltsin era. Some bold voices even champion interim dictatorship in Russia as the only way to ensure stability (McFaul 2003).

The Russian Constitution provides for freedom of religion and the equality of all religions before the law, as well as the separation of church and state. The Russian Orthodox Church currently enjoys privileged relations with the government and its strong overall support. The influx of missionaries over the past several years has led to pressure by groups in Russia, specifically nationalists and the Russian Orthodox Church, to limit the activities of these "nontraditional" religious groups, resulting in the recent adoption of restrictive legislation.

The constitution guarantees Russian citizens the right to choose their place of residence and travel abroad. Some big-city governments, however, have restricted this right through residential registration rules that closely resemble the

Soviet-era *propiska* (a living permit) system. Although the rules were touted as a notification device rather than a control system, their implementation has produced many of the same administrative results as the notorious propiska. The freedom to travel abroad and emigrate is respected, although restrictions may apply to those who have had access to state secrets (U.S. Department of State 2002).

In terms of the economic situation, after the implosion of central planning, Russia is still struggling to establish a modern market economy, modernize its industrial base, and maintain strong economic growth. The 1992-1998 period was marked by a poor business climate, deterioration in already threadbare living standards, and failure to institute modern market reforms, ending in the devastating 1998 financial crisis. Conditions improved markedly in 1999-2003, with annual output growing by an average 6 percent, helped by high world prices for oil, gas, and other commodities, as well as some progress in reforms. Yet serious problems persist. Russia remains heavily dependent on exports of commodities, particularly oil, natural gas, metals, and timber, which account for over 80 percent of exports, leaving the country vulnerable to swings in world prices. Russia's industrial base is increasingly dilapidated and must be replaced or modernized if the country is to maintain strong economic growth. According to an assessment by Russian Prime Minister M. Kasyanov (Kasyanov was replaced by a new Prime Minister, Mikhail Fradkov in 2004), the Russian exports structure has remained unchanged for a long time. Although exports are substantial, manufactured goods account only for 10 percent, minerals and other raw materials for 60 percent, and the rest are metals, chemicals, and other low-tech products (NAG Consulting-Intratrade 2004). Other problems include widespread corruption, lack of a strong legal system, capital flight, and brain drain (CIA 2002). As a result of soaring world prices for commodities, as well as some improvements in domestic performance, the Russian current economic outlook looks good, and there are ambitious plans to double the nation's GDP by 2010.

In the late 1990s to early 2000s, Russian governance was being shaped under increasingly strong international influence, following the nation's newly acquired political-economic and cultural openness. Some recent federal legislative steps to create positive background for further development of the Russian administrative culture include amendments to the Russian Civil Code, a new Labor Code, and a law "On the System of Administrative Service of the Russian Federation" (Grazhdansky Kodeks Rossiiskoi Federatsii 2002).

Meanwhile, Russian entrepreneurs have united under the umbrella of the Russian Union of Industrialists and Entrepreneurs/Employers (RUIE) and adopted some important documents defining their self-governance, mutual strategies, interrelations, and standards of behavior. A stream of well-educated managers with

MBA degrees from leading Russian and overseas universities are already making a difference in changing organizational culture in Russia's enterprises, albeit largely in Moscow and, to a lesser degree, in St. Petersburg. Some of the largest Russian firms have adopted internationally recognized principles of corporate governance and Generally Accepted Accounting Principles (GAAP). For the first time in decades, the 2003 Financial Times Rating included five Russian firms. Increasingly, the boards of directors of Russia's leading public firms have independent directors (including overseas ones), although there is still an overall shortage of qualified candidates.

With these changes and the proliferation of popular awareness, only in the early twenty-first century have the business culture and the business-like administrative culture started taking shape in post-Soviet Russia. Greater political-economic and cultural openness and international business involvement increasingly compel Russian business and administrative cadres to adhere to internationally accepted behavioral norms and business protocol that in many countries outside Russia came about naturally as a result of their long evolution in international business practices. This trend should facilitate Russia's integration in international business, without which its further overall outlook will be bleak.

In this context, two documents significant to the formation of the Russian business and administrative culture should be mentioned. First is the non-binding Charter of the Corporate and Business Ethics (2003)[9] adopted by members of the Russian Union of Industrialists and Entrepreneurs/Employers, which sets up straightforward procedures for conflict resolution, establishes the Commission on Corporate Ethics, and forms a roster of arbiters on corporate ethics. This generates new momentum in the development of an organizational culture not only in the Russian business community itself, but also in a broader environmental context. The second important document is the non-binding Code of Corporate Behavior adopted in 2002, designated for publicly traded stock companies and modeled after the Corporate Governance Principles adopted in 1999 by the Organization for Economic Cooperation and Development (OECD). Filling a void in the Russian administrative law and culture, in August 2002 President Putin issued a decree "On General Principles of Administrative Behavior for Government Employees."[10]

These recent administrative documents, decisions, and other positive developments in Russia are very important initial steps in the right direction. However, implementing them into meaningful cultural changes, e.g., new behavioral norms and patterns in the macro governance and micromanagement of organizations, will take much more time and effort. This includes incorporating them in legislative, organizational, educational milieus, different media, etc., in various segments of the Russian society, including wide grassroots acceptance and support.

Transitional Developments and Their Impact

Information Technologies

Over many centuries, administration systems and processes in Russia were largely based on traditional technologies and top-down schemes. The advent of computers, the Internet, mass media, international travel, exchanges, democracy, and informational pluralism in the 1990s has abolished ideological restrictions and radically changed old-fashioned organizational requirements for administration. After the turbulent and often chaotic decade under Yeltsin, the Putin administration stresses the significance of the global information revolution for Russia's future and is making practical steps in that direction.

Information technologies (IT) are seen as tools for improving governmental performance, efficiency, and transparency in administration and decision-making. On the other hand, the mass proliferation of information technologies and other alternative sources make administrative processes more complicated and challenging by bringing into existence many differing, often conflicting, interests and increasing the social-political price of the governance. According to the 2003 annual e-readiness report, Russia holds the 43rd ranking (out of 60 countries), with an overall score of 3.9 (out of 10 maximum) that unfavorably compares to first place Sweden with an 8.7 score, and the United States, in fourth place with 8.4 points (Economic Intelligent Unit 2003).

The Russian Internet has now been in existence for ten years. Up until the mid-1990s, it was limited mainly to Moscow, St. Petersburg, and some "science cities." By 1997-1998 it had spread to other large cities (with populations of one million and above). Only recently is Internet use beginning to increase in smaller cities (populations 50-100,000). Some estimates indicate that as of mid 2001, the number of Internet users in Russia was 12.8 million, or 8.7 percent of the population. The CIA assessments for 2002 put these numbers at 18 million, or 12 percent of the total population, compared to 165.8 million and 59 percent in the U.S. Women in Russia accounted for over 40 percent of the 4.2 million regular Internet users. Meanwhile, 27 percent of the Russian users, and nearly 40 percent of the most active and regular users, live in Moscow or St. Petersburg, two cities comprising approximately 12 percent of the total population. In these cities, Internet users constitute about 20 percent of the population, compared to 8 percent in the remaining parts of the country. Most of the growth in recent years has been in the number of occasional users (i.e., less than once a week). Hardly any Internet users live in rural areas. The critical limiting factors are low incomes and poor telecom infrastructure (CIA 2002; Perfilev 2002). Because most of the Russian users connect via their existing (and often dilapidated) telephone connections, and the share of the broadband and cable market is small, the functional power of the Internet remains limited.[11]

Along these lines, President Putin is promoting a universal requirement that public officials should be computer literate. At his meeting with Russian IT executives in April 2001, Putin put forward a requirement that by the end of the year all federal government agencies post their business on the Internet and update their web sites on a daily basis.[12] By October 2001, the federal government had begun conducting its public procurement tenders for goods and services on-line, with the goal of opening up the procurement process to promote competition and reduce corruption. The "E-Russia" program calls for the creation of a government-wide Intranet, the integration of agency databases, and a real-time system for drafts and discussion of federal legislation and regulations on-line.

The Russian government also has established a special federal program with the goal of having computers and Internet access available in all higher educational institutions by 2005 and in all secondary schools by 2010. The E-Russia program envisions that 25 million Russians (nearly 17 percent of the total population) will be on-line by 2010. Perhaps most encouraging from administrative and democratic standpoints, taking Russia's history into account, is that the presidential initiative asserts that a widespread IT diffusion is "a prerequisite for the development of civil society based on free access to information through the global Internet" (Azrael and Peterson 2002).

With all the challenging goals and good intentions gearing toward the Internet revolution, Russia still lags far behind many developed nations. In 2003, Russia had 207.57 telephone lines per 1,000 inhabitants, compared with 617.73 in Germany and 668.17 in the United States (CIA 2003).[13] Russia's 5 percent rate of growth in international telephone traffic (measured as outgoing calls) between 1995 and 1998 lagged far behind the 9.5 percent average growth registered worldwide. The number of personal computers in Russia in 2003 (43.59 per 1,000 people) was lower than that of Brazil (46.69 per 1,000) or Mexico (54.33 per 1,000). Three-quarters of the Russians polled in a January 2001 survey had never even used a personal computer. The development of the Russian portion of the Internet (dubbed "Runet") is also behind that of the West and many major developing nations, such as Malaysia. Russia also does not have any major firms or facilities engaged in the production of such IT hardware as PCs. In a RAND survey of trends in the global information revolution, Russia was not even identified as a visible actor in technology development or application (Nationmaster 2003; Azrael and Peterson 2002).

Contrary to the remarkable progress already underway, none of the goals proclaimed for the creation of the E-Russia will be easily or quickly accomplished. Beyond the issues of strategic planning and financing, spending on information technology hardware must be synchronized with investments in "knowledge management" (training and development, textbooks, research, etc.) and other organizational transformations to ensure that the large volume of information that is being generated is used practically and efficiently. For example, efforts by the Soviet government in the late 1980s to develop a unified database to improve central planning and management of the economy failed, in part, because of the government agencies' resistance to sharing information and mending their ways in pursuit of national priorities. In Russia, today, many business executives and government functionaries continue to believe that controlling information is a major tool of power, suggesting that the administrative culture is to be a critical barrier in the impeding proliferation of ideas and executive decisions through the maze of the centralized bureaucratic governance system.

Democratization, Media, and Openness

The nation's large size, complex political administrative structure, and cultural-ethnic composition suggest that in addition to and beyond technological issues, such as the Internet and other IT tools and channels facilitating the dissemination of information, the mass media, especially TV, continues to play an extremely important role in the administrative process.

Russia's Internet users, however limited in numbers, have an access to a range of independent and reputable domestic news and information sites: the RAND survey data suggests that information sites are a high priority of web surfers. By mid 2001, 180 parties and other political movements had established their own web sites. Efforts are under way to provide on-line access to the Russian State Library in Moscow, one of the largest collections in the world. As Internet use increases, more and more Russians are gaining access to a plethora of international media and information sites, such as MSNBC, CNN, and Yahoo. Although, in a broad sense, Russia is not quite ready to embark on using commercial databases, such as ProQuest or LexisNexis, a growing access to various sources of information via free Internet sites vastly improves opportunities for general education and research, professional training and development, and political pluralism and democracy.

As one would expect in an administration in which former and current secret police and intelligence officers hold key government positions, and with a view of the "militocratization" of the Russian administration, a major priority has been placed on defense against the risks that uncontrolled information flows could pose to Russia's political stability and national security. Examples include, but are not limited to, the ongoing war in Chechnya; military, political, and economic

Figure 2.
Russia's Media Sustainability Index: 2001-2002

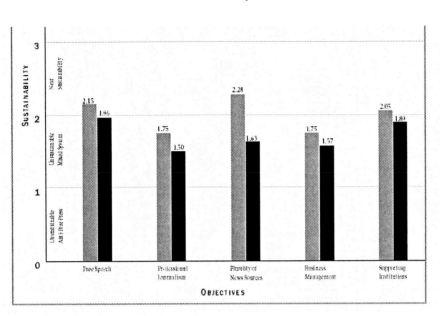

intelligence; and international and domestic terrorism. Under this preoccupation, a variety of steps have been taken in the legislation, presidential administration, and government agencies to enhance the government's ability to monitor electronic communications and ensure that, in Putin's words, the latter are used "with particular responsibility" (as quoted in Azrael and Peterson 2002). Shortly after he was appointed acting president, Putin approved a secret rule permitting the tax police, the Interior Ministry, and parliamentary security services to intercept electronic data communications and e-mail. In July 2000, the government promulgated additional regulations making information about the eavesdropping equipment a state secret and enabling government agencies to monitor communications for up to two days before getting court approval (as required by the Russian Constitution). In January 2002, the president signed legislation on digital signatures putting another national security organ, the Federal Service for Government Communications and Information (FAPSI), in control over on-line transactions (Azrael and Peterson 2002).

These concerns correspond with the IREX Media Sustainability index showing Russia's regress on a 10-point scale from 2.15 points in 2001 to 1.96 points in 2002, and placing the nation's across-the-board rating in a category of "unsustainable mixed system" (United States Agency for International Development 2003). As the chart (Figure 2) suggests, the level of professional journalism and plurality of sources have a major downgrading impact on Russia's Media Sustainability Index.

Russia's post-communist transformation has altered the nation's reputation as the world's top reading country, although the amount of print is still quite high: 5,436 newspapers, 2,409 magazines, 3,420 titles of other periodical and continuing publications, and 46,156 titles of books and brochures (Rossiiskaya knizhnaya palata 1999).

As the rapid liberalization of prices in the early 1990s made newspaper and magazine subscriptions too expensive for the majority of impoverished Russian families, they were forced to drastically reduce their choices to just one or two titles, as opposed to tens of titles often subscribed to earlier under the Soviet system. Thus, Russia has shifted from being a reading nation to a nation of TV viewers. The rise of TV as a major media powerhouse, and the loss of an administrative monopoly on broadcasting has prompted the government to find some ways to regain and retain its control of the national TV channels through licensing or law enforcement schemes (Usatcheva 2000).

Russia's newly acquired post-Soviet political and economic freedoms put the government administration face to face with a variety of different views, positions, and challenges existing in the society. Russia is fundamentally a democracy. Free elections are held and politicians are concerned about their prospects for re-election (and behave accordingly). Federal law requires that elections be contested; candidates cannot legally run unopposed. Another indicator of democratization is the presence and role of political parties. Some 150 political parties, blocs, and movements were registered with the Russian Justice Ministry as of December 19, 1998 (CIA 2002). Russia has abolished its exit visas and other restrictions on international travel for its citizens, which facilitated educational, cultural, and other exchanges, helping to improve mutual understanding and pluralism among the Russian population.

There is growing concern, however, that at the beginning of the twenty-first century, Russia is becoming increasingly unfree. Print and electronic media throughout Russia have been put under control of either federal, regional, or big business interests, which provide alternative (if still biased) perspectives. Whether the replacement of the management (and effectively, the journalistic staff) of the last independent NTV television station outside direct government control was motivated by a personal vendetta against former media baron Vladimir Gusinsky, or a desire to silence an opposing voice, or for legal/financial reasons, the result has been an increased perception among the press that free speech does not fully exist in Russia, and that police and government organs may be used to silence critical or independent media.

President Putin's KGB roots and his reliance on advisors and aides with a similar background create additional concern on the part of many Russians and Russia-watchers about the implications for freedom and democracy.[14] With the disturbing trends unfolding in the media, in the courts, and in efforts to control the Internet, government's desire to limit the political influence of big business and its hatred among the population at large, democracy in Russia is far from entrenched, and freedom seems even less so, with all of these aspects varying, to some extent, by region. Amid the reform fatigue and confusion among the general population stemming from ongoing environmental turbulence and countless changes, the lack of public outcry at newly imposed restrictions and limits on free speech and the press suggest that, up to a certain point, the majority of the Russian people may be willing to trade freedom and tolerance for administrative abuse and the stability that they perceive President Putin as bringing. Perhaps most importantly, because so many of Putin's efforts and reforms are tied up with him personally, as leader, whether their direction is autocratic or democratic, it is uncertain if his successor will follow the same path after Putin's second term in office (he has been re-elected for the second term in March 2004). If Russia does move in the direction of personalized autocracy (the sort of benevolent dictatorship that has worked well for Singapore or S. Korea), it again runs the risk that is faced by personal autocracies—instability and danger when a succession takes place (Oliker and Charlick-Paley 2002). And the probability of such scenario for Russia is high, given the strong existing political support for the pro-presidential party, the unfolding "vertical of power" in the nation's administrative organization, and the presidential supporters and loyalists with the security and military background already broadly implanted in the system.

Internationalization

Internationalization is a powerful factor affecting Russia's transformation. Although not directly related to administrative culture, globalization and international cooperation in political, business, cultural, and professional exchanges facilitates the diffusion of ideas and practical approaches that eventually lead to incremental changes in administration and governance.

Not a global superpower any more, Russia is still a nuclear nation with significant, although diminishing, military and political-economic clout in several global regions, including important ones in the Middle East and Asia. In this context, Russia is a key economic player in the world defense product markets, directly competing with the United States, the United Kingdom, France and other important actors. The major oil producer and the second largest oil exporter in the world after Saudi Arabia, Russia also holds the leading positions in production and exports of steel, aluminum, palladium, and other resources upon which many countries in Europe and across the world are highly dependent. Russia is also a large, albeit risky, market for foreign imports and investments: the nation's prosperity and political economic stability is increasingly dependent on international relations. The recent wave of global terrorism, the proliferation of weapons of mass destruction, and the nation's political leverage with some countries in these areas, also increase the international community's interest in engagement with Russia.

Conversely, as internal priorities are shifting toward democracy and a market economy, they increase Russia's own domestic stake in internationalization, especially from an economic development perspective. To materialize its rich natural resource base into economic wealth, Russia must take full advantage of exporting and international investment activities in the realization of absolute economic advantage and economy of scale. Pragmatically speaking, Russia needs foreign technology and investment. From a consumer standpoint, its political-economic liberalization opens a wide range of advantages: large access to foreign-produced goods and services at lower price, resulting in an increase in the standard of living. By engaging in international trade and investment, Russia and its citizens are also gaining a much broader access to internationally based markets, jobs, educational resources, cultural exchanges, travel, practical experience in business, management, governance, and administration both domestically and overseas.[15]

The data chart below characterizes Russia's global standing and involvement in international business in comparison with the world's selected regions and countries. By all measures presented in Table 1, Russia is holding low positions in

Table 1. Russia's Rankings in Key International Indexes in Comparison With the Best and Worst Performing Countries

	Russia		Three Leaders In the Ranking		Three Outsiders In the Ranking	
	Rank	Score	Rank	Score	Rank	Score
The 2003 Index of Economic Freedom (Heritage Foundation) Out of 156 countries, on a 1 -5 scale. http://www.heritage.org/research/features/index/	135	3.70	#1 Hong Kong #2 Singapore #3 Luxembourg	1.45 1.50 1.70	#153 Zimbabwe #155 Cuba #156 N. Korea	4.40 4.45 5.00
The 2002 Market Potential Indicators for Emerging Markets. (Michigan State University -CIBER) Out of 24 countries, on a 1 -100 scale. http://globaledge.msu.edu/ibrd/marketpot.asp	13	33	#1 Hong Kong #2 Singapore #3 S. Korea	100 98 75	#22 Indonesia #23 Venezuela #24 Colombia	8 7 1
The 2002 E-Readiness (The Economist Intelligence Unit) Out of 60 countries, on a 1 -10 scale. http://www.ebusinesssforum.com/index.asp?layout=rich_story&doc_id=5768	45	3.93	#1 U.S. #2 Netherlands #3 UK	8.61 8.45 8.40	#58 Algeria #59 Kazakhstan #60 Azerbaijan	7.18 7.12 6.83
The 2002 Growth Competitiveness (World Economic Forum) Out of 80 countries http://www.weforum.org/site/knowledgenavigator	64	NA	#1 U.S. #2 Finland #3 Taiwan	NA	# 78 Bolivia # 79 Zimbabwe # 80 Haiti	NA
The 2002 Globalization Index (A.T. Kerney) Out of 50 countries http://www.atkearney.com/shared_res/pdf/Rankings_2002_S.pdf	45	NA	#1 Ireland #2 Switzerland #3 Sweden	NA	# 48 Argentina # 49 Mexico # 50 Pakistan	NA
The 2002 Foreign Direct Investment Confidence Index (A.T. Kerney) Top 25 countries, on a 0 -3 scale. http://www.atkearney.com/shared_res/pdf/FDI_Confidence_Sept2002_S.pdf	17	0.96	#1 China #2 U.S. #3 UK	1.99 1.89 1.51	# 23 Belgium # 24 Taiwan # 25 Austria	0.86 0.85 0.85
The 2003 World Competitiveness Index. (International Institute for Management Development - IMD) http://www02.imd.ch/documents/wcy/content/ranking.pdf Out of 30 countries with over 20 million people population category, on a 1 - 100 point scale.	26	24.58	#1 U.S. #2 Australia #3 Canada	100.0 86.5 84.1	# 28 Indonesia # 29 Argentina # 30 Venezuela	13.2 12.5 9.8
The 2002 Transparency International Corruption Perception Index Out of 102 countries, from 0 (highly corrupt) to 10 (highly clean) http://www.transparency.org/pressreleases_archive/2002/dnld/cpi2002	71 (tied)	2.7	#1 Finland #2 Denmark #3 New Zealand	9.7 9.5 9.5	# 98 Paraguay # 101 Nigeria # 102 Bangladesh	1.7 1.6 1.2

Table 2. Population, Merchandise Export, and Foreign Direct Investment Per Capita

	2001		2000
	Population, millions**	Merchandise Exports Per Capita, $US	FDI Inflows Per Capita, $US
World	6,132.8	1,005	190
Russia	144.8	713	19
China (PRC)	1272.0	209	30
Czech Republic	10.3	3.240	445
Germany	82.2	6,929	2,301
Hungary	10.2	3,018	166
Japan	127.1	3,184	65
Poland	38.7	917	241
U.S.A.	284.0	2,574	1,013

Calculated on the basis of the World Development Report 2003, pp.234-243.

the world's charts and having a sizeable score handicap with the leading countries. The 135th rank (out of 156) in economic freedom, the 45th (out of 60) in e-readiness, the 63rd (out of 80) in growth competitiveness, the 45th (out of 50) in globalization, the 26th (out of 30) in competitiveness, and the 71st (out of 102) in a perception of corruption. These statistics are quite revealing in reflecting Russia's problems with weak governance and outdated administrative culture and point to the daunting reformation work ahead.

Richly endowed in mineral resources, the world's largest country in territory (12 percent of the world total) and the seventh largest in population (2.4 percent of the world total), Russia's share in world economy, trade, and investment is disproportionately low. For instance, in 2001 it contributed only 0.8 percent to the world's great national income (GNI), generated 1.7 percent to world exports, and attracted 0.2 percent of the world's foreign direct investment (FDI) inflows in the year 2000. In contrast, during the same year, the United States (having 6.7 percent of the world's territory and 4.6 percent of the world's population) contributed 31.3 percent to the world's GNI, 11.9 percent to world exports, and attracted 24.64 percent of the world FDI inflows (World Bank 2003). In the per capita merchandise trade and FDI inflows (Table 2), Russia is also trailing other countries.

In the beginning of the twenty-first century, Russia is the only big country remaining outside the World Trade Organization (WTO). Along with pending plans in the Putin administration to secure WTO membership by 2005, there are also some serious doubts in and outside of Russia concerning whether the country will be able to qualify and get ready for the WTO by 2005. Russia's membership in the EU, another important trading block (implicitly logical and necessary from many viewpoints), has not even been discussed yet with the EU. For many in the EU, Russia is too big, too unpredictable, and too different from other EU members.

Will Russia internationalize and will its internationalization lead to sustainable changes in the nation's administrative culture? A short answer to this complex and relatively new question is definitely "yes." However, as it is contingent upon many developments, Russia's internationalization is likely to be gradual, limited, and less dynamic compared to other countries.

Over the past several decades, Russia's large geographic size and relative isolation from the world formed a barrier to internationalization, which has been partially offset by advances in transportation and communications. Recent changes mainly affect key metropolitan cities, such as Moscow and St. Petersburg, leaving the rest of the country's administrative culture outside immediate international impact.

The tradition of authoritarian leadership and high centralization in governing Russia that has been evolving over a dozen centuries does not show signs of weakening. In addition to the continuing concentration of political-economic and administrative power in Moscow under the Putin administration, there are also multiple indications of further centralization and subjugation of independent media by the government. Putin's second presidential term is likely to further this trend.

Objectively, the ruling political, business, and security elites who are governing the country, controlling resources, and enjoying numerous privileges, are not interested in losing their power and personal pursuits inherent with internationalization. Under the guise of patriotism and nationalism, these elites seek to reinforce their powers and strategic positions in the administrative establishment. Reservations toward internationalization are particularly strong in Russian provinces, where the level of general and professional education, political and cultural awareness, competitiveness, and problem solving capabilities related to an international involvement scenario are still low and lagging behind those in the capital cities. Internationalization is likely to bring additional complexities in administration in the forms of alternative sources of information, independent thinking and ideas, a need for decentralization, grass-roots participation, the sharing of power, transparency, accountability, increased legalization and liabilities, responsibilities, and many other challenges.

Apart from a common rationale for internationalization, the Russian ruling elites have no immediate urgency to effect change as long as their short-term interests do not suffer. High self-sufficiency in natural resources, a large domestic market allowing for relative efficiency without wide internationalization of the economy, a line-up of outside countries dependent on Russian oil, gas, and other raw materials (including many countries in the world's major centers of power), and other factors work against Russia's large-scale internationalization. In other words, the Russian administrative establishment will be more inclined to support limited internationalization in the short-term, with many protectionist restrictions shielding domestic industries, regions, and forms of economic cooperation from foreign involvement.

Given that Russia is a part of Eurasia, the Newly Industrialized Countries (Hong Kong, Singapore, South Korea, Taiwan, as well as Israel) and their accomplishments in economic acceleration and a process of governance is particularly interesting for Russia, because in these countries, the state (government) played the role of key architect in the development of their market economy (a "state controlled" type as noted in Figure 1). China also serves as another model for emulation.

What form of business cooperation within the international context would be the most beneficial for Russia that could add additional momentum in the development of the nation's administrative culture? Russia is not an equal international business player in the developed world and, as a result, a continuing emphasis on the export of raw materials and extracting industries, however profitable short-term, is not an effective answer to Russia's long-term development needs. A greater focus on human and intellectual resources should become a high priority. Specifically, these priorities should include investment in professional education and personnel training and development through the financing of curriculum development projects based on advanced experience in various nations; bringing more international joint ventures and other forms of business cooperation to Russia to promote a better understanding of effective management and governance by the Russian cadre; inclusion of the best representatives of overseas business in boards of directors of Russian companies (specifically in medium size companies in the Russian provinces); creation and development of the venture funds needed to support innovative entrepreneurial high potential enterprises by Russian entrepreneurs; and joint research/consulting projects geared toward norms of business cooperation and corporate interrelations.

NOTES

1 Dmitry Serbinenko, a student at the People Friendship University in Moscow, Russia, and a 2002-2003 Russian Presidential fellow at Loyola Marymount University in the United States, assisted in data collection for this chapter.

2 While lack of good roads in governing the nation has been partially offset by the latest information technologies, Russia's inadequate infrastructure, in combination with vastness, continue to be a hindrance to political-economic developments and administrative culture. This is because of the limited local access to conventional

3   Having legally abolished the serfdom in 1861, Russia, in essence, has continued to be a predominantly peasant country well into the late 1920s and early 1930s, when Joseph Stalin unleashed a wide-scale industrialization campaign. Under this campaign, millions of peasants were moved from villages to cities. Millions of the remaining peasants continued to be communist serfs because of the harsh restrictions on migration and the living permit system.

4   For more detail, please refer to Library of Congress Country Studies (2003).

5   "Dictatorship of the proletariat" was a fundamental principle of the communist doctrine that was institutionalized in the Communist Party ideology, Charter, and Program. Additionally, party membership was a mandatory requirement in the personnel selection for top administrative positions in the party and government bodies, and for arrangements for family medical care and other benefits.

6   According to the preliminary results of the first Russian National Census, since 1989 more than half of Russia's 155,290 villages are abandoned or populated by 50 or fewer stragglers. In the summer of 2003, the Russian government announced relocation of some 600,000 people from remote parts of Siberia and the Arctic, the biggest population relocation since the Stalin era. Their further life and work in these areas under the market economy cannot be sustained any longer without significant government subsidies (Paton 2003; Conant 2003).

7   The official name of the largest of the fifteen union republics of the Soviet Union. Inhabited predominantly by Russians, the RSFSR comprised approximately 75 percent of the area of the Soviet Union, about 62 percent of its population, and more than 60 percent of its economic output (Library of Congress Country Studies 2003).

8   During 2001-2003, the Elite Studies Department at Russia's Sociology Institute has conducted a survey entitled *Putin's Elite* based on 3,500 biographies of the Cabinet members, the Parliament, regional government elite, and business leaders. The survey points to a new "militocracy" trend in the Russian ruling establishment. Across all groups of Russian elites under the study, people with military backgrounds comprise 15 to 70 percent of the total. More than 35 percent of all deputy ministers appointed by V. Putin since 2000 come from the military-security sector. More than a quarter of Russia's highest-ranking officials today are graduates of military academies. Representation of the military among regional

governors over the last two years has doubled. The militocracy has supplanted the Yeltsin-era elite of civilian officials with advanced and professional degrees. Today, the number of state leaders holding such degrees has declined from 50 percent to 20 percent (Karatnycky 2003; Kryshtanovskaya 2003).

9 For more detail, please refer to the RUIE web site: www.rsppr.ru

10 For a full Russian text of these documents please refer to the following web sites: http://www.goscomzem.ru/leg_069.htm; fedcom@online.ru; www.rid.ru.

11 Out of the overall amount of American users, 54 million households dial into the Internet, 11 million use cable modems, and 5.4 million have DSL connections (Taylor 2003).

12 Although this requirement is unrealistic for Russia given the scope and depth of the problem (including limited resources and a lack of momentum to achieve this task overnight), this initiative points in the right direction.

13 There were 35.5 million main telephone lines and 17.65 cellular phone users in Russia vs. 181.6 million and 158.7 million respectively in the United States (CIA 2003).

14 There is a bitter irony in that in 2003, YUKOS, one of the biggest Russian oil companies, was declared by *Fortune* magazine to be one of the world's most efficient and transparent companies in the world (Rosbalt 2003). YUKOS is currently under the widely publicized investigation on alleged multiple criminal charges that are believed to be politically motivated. Many Russian observers attribute them to the independent business strategy and public relations course by YUKOS and its chairman, Mikhail Khodorkovsky. Despite the multibillion financial losses inflicted to YUKOS, the Russian stock market, and the overall investment climate within just a few days of the investigation, powerful government interests proceeded with the investigation, with the political goal of demonstrating their power.

As an example of Russian administrative resolutions, the following scenario may follow: Vladimir Putin can scold law enforcement agencies for using clumsy methods when investigating complex financial cases, and the representatives of big business for occasionally "abusing," in the opinion of the authorities, their powerful economic resources when lobbying their political interests. Perhaps some other oligarchs will also be affected. In order to maintain balance, a "tactical" political jab might be made at, for example, Anatoly Chubais, head of RAO Unified Energy Systems of Russia, who has become used to such "attacks." No doubt, this move will be popular with the people; it will show that all are equal before the law in Russia, including the "new St. Petersburgers" (Putin's team) and their opponents (Mite 2003; Johnson 2003)

15 For example, in April 2002, Russia adopted its own non-binding Corporate Management Code. The Code, modeled after the Corporate Governance Principles by the Organization for Economic Cooperation and Development (OECD), has been developed by Coudert Brothers, a reputable Western law firm, with the financing provided by the Japanese government via the European Bank for Reconstruction and Development.

REFERENCES

Akhiezer, A. 2002. "Spetsifika rossiiskoi politicheskoi kultury i predmeta politologii" (Specifics of the Russian Political Culture and a Subject of Political Science). (Istoriko-kulturnoe issledovanie). *Pro et Contra. Politicheskaya kultura.* Biblioteka publikatsii Moskovskogo Tsentra Karnegi. Accessed April 24, 2003 (http://pubs.carnegie.ru/p&c/Vol7-2002/3/pdf/v7n3-03.pdf).

Azrael, J. and Peterson D. 2002. "Russia and the Information Revolution." *RAND Center for Russia and Eurasia.* Santa Monica, CA: RAND. Accessed June 20, 2003 (http://www. rand.org/pblications/IP/IP229/IP229.pdf).

Brokgauz, F. A. and I. A. Efron. 2002. "Entsiklopedicheskii slovar." *Sovremennaya versia.* Moscow: Russia.

Vartanova, E. 2002. *"Media v postsovetskoi Rossii: ikh struktura i vliyanie"* (Media in the Post-Soviet Russia: Its Structure and Impact). *Pro et Contra. tom 5. No.4. Osen'* 2000. p.61-81. Accessed December 4, 2002 (http://pubs. carnegie.ru/p&c/Vol5-2000/4/v5n4-03.pdf).

CIA. 2002. *The World Factbook.* Accessed July 14, 2003 (http://www.cia.gov/cia/publications/factbook/geos/rs.html).

Conant, E. 2003. "Ghosts of the Heartland." *Newsweek,* Atlantic Edition. Accessed July 14, 2003 (http://www.cdi.org/russia/johnson/7246-17.cfm).

Economic Intelligence Unit. 2003. "The 2003 E-readiness Ranking." *The Economist.* Accessed July 19, 2003 (http://graphics.eiu.com/files/ad_pdfs/eReady_2003.pdf).

Gratchev, M., N. Rogovsky, and B. Rakitski. 2001. "Leadership and Culture in Russia: The Case of Transitional Economy." Accessed January 2003 (http://www.haskayne.ucalgary.ca/GLOBE/Public/publications_2001.html).

Grazhdansky Kodeks Rossiiskoi Federatsii (Civil Code of the Russian Federation). 2002. Moscow, Russia, Yuridicheskaya Literatura.

Hofstede, G. 1997. *Cultures In Organizations: Software of the Mind.* London: McGraw Hill.

Javidan, M. and R. House 2001. "Cultural Acumen For the Global manager: Lessons From Project Globe." *Organizational Dynamics* 29(4):289.

Johnson, David, ed. 2003. "YUKOS Case to Be Settled" *Johnson's Russian List* 7259(2). Accessed July 21, 2003 (http://www.cdi.org/russia/johnson/7259-2.cfm).

Karatnycky A. 2003. "Jobs For Boys: Putin's New Militocracy." *The Wall Street Journal*, June 13. Accessed June 20, 2003 (http://www.cdi.org/russia/johnson/7221-12.cfm).

Klyuchevsky, V. 1911-31. *The Course of Russian History*. 5 vols. Translated by C. J. Hogarth. New York: Dutton.

Korchagina, V. 2002. "Study: Bribery a $36 b Business." *The Moscow Times*, May 22.

Kryshtanovskaya O. 2003. "Putin's People. Does our Future Include a Militarized Russia and Authoritarian Rule?" *Vedomosti,* June 30. Accessed June 30, 2003 (http://www.cdi.org/russia/johnson/7245-1.cfm).

Lawrence, P. and C. Vlachoutsicos. 1990. *Behind the Factory Walls. Decision Making in Soviet and U.S. Enterprises*. Boston, MA: Harvard Business School Press.

Lewis, R. 1999. *When Cultures Collide. Managing Successfully Across Cultures*. London: Nicholas Breadley Publishing.

Library of Congress Country Studies. 2003. *Russia*. Accessed July 17, 2003 (http://lcweb2.loc.gov/frd/cs/rutoc.html).

McFaul, M. 2003. "The Real Vladimir Putin." *The Wall Street Journal,* July 9. Accessed July 9, 2003 (http://www.cdi.org/russia/johnson/7247-9.cfm).

Media Sustainability Index (MSI). 2002. Russia. *International Research and Exchange Board* (IREX). Accessed June 6, 2003 (http://www.irex.org/msi/2002/country/Russia.pdf).

Mite, V. 2003. "Russia: Critics Call Kremlin's Yukos Investigation Politically Motivated." CDI Russia Weekly 265(1). Available at (http://www.cdi.org/russia/265-1.cfm).

NAG Consulting-Intratrade. 2004. Accessed August 19, 2004 (http://www.russia export.net).

Nationmaster. Available at (http://www.nationmaster.com/graph-T/med_per_com_cap).

Normativnyie i rasporyaditelnye dokumenty (Government Documents). 2003 http://www.goscomzem.ru/legal.htm (accessed July 10, 2003).

Oliker, O. and T. Charlick-Paley. 2002. "Assessing Russia's Decline: Trends and Implications for the United States and the U.S. Air Force." RAND.

Perfilev Y. 2002. "Territorial Organization of the Russian Internet-Space." *In The Internet and Russian Society.* Moscow: Moscow Carnegie Center. Accessed July 20, 2003 (http://www.cdi.org/russia/johnson/7069-8.cfm).

Russkaia gosudarstvennost: tabel o rangakh (The Russian Statehood: The Table of Ranks). Accessed June 17, 2003 (http://voskres.ru/gosudarstvo/army/ range-table.htm).

Rossiiskaya knizhnaya palata. 1999. *Pechat' Rossiiskoi Federatsii v 1998 godu* (The Russian Book Clearing House. Print in the Russian Federation in 1998). Moscow, Russia.

Rosbalt. 2003. "Voted World's Most Efficient Company by Fortune Magazine." *Fortune*, July 17. Accessed July 17, 2003 (http://www.cdi.org/russia/johnson/7254-14.cfm).

Shikhirev, P. 2000. *Vvedenie v rossiskuyu delovuyu kulturu* (Introduction to the Russian Business Culture). Moscow, Russia: Novosti.

Smelser, Neil J. and Paul B. Baltes. 2001. *International Encyclopedia of the Social and Behavioral Sciences*. New York: Elsevier.

Taylor, C. 2003. "Budget Broadband" *Time,* July 28.

The World Bank Group. 2003. *World Development Report 2003*. Accessed August 19, 2004 (http://econ.worldbank.org/wdr/).

Transparency International. 2002. *Corruption Perceptions Index 2002*. Accessed February 12, 2003 (http://www.transparency.org/pressreleases_archive/2002/2002.08.28.cpi.en.html).

United States Agency for International Development. 2003. *Media Sustainability Index, 2003*. Washington D.C.: IREX Media. Available at (http://www.irex.org/msi/2003/MSI03-Russia.pdf).

U.S. Department of Commerce. 2002. "Commercial Overview of Russia." *BISNIS* Accessed August 19, 2004 (http://www.bisnis.doc.gov/bisnis/bisnis.cfm).

U.S. Department of Commerce. 2002. "Russia. Country Commercial Guide." Accessed May 12, 2003 (http://www.usatrade.gov/Website/CCG.nsf/ CCGurl/CCG-RUSSIA2002-CH-10).

U.S. Department of State. 2002. "Background Note. Russia." *Bureau of European and Eurasian Affairs.*

Chapter 6

ADMINISTRATIVE CULTURE IN THE MIDDLE EAST: THE CASE OF THE ARAB WORLD

Joseph G. Jabbra and Nancy W. Jabbra

I. Introduction

The growth of government activities in the Arab world after independence was accompanied by an increase in the size and importance of bureaucracy. With full control over the public purse, the Arab state became responsible for charting social and economic development policies and for the bureaucracy empowered to implement them. The challenge of Arab bureaucracies to transform their societies rapidly from traditional to modern entities has contributed to their size and vested them with an intense concentration of powers. In turn, their size and their acquired powers have increased the opportunity for corruption, unethical conduct, and the misuse of public office for personal profit. Moreover, within the context of this new administrative culture, attempts at reforming the bureaucracy in the Arab world have not been successful.

In his book, *Politics Without Process: Administering Development in the Arab World,* Jamil E. Jreisat (1997:20-21) provided many reasons for the failure of administrative reforms with a particular focus on the inadequate administration of development, the problems of poor leadership, and the insufficient institutional capacity. Moreover, on the basis of a survey of recent administrative reform programs in several Arab states, Jreisat (1997:89) added that the politicization of public administration has compounded democratic corruption among public servants who lack the requisite management skills to implement and monitor development efforts. The administrative reforms that were implemented in the Arab world lacked concrete means of carrying out the programs and measuring the results. Instead, programs have been limited to applying "band-aid approach to a heavily bleeding patient" (Jreisat 1997:89). Furthermore, there are no appropriate safeguards and proper checks and balances to protect the Arab public from bureaucratic abuses. Thus, in carrying out their official responsibilities, Arab public servants are not accountable for their actions and behavior.

II. The Deceiving Administrative Culture of Formal Control Mechanisms

The poor performance of bureaucracy in the Arab world and the inability of Arab governments to reform bureaucracy seem puzzling. A cursory examination of Arab bureaucracy would point to the presence in the Arab World of a special administrative culture that is reflected in the significant number of formal control mechanisms designed to insure accountability and integrity.

The first formal control mechanism is internal and governed by the pyramidal structure of the bureaucracy whereby each administrative layer is accountable to the next higher one. Moreover, the behavior of public servants, their rights, responsibilities, and positions are regulated by laws enacted by either a legislative branch and promulgated by presidential decrees, or enacted by royal decrees upon the recommendation of the Council of Ministers, which, in the absence of a legislative assembly exercises both legislative and executive powers (Al-Farsi 1978:94-95).

The second kind of control mechanism is external and comprises political, administrative, juridical, and non-official "watchdogs" who presumably strive to make sure that the bureaucracy is accountable, efficient, and productive. In Lebanon for example, the political heads of the departments are the ministers, who are accountable for their departments to the cabinet; in turn, the cabinet is accountable to parliament collectively and individually, for the bureaucracy. Members of parliament are elected politicians, are required to monitor the bureaucracy, apply pressure on the cabinet, and explain any irregularities in the behavior of public servants. The pressure may be increased by bringing the matter to the public's attention. On a number of occasions, the pressure of parliament serves to bring about much needed administrative reforms.

Administrative watchdogs play a similar role. For example, the Civil Service Commission, created in 1959, is in charge of developing and maintaining a strong and capable civil service. Its responsibilities include recruitment, training, promotion, transfer, and retirement matters. In addition, it hears complaints from civil servants in relation to transfer requests and disciplinary matters involving penalty or dismissal (Grassmuck and Salibi 1964:4).

The Central Inspection Administration, created in 1961, sets and administers inspection policies aimed at improving procedures, reducing costs, and increasing efficiency. Its jurisdiction extends over all divisions of the administration, with the exception of the army and the judiciary (Kisirwani 1971:173).

The Council of State serves as a court of appeal and cassation for administrative cases assigned by a special law to other courts. In 1965, the General Disciplinary Council for Public Officials was established to deal with all administrative infractions except by members of the Civil Service Commission, the Central Inspection Administration, security forces, autonomous agencies, and municipalities (Salem 1973:59).

Finally, open hearings, interest groups, and organized citizens' participation and pressure attempt to keep public servants accountable and prevent them from using their public office for personal gain.

As in Lebanon, government departments and central agencies in Egypt are accountable to their ministers. In turn, the ministers are accountable individually to the cabinet and collectively to the national assembly for the actions and behavior of public employees working within their ministries. In reality, the cabinet is responsible to the President of Egypt, whose office wields enormous powers.

Cabinet committees and central agencies presumably monitor the accountability of public employees. Ministerial committees were established by the Council of Ministers to coordinate and account for the execution of public policy in planning, legislation, organization and administration, economic affairs, human resources, and local administration. Independent central and control agencies (e.g., Central Agency for Training, Central Agency for Organization and Administration, Central Auditing Agency, etc.) perform the same functions (Ayubi 1980:200).

Administrative vigilance is also provided by the Council of State, The Administrative Parquet Department (Al-Niyaba Al-Idariyyah), the Administrative Inspection Department (Al-Raqaba Al-Idariyyah), the Ministry of State Department, and the Secretariat of the President.

The Council of State was established in 1946 and is the supreme administrative court. Patterned after the French Council of State, it consists of a judicial section and a consultative section on administrative regulations and their interpretation. Created in 1954, the Administrative Parquet Department overseas procedures of control and investigation of administrative violations and hears complaints and calls for disciplinary action against public officials. The Administrative Inspection Department inspects the work of public officials and ensures the proper application of laws and the correction of any errors in administrative, technical, or financial procedures. Finally, the General Secretariat of the Presidency serves as a channel of communication and the liaison between the President's Office and the various ministries and is indirectly involved in administrative control activities (Ayubi 1980:201).

In Saudi Arabia, the King exercises his supervision and control of the Saudi bureaucracy through the Council of Ministers and his Private Office. The Council of Ministers, established in 1953, is the most powerful, central, and dynamic institution in the Kingdom of Saudi Arabia. It is responsible to the King for all its activities and those of the bureaucracy, which serves as its agent. Through their respective ministers, departments are accountable for the action and behavior of their employees to the Council of Ministers and to the King. Central and independent agencies are accountable directly to the King. Although their heads possess ministerial powers, they do not normally participate in the deliberations of the Council of Ministers (Al-Awaji 1971:126-131).

The following will serve as illustrations:

The Civil Service Board, established by a royal decree in 1977, attends to civil service matters (e.g., personnel, salary, position classification, etc.) in all ministries, public agencies, and corporations, and strives to ensure accountability and high quality performance among public employees. To this end, it continually makes policy recommendations to the Council of Ministers (Al-Mazrua 1980:290).

The General Bureau of Civil Service reports to the Civil Service Board and has a mandate to enhance the accountability and efficiency of Saudi public servants; it supervises closely the execution of civil service laws, regulations and resolutions, and carries out research in the area of position classification, compensation, allowance, and awards; it makes recommendations to the Civil Service Board, which is required to submit to the King an annual report on the state of the Saudi civil service (Tawati 1976:120-123; Al-Mazrua 1980:291-292).

The Institute Of Public Administration was created by a royal decree in 1971 to provide training for Saudi public servants and enhance accountability among them. Article II of its statute states clearly that the objective of the Institute of Public Administration is: "To promote the efficiency of civil servants and to qualify them theoretically and practically to be able to assume their responsibilities in a way that will promote the level of administration and foster the development of the national economy."

The High Committee for Administrative Reform was established as a continuing body by the Council of Ministers in 1963 (resolution 520) to spearhead the administrative reform, reorganize existing government agencies, create new departments, and develop new and effective work systems and methods for the purpose of improving efficiency and accountability among Saudi public servants. In carrying out its responsibilities, the High Committee is helped by the Staff Committee for administrative reform and by a Secretariat (Al-Mazrua 1980:327-333).

The Central Department for Organization and Management was established by a royal decree in 1966, with a mandate to foster efficiency and effectiveness in the Saudi public service, make Saudi public servants accountable for their actions and behavior, monitor the execution of reform recommendations adopted by the High Committee for Administrative Reform, and initiate needed administrative development (Al-Mazrua 1980:333-338).

Finally, the Grievance Board, created in 1954, represents an extension of the traditional practice of direct accessibility to the King by any citizen who has a grievance against the bureaucracy (Al-Ghamdi 1982:142-144).

Variations of the above formal administrative structures can be found throughout the Arab World as well as in non-Arab Middle Eastern countries (e.g., Iran, Israel, Turkey) (Farazmand 1989; Farsoun and Mashaekhi 1992; Perez and Dorn 1997). In fact, in a number of cases, these structures are similar to and even patterned after those of bureaucracies in Western democracies. If this is the case, why have public bureaucracies been, on the whole, inefficient and ineffective in the Arab World and why have Arab leaders failed to reform them? The answer to these questions can be found in a more careful and detailed analysis of Arab public bureaucracies, which would show the superficial and deceiving character of the administrative culture of formal control mechanisms.

III. The Real Administrative Culture in the Arab World

The concern of Arab governments, since Word War II, to develop and modernize their countries has led them to adopt Western management philosophies and administrative structures. This exercise proved unsuccessful because Western innovations were implanted in an environment that continues to be influenced by a pervasive and powerful traditional administrative culture, a culture that draws its strength from two main sources: (1) administrative and structural, and (2) social and behavioral.

The Administrative and Structural Source

Six traditional cultural streams nurture this source. They are: overcentralization, outmoded systems, administrative expansion, overstaffing, rigidity and complexity of rules, and salary structure.

Overcentralization

Overcentralization of administrative structure and overconcentration of authority characterize bureaucracies in the Arab World. First, authoritarian superiors and top managers are usually accompanied by passive subordinates. Second, lengthy lines of command result in both weak control and distortion of orders. Third, subordinates rely excessively on their superiors and send them minor administrative problems for resolution. Consequently, senior public servants become occupied by administrative minutiae instead of spending their time on more important matters.

Fourth, subordinates often do not have enough to do and their talents are not fully utilized. Fifth, influence peddling and corruption tend to thrive. Finally, citizens waste time and money by having to travel often to the capital to crowded offices in order to finalize their transactions. The Egyptian administrative system, for example, is overcentralized and authority is concentrated in the hands of top bureaucrats. In fact, centralization in government organizations became the preferred Egyptian solution for any problem of coordination (Ayubi 1977:18).

The rapid structural changes that took place in Egypt between 1952 and 1970 gave rise to a complex and overcentralized organizational structure, which was cumbersome and unwieldy (Ayubi 1980:234-235). Moreover, all the major steps taken by the Egyptian central government to improve local governments failed to decentralize the system and to delegate more authority to local government officials. Even in public enterprises, there is a general tendency toward centralization (Abdo-Khalil 1983:67). Egyptian officials are always trying to concentrate more power in their own hands. In an editorial in 1982, the *Egyptian Gazette* (a government journal which publishes all statutes and decrees) stated that "with such material and moral accoutrements adorning the post of manager, it is only natural that officials should be vying with one another to attain this post through all means available, not excluding hypocrisy, bribery, backbiting, double-dealing and deception."

Palmer, Yassin, and Leila (1985:323-337) provided an empirical assessment of the excessive centralization in the Egyptian bureaucracy. Their conclusions supported Ayubi's (1980) thesis that the centralization of authority in the Egyptian bureaucracy was a major problem. They also concluded that the sources of centralization in the Egyptian bureaucracy were rooted both in the pragmatic realities of bureaucratic life and in the broader dimension of Egyptian culture. Similar illustrations exist in the rest of the Arab World (Munla nd:11; Bashir 1965:47; Al-Bilani 1966:263; Grassmuck and Salibi 1964:5; Nakib 1972:132; Al-Awaji 1971:206, 209; Saudi Ministry of Planning 1975:571; Chackerian and Shadukhi 1983:319-322).

Outmoded Systems

Despite the substantial amounts of money Arab countries spend on modernizing their bureaucracies, most of them still have dated administrative structures, outmoded systems and procedures, and old technical and physical facilities. All of these foster an administrative culture characterized by an unsystematic flow of information, poor coordination, lack of comprehensive planning, difficulty with control and supervision, red-tape, and inefficiency.

In the Lebanese bureaucracy, for example, outmoded technical systems and procedures are still used in financial information and program training. Typewriters, calculators, and computers are not sufficiently available and inadequate physical and storage facilities are standard. Government buildings lack central heating and adequate lighting and furnishing. The offices of many directorates are dispersed throughout the capital city of Beirut, contributing to low morale among public servants and making control, supervision, and accountability difficult to enforce (Salem 1973:59). A similar situation prevails in the Egyptian bureaucracy (Ayubi 1982:292).

In contrast to Lebanon and Egypt, Saudi Arabia has had enough oil revenues to build modern physical facilities and provide state-of-the-art equipment. However, experts continue to complain about the absence of science, technology, management by objectives, scientific management, and organizational development (Al-Khaldi 1983:44-45).

Moreover, working conditions, filing systems, office layouts, maintenance services, and typing and copying facilities are still inadequate. Lengthy, cumbersome, and outdated procedures continue to hamper the normal flow of work and do not encourage efficiency and accountability (Al-Hegelan 1984:12). Even in recruitment, the methods used to advertise positions are inadequate and ineffective. Often, vacancies are not advertised at all, and even when they are, they do not specify the qualifications or duties and responsibilities. The same applies to entrance examinations and assessment for transfers and promotions (Binsaleh 1982:130).

Expansion

The emergence of the Arab state in the post World War II era as the chief employer and provider caused a rapid, unexpected, and unplanned expansion of the bureaucracy, which hampered the development of a strong sense of accountability among public servants. This situation made proper control, coordination, and supervision extremely difficult to achieve; it also caused overstaffing and underemployment, lack of clearly defined lines of responsibility, and, in some cases, lack of qualified personnel.

For example, the 1950s was a turning point in the history of Saudi Arabia. With oil revenues increasing, the bureaucracy began to expand rapidly to provide Saudi citizens with the services they needed. The new and rapid expansion of the bureaucracy did not provide an environment conducive to the internalization and development of accountability among the new Saudi public servants. The reasons were simple: control, coordination, and planning were inadequate, particularly at the implementation level, despite the existence of agencies for these functions; procedures for responding to the pressing needs of the population were outdated;

and the functions, positions, and responsibilities for public servants were not clearly defined in organizational manuals (Al-Sadhan 1980:80) Hence, a total state of confusion would at times cripple public agencies and departments, bringing administrative transactions to a standstill (Warner 1964:6; Al-Awaji 1971:18). Similar problems are found in other Arab countries (Grassmuck and Salibi 1964:18; Ayubi 1982:326).

Overstaffing

Overlapping and lack of qualified personnel in key government areas do not promote a culture of accountability among Arab public servants. In Lebanon, for example, the promotion policy contributed significantly to overstaffing. Promotions were made annually between ranks regardless of whether there were vacancies for those promoted (Nakib 1972:105). Overstaffing of the Egyptian bureaucracy reaches extreme dimensions at most levels and estimates of excess workforce are about 15 percent of all employees (Al-Ahram Al-Iqtisadi 1979). Overstaffing results from the steady pressure on the government to provide employment and from the bargaining attitude of top officials, who exaggerate their personnel needs in order to increase prestige and opportunity for promotion. According to Ayubi (1980:247), sectoral and geographic overstaffing contributes to bureaucratic inflation, idleness, cynicism, and disguised unemployment in the Egyptian bureaucracy and thus creates a hostile cultural environment for accountability among public servants.

The lack of qualified personnel is a more serious problem in Saudi Arabia (Tawati 1976:6; Alnimir 1981:26; Al-Ghamdi 1982:66). As the Saudi public service expanded rapidly in response to rising oil revenues and the desire of the royal family to provide Saudi citizens with new services, the unavailability of qualified Saudi personnel proved to be a major handicap in building an accountable and responsible bureaucracy (Ford Foundation 1963:3; Al-Awaji 1971:219; Sadik 1965: 196).

The government of Saudi Arabia broached this problem in three ways. First, it began hiring non-Saudis, largely from the Arab countries. Second, it established the Institute of Public Administration in the early 1960s to train public employees. Finally, and most seriously, it tried to compensate for the lack of qualified personnel by overstaffing government offices with people who did not have the proper training to serve the public responsibly. The problem was further compounded by mismatching between the qualifications of public employees and requirements of their positions (for more details on the above, see Al-Awaji 1971:221-222; Tawati 1976:4; Binsaleh 1982:24; Al-Khaldi 1983:193).

Rigidity and Complexity of Rules

Public servants subject to rigid and complex rules seldom take initiatives, nor can they be accountable for their actions and behavior. In Arab bureaucracies, rigidity stems from overcentralization of authority and a legalistic approach to administrative decision making and procedures, which do not allow much room for innovation. In fact, rigidity leads to a tendency among Arab public servants to avoid responsibility, especially when they are faced with new problems that are not foreseen and regulated by law. Moreover, laws and regulations which govern administrative behavior are often rigid and confusing (Lebanon Civil Service Commission 1969a; Ayubi 1977:17; Attrabi 1982; Murad 1983:31).

The Saudi bureaucracy, for example, suffers from rigidity and complex rules and regulations. Thus, before a matter can be sent to a top bureaucrat for his signature and directive, it is subjected to a lengthy and time consuming procedure involving the approval of several officials within the agency, each of whom may go through a similar exercise (Al-Ghamdi 1982:286; Al-Hegelan 1984:12; Alnimir and Palmer 1982).

Salary Structure

Salary structure is a sensitive issue in the administrative culture of Arab public servants. It has a direct effect on an employee's efficiency, accountability, and moral conduct. It also influences the government's ability to recruit and maintain qualified personnel. For example, the low salary structure for public employees in Lebanon, especially after the conclusion of the 1975 civil war, is leading to two serious results. First, competent people receive more attractive salary offers from the private sector and stay away from or leave the Lebanese public service. Second, those who join or stay in it are afflicted with low morale and forced to look for other income to compensate for their low salary (Lebanon Civil Service Commission 1969b:2; An-Nahar 1969:3). Moreover, the automatic salary increases, which are granted indiscriminately and not on merit, are another reason for the unwillingness of the employee to work harder or to show more innovation and accountability in carrying out his/her responsibilities (Nakib 1972:107).

The salary structure for Egyptian bureaucrats is also low, and most Egyptian public servants have poor salaries (CAOA 1969:15). The low salary structure and the relative deprivation of Egyptian bureaucrats produce in many higher officials a perpetual obsession with obtaining higher salaries (Al-Salami 1968). This obsession causes public employees to join the private sector for better salaries or to practice corruption to compensate for their low remunerations (*Rose Al-Yousef* 1966).

Despite improvements in the compensation scale for Saudi public servants, the problem of inadequate salaries continues to contribute greatly to the problems of turnover and low standards of morality and personal integrity (Tawati 1976:156-171). Rising expectations, rapid social transformations, as well as economic and inflationary pressures continue to tempt government employees to seek different sources of income by going into business or joining corporations and doubling their salaries. As we will see in the next section, low salaries and rising expectations may lead to an administrative culture marked by laxity in moral standards and personal integrity. They may also lead to corruption, graft, and profiteering (Tawati 1976:171; Abussuud 1979:163-166). In both cases, high standards of performance and accountability among Arab public servants suffer a great deal.

The Sociocultural and Behavioral Source

Traditional customs, attitudes, and behavior that are deeply imbedded in Arab public servants include nepotism and favoritism, patron-client relationships, corruption, avoidance of responsibility, and lack of adequate training.

Nepotism and Favoritism

The family continues to rival the state as the focal point of loyalty and security in Arab countries. In fact, accountability to one's family often takes precedence over accountability to the state and thus leads to a culture and practice of nepotism. Moreover, loyalty to the family is paralleled by a strong devotion to one's village and friends, thus leading to a culture of favoritism. Neither is conducive to a culture of accountability among Arab public servants. For example, family, friendship, and geographical ties are strong in Lebanon and loyalty to them is the hallmark of the Lebanese bureaucracy (Nakib 1972:101). Thus, despite the professionalization of the Lebanese civil service, it is not only permissible "socially," but also mandatory for a *zaim* (political leader) to appoint family members and friends to prestigious posts in the Lebanese bureaucracy. Consequently, the qualified child of an ordinary Lebanese citizen experiences difficulty in finding a post in the bureaucracy when competing with an equally or less qualified child of a prominent leader or the child of a friend of a prominent leader. Thus, nepotism is a major hindrance to the growth of a culture of accountability in the Lebanese bureaucracy. A public servant who owes his or her appointment to a family zaim or a friend is likely to delay, derail, or obstruct regular administrative procedures in order to repay the debt (Salem 1973:88-89).

Because of loyalty to family, Saudi public servants practice nepotism and are biased when assigning jobs and distributing benefits (Lipsky 1959:45). This is confirmed by Louis G. Korninghauer's observationt: "Since the entire social structure has been based on kinship, it is not surprising to find a certain amount of influence being exercised in favor of relatives. In this society it is taken for granted that an individual will use his position to benefit his relatives" (1963:1). The same conclusion can be drawn concerning an administrative culture of loyalty to one's friends, village, and region (Al-Awaji 1971:230-242).

The Patron-Client Relationship

A culture of unethical and irresponsible practices in the bureaucracy may result from a strong patron-client system. In Arab countries, as well as most developing societies, where identification with the national community and its laws is still weak, protection is sought outside the family through ties with powerful protectors or patrons (Jabbra and Jabbra 1983:133). This system of relationships has encouraged the development and institutionalization of an administrative culture of disrespect for accountability and regulations. Patron-client relationships, patronage, and influence go hand in hand with a culture of unethical conduct and a climate where personal profit and private loyalty take precedence over public duty. For example, before the 1975 civil war in Lebanon, the Lebanese public service was plagued by absenteeism, which was assiduously practiced by public servants who felt they could be away from their jobs during working hours because they enjoyed the protection of their patron. This behavior resulted in delays in the processing of administrative transactions and inconvenience to Lebanese citizens, who were forced to resort to bribery to buy what should have been their right (Jabbra and Jabbra 1983:133-134).

In order to remedy the problem of absenteeism, the Lebanese government introduced a new public measure, whereby timeclocks were installed in all public institutions; all civil servants were required to record their time of arrival and departure. However, protected by a system of patron-client relationships, public officials devised a trick to beat the system. They either alternated in punching each other's timecards or they asked their janitors to do it for them. The Lebanese press reported that on 19 March 1971, when the Minister of Information paid a surprise visit to the officials in his ministry, he found all unit chiefs absent, although their time cards showed them to be present (*An-Nahar*, September, 1969). Lebanon's Civil Service Commission has observed repeatedly that in the Lebanese civil service, a culture of private interest and loyalty to patrons take precedence over public duty (Lebanon Civil Service Commission 1966, 1967, 1968). In 1971, Kisirwani

(1971:128) reported that the results of his data confirmed that at least 40 percent of Lebanese public employees left their jobs daily for one hour or more to run private errands.

Another manifestation of an institutionalized culture of unethical practices, promoted in Lebanon by the patron-client system, was the processing of illegitimate transactions (Jabbra and Jabbra 1983:134), and the use of *wastah* or "pull" by a zaim to help his clients outside the appropriate administrative channels (Al-Haj 1972:8). The patron-client relationship and the wastah have always been prevalent in other Arab countries with similar negative effects on their administrative cultures (Ayubi 1977:29; Ayubi 1980:157, 466; Lipsky 1959:163; Al-Awaji 1971:233; Al-Khaldi 1983:41).

Corruption

Because it means the use of public office for personal gain, corruption is a serious cultural flaw in Arab societies and their bureaucracies. Corruption has many causes: weak commitment to the national interest and the common good; changing economic status of public servants, which makes their salary insufficient to satisfy their rising expectations and love of ostentation; the confusing network of government institutions and regulations; and an oversupply of graduates seeking a limited number of available positions, thus opening the door for bribes. All of these factors have given Arab public servants a golden opportunity to cultivate the art of bribery and corruption by systematically using their public offices to promote and protect their private interests.

For example, although it is difficult to collect hard facts about a culture of corruption in Saudi Arabia, one can identify several factors that account for its prevalence among Saudi public servants (Alnimir 1981:27). First, the Saudis public spirit and loyalty to the national interest is weak because of the commitment to parochial and particularistic values (Al-Awaji 1971:242-243). Saudi public servants are expected to use their public positions in order to maximize their personal interest. In the words of Lipski, "It is keeping with old practice in the area for officials at all levels to take advantage of their position to enrich themselves. Those who did not do so would be regarded as stupid and eccentric" (1959:178).

Second, Saudi public servants are excessively impressed by the achievements of their counterparts in Europe and North America. The rising expectations concerning consumer goods such as cars and appliances have caused many Saudi public servants to seek extra financial resources by methods that are not sanctioned by law. In his 1971 doctoral dissertation, Al-Awaji (1971:243) reported a discussion with a highly educated Saudi official who was then pursuing graduate studies in the United States. The official stated that the fixed monthly salary no longer satisfied the needs of Saudi public servants and corruption was too complex to be resolved by his own refraining from it.

Third, the over-centralization of authority in the hands of a few officials also facilitates corruption. The lack of an effective system of control and supervision and the lack of accountability nurture a culture of corruption. In the early 1960s, the government of Saudi Arabia, in an effort to control corruption, issued a form headed "Where Did You Get This?" on which government employees were to list all their properties so that the government could compare their income with their holdings. Unfortunately, no one bothered either to fill out the forms or to collect them, and the regulation was forgotten (Al-Tawail M. A. 1970:46). Similar illustrations can be found in other Arab countries (Kisirwani 1971:79-86; Jabbra and Jabbra 1983:134-135). It is important to note that this culture of corruption is not limited to Arab public servants. It can also be found in other non-Arab developing societies and constitutes a major challenge in their efforts to build more efficient administrative structures and develop a climate of honesty and integrity among public servants.

Laxity and Avoidance of Responsibilities

Laxity and avoidance of responsibility constitute two additional and serious flaws in the administrative culture of Arab bureaucracies. For example, in Lebanon, bureaucrats often come to work late, show little interest in their jobs, go home early, and take maximum advantage of loose regulations affecting leave with pay. In addition, laxity characterizes the upper levels of bureaucracy (Salem 1973:90). According to Al-Bilani, "although they (top bureaucrats) are expected to be leaders and pace-setters, their behavior does not differ from that of other subordinates, except that they sign more documents"(Al-Bilani 1966:258). In the Egyptian bureaucracy, there is a small minority of public servants who are committed to their jobs, however, the attitude of the majority toward hard work is very lax. According to Ayubi (1982:289), Egyptian public servants arrive late to their offices and by noon many of them are getting ready to go home. Moreover, a significant number may not go to work at all. Ayubi (1980:293) adds that only 15 percent of all Egyptian employees arrive at their offices punctually, and most of these are in the security and order departments. The cost of lost working hours is estimated at 4 million Egyptian pounds every month. When at work, Egyptian public servants appeared to do everything other than attend to their jobs. On average, the Egyptian public servant works an estimated 20 minutes to 2 hours every working day (Ayubi 1980:293). Obviously, there is no culture of integrity, probity, and accountability, and no one seems to care much.

While supervisors vie to concentrate more power in their own hands, subordinates in the Egyptian bureaucracy tend to shun responsibility and send all transactions to their superiors for clearance. According to Palmer, Yassin, and Leila (1985:331-333), this avoidance of responsibility contributes to the concentration of authority in the hands of supervisors, lack of innovation among subordinates, and refusal to take responsibility to settle a conflict or to take a risk. Subordinates seem to be satisfied with this situation and they do little to arouse the ire or suspicions of their supervisors. Moreover, more responsibility means more work. In the eyes of the subordinates, this is not justified because of their low salaries. Finally, the subordinates' tendency to avoid responsibility may also be the result of poor training and a related lack of the necessary skills.

Lower employees and subordinates in the Saudi bureaucracy also avoid responsibility and decision making; they are consumed with detailed and specific rules and regulations which do not allow for innovation (Al-Khaldi 1983:43; Alnimir and Palmer 1982:95-96). A survey conducted by Alnimir (1981:95) demonstrated that only 6.1 percent of the respondents were willing to take risks in making decisions in their jobs. Not only do Saudi public servants wish to avoid conflict and maintain job security, they feel that their superiors will use their authority over them unfairly. Despite an effort by the government to improve their lot, Alnimir (1981:36) concludes that public servants in general, lack enthusiasm and the desire to innovate. Their avoidance of responsibility is clearly illustrated by their unwillingness to move to areas where their skills are most needed, and their unwillingness to work, at least temporarily, in an uncomfortable rural environment; they are dissatisfied with the salary structure, they are often fatalistic; they prefer ascriptive values over achievement, and they suffer over the area of nonmaterial incentives, such as recognition, achievement, responsibility, advancement, working conditions, and interpersonal relations (Al-Awaji 1971:70-75; Abussuud 1979:160; Alnimir 1981:98; Al-Khaldi 1983:42; Alnimir and Palmer 1982:97-98). An administrative culture in which a tendency to avoid responsibility flourishes is most unfavorable to the development of efficiency, effectiveness, and accountability among public servants.

Lack of Adequate Training

Finally training, which was intended to improve the performance of public servants in Arab countries, has ironically proved to be an obstacle to a culture of efficiency, effectiveness, and accountability (Iskandar 1964:88-94; Bashir 1965:359-365; Nakib 1972:111; Ayubi 1977:54). For example, because of the vast revenues from oil, beginning in the early 1950s, government activity has increased steadily in

Saudi Arabia, giving Saudi public servants responsibilities for which they were not prepared. In response to complaints that civil servants were poorly skilled, in 1961 the Saudi government established the Institute of Public Administration to train Saudi public servants to carry out their responsibilities competently and accountably.

However, despite Saudi Arabia's attempt to promote an educational culture in the training programs, the quality of government employees has not improved significantly (Tawati 1976:208-211). According to Al-Hegelan (1984:13), the lack of adequate training is still a major problem for the Saudi bureaucracy; most Saudi public servants still consider training a waste of time or a way to avoid responsibility. Training excursions outside the country are not based on the needs of a civil servant or those of his administrative unit for a specific kind of training; rather they are granted as a form of compensation.

Several factors account for the poor quality of training among Saudi civil servants. First, early on in the 1950s and throughout the 1960s, methods of recruitment and selection were poor. Consequently, many improperly trained Saudis joined the bureaucracy. Second, government educational programs have been mainly concerned with the number of schools and not with the quality of education. Third, because of the high salaries offered by the private sector, the government faces serious difficulties in recruiting qualified technical personnel. Fourth, despite the establishment of the institute of public administration, there is still a shortage of educational and training institutions available to government officials at all levels. Finally, government managers discourage training and development of their employees, not only because such training usually requires an employee's absence from an already understaffed unit, but because of possible future competition for their own positions.

Whatever the reasons, it should be clear that the prevalent administrative culture of poorly trained public employees will not help public servants in the Arab World carry out their responsibilities efficiently and accountably.

IV. Conclusion

The prevalence of this informal administrative culture (El-Fathali and Chackerian 1983:193-209) imposes a heavy financial burden on Arab countries and hinders their economic, social, and political development. Replacing it with a more positive administrative culture will depend upon the understanding of Arab governments and Arab leaders that the currently prevalent administrative culture is embedded in the socioeconomic, political, and behavioral settings of Arab societies. In other words, Arab bureaucracies are part of Arab societies. It would be difficult to reform the former without changing the latter. Therefore, an administrative culture that is truly conducive to efficient, effective, and accountable public service in Arab societies will only be attained when the current administrative culture is modified. And, because the latter is rooted in the general Arab social settings within which bureaucracies have to operate, reform measures must be directed at a new form of socialization to be implemented both within Arab bureaucracies and among the Arab public at large. Reforms must establish and enforce a code of conduct for public servants (for more detail see Jabbra 1976, 1989; Jabbra and Jabbra 1983, 1997).

The socialization approach recommended by Jabbra and Jabbra may be complemented and reinforced by Ayubi's (1990:42-48) contingency approach. Ayubi counsels Arab governments and scholars of public administration to begin by carefully studying the successes and failures of Arab bureaucracies, to compare their experiments to those of other developing societies, and to dwell on and celebrate successes; for successes are contagious and inspiring while failure and disappointment is discouraging. According to Paul (1982:4-5), "the insights and understanding to be gained from high performers will be far more valuable than the incremental gains to be derived from further investigations of low performers about which we already know a great deal."

We are confident that the coordinated implementation of both approaches will provide Arab governments with a better opportunity to reform their bureaucracies and modify and gradually replace their current administrative culture with a more effective one that would combine the best from the traditional and modern, the old and the new.

REFERENCES

Abdo-Khalil, Zeinab M. 1983. "Public Sector Administration in Egypt." Ph.D. Dissertation, Claremont Graduate School, Claremont, CA.

Abussuud, Alawi N. 1979. "Administrative Development and Planning in Saudi Arabia: The Process of Differentiation and Specialization." Ph.D. Dissertation, University of Maryland.

Al-Ahram (Egyptian daily newspaper). 1979. *Al-Ahram Al-Iqtisadi* (economic supplement), 10 September.

Al-Awaji, Ibrahim Mohammad. 1971. "Bureaucracy and Society in Saudi Arabia." Ph.D. Dissertation, University of Virginia.

Al-Bilani, Bashir. 1966. "Mustakbal Al-Idarah Al-Lubnaniyyah Wa Al-Inma" (The Future of the Lebanese Administration and Development.) In *Al-Dawala Wa Al-Inma (State and Development),* edited by Nadwat Al-Dirassat Al-Inmaiyyah. Beirut: Dar-Al-Ilm Lil-Malayeen.

Al-Farsi, Fouad. 1978. *Saudi Arabia: A Case Study in Development.* London: Stacey International.

Al-Ghamdi, Abdullah A. 1982. "Action Research and the Dynamics of Organizational Environment in the Kingdom of Saudi Arabia." Ph.D. Dissertation, University of Southern California.

Al-Haj, Louis. 1972. "Min A´rad Al-Da´" (From the Symptoms of the Disease). *An-Nahar,* 17 March.

Al-Hegelan, Abdul-Rahman. 1984. "Innovation in the Saudi Arabian Bureaucracy: Survey Analysis of Senior Bureaucrats." Ph.D. Dissertation, Florida State University.

Al-Khaldi, Abdullah M. 1983. "Job Content and Content Factors Related to Satisfaction in Three Occupational Levels of the Public Sector in Saudi Arabia." Ph.D. Dissertation, Florida State University.

Al-Mazrua, Suliman A. 1980. "Public Administration Trends and Prospects in the Context of Development in Saudi Arabia." Ph.D. Dissertation, Claremont Graduate School, Claremont, CA.

An-Nahar (Lebanese daily newspaper) 1969. *Lebanon, the Civil Service Commission: A Study of An-Nahar.*

Alnimir, Saud M. 1981. "Present and Future Bureaucrats in Saudi Arabia: A Survey Research." Ph.D. Dissertation, Florida State University.

Alnimir, Saud, and M. Palmer. 1982. "Bureaucracy and Development in Saudi Arabia: Behavioral Analysis." *Public Administration and Development* 2(1).

Rose al-Yousef 1966, No. 1971, 21 March.

Al-Sadhan, Abdulrahman M. 1980. "The Modernization of the Saudi Bureaucracy." In *King Faisal and the Modernization of Saudi Arabia*, edited by Wellard E. Beling. Boulder, Colorado: Westview Press.

Al-Salami, Ali. 1968. In *Al-Ahram Al-Iqtisadi,* no. 308, 15 June.

Al-Tawail, M.A. 1970. "The Procedure and Instruments of Administrative Development in Saudi Arabia." M.A. Thesis, University of Pittsburgh.

Attrabi, H. A. 1982. *Egypt: Problems and Solutions* (in Arabic). Cairo: Madbouli.

Ayubi, Nazih M. N. 1982. Bureaucratic Inflation and Administrative Efficiency. *Middle Eastern Studies* 18(3).

———. 1977. *Al-Thaura Al-Idariyyah* (*The Administrative Revolution*). Cairo: Center for Political and Strategic Studies.

———. 1980. *Bureaucracy and Politics in Contemporary Egypt*. London: Ithaca Press.

———. 1990. "Policy Developments and Administrative Changes in the Arab World." Pp. 23-53 in *Public Administration in World Perspectives*, edited by O. P. Dwivedi and Keith M. Henderson. Ames: Iowa State University Press.

Bashir, Iskandar. 1965. "Major Problems of Local Government in Lebanon." Paper presented in the seminar on local government in the Mediterranean countries. Beirut, 10-15 May, 1965.

Binsaleh, Abdullah M. 1982. "The Civil Service and its Regulation in the Kingdom of Saudi Arabia." Ph.D. Dissertation, Claremont Graduate School.

CAOA. 1969. *Annual Report 1963-1968*. Cairo.

Chackerian, Richard, and Shadukhi Suliman. 1983. "Public Administration in Saudi Arabia: An Empirical Assessment of Work Group Behavior." *International Review of Administrative Sciences* 3:49.

El-Fathali, Omar, and Richard Chackerian. 1983. "Administration: The Forgotten Issue in Arab Development." In *Arab Resources: The Transformation of a Society*, edited by I. Ibrahim. Washington D.C.: Center for Contemporary Arab Studies.

Farazmand, Ali. 1989. *The State, Bureaucracy, and Revolution in Modern Iran*. New York: Praeger.

Farsoun, Samih K., and Mehradad Mashayekhi, eds. 1992. *Iran: Political Culture in the Islamic Republic*. London: Routledge.

Ford Foundation. 1963. *The Aspects which Affect the Administrative Reorganization in Saudi Arabia*. Riyadh: Ford Foundation.

Grassmuck, George, and Kamal Salibi. 1964. *Reformed Administration in Lebanon*. Beirut: Catholic Press.

Iskandar, Adnan. 1964. "The Civil Service of Lebanon." Ph.D. Dissertation, American University of Beirut.

Jabbra, Joseph G. 1976. "Bureaucratic Corruption in the Third World: Causes and Remedy." *The Indian Journal of Public Administration* November-December.

———. 1989. "Bureaucracy and Development in the Arab World." *Journal of Asian and African Studies* 24(1-2).

Jabbra, Joseph G., and Nancy W. Jabbra. 1983. "Public Service Ethics in the Third World: A Comparative Perspective." In *The Public Service: Comparative Perspectives*, edited by Kenneth Kernaghan and O. P. Dwivedi. Brussels: International Institute of Administrative Sciences.

Jabbra, Joseph G., and Nancy W. Jabbra, eds. 1997. *Challenging Environmental Issues: Middle Eastern Perspectives*. Leiden: Brill.

Jreisat, Jamil E. 1997. *Politics without Process: Administering Development in the Arab World*. Boulder: Lynne Rienner.

Kisirwani, Marun Y. 1971. *Attitudes and Behavior of Lebanese Bureaucrats: A Study in Administrative Corruption*. Ph.D. Dissertation, Indiana University.

Korninghauer, Louis G. 1963. *Civil Service in Saudi Arabia, A Report*. Riyadh: Ford Foundation.

Lebanon, Civil Service Commission. 1966, 1967, 1968. *Annual Report*. Beirut.

Lipsky, G. A. 1959. *Saudi Arabia: Its People, Its Society, Its Culture*. New Haven: HRAF.

Munla, Hasan. n.d. *Bahth fi Al-Markaziyyah wa Al-lamarkaziyyah, An-Nahar, Economic and Financial Supplement*. Beirut.

Murad, Magdi W. 1983. "The Egyptian Public Sector: The Control Structure and Efficiency Considerations." In *Public Administration and Development* 3(1).

Nakib, Khalil A. 1972. *Bureacracy and Development: A Study of the Lebanese Civil Service*. Ph.D. Dissertation, Florida State University.

Palmer, Monte, El-Sayeed Yassin, and Ali Leila. 1985. "Bureaucratic Flexibility and Development in Egypt." *Public Administration and Development* 5(4).

Paul, Samuel. 1982. *Managing Development Programs: The Lessons of Success*. Boulder, Colorado: Westview Press.

Peretz, Don, and Gedeon Doron. 1997. *The Government and Politics of Israel*. Boulder, Colorado: Westview Press.

Sadik, Mohammed T. 1965. *The Development of Government and Administration in Saudi Arabia*. Riyadh: Institute of Public Administration.

Salem, Elie A. 1973. *Modernization without Revolution: Lebanon's Experience*. Bloomington: Indiana University Press.

Government of Saudi Arabia, *Saudi Ministry of Planning, 1975-1980*. Riyadh.

Tawati, Ahmad M. 1976. *Civil Service of Saudi Arabia: Problems and Prospects*. Ph.D. Dissertation, West Virginia University.

Warner, S. E. 1964. *Proposed Accounting Development Program for the Government of Saudi Arabia*. Riyadh: Ford Foundation.

Chapter 7

NATIONAL CULTURE, CORRUPTION, AND GOVERNANCE IN PAKISTAN

Nasir Islam

A country's culture consists of shared products both material and non-material. It consists of the shared values, norms, institutions, artifacts, symbols, understandings and traditions (Deresky 2003:84). Culture is the learned and shared ways of thinking and acting among a group of people or a society. Hofstede (1980:70-73) refers to the concept of culture as the software of the mind, a sort of mental programming. Kroeber and Kluckhohn define culture in terms of human orientation to fundamental modes of actions, leading to value assumptions that form the core of human cultures (Kroeber and Kluckhorn 1963). Culture thus influences our daily lives in the way we eat, dress, greet and treat one another, teach our children, manage organizations, and solve problems. Humans are not born with an innate culture. Rather, they are born into a society that teaches them the collective ways of life we call culture. Culture enables human beings to adapt to their ever-changing environment.

Societal standards and norms are derived from values. Values can be seen as shared ideas about what is good, right, and desirable. The difference between values and norms is that values are abstract whereas norms are behavioral rules or guidelines for people in a particular kind of situation. The values of a society are important because they influence the content of its norms (Robertson 1981:61-62). If a society values small populations, it prescribes a small family. If a society values human life, it abolishes capital punishment. In principal, all norms can be traced to basic social values. The norms that prescribe corporate downsizing, for example, reflect a high value placed on productivity and efficiency.

Most anthropologists and sociologists tend to agree that culture cannot be genetically transferred. Culture is learned behavior. It represents deeply ingrained influences on the way people from different societies think, behave, and solve problems. As a group learns, adapts, and integrates, the practices are validated and taught to new members as methods of thinking, perceiving, feeling, and behaving.

Consequently, the patterns of shared basic assumptions continue to develop among a given group (i.e., a corporate entity, a region, or a country). Managers must give special attention to the cultural variables because the way people behave in organizations depends on culture and not official rules (Deal and Kennedy 2000:40). Underlining the importance of values, Trompenaar and Hampden-Turner have argued that "a deep structure of beliefs is the invisible hand that regulates economic activity" (Hampden-Turner and Trompenaar 1993:4).

There are various levels of culture: national, regional, and corporate. Researchers choose a level depending on the focus of analysis in a given study. This paper concerns the national level of government in Pakistan. Thus, norms, values, symbols, organizations, and institutions at the national level will be the primary focus of this study. The author has chosen Hofstede's four dimensional model of national culture as a framework to organize and analyze data, information, and reflections. Hofstede has been by far the most influential scholar in the development of a theory of national culture (Gatley, Lessem, and Altman 1996:98; Cray and Mallory 1998:49; Redding 1994). His four dimensional model of national culture has been widely used by researchers to compare national cultures (Sondargaard 1994:447-56).

A Framework for Analysis: Hofstede's four Dimensions of Culture

Hofstede posits the following four dimensions of culture: power distance, individualism-collectivism, uncertainty avoidance, and masculinity (Hofstede 1980:92-96).

Power Distance is a measure or indicator of the extent to which a society tolerates the unequal distribution of power in organizations.

The **Individualism-Collectivism** dimension refers to the degree to which people in a country have learned to act as individuals rather that as members of a cohesive group.

Masculinity represents the degree to which masculine values such as assertiveness, performance, success, and competition prevail over feminine values such as the quality of life, maintaining warm personal relationships, service, caring, and solidarity.

Uncertainty Avoidance is the degree to which people in a country prefer structured over unstructured situations (Hofstede 1980:92-96).

In the pages that follow, this paper will elaborate on Hofstede's cultural dimensions as posited above and use them to frame the information and data concerning Pakistan's administrative culture. The paper will use Hofstede's findings and conclusions about the national culture of Pakistan as the departure point for a more reflective and in-depth analysis of administrative culture. The paper assumes that despite a good deal of diversity in regional/provincial cultures, Hofstede's conclusions are generally applicable, and three of his four dimensions hold true for all regions of Pakistan. In a study of managers of British, Sudanese, and Pakistani origin, Shackleton and Ali (1990:114-116) corroborated the findings of Hofstede for at least two dimensions—power distance and uncertainty avoidance (there may be some differences in the masculinity/femininity dimension between the tribal regions of Balochistan and NWFP, on one hand, and the Punjab and Sindh on the other). We also assume that national cultures and administrative cultures are mediated by history, traditions, and leadership. Therefore, before an analysis of the administrative culture is offered, the paper will present a brief history of the public service traditions and their colonial and post-colonial antecedents.

Colonial and Post-Colonial Traditions of Pakistan's Public Service

The administrative system that Pakistan inherited from the colonial state remained intact at least until 1973. The system consisted of three crucial institutions: an elitist public service, the secretariat, and the district administration. From 1948 to 1973, the government of Pakistan undertook five major reform efforts and brought some important changes to this troika. All the reports resulting from these efforts, except one, were classified and never made public. The legacy of the vice-regal system of administration remained intact for 25 years.

The public service structure inherited from the colonial period was based on rank classification, grouping all government positions into four broad classes: Class I, II, III, and IV. The fourfold Hindu caste system—Brahmins, Kashatriya, Vaishiyas, and Sudras—has often been used as a metaphor for this elitist structure. Vertical movement between these classes was rather rare. Class I consisted of two all-Pakistan Services called the Civil Service of Pakistan (CSP) and the Police Service of Pakistan (PSP). It also included some dozen functional cadres called the Central Superior Services, including the Pakistan Audit and Accounts Service, Pakistan Income Tax Service, Pakistan Customs and Excise Service, and the Pakistan Military Accounts Service.

The CSP was the direct descendent of the famous ICS (Indian Civil Service), the steel frame of the Raj. It was comprised of the 83 Muslim and 53 British members of the colonial cadre who opted to serve in Pakistan, at the time of the partition (Braibanti 1963:364-567). Like its predecessor, the CSP provided the hierarchical chain of command linking the district administration to the provincial secretariat and the central government. In a federal system, this was an innovation or perhaps an anomaly. Being an all-Pakistan cadre, the members of the

CSP could be posted to all levels of governments—local, provincial, and federal. They could also be posted to head the state enterprises. A system that reserved policy level posts for the cadre provided the members the opportunity to gain quick promotions.

The only point of entry to the CSP as well as the other Central Superior Services was through a competitive examination at the lowest level. Young university graduates before the age of 24 were eligible to take the examination. Eighty percent of the positions were filled based on a provincial quota related to population. The other 20 percent were open to all candidates on a merit basis—their rank in the competition. There was no lateral entry into any of these cadres; nor was there lateral movement between the cadres. Assignment to the cadres was based on the candidate's initial standing in the examination. It was like being born into a caste. The CSP, like its predecessor the ICS, was steeped in classical generalism, and its exclusivity and training created an amazing *esprit de corps*. In Pakistan, the CSP enjoyed enormous prestige and power. According to Asaf Hussain, the CSP not only inherited the ICS tradition but also internalized them through training and indoctrination (Hussain 1979:62).

In 1973, under Prime Minister Bhutto, the civil service structure was finally reformed. Castes, like classes, were abolished. All positions in the public service were grouped into 22 Basic Pay Scales (BPS), thus abolishing some 600 different pay scales. The reform abolished the CSP and merging the provincial generalist services with the former CSP created a District Management Group (DMG). Similarly, the Police Group replaced the PSP. Other services were transformed into such groups. For a short while, even lateral entry was allowed into the elite groups but was later discontinued. The reform also led to the creation of a Secretariat Group to staff the policy-making positions at the Secretariat level. This diluted the power of the CSP, which formerly enjoyed a monopoly over these positions. Charles Kennedy (1987:106) believes that these reforms attained some of their main objectives. They diluted the elite character of the civil service structure, eliminated the reservation of posts for the CSP, and reduced the salary differentials between various cadres. However, the overall importance of the cadre system and the relative elite character of the cadres persisted. After the fall of Bhutto and reinstallation of another military regime, the reform agenda of the Bhutto period was abandoned. Bureaucracy re-emerged as a powerful influence on the policy process. The CSP was not revived but the DMG acquired some of the underpinnings and elite character of its predecessor (Islam 1989:278). The former CSP members of the generalist cadre were able to stall the recommendations of the Anwar-ul-Haq Commission (Haq 1980:21-24), which may have further eroded their prestige.

The Central and Provincial Secretariats are constituted by the Ministries and Divisions, crefated on functional basis. A Secretary to the Government heads a Division. A Federal Secretary is a BPS 22 grade official. The additional Joint and Deputy Secretaries and Section Officers support them. The Cabinet Secretary is in charge of the Cabinet Secretariat and occupies the highest position in the public service. Despite the creation of the Secretariat Group, the DMG members have come to dominate the senior positions. Policies are formulated in the secretariat divisions and implemented by directorates known as "attached departments." Experts and functional specialists staff these positions. This creates a net dichotomy between policy and implementation and often leads to a conflict between senior specialists in the attached departments and relatively young section officers and deputy secretaries. Many reform committees and commissions have recommended the abolition of this artificial distinction and the transformation of the secretariat into the personal staff of the Minister. The powerful generalist lobby has been successful at blocking such proposals.

The District Administration, until recently headed by a DMG officer, is the third element in the administrative troika that runs the country. The district has been the focus or hub of the territorial management—maintaining law and order, dispensing justice, collecting revenue, and coordinating the development programs of the functional department (Gable 1964:1-19). The DMG officer heading the district was called the DC (District or Deputy Commissioner). The office of DC has been romanticized in the administrative folklore of the Indo-Pak sub-continent. This involves legendary young men out of Cambridge and Oxford who formed the steel frame of the Raj in India. They spent 14 days a month on horseback and toured their districts. They learned the local languages and became amateur anthropologists. Above all, they dispensed evenhanded justice to the oppressed people of the rural India and kept a balance between the Hindus and the Muslims. They also exercised absolute authority and were responsible only to the Chief Secretaries and Governors for the Raj. They were paternalistic, authoritarian, and elitist and their successors the CSP/DMG in Pakistan espoused the same traditions. They did not take orders from the local politicians. The ICS reigned supreme in India. In their view, politics (or policy) was confined to Westminster or later to Islamabad. The elitist traditions of the ICS/CSP, the policy administration dichotomy of the secretariat, and the district administration are thus the institutions that constitute the key elements of the British colonial heritage in Pakistan (Islam 1989; 1990).

The CSP and, to a lesser extent, the DMG (and other senior levels) have been the carriers of this tradition and ethos. This is a tradition of disciplined, rationally disposed, but authoritative individuals. It emphasized the comprehension of order, intellectuality, law, objectivity, and rational analysis. Below this group is perhaps a larger group of Grade 17-19 officers. They are conversant with rules and procedures but the other qualities have not perhaps evenly permeated this group. Then there is the third and much larger group of the remaining public servants—the plebs of the bicycle bureaucracy. Among them, the values of an impersonal and rational bureaucracy have only marginally permeated (Braibanti 1963:382-383). This analysis, to a large extent, remains valid

More recently, the office of the DC has been abolished. According to the National Reconstruction Bureau (2001:6), its latest incarnation is the District Coordination Officer (DCO). The DCO will be responsible for the day to day administration to an elected district administrator, called the Nazim. For Technical issues, the DCO will be responsible to the Chief Secretary of the province. Many functions of the former DC have been given to the Nazim. This latest reform has been carried out in the context of the government's devolutionary program. It is a serious blow to the elitist character of the DMG Group. It is too early to determine the real impact of this reform on the elitist DMG group and the provincial bureaucracy.

Power Distance in Pakistani Administration

Power Distance signifies the degree of inequality that people in a given society would consider normal. It represents the willingness of people to accept status and power differences among its members. It reflects the degree to which people are likely to respect hierarchy and rank in organizations. The degree of tolerance for power distance will influence the relationship between management and employees, how responsibilities are assigned, and how discipline is maintained.

A high power distance society accepts wide differences in power in organizations. Employees show a great deal of respect for those in authority. Titles, rank, and status carry a lot of weight. In countries with large PDI scores (e.g., Hong Kong), subordinates feel dependent on their superiors and are afraid to express disagreement. The notion of concentration of authority suggests that a high Power Distance country would prefer centralization of organizational structures and a greater number of hierarchical levels.

Subordinates who feel dependent or fearful of a boss will either prefer an autocratic/paternalistic boss or reject this person outright. A manipulative or autocratic style is compatible with high power distance, and we find high power distance scores in Arab, Far Eastern, and Latin countries. A low power distance culture plays down inequalities as much as possible, but employees are not fearful or in awe of the bosses. Persons living in low Power Distance countries would prefer less centralization of organization structures. In low scoring PDI countries (e.g., the United Kingdom and United States) there is more of a contractual relationship between subordinates and supervisors and less dependence on the supervisor. Low power distance orientation leads to employee demands for participative leadership. This style of leadership tends to be more effective in low Power Distance cultures like Norway, Finland, Denmark, and Sweden (Hofstede 1980:158).

Pakistan has a moderately high score on power distance. It ranks 18th in a group of 52 countries according to Hofstede's Power Distance Index (PDI). Austria has the lowest PDI and Panama and Guatemala score the highest at 95. Most of the Anglo-Saxon and Scandinavian countries score toward the low end of the continuum. This signifies that Pakistanis tolerate a rather high degree of inequality. Inequality begins in the family. According to Ziring, "the family patriarch has unlimited power and is entitled to great respect" (Ziring 1971:150). In rural areas, the authority of the feudal landlords is accepted unquestionably. Most people in the villages tend to be submissive and readily accept the power of the landlords (Ziring 1971:145-147). The relationship between government and the people is also characterized by high power distance. According to the Pay and Services Commission, the public bureaucracy employs paternalistic methods of administration and the people are accustomed to accept oppression without complaining (The Government of Pakistan 1962:74). Akhtar Hameed Khan, an astute observer of Pakistan's rural development also supports this view. In his words, "power is concentrated in a small governing class who regard themselves as guardians of the people" (Khan 1984:180).

They have organizations where hierarchy is very important. The corner stone of Pakistani bureaucracy remains a rigid pattern of hierarchic rank (Kennedy 1987:10). This system allows little opportunity of upward mobility. Military organizations are respected and accorded a great deal of prestige. I believe that Hofstede's Power Distance Index (PDI) underestimates the tolerance for inequality in Pakistani society, particularly in public sector organizations. If Hofstede's sample had included the managers from public sector, Pakistan's score would have been even higher.

The high PDI orientation is evident in the administrative structures and classification of the public services in Pakistan. All civil servants are grouped into 22 Basic Pay Scales (BPS) or grades. The BPS 17 through 22 is considered the officer class. This category accounts for only 9.8 percent of the public servants in the provinces and about 5 percent in the federal government. Seventy-one percent of the public servants are in the lowest grades (grades 1-7). This steep pyramidal structure offers little opportunity of mobility between the lower scales and officer class. It is almost impossible for a clerical employee (BPS 8-16) to be promoted to the ranks of the officer class (BPS 17-22). Power and authority are centralized at the top of the organizational structures (The World Bank 1998:11-12).

In addition to this vertical classification, the public service has been organized into functional groups or cadres. All-Pakistan cadres, including the District Management Group (DMG) and the Police Group, remain the most prestigious because of the power and privileges they enjoy. Most of the senior policy making positions—Secretary and Joint Secretary to government, Heads of the state enterprises—are "reserved" for the members of this group. Until recently, the members of the DMG cadre were posted as the Divisional Commissioners and the District or Deputy Commissioner (DC) —the most revered, romanticized, and powerful positions in the territorial administration of the country. Government's most recent experiment in devolution may have made a dent in the elite position of the DMG cadre. It is interesting to note that the Foreign Service Group is not the first choice of the majority of the candidates for civil service examinations. It is not perceived to have the power and authority that confers status within the local community. The people's usual refrain about the Foreign Service is *Jungle main more nacha, kiss ne dekha* (The peacock danced in the forest, nobody saw it?)

All the policy-making powers are concentrated in the federal and provincial Secretariats where the Secretary to the government heads a Ministry or a Division. Most often, the people from the DMG and The Secretariat Groups occupy these jobs. Even the routine decisions appear to be made by the top administrators. Over the years, the administrative culture of government has evolved in favor of increased centralization of authority. The Secretary or a central authority makes routine decisions like the recruitment of clerical staff, postings, and transfers of teachers and other lower level personnel. The personnel decisions concerning BPS 17-22 employees often require the intervention of the Prime Minister or the Chief Ministers. Foreign travel by the federal officials requires the approval of the highest level of government. They have disproportionately high compensation packages as compared to the lower level employees. A World Bank Study concluded that the Government of Pakistan has an over-centralized structure, management, and rules inappropriate for public sector activities. (The World Bank 1998:1) The Secretaries (to government) are given luxurious homes, cars, drivers, and servants along with their salaries. A World Bank estimate of the total annual remuneration of BPS 22 Secretary puts it at around Rs1.2 million. This appears to be substantially less than the top management salaries in the private sector, yet quite steep in comparison with the benefits of BPS 1-7 employees (The World Bank 1998:1). The tolerance for high Power Distance has led to a tradition of sycophancy throughout the Pakistani government and administrative system. The tradition of Mughal *darbars* (courts of the Mogul Kings), vice-regal ethos of the colonial period, dictatorial regimes, centralization of power and privilege in the higher civil service, and the importance attached to hierarchy have all reinforced the phenomenon. According to Iqbal Akhund (2000:323), a senior Pakistani diplomat and a former advisor to the Prime Minister, "sycophancy is virtually an institutional feature of Pakistan's governance." In Pakistani politics and government, there are frequent stories of careers being made based on the use of flattery.

Sherbaz Khan Mazari, a former Prime Minister of Pakistan, recounts in his autobiography how Zulfiqar Ali Bhutto had endeared himself to then President Iskander Mirza through the "gazelle shoots" organized by his family in their Larkana estates. These occasions remain the vital links through which a Sindhi feudal lord establishes and maintains links to power holders and power brokers. Bhutto, an obscure and unknown Karachi lawyer, was then rewarded by being chosen to head the Pakistani delegation to the U.N. and, later, appointed Minister in Ayub's cabinet. Mazari (1999) goes on to quote from a letter that Bhutto later wrote to Mirza expressing his "imperishable and devoted loyalty." The letter ended with a classic sycophant's refrain: "When the history of our country is written by objective historians, your name will be placed even before that of Mr. Jinnah. Sir, I say this because I mean to, and not because you are the President of my country" (Mazari 1999:77). Subordinates tend to use extreme flattery to bridge the power distance with their superiors. There is no tradition of "speaking truth to power." The false flatterers constantly try to second-guess the boss's preference and reinforce it with flattery.

Individualism-Collectivism in Pakistan

Individualism refers to the degree to which people in a country have learned to act as individuals rather than as members of cohesive groups such as family, kinship, or lineage groups. This dimension concerns the degree of horizontal dependence of individuals upon the group. According to Hofstede, "individualism pertains to societies in which the ties between individuals are loose. Everyone is expected to look after himself or herself and his or her immediate family. Collectivism as its opposite pertains to societies in which people from birth onwards are integrated into strong, cohesive in-groups, which throughout peoples' lifetime continue to protect them in exchange for unquestioning loyalty" (Hofstede 1980:316-17). The workplace in highly individualistic cultures is largely contractual or transactional, and work is controlled and organized with reference to individuals and assumed economic rationale and self-interest. Collectivist cultures emphasize dependence upon the organization to provide training, good physical conditions, and to enable a full use of skills. In collectivist societies, the employment relationship is morally based and management of groups is salient with personal relationships prevailing over the task. Trust is the essential requirement for successful cooperation. In these countries, it is important for the organization to establish linkages between private and work life.

It appears that managers in collectivist societies should exhibit a high degree of concern for employee welfare. Collectivist societies are characterized by a focus on the group (i.e., extended family, caste, lineage groups, or tribes). Individuals feel committed to the group and bear responsibility to the group. They derive pleasure and satisfaction from group achievement.

Pakistan scored very low on individualism and, conversely, very high on collectivism in Hofstede's study along with many countries of Central and South America—Costa Rica, Ecuador, Guatemala, Columbia, and Venezuela. Pakistan remains essentially a collectivist country. Out of a group of 52 countries in Hofstede's sample, Pakistan ranked 38th on individualism. The United States was the most individualistic with a score of 91, and Guatemala the least with a score of 6. Pakistan's score of 14 was just above five other countries (Hofstede 1980:158, 166-167). This is confirmed by the observations of various analysts, such as Kochanek, Braibanti, and Wiess, concerning Pakistan's sociocultural environment. Describing the influence of family on the individual, Wiess declares "there is a great deal of social pressure on an individual to share and pool resources (e.g., income, political resources and personal connections)" (Weiss 1991:22). Kochaneck maintains that the family networks in Pakistan are "extremely strong and are a primary focus of loyalty" (Kochaneck 1983:31).

The most significant manifestation of Pakistani collectivism, then, is the central importance of family and kinship structures. Rural Pakistan remains dominated by a value system based on kinship, *zat* (lineage group), and tribe. All sections of society function within the context of these social structures and values attached to them. Though the norms, values, and institutions vary somewhat from region to region, the central place of the family and kinship remains constant. In Punjab and Sindh, for example, the dominant social organization consists of kinship networks called *Biraderis* literally meaning "brotherhoods." These are people who trace their lineage from a common ancestor (see Kochanek 1983; Braibanti 1963; Weiss 1991). In the NWFP and Balochistan, the tribal structures replace the *biraderis*.

These kinship structures are so strong that they extend to town and cities, penetrating the corporations, public bureaucracy, and the political system. The individual is closely integrated into these networks and they determine his/her status, mobility, and success. Family networks are the primary focus of loyalty. Their strength is reinforced by endogamous marriages between cousins. The latter enable the family to retain land and assets within the family and build clan networks.

The kinship structure creates a set of strong mutual obligations to one's kin. One owes employment to one's relatives regardless of competence; support in feuds and conflicts irrespective of any criteria of justice; and favors if one happens to be in a position of authority (Kochanek 1983:31). Wiess (1991) found that everyone involved is aware of family obligations particularly to acquire jobs for one's kith and kin (Wiess 1991:23). The scope of these obligations often extends beyond the extended family to the kinship or lineage group. The fulfillment of these obligations plays a fundamental role in maintaining the solidarity and status of the *quom* (lineage group) to which one belongs. A social structure that places such a premium on family and kinship inhibits the development of loyalties to larger professional organizations or associations. Rules and norms based on family and kinship take precedence over professional or rational codes of conduct or even laws. Any action in pursuit of the welfare of the family or the in-group is acceptable. The practice of helping your kin group to find jobs has lead to the emergence of caste base informal networks in public bureaucracy.

Ralph Braibanti, a Public Administration advisor to the government of Pakistan, considered the intrusion of caste, communal, and familial considerations in bureaucratic decision-making a fundamental factor (Braibanti 1963:388). Even in cases where these factors did not matter, the perception prevailed that they did. Thus, every action of promotion, discipline, and severance was viewed as capricious and based on cliquish animosities resulting from these ascriptive affiliations.

Family and kinship-based social structures have given rise to the culture of *Sifarish*. This Urdu word literally means "a recommendation" or "a connection." In some ways, it resembles the Chinese system of *Guanxi*. Short of straight bribing, it has become the standard means of getting things done from public functionaries. Ordinary public services, which should be provided to the citizens by right in developed societies, are procured through *Sifarish*. Getting a passport, renewing a driver's license, clearing goods from the customs, getting a telephone connection, admission to schools and universities, sometimes even making an airline reservation need *Sifarish*. It involves finding a relative or a close friend who knows the functionary or has some influence to get the job done. In the rural areas, access to water, electricity, fertilizers, sanitation, health services, and roads must all be procured through *sifarish*. It makes a mockery of any rational system of service delivery based on rational criteria. The decision makers who feel compelled under family and kinship pressure to oblige their clients bend and break the rules. Those who do not play the *sifarish* game risk having a "bad reputation" or even to face ostracization. Some departments have developed an institutionalized system so that the important officials can oblige their favorites. Pakistan International Airline is widely rumored to have allocated a quota of seats to various ministries and departments on every flight. They are kept available until the last minute. The universities and prestigious colleges have a quota of seats for important officials like the Governors of the provinces.

Uncertainty Avoidance and Public Bureaucracy

Uncertainty Avoidance (UA) is the cultural tendency to feel uncomfortable with uncertainty and risk in everyday life. It reflects the degree to which people in a country prefer structured over unstructured situations. From an organizational perspective, it reflects the degree to which people are likely to prefer structured or unstructured organizational situations. It also reflects the propensity to take risks as well as the attitude toward change and innovation. Cultures that rank relatively low on UA feel much more comfortable with the unknown. High uncertainty avoidance cultures prefer formal rules and structured organizations and any uncertainty expresses itself in higher anxiety than that of low uncertainty avoidance cultures. The degree of uncertainty avoidance will impact on management preferences, decision making, and the relationship between management and employees.

High uncertainty avoidance is characterized by emphasis on clear formal rules. Leaders or top managers are considered as "experts" because of their supposed mastery of rules. Learning is highly structured and formalized. Precision and security are important. In such organizations there is usually a low turnover rate. There is a great deal of resistance to change.

Pakistan ranks fairly high on Hofstede's Uncertainty Avoidance index with a rank of 21 among 52 countries. Its average score in the index is 70, while the highest scoring country was Greece with a score of 112 (Hofstede 1980:132-33). Pakistan's high uncertainty avoidance manifests itself in many of its administrative institutions and practices. The highly hierarchic structures with centralized power are used as the principal means to coordinate and resolve conflicts. Though Pakistan has a federal form of government yet most of the power is concentrated at the central level. The presence of senior cadres of the central government (described above) seriously undermines the federal character and autonomy of provinces. Power to impose taxes is largely concentrated at the centre. Consequently, the provinces are dependent on the central government for resources.

Hierarchy is often used to reduce uncertainty. All kinds of routine decisions are pushed up the hierarchy. Perhaps the most significant aspect is the emphasis given to formal rules and regulations. Every department is saddled with a plethora of rules, regulations, and procedures that lead to unnecessary delays in making decisions and the delivery of services. Ironically, the propensity to avoid uncertainty and the collectivist orientation (discussed above) result in a paradoxical situation. As more and more rules are created to avoid uncertainty, more ingenious ways of circumventing the rules are found under pressures of collectivist orientation. Rules are selectively enforced and bent to favor relatives or friends. Often, when the rules are enforced, they are used deliberately to stall a decision to give time to favorite clients or solicit a bribe.

The Masculinity-Femininity Dimension in Pakistan's Administrative System

The Masculinity-Femininity dimension refers to the degree to which the gender roles in a society are differentiated. Masculine culture emphasizes assertiveness, task orientation, performance, success, and competition. Feminine culture, on the other hand, espouses such values as the quality of life, maintaining warm personal relationships, service, caring, and solidarity. Work goals that satisfy needs such as advancement and earnings are important to the masculine cultures in which the work ethos is to live in order to work. Conflicts are resolved through combat. It is important to be aware of the impacts of a masculine approach to conflict when dealing with a feminine culture. Motivations relate to goals and achievement. Heroes are seen as assertive/decisive, which suggests a positive relationship between masculine culture and frequent use of hierarchical authority by the managers.

Paraphrasing Hofstede, feminine societies are characterized by concern for others and emphasize relationships among people. They value group decisions, equality, and solidarity. They attach importance to the quality of life rather than material acquisition. In these societies, men and women both are looked upon as nurturers and gender based occupational segregation is discouraged. In a feminine managerial organization, interpersonal goals such as "a friendly atmosphere" and "cooperation" satisfy the social ego. A feminine work culture has an ethos that promotes working in order to live. Conflicts are resolved through compromise, meaning that masculine managers working in a feminine culture must realize the importance of compromise in negotiations and work assignments, and motivational systems are welfare and socially orientated. Heroes in a feminine culture tend to be intuitive and consensus seeking. This suggests that greater degrees of involvement of subordinates in decision making will fit best with the feminine culture (Hofstede 1980:200-201).

Pakistan scores moderately high on masculinity. Its score in the index is 50, as compared to Sweden (the most feminine) and Japan (the most masculine), scoring 5 and 95 respectively. In Pakistan the gender roles are highly differentiated. The prevailing pattern of gender based division of labor in Pakistan supports Hofstede's findings of three decades ago. Women's participation in the labor force remains low at 27 percent (1997). This is the lowest among the major South Asian Countries. Women's participation rate, however, has risen faster than men's participation rate since 1980 (The Mahbub-ul-Haq Human Development Centre 2000). Out of necessity, women among the middle and lower classes have had to contribute economically to family income; the result is that more and more women have joined the labor force (Wiess 1994). Pakistan ranks 115 according to the Gender Related Development Index (GDI) of the UNDP among the 173 countries included in the ranking. Women account for 25.1 percent of the professional and technical workers and 8.0 percent of the administrators and managers. Female literacy rates (28.9 percent), as well as the gross enrollment (28 percent), are half of that of the men (UNDP 2000:163-167).

There is a high degree of gender imbalance in Pakistani public service. With the exception of the Ministry of Education (51 percent of women at middle levels) and the Ministry of Health (30 percent of women at the middle levels), the proportion of women at the middle levels remains very small. Compared to some 800 men serving in the BPS scales 20 and above, there are only 19 women holding posts in these grades. The current military regime has appointed several female ministers and many women to senior positions including the Cabinet Secretary, the Ambassadors to Washington and London, and the Secretary to the Women's and Social Welfare Division. Under the government's devolutionary reform, 33 percent of the seats in local bodies have been reserved for women. Some 36000 women councilors have been elected to various local bodies.

Cultural norms continue to inhibit women's access to education in general and higher education in particular. Gender differentiation of roles assigns women to domestic roles and encourages an early marriage, having a family and taking care of children and domestic work. In Pakistan one often sees young women who have qualified as doctors, teachers or nurses staying home after marriage and taking care of the children. Gender differentiation also leads to "ghettoization" of the workplace. Large numbers of women work as elementary school teachers, nurses, para-professionals, and secretaries. In Pakistan, the institution of *purdah* is responsible for the exclusion and segregation of women. It restricts the interaction of women with the non-kin males and, in some regions, restricts their movements outside the family compounds, thus limiting women's roles again to the domestic and segregated spheres (The Mahbub-ul-Haq Human Development Centre 2000:30). In Balochistan and the NWFP where the institution of Purdah is much stronger, it is sometimes difficult to find women to fill jobs of health para-professionals or primary school teachers. The large-scale presence of women in local bodies is likely to change the culture of the workplace. It could create a lot of trouble in these institutions. Women are already having problems in claiming their office space and separate toilets.

Corruption and the Public Service

Corruption has a long history in Pakistan. For example, during the first martial law regime, 526 officers were compelled to retire or were removed from service on charges of corruption. This group included 84 officers of the elite All Pakistan (CSP and PSP) and Class I Services. All kinds of anti-corruption measures were announced by the military government in an effort to reform the bureaucracy (Ziring 1971:12-13). During the first democratically elected government of Mr. Bhutto, from 1971 to 1977, "Death to Bribery" was a popular slogan (Ahmed 1974:144). During the second martial law regime, General Zia-ul-Haq himself complained about the widespread corruption in his government (Haq 1982:1).

Corruption continued nonetheless. Over the last five decades, corruption became part of the administrative culture in Pakistan. It became pervasive at all levels of administration—from the highest echelons of the government to the lowest levels of the bicycle bureaucracy in the field. During the early years of Pakistan's existence, *Rishwat Khor or Rashi*, the Urdu words for "corrupt officials," were used in the pejorative sense, with a hushed tone and a wink. They indicated strong disapproval. Overtime, these words have practically disappeared from the social lexicon. During the 1950s and 1960s, the preferred choice of most candidates in the Central Superior Services Examinations was the elite Civil Service of Pakistan (CSP) and the Foreign Service. During the 1980s and 1990s the Customs and Income Tax Services became the premium choice. Bribery and corruption have become a way of life in Pakistan.

In many departments of government, corruption became institutionalized. In the Public Works Department (PWD), a percentage of the total value of a project was often paid to various levels of officials for moving a file up the hierarchical line of command. WAPDA (the Water and Power Development Agency) became so notoriously corrupt that the Army had to be called in to administer the agency. Ironically an army general who came to set things right is now under investigation by the National Accountability Bureau. Transfers and postings to certain police stations that offered lucrative opportunities to extract money were made by auction to the highest bidder. The Customs Service became so corrupt that a Swiss Agency had to be engaged to assess customs at the departure points abroad. Ironically, the agency had to pay a hefty bribe to Asaf Zardari, (Prime Minister's husband and a Minister in her cabinet) for winning the contract. The parent agency of the Customs Department, the Central Board of Revenue (CBR), was labeled in the press as "holding a unique place in Pakistan's corruption-infested bureaucracy" and was characterized as "rotten to the core" (*The Herald* 2000:44). The CBR has never met its target in revenue collection. According to the press reports, the CBR Chairman,

Riaz Hussain Naqvi, had reported to General Musharraf that only 1/10 of the CBR staff was honest and that he would like to sack the rest of the 90 percent (Zaidi 2000). The collectorates of the CBR in major industrial cities have paid back billions of rupees in fraudulent refunds. In 1999-2000, for example, Rs4.19 billion was paid out against a gross collection of Rs4.89 billion in Karachi West. In Lahore and Faisalabad, Rs5.1 billion and Rs3.96 billion were similarly paid out against gross collection of Rs10.5 billion and Rs4.9 billion respectively (Zaidi 2000:46).

Bribery at the service delivery point is routine and commonplace. Clearing customs, obtaining a driver's license, getting a passport, an identity card, an electricity connection, a telephone connection, registering a police report (F.I.R.) and any government permit, could all be obtained expeditiously through a bribe, if not through *Sifarush*.

Pakistan's decade of democracy turned out to be a decade of grand corruption. Every elected government during this period was dismissed on corruption charges. The governments under Prime Ministers Bhutto and Sharif set records of corruption. Both these leaders were charged with siphoning off hundreds of millions of dollars into dummy corporations and pricey real estate ventures abroad. The stories of their legendary corruption have been published in the national and international press (Grey and Syal 1998). In a recent survey, 88 percent of the respondents felt that political leaders had become more corrupt during the last five years and 33 percent admitted to giving bribes (The Mahbub-ul-Haq Human Development Centre 1999:162). In another survey, over 95 percent believe that bureaucrats and politicians were corrupt. Seventy-six percent thought that the generals were more corrupt now than 15 years ago (*The Herald* 1997:152-4). The *Human Development Report in South Asia 1999* noted: The moral foundations of the state have been eroded by electoral fraud, advent of money politics, the criminalization of the political system and increasing corruption in public life (The Mahbub-ul-Haq Human Development Centre 1999:442-447).

Pakistan is considered one of the most corrupt countries in the world. Table 1 gives Pakistan's rankings according to the now famous *Transparency International Index*.

Table 1. Corruption in Pakistan: Transparency International Rankings, 1996-2003

Year	Rank	Score	Countries
1996	53	1.00	54
1997	48	2.6	52
1998	71	2.7	85
1999	87	2.2	99
2001	79	2.6	91
2002	77	2.3	102
2003	92	2.5	133

Source: Compiled from the Transparency International Indices.

The data presented in Table 1 is based on the perceptions of foreign businessmen. There are also some methodological weaknesses in sampling procedures. However, the widespread anecdotal evidence and widely published information in the press about specific cases corroborates the findings of Transparency International about the degree of corruption prevalent in the country. The figures show a little improvement since 1996. In that year, Transparency International ranked Pakistan as the second most corrupt among 53 countries examined, second only to Nigeria. This was during Bhutto's second term when her first husband Mr. Zardari had been promoted by the local press from "Mr. 10 percent" to "Mr. 20 percent" (*The Globe and Mail* 1998:D4). In another survey of Corruption in South Asia, Transparency International found significantly higher levels of the reported incidence of corruption in Pakistan than the other South Asian countries. Police, land administration, and taxation were considered to be the most corruption prone sectors of public administration (Transparency International 2002:2, 15-16).

> The government of Pakistan noted in its *Pakistan 2010 Vision Statement*: Corruption pervades all three branches of government: the executive, the legislature, and the judiciary. The result is that none of three branches acts as a check upon the misfeasance of the other two. The powers to appoint or reward public officials is use arbitrarily, public property is handled in a cavalier fashion, the system ignores and often rewards the financial corruption and the misuse of powers, financial institutions have been burdened by unserviceable loans, public lands have been doled out in return for political favor or financial favors, and public institutions are badly managed and respond neither to citizen needs nor to financial imperatives. (The World Bank 1998:2)

Families often become the source or the motive for corruption at all levels of administration. The immediate and extended families of political leaders and senior bureaucrats are invariably involved in the *Sifarish* game, rule breaking, corruption, and shady wheeling and dealing. President Ayub's sons became notorious for receiving government largesse. One of his sons and his father-in-law built an industrial empire during the President's tenure. Asif Zardari, Benazir Bhutto's husband has been charged with many counts of corruption in several cases pending in the courts in Pakistan and abroad. Prime Minister Sharif's family was alleged to have amassed millions of pounds in off shore accounts and London properties. There are many cases pending against him and his family in the courts under the jurisdiction of the National Accountability Bureau. These cases are dormant because Nawaz Sharif made a deal sponsored by the Saudi government and has been in exile in Saudi Arabia (Shah 2001:579).

Conclusions

This author believes that a tolerance for high power distance, collectivism, high uncertainty avoidance, and masculinity combine to contribute to a dysfunctional administrative system. High power distance accounts for centralized, hierarchical, and authoritarian structures. These organizational attributes, in turn, inhibit the development of transparency and accountability. The tolerance for inequality accounts for a compensation system that hardly allows a minimum living wage for a vast majority of low level employees. This is a major reason for petty corruption in the delivery of services. Concentration of authority at higher levels bestows a lot of discretionary power on senior officials and politicians. Discretionary power without adequate accountability is a great temptation to misuse public power for private purposes.

A predominantly masculine culture promotes acquisitive values and leads to greed. It emphasizes money, power, status, and aggressiveness. These values tend to contribute to corruption and the misuse of power. Thus, the masculine culture contributes to the grand corruption at the higher echelons of the government. In a highly collectivist society, politicians and officials are bound in a network of obligations and counter obligations. This contributes to nepotism, favoritism, and cronyism; thus paving the way for corruption. Pakistani culture's collectivist orientation is, perhaps, a major contributor to the pervasive corruption. Saving the family honor and enhancing the family status take precedence over rational norms. Supporting family members through thick and thin is a primordial obligation. The Pakistani society's propensity toward high uncertainty avoidance leads to the creation of elaborate rules and procedures. Applying these rules to individual cases and their interpretation is another source of discretionary power. In a society where the universal application of rules is anathema, their selective application leads to not only injustice, but also corruption and nepotism.

Corruption skews priorities, reduces allocative efficiency, compromises the quality of programs, undermines accountability, and reduces transparency. Corruption in the police and judiciary leads to gross injustice and the violation of human rights. A World Bank official points out that the Pakistan's GDP per capita would have been significantly higher if corruption had been reduced (The Mahbub-ul-Haq Human Development Centre 1999:98).

Pakistan's current quasi-democratic regime has undertaken a massive program of devolution, administrative reform, and accountability. There is some empirical evidence that a greater share in public expenditures for local and state governments may reduce incentives for corruption and decentralization may increase accountability (The World Bank 2002:108). Some of the structural changes, if implemented effectively, will go a long way to address the problem of corruption. The institutional change, however, takes root very slowly, particularly when a change in attitudes, values, and norms is involved. The government also created a National Accountability Bureau to pursue and bring to justice the corrupt public officials. The bureau has been pursuing corrupt officials and politicians for the last six years. It has been successful in recovering hundreds of millions of rupees from the corrupt public officials but has failed, so far, to convict any individuals of major significance in the courts.

REFERENCES

Ahmed, Muneer. 1974. *Aspects of Pakistan's Politics and Administration.* Lahore, Punjab: South Asian Institute, Punjab University.

Akhund, Iqbal. 2000. *Trial and Error: the Advent and Eclipse of Benazir Bhutto.* Karachi: Oxford University Press.

Braibanti, Ralph. 1963. "Public Bureaucracy and Judiciary in Pakistan." In *Bureaucracy and Political Development*, edited by Joseph J la Plombra. Princeton, NJ: Princeton University Press.

Cray, David and Geoffrey R. Mallory. 1998. *Making Senses of Managing Culture.* London: International Thompson Business Press.

Deal, Terrance E. and Allen A. Kennedy. 2000. *The New Corporate Cultures.* Cambridge, MA: Perseus Publishing.

Deresky, Helen. 2003. *International Management: Managing Across Borders and Cultures.* Upper Saddle River, NJ: Prentice Hall.

Gable, Richard W. 1964. "District Adminsitration: Its Development and its Challenges." In *District Administration in West Pakistan*, edited by Inaytullah. Peshawar: Pakistan Academy for Rural Development.

Gatley, Stephen, Ronnie Lessem, and Yochanan Altman. 1996. *Comparative Management.* London: McGraw Hill Europe.

Grey, S and R. Syal. 1998. "The Hunt for Benazir's Booty," in The Sunday Times, 12 April

Hamden-Turner, Charles and Alfons Trompenaar. 1993. *The Seven Cultures of Capitalism.* New York, NY: Doubleday.

Haq, Anwar-ul. 1980. *Commission on Administrative Reform: Report, Part II.* Islamabad: Government of Pakistan.

Haq, General Zia-ul. 1982. *The Dawn Overseas* 6:1-6.

Hofstede, Geert. 1980. *Culture's Consequences: International Differences in Work Related Values.* Newbury Park, CA: Sage Publications.

Hussain, Asaf. 1979. *Elite Politics in an Ideological State.* Folkston, Kent: Dawson.

Islam, Nasir. 1989. "Colonial Legacy, Administrative Reform and Politics: Paksitan 1947-87." *Public Administration and Development,* edited by O.P. Dwevedi. 9(3)June-August.

———. 1990. "Pakistan." In *Public Administration in Developing Countries: an International Handbook*, edited by V. Subramaniam. New York, NY: Greenwood Press.

Kennedy, Charles H. 1985. "Prestige of Services and Bhutto's Administrative Reforms in Pakistan, 1973-84." *Asian Affairs* 12:25-43.

Kennedy, Charles H. 1987. *Bureaucracy in Pakistan.* Karachi: Oxford University Press.

Khan, Akhtar Hameed. 1985. *Rural Development in Pakistan.* Lahore, Punjab: Vanguard.

Kochanek, Stanley A. 1983. *Interest Groups and Development*, Karachi: Oxford University.

Kroeber, A. L. and C. Kluckhohn. 1963. *Culture: A Critical Review of Concepts and Definitions.* New York, NY: Vintage/Random House.

Mazari, Sherbaz Khan. 1999. *A Journey to Disillusionment.* Karachi: Oxford University Press.

National Reconstruction Bureau. 2000. "Local Government Plan 2000." *Dawn*, 16 August, 2000. Internet Edition available at http://www.dawn.com/events/plan2000/ plan.htm.

Redding, S. G. 1994. "Comparative Management Theory: Jungle, Zoo or Fossil Bed." *Organization Studies* 15:323-59.

Robertson, Ian. 1981. *Sociology.* New York, NY: Worth Publishing Inc.

Shackleton, V. J. and A. H. Ali. 1990. "Work Related Values of Managers: A Test of Hofstede's Model." *Journal of Cross-Cultural Psychology* 21:109-18.

Shah, Sajjad Ali, 2001, *Law Courts in a Glass House*, Karachi: Oxford University Press.

Sondargaard, M. 1994. "Hofstede's Consequences: A Study of Reviews, Citations and Replications." *Organization Studies* 15:447-456.

The Globe and Mail. 1998. January 24, Toronto, section D.

The Government of Pakistan. 1962. *Report of the Pay and Services Commission.* Karachi: Government of Pakistan.

Zaidi, Mubahsir, 2000. "Inside the CBR (Special Report)," *The Herald,* July, pp. 44-50.

The World Bank. 1998. *Pakistan: A Framework for Civil Service Reform in Pakistan.* Report No.18386. December 15.

The World Bank. 2000. *World Development Report 2000.* New York, NY: Oxford University Press.

The Mahbub-ul-Haq Human Development Centre. 2000. *Human Development in South Asia 2000: the Gender Question.* Karachi: Oxford University Press.

———. 1999. *Human Development in South Asia.* Karachi: Oxford University Press.

Transparency International. 2002. *Corruption I n South Asia.* December.

UNDP. 2000. *Human Development Report 2000.* New York: Oxford University Press.

Wiess, Anita M. 1991. *Culture, Class and Development in Pakistan.* Boulder, Co: Westview Press.

———. 1994. "Challenges for Muslim Women in a Post Modern World." In *Islam, Globalization and Post-Modernity*, edited by A. S. Ahmed and H. Donnan. New York: Routledge.

Ziring, Lawrence. 1971. *The Ayub Khan Era.* Syracuse: Syracuse University Press.

Zaidi, Mubashir. 2000. "The Rot Within." *The Herald*, July, pp. 47-48.

Chapter 8

WHITHER CHINA'S ADMINISTRATIVE CULTURE IN THE TWENTY-FIRST CENTURY?

Stephen K. Ma

I. Introduction

In September 2000, Cheng Kejie, a Vice Chairman of the Standing Committee of China's People's Congress was executed for corruption. In October 2001, Li Jizhou, a Vice Minister of China's Public Security was sentenced to death for bribery-taking, dereliction, and other crimes. Cheng and Li were respectively the highest ranking government officials in legislature and law enforcement to be convicted since the founding of the People's Republic of China (PRC) in 1949. Though the hush money they pocketed amounted to tens of millions of Chinese *Yuan*, both cases surprised few people, if any, as corrupted bureaucratic behavior has been chronic and contagious in the past two decades. In fact, despite the efforts by the post-Mao leadership to fight against corruption, it does not seem to be well contained. Rather, as an old Chinese saying describes, "not even a prairie fire can destroy the grass, it grows again when the spring breeze blows." He Qinglian, a well-know Chinese scholar on corruption, believes that "[s]tarting in 1998, China's corruption began a transition from organizational corruption to institutionalized corruption" (Kuhn 2000). Has China's administrative culture entered a new stage of deterioration in the twenty-first century? To answer the question, this chapter reviews the background of change of China's administrative culture and the major development in the authorities' efforts to rebuild proper administrative culture. The chapter also addresses certain issues in the process and its possible future development.

II. Change in Administrative Culture

Every organization, including China's administrative apparatus, has its own culture, which is "a persistent way of thinking about the central tasks of and human relationships within an organization. Culture is to an organization what personality is to an individual." The perceptions supplied by an organizational culture "can lead an official to behave not as the situation requires but as the culture expects" (Wilson 1989:110).

What, then, was the culture of China's public administration during the first three decades since the founding of the People's Republic of China? Did the nation's administrators behave as expected by its administrative culture?

Administrative culture was never a big issue in Mao's China. During those years, as Lucian Pye has pointed out, "officials in the state bureaucracies have had to learn to uphold ideals of loyalty and obedience while creating the impression of being imaginative in figuring out how established policies can be carried out more efficiently. They have had to worry about the sin of bureaucratism (*guanliaochuyi*), the tendency to loose touch with the masses and become absorbed with questions of rank and status" (Pye 1984:179). In other words, it was a culture of loyalty and obedience that predominated in China's public administration.

Things have quickly changed since the end of 1978 when Deng Xiaoping launched his second revolution, sending China's behemoth administrative apparatus onto the uncharted path of reform and openness to the outside world. A new administrative culture was emerging in the process.

Unrestrained behavior proliferated as the two tools indispensable for the Party's control over state bureaucracy—ideology and organization—were undermined by Deng's reformist policies. While the "Cultural Revolution" yielded such unintended consequences as emasculated political control, de-Maoization in the post-Cultural Revolution era has been designed to depoliticize part of the system. Deng's pragmatism, which has replaced Mao's belief in ideology and politics in post-Mao China, openly depreciated the role of ideological indoctrination and political organization. On the other hand, personal gains were emphasized as Deng decided to encourage the nation's modernization by motivating the Chinese people through material incentives. His suggestion that "some people will become prosperous first, and others later" was tempting and tantalizing (*Time* 1985:35). The emphasis on economic prosperity has opened a Pandora's box of human greed, which, with its unexpectedly strong momentum, will turn out to be very difficult to hold back. Under the pretext of "listening to the Party," the government bureaucrats were eager to move toward "listening to the purse." The pursuit of self-interest and material good has quickly become a main concern among an increasingly large number of government officials. A new, recalcitrant administrative culture of pursuit of personal profit through public office has emerged (Ma 2001:145-157). The corrupt conduct of public administration in post-Mao China has grown rotten and rampant. The issue of administrative ethics is haunting the nation's leadership as never before in the history of the PRC.

B. Guy Peters believes that the conduct of public administration is a function of changes at three distinct levels: political, societal, and administrative (Peters 1989:40). Further probing the issue, Gerald Caiden suggests "there are multitudinous factors contributing to corruption." A list of them includes psychological, ideological, external, economic, political, sociocultural, and technological factors (Caiden 2001:21-26). These factors have greatly influenced ways of thinking and behaving among millions of Chinese government officials, resulting in a new administrative culture in the world's most populous nation.

From the psychological point of view, "the root cause of corruption is found in the defects of human character inherent in the human condition; few are above temptation" (Caiden 2001:23). The reformist policies placed Chinese bureaucrats in a new, tempting environment where the society was characterized by material gain and where government officials were faced with numerous opportunities to profit personally through public office. As upstart millionaires flaunted their expensive cars and luxurious houses, the temptation to catch up was hard to resist.

As Caiden points out, "there are ideologies that endorse corruption or prevent remedial action" (Caiden 2001:23). Deng was well known for his belief that "whether a cat is black or white, it is a good cat as long as it catches mice." It would be unfair to claim that this notion of "cat" endorses corruption. The tenet does, however, strongly suggest that the ends are more important than the means. When he advanced the policy of allowing some to get rich first, people answered his call and strove to achieve personal prosperity.

External influence cannot be ignored. According to Caiden, "corruption is contagious. As no society is isolated or cut off from any other, corruption crosses boundaries" (Caiden 2001:23). Deng's era began with opening China to the outside world. The main purpose of this policy was to be exposed to civilizations around the world and to benefit from the experiences of industrialized nations. No matter how selective and how well controlled the learning process could be, the sham could be passed off as the genuine. Corrupted behavior among government officials in those countries could be treated as a right, an acceptable, or even a clever way of doing business. For others, the ways and means of bureaucratic corruption there simply opened their eyes. They quickly learned the trick and followed suit.

Economy also plays a certain role. Caiden explains that "scarcity is clearly a key source of corruption…Public monopolization of scarce resources only exacerbates the situation: public officials may run their public businesses as private concerns" (Caiden 2001:24). A new term, *guandao,* was added to the Chinese vocabulary in the late 1980s. It refers to the activities of government officials who took advantage of the scarcity of particular goods and resold them at a profit. The phenomenon was widely resented. Though its elimination was a major theme in student demonstrations during the spring of 1989, *guandao* became a part of China's new administrative culture.

Power corrupts and, according to Caiden, "public officials are powerful because they determine in large part the personal fortunes of everyone affected by their decisions...Hence, corruption seeks out key decision makers and the most powerful officials" (Caiden 2001:24). This seems to explain, among other things, why more and more high-ranking government officials were caught accepting enormous bribes regardless of the authorities' determination to fight against the corruption. For example, six senior administrators at the level of governor/minister, including Li Jiating, the Governor of Yunnan Province, were brought to justice in 2001 (*Renmin Ribao,* Overseas Edition, March 12, 2002).

Socioculturally, "internal socialization and peer group pressure ensure that public officials go along with or at least keep quiet about deviance" (Caiden 2001:25). Indeed, internal socialization or peer socialization transformed administrative culture in a way unprecedented in the history of the PRC. Shengyang, the capital city of Liaoning Province in Northeast China, gained infamy overnight for a corruption case involving a large number of municipal government officials including members of the city's top leadership. The case caught the attention of the Central Government as early as the beginning of 1999. Yet, a seventeen month long investigation by the Provincial Government of Liaoning into the case still made "no substantial progress" because of internal socialization or peer socialization. As a result, the case had to be taken over by the Provincial Government of Jiangsu and moved to its capital city Nanjing, hundreds of miles away from Shenyang (*Yangzi Wanbao,* February 19, 2002; See also Pomfret 2002).

Technology can influence corruption. Indeed, "faulty technology and faulty administrative systems are also to blame for corruption as they permit those inclined to corruption to remain unseen and unknown, to evade detection, and to escape investigation" (Caiden 2001:25). The more faulty the administrative systems, the more captivating the bureaucratic corruption. With flaws, defects, and loopholes in the systems, those beguiled by corruption will also find escape from justice easier. As China's Xinhua News Agency reported in January 2001, more than four thousand officials, suspected of or accused of corruption, succeeded in absconding with more than five billion *Yuan.* Having caused a grave drain on the state coffer, few were brought to justice as many fled the county (*Renmin Ribao,* September 2, 2002).

All of the above factors have helped to bring about the emergence of a new administrative culture in China, which was becoming increasingly individualistic and materialistic, advocating and admiring money-making and pleasure-seeking. As suggested by Hu Angang, a Chinese economist, "in dollar value, China is the most corrupted country in the world" (Pomfret 2002). J. S. Ott observes that organizational culture is a force behind organizational activity. It energizes organizational members to act. More importantly, it not only serves as a unifying theme that expedites meaning, direction, and mobilization of them, but also serves as a control mechanism that encourages or prohibits behaviors (Ott 1989:50).

Serving as a force behind the widely spread unhealthy administrative behavior, the new administrative culture was characterized by several new features. As pointed out in an article published by China's Central Party School, these features include: corruption by collectives; corruption at higher levels of administrative hierarchy; corruption in the areas of personnel management and law enforcement; corruption in capital-intensive areas; corruption assisted with high technology; and corruption in collaboration with international criminals (*World Journal,* August 19, 2003).

The new administrative culture has energized members' action, encouraging and emboldening more bureaucrats to pursue personal interest by taking advantage of public office. This explains why over 800,000 administrators were expelled from the Party within one year between July 2002 and June 2003. In addition, more than four thousand bureaucrats either disappeared or fled the country (Luo Bin 2003:9).

The new administrative culture has also offered a unifying theme of taking the lead to achieve prosperity for China's forty-two million civil servants. Many of them enjoy a much higher standard of living than average Chinese people. One report suggests that the real purchasing power and living condition of *Chu Zhang,* a mid-ranked bureaucrat, in such cities as Shanghai, Guangzhou, Shenzhen, Zhuhai, Fuzhou, and Dalian, has actually surpassed that of a government minister or a mayor in Great Britain, Germany, or Italy (Li Zijing 2003:14).

Finally, while encouraging certain behaviors among state bureaucrats, the new administrative culture has also discouraged some other behaviors among them. The above-mentioned Shengyang case has illustrated how the new administrative culture contributed further to internal socialization and peer pressure, which led to many public officials going along with corruption or at least keeping quiet about deviance.

III. Attempts to Curb Unhealthy Change in Administrative Culture

In order to keep a rein on the huge army of state bureaucrats, the Chinese authorities turned to the enactment of ethical codes for government officials. Codes of ethics are systematic efforts to define acceptable conduct. Generally speaking, they serve three purposes. The first is to provide "guidance to public officials on doing good and avoiding evil." A second aim is to instill "confidence in government and elevate the standards of administrative behavior in public organizations." In addition, codes of ethics also "provide guidance to decision makers dealing with situations where values may be in conflict" (Plant 1994:221). In other words, administrative codes of ethics are designed to address the issue of administrative culture.

New codes could help to inculcate a sense of obligation into the minds of government officials. Deng's modernization has de-Maoization as a component of the program. Mao is no longer treated as a God and his thoughts as golden rules. Contrary to Mao's egalitarian ideas, Deng has been urging people to pursue self-interest by getting rich first. The ideological confusion has led to a crisis of confidence. A lack of confidence in the system and the uncertainty about one's life goals are haunting hundreds of millions of Chinese, including those who serve in the state bureaucracy. Many state cadres, who are supposedly public servants, do not feel obligated to serve the state and the public interest.

As early as 1928, a board of inquiry in the United Kingdom stated that "the first duty of a civil servant is to give his undivided allegiance to the state at all times and on all occasions when the state has a claim on his service" (Waldo 1994:176-190). The Chinese authorities in post-Mao China certainly like very much to see the nation's civil servants fulfill this duty faithfully. Actually, government officials in any country in the world are expected to recognize and observe their obligation to the state, although the degree of their response may vary. The civil servants of China are no exception. Codes of professional ethics could assist in guiding them toward that goal in an environment of ideological confusion and crisis of confidence.

Moreover, the Chinese authorities obviously intended to regain legitimacy for the regime by means of establishing guidelines for administrative behavior. Many cadre-related groups "hoped to assure the Party's revolutionary legitimacy for the future" through purging corruption (White III 1989:13). One of the demands raised during the student pro-democracy demonstrations in the spring of 1989 was that corruption had to be curbed or otherwise it could bankrupt the regime. With the regime's survival at stake, they have had to deal with the problem of bureaucratic corruption.

Two types of corruption exist. One assists in the enhancement of the wealth of the officeholder; the other helps to maintain or expand his/her personal power (Bollens and Schmandt 1979:17). The codes of ethics in post-Mao China basically deal with the first type of corruption, which is an inevitable though not intentional consequence of the call to "get rich first." Beginning in 1993, when the Chinese authorities decided to launch the anti-corruption campaign (Li 1995:58-61), a series of codes of ethics designed to set guidelines for Party and state bureaucracy was established. It included the first and second "five rules" on anti-corruption and self-restraint by leading cadres, developed by the Party's Central Commission for Discipline Inspection in August 1993 and March 1994 respectively. Both codes prohibit cadres at or above the county level from getting involved in commercial activities; accepting such benefits as gifts, bonds, credit cards and club memberships; using luxury cars; buying houses at special prices; squandering public money; and defaulting on state loans. Later, four additions were made to the two "five rules." The added codes that forbid state cadres from building private houses, using vehicle license plates designated for police or foreigners, reimbursing entertainment, and attending banquets that may influence official business.

Apparently, these codes failed to deter unhealthy bureaucratic behavior effectively. The authorities decided to come up with more specific codes targeting certain aspects of corruption. In September 1994, the General Office of the Party's Central Committee and the General Office of the State Council issued "The Rules on the Use and Administration of Vehicles in Party and Government Institutions" (*World Journal,* October 17, 1994). Vehicles supplied to ministers, governors, and officials at that level should not be equipped with engines of over 3.0 liters. Those ranked below them such as vice-ministers or vice-governors may only use vehicles with engines of under 2.5 liters and must gradually switch to domestic ones.

In December of that year, the State Council issued specific rules concerning gifts. No government officials may accept gifts worth more than two hundred *Yuan* in their official dealings with foreign nationals or organizations. Months later, the General Office of the Party's Central Committee and the General Office of the State Council also issued "The Rules on Registration of Gifts in Domestic Activities among Party and Government Personnel" (*Renmin Ribao,* Overseas Edition, May 19, 1995).

Like millions of average Chinese, many state cadres consider the newly opened stock market a shortcut to quick money and want to make a profit there with the help of their networks. To bar them from playing in the stock market, the Party's Central Commission for Discipline Inspection decided in August 1993 to ban Party and government officials from stock trading and other market pursuits.

In order to keep track of bureaucrats' personal financial situations, the General Office of the Party's Central Committee and the General Office of the State Council, in April 1995, issued "The Rules on Filing an Income Disclosure by Leading Party and Government Cadres at the County/Division Level" (*Renmin Ribao,* Overseas Edition, May 25, 1995). Though a semi-annual disclosure is now required of those covered by the codes, the information remains confidential, which raises doubts about the effectiveness of the measure.

There are also codes on travel abroad. Late in 1993, the authorities issued a notice, attempting to slow the flow of state-funded delegations of cadres going abroad. Still, groups of visiting Chinese government officials are often seen in many tourist destinations in the United States and many other countries.

How to curb the bureaucratic addiction of eating and drinking wantonly at the public expense is a perennial problem in China. The central government issued thirty-two directives in this regard in 1992. They were of no avail. The cost of state-funded banquets reached a whopping 100 billion *Yuan* in 1993 (Huang 1995:93-97). Indeed, "The Rules on Barring Industrial and Commercial Administrators from Attending Banquets which may Influence the Proper Conducting of Official Business," issued in early 1995, were just an additional attempt to tackle the vexing bureaucratic pathology (*Renmin Ribao,* Overseas Edition, March 22, 1995). The codes cover only cadres at bureaus of industry and commerce. However, many Party and government agencies at the central level soon followed suit and established their own rules on accepting invitations to banquets.

In early 1997, the Office of Law and Regulations under the CCP's Central Commission for Inspection published a booklet entitled *Codes of Conduct and Related Rules and Regulations for a Honest Government* with a first printing of 300,000 copies. An inclusion in the volume is a 1997 circular issued by the General Offices of the CCP and the Central Government stipulating that all leading cadres at or above the level of deputy county head had to report to their superiors on important matters in their personal lives. Apparently, the authorities felt that more measures were required to keep state bureaucracy in line, no matter how intrusive they might be.

The official request of a self-report was hardly sufficient in restraining corruption. Therefore, in November 1998, the CCP Central Committee and the State Council issued a document entitled *The Stipulations on the Establishment of the System of Responsibility for the Atmosphere within the Party and Honest Government*. The document consists of five chapters. What merits special attention is Chapter Four devoted to the "investigation of the responsibility" (*zeren zhuijiu*) of those leading cadres who are held accountable for: (a) failing to stop, probe into, and/or to deal with unethical behavior properly in their jurisdiction; (b) having cases in their jurisdiction that caused serious damage to state property; (c) failing to recruit or promote well-behaved administrators; (d) inciting, instructing, or even forcing subordinates to behave unethically; (e) inciting, instructing, or conniving at subordinates' interference with investigation of bureaucratic unethical behavior; (f) concealing the knowledge of unethical behavior by spouses, children, or colleagues and failing to report it to the proper authority.

Any government official who is found having any of the above problems will be subject to either disciplinary measures by the Party or criminal sanction by the judiciary or both (*Renmin Ribao,* December 4, 1998). By holding administrators accountable for their subordinates' unethical behavior, the post-Mao leadership was trying to send another, more serious, signal to the state bureaucrats that they had better watch their words and deeds, as well as those of their subordinates, with great care or else neither party may escape punishment.

The behavior of a number of judges was equally problematic. There were judges who were actually "illiterate, knew nothing about laws and behaved like gangsters" (*Renmin Ribao,* Overseas Edition, November 2, 2001). In October 2001, the Supreme People's Court issued *The Basic Codes of Professional Ethics for Judges* in order to establish uniform behavioral guidelines for the nation's more than two hundred thousands judges. The codes stipulate that judges must ensure judicial integrity, improve judicial efficiency, be honest in performing official duties, uphold judicial protocol, strengthen self-cultivation, and restrain activities in after-hours. Clearly, the codes seek to govern judges' behavior in and out of court, behavior beyond employment, as well as behavior after retirement.

In February 2002, the Ministry of Personnel issued *The Codes of Conduct for State Civil Servants*. The codes cover eight areas, asking employees to do the following:

(a) be firm politically;
(b) be loyal to the state;
(c) be diligent in administration;
(d) be respectful to laws and regulations in conducting official duties;
(e) be steadfast and innovative;
(f) be honest and upright;
(g) be united and cooperative;
(h) be correct in behavior (*Renmin Ribao,* February 27, 2002).

In sum, all of these codes of ethics, designed to promote a positive image of public administration in an era of reform, have illustrated the efforts by the post-Mao China's leadership to deal with a new, recalcitrant administrative culture.

IV. Positive and Negative Impact

The anti-corruption campaign and the efforts to reestablish an honest administrative culture did produce some positive impact. On the side of the state, the bureaucratic prerogatives began to decline. As part of the "new class" described by

Djilas, the government bureaucrats used to enjoy plenty of privileges without restraint, including the privilege to take into their own possession and dispose of state property freely (Djilas 1957:37-69). The ethical codes serve as unequivocal warnings for them that such privileges can no longer be taken for granted. The state cadres now have to think twice before they act as even high-ranking officials can be caught and prosecuted if they are involved in corruption. For example, according to *Zhongguo Xinwen Zhoukan* (*China News Weekly),* the number of high-ranking administrators who had been prosecuted kept climbing. The state investigation netted twelve officials at the provincial/ministerial level in 1998. The next year witnessed seventeen cadres at that level being charged with corruption. The number grew to twenty-two in 2000. In addition to Cheng Kejie, who was mentioned earlier in the chapter, that year also saw the imprisonment of Qin Changdian, the former Vice Chairman of the Standing Committee of the Municipal People's Congress of Chongqing; Zhou Wenji, the former Vice Chairman of the Region's Chinese People's Political Consultative Conference of Ningxia; Li Daqiang, the former Vice Governor of Hubei; Xu Penghang, the former Vice Chairman of the State Commission on Science, and Industry for National Defense; and Wu Wenying, former Chairwoman of the National Association of Textile, to name just a few (*World Journal,* November 17, 2001).

Moreover, the anti-corruption campaign has also rendered bureaucratic personal connections less functional. The informal organization connections through years of friendship, courtship, or bribery might no longer be reliable in rescuing them from trouble. When investigators searched two villas belonging to Mu Suixin, former Mayor of Shengyang, the capital city of Liaoning Province, they found $6 million worth of gold bars hidden in the walls, 150 Rolex watches, computer files documenting years of illegal activities, etc. Few were surprised at the finding as "corruption is routinely the top complaint of people queried in internal government polls" (Pomfret 2002). The case involved more than one hundred people including Mu and Ma Xiangdong, the former Executive Vice Mayor. What puzzled most of the observers was the unprecedented decision by the Central Government to have the case tried in two cities: Shengyang and Nanjing, the capital city of Jiangsu Province located hundreds miles north of Shengyang. It turned out that Ma's wife Zhang Yafei, Vice President of a medical college and Principal of a hospital, was so skillful in taking advantage of their local connections that Ma, though in custody, remained well informed about the intentions and strategies of the prosecution. In order to stay informed, she spent over one million *Yuan* on bribery within the period of one year. Authorities were forced to relocate the trial to another city, far away from Ma and Zhang's network of informal organization (*Yangzi Wanbao*, February 19, 2002).

On the side of the society, the public became aware of behavioral guidelines against which they could measure government officials' performance. They began to take the role of watching their civil servants more seriously. Their voices became louder. They grew more courageous in targeting bureaucratic corruption. For example, the July 7 mine accident in Nandan County of Guangxi Region involving over eighty deaths was kept secret for more than ten days. It was the news media that managed to break the cover-up and made it public. Several principal leaders of the county government were arrested as a result (*Beijing Qingnian Bao,* December 9, 2001).

There was also some negative impact. For many in society, codes seemed to be useless. As more corrupted bureaucrats were exposed, the public could not help asking whether the ethical codes just remained on paper. Moreover, the more the public learned about the seamy side of the regime, about bureaucrats' scandalous behavior, and about the administration's ignominious culture, the less confidence the public had in the state bureaucracy.

As for China's law enforcement, the picture looks even more dismal. The prime tool in the battle to control bureaucratic misconduct ought to be law enforcement. When the law is upheld, when everybody has equal access to it, and when the public trusts enforcement agencies, only then will China be able to "do much to clean up the rest of government and keep all other public officials honest" (Caiden 1990:58-60). Unfortunately, agencies of China's law enforcement, which constitute a major force in the struggle against bureaucratic corruption, have become no less corrupt. For example, in comparison with 1994, officers in law enforcement that were involved in criminal cases increased by almost forty per cent in 1995 (*Renmin Ribao,* Overseas Edition, March 13, 1996). In the Xiamen smuggling case, which has so far implicated more than two hundred officials of the municipal government including almost the entire Party and government leadership of the city, the Director of the Municipal Bureau of State Security has had the audacity to assist in a deputy mayor's escape (*World Journal,* January 12, 2000). Meanwhile, the number of corrupt bureaucrats who manage to escape from investigation and prosecution is anyone's guess. And the question many people have is why isn't China's administrative culture improving in light of the enactment of an increasing number of ethical codes?

V. Whither China's Administrative Culture in the Twenty-First Century?

The newly promulgated codes of ethics have obviously not resolved the issue of a recalcitrant administrative culture in post-Mao China. Though these codes have been widely publicized, the situation continues to deteriorate steadily. A main reason why the enactment of ethical codes failed to bring about an honest administrative culture is the lack of a multitudinous approach to the issue. Mark Nadel and Frances Rourke believe that administrative behavior is a function of a variety of factors. Therefore, it requires work from different perspectives. A single strategy cannot improve administrative culture. To refine administrative ethics, they have listed four areas that must be addressed. There must be efforts coming from such external/formal actors as political executives, elected legislatures, courts, and ombudsmen. There must be external/informal pressures applied to the bureaucracy by public opinion, media, pressure groups, electorate, and university public administration programs. There should also be certain internal/formal means such as public hearings and inquiries that could help keep government officials accountable. Finally, internal/informal measures such as professional standards and codes must be taken in order to serve as guidelines for administrative culture (Nadel and Rourke 1975:416).

Though the development of a new administrative culture in post-Mao China over the past twenty years has been far from encouraging, and though many of the steps taken by the authorities have failed to curb negative bureaucratic behavior, it should be pointed out that both the state and society have realized the importance of an honest administrative culture. There were efforts on both sides to try to rein in the nation's humongous state bureaucracy. For example, public hearings were held to receive public input on pending policy and/or programs. A July 2001 State Planning Commission decision stipulated that certain prices must be decided upon after public hearings. It gained such popularity that it became one of the nation's twenty-one hottest terms in 2001 (http://www.peopledaily.com.cn). China's electorate is no longer an obedient subject. There were nearly half a million cases in which the average citizens took the government officials to court in the past five years. The percentage of lost cases declined from 36 percent in 1992 to 29 percent in 2001 (http://www.peopledaily.com.cn). Open meetings were experimented with in the municipal government of Xiamen, a coastal city of Province Fujian, in order to open the decision-making process of government to the public and to help the public retain control over those who are supposed to be their servants (*World Journal,* June 30, 2003). The pressure on administration by the society could no longer be ignored.

Mr. Yanyong Jiang, a retired medical doctor in a military hospital, decided to do the whistleblowing when the government claimed that the SARS was not spreading dangerously in the country (Beech 2003:63). His brave action shocked the world, brought down the nation's Minister of Health and the Mayor of Beijing, and, more importantly, led to change in bureaucratic behavior and administrative culture (Ratnesar and Beech 2003:54-56). The case has had several implications.

First, external pressure from media did have an impact. (*Time* magazine broke the story fist.) Second, internal professional standards encouraged employees like Dr. Jiang to follow the guidelines in fighting against bureaucratic abuse of power. Third, external pressure in the form of politicians' involvement, in this case the involvement of the new generation of China's leadership headed by Party's General Sectary Hu Jintao and Prime Minister Wen Jiabao, could be considered essential in facilitating change toward a healthy and honest administrative culture (Pomfret 2003).

It seems that the new generation of China's leadership headed by Hu and Wen have realized the importance of a healthy and honest administrative culture within the state bureaucratic apparatus. They have also showed their willingness to challenge bureaucrats' resentment and resistance. In arguing for the possibility of change, Stephen Robbins suggests that "changing an organization's culture is extremely difficult, but cultures can be changed" (Robbins 2001:530). He has also listed certain conditions required to bring about cultural change: a dramatic crisis; turnover in leadership; young and small organizations; and weak culture. In his view, "cultural change is most likely to take place when most or all" of these conditions exist (Robbins 2001:530). SARS certainly posed a dramatic crisis for China in 2003. The Party's Sixteenth Congress in November 2002 resulted in leadership turnover. Hu and Wen emerged as the nation's top leaders. And, leadership, whether in public or private sectors, is seen as a key factor in the maintenance or changing of organizational culture (Grosenick and Gibson 2001:249). Clearly, the existence of these two conditions serve as powerful catalysts for the movement toward a healthy and honest administrative culture in China.

On the other hand, the nation's bureaucratic machinery is a colossal organization. A culture nurtured over the past two decades and perpetuated by a large number of members of the bureaucracy is by no means amenable to easy and quick change. Therefore, the cultural change in China's public administration is likely to be a tremendously painful undertaking. It remains to be seen whether the new generation of China's leadership will be able to beat the odds and transform the nation's administrative culture successfully. Though setbacks may occur in the years to come, there is little doubt that at least some improvement will take place eventually. To borrow from Robbins again, "cultural change is a lengthy process—measured in years rather than in months. But cultures can be changed!" (Robbins 2001:530).

REFERENCES

Time. 1985. "An Interview with Deng Xiaoping." November 4, p.35.
Beech, Hannah. 2003. "Unmasking a Crisis." *Time*, April 21, 2003, p.63.

Bollens, John, and Henry J. Schmandt. 1979. *Political Corruption: Power, Money, and Sex.* Pacific Palisades, California: Palisades Publishers.

Caiden, Gerald. 1990. "Abuse of Public Trust: Fact or Way of Life?" *USA Today Magazine*, July 1990, pp.58-60.

——. 2001. "Corruption and Governance." Pp. 21-26 in *Where Corruption Lives,* edited by Gerald E. Caiden, O. P. Dwivedi, and Joseph Jabbra. Bloomfield, Connecticut: Kumarian Press.

Djilas, Milovan. 1957. *The New Class: An Analysis of the Communist System.* New York: Praeger Publishers.

Grosenick, Leigh E. and Pamela A. Gibson. 2001. "Government Ethics and Organizational Culture." Pp. 249 in *Handbook of Administrative Ethics,* 2d ed, edited by Terry L. Cooper New York: Marcel Dekker.

Huang, Bailian. 1995. "*Lun Shehuizhuyi Shichang Jingji Tiaojian xia Fanfubai de Jiben Silu*" (On the Basic Thoughts of Anti-corruption under the Conditions of Socialist Market Economy). *Shehui Kexue Yanjiu*, April 1995, pp.16-20.

Kuhn, Anthony. 2000. "China Executes Ex-Official for Corruption." *Los Angeles Times,* September 15.

Li, Xueqin. 1995. "Fan Fubai de Qushi yu Qianjing" (The Trends and Prospects of Anti-corruption). *Qianxian*, April 1995, pp.11-14.

Li, Zijing. 2003. "ZhongJiwei Jinghu Jing Zhe Liao Cha Heiqian" (The Central Commission for Discipline Inspection Work Teams Moved into Beijing, Zhejiang, and Liaoning to Look Into Black Money). *The Trend Magazine,* July 2003, p.14.

Luo, Bing. 2003. "*Hu Jintao Tancheng Zhizheng Weiji*" (Hu Jintao Admits to Regime Crisis). *Cheng Ming,* August, 2003, p.9.

Ma, Stephen K. 2001. "The Culture of Corruption in Post-Mao China." Pp. 145-157 in *Where Corruption Lives,* edited by Gerald E. Caiden, O. P. Dwivedi, and Joseph Jabbra. Bloomfield, Connecticut: Kumarian Press.

Nadel, Mark, and Frances Rourke. 1975. "Bureaucracies." P. 416 in *Handbook of Political Science,* Vol.5, edited by Fred Greenstein and Nelson Polsby. Reading, MA: Addison-Wesley.

Ott, J.S. 1989. *The Organizational Culture Perspective.* Chicago: Dorsey Press.

Peters, B. Guy. 1989. *The Politics of Bureaucracy*, 3d ed. New York: Longman.

Plant, Jeremy F. 1994. "Codes of Ethics." In *Handbook of Administrative Ethics,* edited by Terry L. Cooper. New York: Marcel Dekker.

Pomfret, John. 2002. "One Corrupt City Reflects Scourge Plaguing China." *Washington Post*, March 6, 2002.

——. 2003. "Outbreak Gave China's Hu an Opening: President Responded to Pressure Inside and Outside Country on SARS." *Washington Post,* May 13, 2003.

Pye, Lucian W. 1984. *China: An Introduction,* 3d ed. Boston: Little, Brown & Company.

Ratnesar, Romesh and Hannah Beech. 2003. "Tale of Two Countries: A Time Investigation into What Went Wrong." *Time,* May 5, 2003.

Robbins, Stephen P. 2001. *Organizational Behavior*, 9th ed. Upper Saddle River, New Jersey, Prentice-Hall.

Waldo, Dwight. 1994. "Public Administration and Ethics." Pp. 176-190 in *Current Issues in Public Administration,* 5th ed, edited by Frederick S. Lane. New York: St. Martin's Press.

White III, Lynn T. 1989. *Politics of Chaos: The Organizational Causes of Violence in China's Cultural Revolution.* Princeton, New Jersey: Princeton University Press.

Wilson, James Q. 1989. *Bureaucracy: What Government Agencies Do and Why They Do It.* New York: Basic Books.

Wolf Jr., Charles. 2001. "Communist Ideologues Struggle to Make Room for Capitalists." *Los Angeles Times,* February 11.

Chinese Language Newspapers & Journals

Beijing Qingnian Bao
Fuyin Baokan Ziliao (Zhongguo Zhengzhi)
Renmin Ribao
Renmin Ribao (Overseas Edition)
World Journal
Yangzi Wanbao
Zhongguo Xinwen Zhoukan

Website

http://www.peopledaily.com.cn/GB/shenghuo/76/123/20020116/649280.html
http://www.peopledaily.com.cn/GB/shehui/46/20030215/923792.html

Chapter 9

PUBLIC SERVICE REFORMS AND THE NEW PARTNERSHIP ON AFRICAN DEVELOPMENT (NEPAD): MOVING FROM TACTICAL TO STRATEGIC RESPONSES

Bamidele Olowu and Ejeviome Eloho Otobo

In 2001, African countries embarked upon an important development initiative that is aimed at transforming the continent's prospects for economic progress. The New Partnership for African Development (NEPAD) is conceived as a partnership between African leaders and their own people, on one hand, and Africa and the rest of the international community, on the other. NEPAD is the latest in a long line of comprehensive programs for Africa's development adopted by African governments. The previous major plans included the Lagos Plan for Action, 1980; the African Priority Programme for Economic Recovery, 1985; the Abuja Treaty establishing the African Economic Community, 1991; and the Cairo Agenda for Action 1995.[1] NEPAD is, however, distinguished from its predecessors by many important features as will be described in the next section.

This paper reviews the objectives of NEPAD and highlights the implications for the reform of public services in the continent, drawing particular attention to the need to restore leadership in the public service, generally, and in the civil service, in particular.

African public services were not always as parlous as they are at present. They displayed high institutional performance and pride in the immediate post-independence years. Even so, African countries felt the need to undertake public service reforms very early after attaining independence, in an effort to respond to the policy needs of that era. Public services in the region have experienced two broad waves of reform.

In the immediate post-independence period, many countries attempted to transform the colonial-oriented public service into a development-oriented one. This meant centralizing and expanding public service dominance over the economy and society. This was the first wave of administrative reforms that swept the continent and much has been written about the achievements and limits of this wave (see African Association for Public Administration and Management 1984).

It would seem that much greater gains were made in changing the personnel from expatriate to indigenous personnel than in transforming the organizational structure and operational capacities for improved performance. In Kenya, for instance, the Ndegwa Commission (1970-1971) was expected to restructure the public service as was the Udoji Commission (1972-1974), in Nigeria. Though ambitious in terms of their recommendations, no serious restructuring of public services occurred and the impact on performance was minimal.

Yet, they succeeded remarkably with respect to Africanization. Tanzania, for instance, a country that inherited a small, educated population at independence, was able to raise the proportion of its nationals holding senior and middle level positions from 12 percent to 90 percent within 10 years (1961-1970). However, such rapid Africanization also meant that the top leadership of the public service was not able to predict or manage the economic crises that followed the two oil shocks in the 1970s. The result was negative growth and a shortage of production, which led to the adoption of structural adjustment programs as touted by the international financial institutions (African Association for Public Administration and Management 1984). An important characteristic of these first wave reforms is that they were formulated and implemented by African governments themselves.

With the structural adjustment programs (SAPs) came the second wave of public sector reforms in Africa. Whereas the first wave of reforms sought to expand and centralize operations within the public service, the new reforms sought to achieve the opposite results: to reduce size and scope of the public service and reduce the cost of operations. The second wave of reforms has been classified into "three generations" by the World Bank, an institution that has played a crucial role in these donor-led reforms. First generation reforms were preoccupied with fiscal balance, primarily the privatization of public enterprises and reduction in other public services. Later, they included personnel retrenchment and the rigorous census of personnel to eliminate the so-called "ghost workers." These reforms did not achieve much. In fact, many believe that the reforms might have harmed the civil services as they facilitated the exit of the few available senior personnel who were the first to leave the public services (Lindauer and Numberg 1994; Haque and Aziz 1999; Olowu 1999).

Second-generation reforms attempted to build capacity. Organizations such as the African Capacity Building Foundation (ACBF) were created to advance this cause in the region. Essentially, these reforms sought to link civil service reforms (CSR) with wider reforms in the public sector, especially decentralization and, to some extent, the reform of the judicial and legislative organs of government. They also attempted to refocus the remit of government organizations to only those that were considered essential activities that could not be conducted by other non-state organs. This meant the enhancement of policy-making and implementation capacities of governments to provide an enabling environment for achieving social goals through inter-organizational cooperation rather than the direct production of services by government agencies. Human resource development, including training and sensitization workshops, and the creation of policy centers within and outside the government were some of the hallmarks of this set of reforms.

This has led to a third generation of reforms, ones that focus on the delivery of services through delegated agencies of large, centralized ministries. These reforms reflected the influence of the so-called new public management (NPM), which advocated subjecting some public sector operations to the discipline of the market place or contracting out to markets and/or delegating some public sector functions into separate organizational entities. The major institutional embodiment of this approach has been the executive agency model (Adamolekun and Kiragu 1999; Stevens and Teggenmann 2003).

One consensus from these reforms is that they have failed to attract and retain the brightest and the best in the civil services. Countries in the region have continued to experience continuous internal and external brain drain from the civil service. Whereas second wave reforms have focused on how to remove excess junior and unrequired skills from the service, the task of attracting and/or retaining the critical required skills have not been properly focused until recently in a few countries. The good news, though, is that there is some agreement that this issue constitutes an important, if not the most crucial, aspect of PSR in Africa (Haque and Aziz 1999; Olowu 1999, 2003; Kiragu and Mukandala 2003).

A recent review of the administrative and civil service reforms programs initiated by the World Bank notes that only about one third achieved satisfactory outcomes. And, even when desirable, the outcomes were often not sustainable. Most of this work has been in the Africa region and the review also explains that "downsizing and capacity building initiatives often failed to produce permanent reductions in civil service size and to overcome capacity constraints in economic management and service delivery. In later reform programs there is little evidence that civil servants began to 'own' and adhere to formal rules such as codes of ethics" (World Bank Website 2003:1).

In this chapter, we argue that the measures being taken reflect a tactical rather than a strategic approach to solving the important problem of building capable public services. The main argument being offered here can be summarized briefly: if NEPAD is to succeed, a new approach to the reform of the public service is needed. The primary focus of such reforms must be the civil service, the administrative core of the public service. It should have a strategic orientation, drawing on some current best practices from around the world. This chapter, therefore, starts by reviewing the objectives of NEPAD and its implications for national level governance and assesses the second wave public sector reforms. The article then outlines some crucial elements for a new, effective approach to public service reforms. Though the review of the reforms will examine the public service broadly defined, encompassing the civil service, public enterprises, and local government; the discussion of the strategic response will focus exclusively on the civil service.

Objectives of NEPAD and Implications for National Level Governance

The New Partnership for Africa's Development was inspired by the vision of launching Africa on the path of sustainable growth and development at the beginning of the new millennium. It is the product of a merger of two separate proposals: the Millennium Partnership for African Recovery Programme (MAP) devised by the Presidents of Algeria, South Africa, and Nigeria; and the Omega Plan, proposed by the President of Senegal. The merged plan was presented to, and adopted at, the Lusaka Summit of the Organization of African Unity (OAU)[2] in July 2001. Initiating this plan at this high political level is one of the outstanding features of NEPAD.

NEPAD is a comprehensive, integrated framework for Africa's development. NEPAD outlines a program of action focused on key priorities in Africa's development. NEPAD's main long-term objective is "to eradicate poverty in Africa and to place African countries, both individually and collectively, on the path of sustainable growth and development and thus halt the marginalisation of Africa in the globalization process" (NEPAD 2001:14). A second long-term objective is to promote the role of women in all activities. Its major goal is to achieve and sustain an average gross domestic product growth rate of over 7 percent per annum for the next 15 years. It is also committed to the achievement of the Millennium Development Goals in Africa by 2015. Specifically, it is committed to cutting the proportion of people living in extreme poverty by half; enrolling all children of school age in primary schools; making progress toward gender equality and eliminating gender disparities in primary school enrolment; reducing infant and child mortality by two-thirds; reducing maternal mortality by three-quarters; providing access to all who need reproductive health services; and implementing national strategies for sustainable development by 2005, so as to reverse loss of environmental resources by 2015 (NEPAD 2001:14).

NEPAD acknowledges certain pre-requisites for sustainable development. These include peace, security, democracy, good governance, human rights, and sound economic management (NEPAD 2001). To reinforce democracy and governance and facilitate effective implementation of the various standards and codes, NEPAD targets capacity building initiatives focusing on administrative reforms, strengthening parliamentary oversight, promoting participatory decision-making, adopting effective measures to combat corruption, and undertaking judicial reforms (NEPAD 2001).

NEPAD also identifies selected sectoral priorities. These include infrastructure development (encompassing ICT, energy, transport, and water sanitation); human resources development (education, skills development, reversing the brain drain, and health); agriculture; the environment; culture; science and technology; capital flows and market access.

NEPAD differs from previous development initiatives in giving explicit recognition to governance as an important factor in economic development. An innovative and central feature of NEPAD is the establishment of African Peer Review Mechanism[3] (APRM), an institutional mechanism for monitoring and reporting on member States' compliance with the codes and standards on political, economic, and corporate governance. The APRM aims to foster the adoption of policies, standards, and practices that enhance political stability and growth. The African Peer Review Mechanism will be based on a number of indicators encompassing four areas: democracy and political governance; economic governance and management; corporate governance; and socioeconomic development. The peer review will be conducted in five stages. The first stage will entail an analysis of the governance and development environment in the country to be reviewed; the second stage will be a visit to the country by the panel of eminent persons' review mission; the third is the preparation of the mission findings and discussion of the draft report with the representatives of the Government of the country being reviewed; the fourth is the discussion and consideration of the findings by the Heads of State and Government of the participating countries; and the final stage involves the public presentation of the review reports.

The implementation of NEPAD poses several major challenges for African countries. The United Nations (2002) has highlighted three of these. The first is building and strengthening the capacity of African countries to implement the program. National capacity is an important precondition of ownership and requires a critical mass of experts to plan, manage, and deliver the desired outcomes. A related challenge is to translate NEPAD priorities into policies and programs at the regional, sub-regional and country levels. This requires commitment as well as capacity to implement. A third major challenge is mobilizing financial resources in order to implement the programs. These challenges will affect African public services, which are the main instruments for the implementation of NEPAD.

In as much as the public service is the institution of choice—indeed, it is the key instrument in realizing the objectives of NEPAD—African governments face an urgent need to build well functioning and capable public services that can better support the state to achieve the goal of better governance and sustainable development in Africa.

The Mixed Record of Public Service Reform

Programs of public sector management reform abound in all segments of the public service: privatization of public enterprises, decentralization to local governments, and different shades of civil service reform (CSR). The most significant achievements have been in public enterprise reform and some countries (e.g., Uganda, South Africa, Nigeria, and Tanzania) have decentralized to local governments or to executive agencies. The latter have become important elements of the administrative innovational landscape in countries such as Zambia, Ghana, South Africa, Tanzania, and Kenya, with some outstanding results and lingering problems: a lack of required autonomy, compromised accountability, the unpredictability of politics, etc. (see Phiri-Mundia 2003; Mutahaba and Kiragu 2002 and Table 1 for a tentative balance sheet). Except in a few selected countries (e.g., South Africa, Mauritius, Botswana, Seychelles, Namibia, and a few Francophone countries that spend a substantial sum on their civil services), these reforms have not succeeded in halting the continuing degradation of the public service in terms of qualitative leadership. The problems are particularly severe in the civil service. Recent surveys across the continent note that top African bureaucrats feel they are no longer responsible for the formulation of public policies for their countries as that assignment has effectively been taken over by Bretton Woods Institutions (BWIs). This is in sharp contrast to their counterparts in Asia and Latin America. Furthermore, as wage levels and quality personnel decline, bribery and corruption levels have increased. This has been accompanied by a decline of service provision and delivery in the majority of countries (Court, Kristen, and Weder 1999; Lienert 1998).

It seems many national governments do not appreciate the seriousness of public service degradation. In many countries, there is a continuing fascination with new policy initiatives—every new government promises change—but little attention is devoted to developing an effective instrument for translating these ideas into concrete policies and programs that positively affect the lives of citizens. Studies of the policy process in two African countries showed that over two-thirds of cabinet decisions were never implemented (Schiavo-Campo and Sundaram 2001:82; Garnett et al 1996; see also Olowu and Sako 2002).

Compared with all other sectors of the public service—public enterprises and local governments—it can be argued that reforms of the civil service have had the least impact or success. The severe hemorrhaging of the civil service, especially at the very top, has continued unabated. Even countries considered "good performers" by the BWIs—Ghana and Uganda—have only improved "slightly but do not seem to perform particularly well" (Stevens and Teggenmann 2003).

However, the civil service, in particular the higher civil service, is expected to perform three crucial roles: assist in formulating policies including the appropriate regulatory framework for state and non-state institutions, program the implementation of policies and programs, and ensure the accountable use of public resources (Table 2). In other words, higher civil servants provide leadership for the rest of the public service at national as well at regional and local levels.

What makes this loss devastating is that the civil services in many African countries used to be prime performers. A recent study of Ugandan and Nigerian public services shows that these two countries whose civil services are still relatively in a bad shape today were actually regarded in the late 1950s and early 1960s as excellent performers. In those golden years, they had relatively small civil services that had a strong commitment to the key attributes of meritocracy, objectivity, excellence, and highly competitive conditions of service. But politicization by single party and military autocracies, followed by several years of effort to roll back the state, have led to a severe loss of the best and brightest employees as well as a loss in pride and performance in public service generally (Olowu 2001).

Most countries have reacted to this problem tactically. They have created service enclaves or executive agencies that separate important services from this overall decline of the civil service. In Africa, the revenue agencies have been prime targets (Devas et al 2001). These are separated from the rest of the civil service and given performance contracts. Some other countries have continued to seek expatriate replacement, mostly through donor-financed technical assistance. The problems of this approach have been well documented (Berg 1993). Some other countries have created senior executive services (SES) to provide leadership; the implementation of this model in Ghana has not been particularly successful (Adamolekun 2002; Stevens and Teggenmann 2003).

Diagnosing the Failure of Old and Current CSRs—Tactical Approaches

The problem of current African CSRs is primarily one of defective design. First, their factual basis is wrong; African civil services are not simply overextended, they are poorly structured. Africa has the least number of civil servants per population among the world's regions: 2 percent of the population compared with the OECD's 7.7 percent and the global average of 4.7 percent (Schiavo-Campo and Sundaram 2001). Second, the diagnosis and prognosis of current CSRs are equally wrong-headed; the primary task is not to reduce cost but to raise investment in favor of the civil service and raise productivity or performance in the civil services. Indeed, there is a need to reduce numbers, to eliminate the large numbers of low-paid officials who should not have been there in the first place. There is also a need to redefine the scope and mission of public service organizations so that some of the tasks currently performed poorly by central government organs can be privatized, decentralized, or outsourced (Olowu 1999, 2003: Smoke 2003).

However, downsizing alone will not result in any substantial reduction of costs as new professional and management skills need to be brought into the service. Such new skills will be required not only for the civil service but also for an important, but often neglected, source of expansion of the public service: the growth of regulatory bodies that have been established in African countries in the aftermath of the privatization of public enterprises.

Recent research on the subject shows that poor pay results in the loss of the top cadres of the public service (Kiragu and Mukandala 2003). However, this is not the only consideration. Another factor is excessive politicization of the top echelon of the public service. Fortunately, for many countries, the latter problem is being corrected with the return to pluralist democracy. There is no doubt that this process must be deepened through structural and educational strategies aimed at replacing a culture of autocracy with one of democracy. Recognizing that it took over a century for Western countries to institutionalize meritocracy, democratizing governments in Africa should be encouraged and should recommit themselves to the articulation of clear ethical norms that are both democratic and developmental for the management of the civil and public services. None of the above can happen without a highly mobilized citizenry and civil society campaigning for better public services. Public services in all parts of the world have tended to improve as a result of pressure from the public. (For history of for instance: British, American and French civil services, see Young 1958, Mosher 1968, Rouban 1975). It is this public voice that needs to be enhanced in Africa, a continent familiar with repression where those in power have always abused the citizens' trust. Hence, what is required is a polycentric political structure; distinct and autonomous roles for each unit of governance; effective means of contestation and checks and balances within the framework of a unified legal order; and strong incentives for rational cooperative action. African Ministers of Public Service have come up with a set of public service ethical codes, but these will be realized only within the framework of effective structures and systems.

Toward a New Genre of Public Service Reform

Any credible new effort aimed at public service reform in Africa must therefore innovatively grapple with six major issues: (a) funding of the public service, (b) pay for public servants, (c) recruitment, (d) public service capacity building, (e) enhancing the process of policy making and coordination, and (f) redesigning external support for public sector reforms. Most of these will sound like some of the key elements of current reform efforts, which reflect the influence of the new public management (NPM) on the design and implementation of public sector reforms that has spread from the industrialized nations to Africa. To the extent that NPM focuses on the importance of entrepreneurial managers in the public service, we agree with the idea that new and sustained effort must be given to how to attract and retain effective political and administrative leadership for the African civil service. It is the sine qua non for reforming public institutions in the knowledge-based twenty-first century, as is already being articulated and promoted for OECD countries (OECD 2001). The problem is that reform agendas for African countries did not place a premium on this issue until the most recent times and even then only in a few countries.

Funding of the Public Service

Increased funding is imperative to re-building Africa's civil service, which should focus on three critical areas: higher pay, institutional and human capacity building, and the modernization of office infrastructure. The combination of the economic crisis of the 1980s and cutback management of the early phase of the second generation of reform has left a legacy of under-funding and neglect in these areas. Instead of focusing on how to mobilize additional resources, donor-initiated/supported reforms have tended to focus disproportionately on how to reduce expenditures. The result is that the typical African civil service today exhibits the characteristics of low pay, antiquated office equipment, and weak capacity for policy analysis, planning, and implementation. It is a measure of the dismal record of the current reform efforts that they have not wrought significant positive changes in these critical aspects of the civil service. This needs to be reversed.

One consequence of the lack of critical mass of policy analytical and technical capacity in African civil services is the fairly high dependence on foreign experts to undertake the task of policy analysis, project formulation, and implementation. Initially, technical experts were seconded from bilateral donors as part of their technical cooperation programs, but multilateral financial institutions also increasingly provide technical experts.

Finding financing sources for the scale and level of investment required in the civil service in the short, medium, and long terms ought to be a major pre-occupation of any serious reform of the civil service. Of course, quality civil services are expensive. Yet, they are necessary. Possible financing sources, presently, have been sought principally from donor partners and international finance institutions, but this has been at the price of adopting reform ideas that undermine rather than build sustainable capacity in the long term. There are several possible avenues for increasing funding for re-building African civil services. One is to devote some percentage of the proceeds from privatization. A second possibility is for Africa's development partners to convert technical assistance resources to capacity building in Africa,[4] with much of that devoted to civil service capacity building. These two sources will be necessary for the short to medium term. In the longer term, there has to be a more deliberate effort to commit tax resources to development of the civil service. Data from the World Bank's development indicators (2002) show that among the world's regions, African countries have substantial levels of inequality (second only to Latin America). Large numbers of rich, informal, and private sector operators are not captured in the tax net; present tax sources are indirect forms. In other words, there is much greater potential here, even within the present income levels, but most governments are reluctant to embark on these activities as they might undermine their own economic interests (e.g., higher properties and income).

More importantly, such a move would mean that they may be forced to be more accountable to their own citizens rather than to donors and multilateral financial institutions—as is the case presently (Moore 1998; Rakner and Golpen 2003).

Pay for Public Servants

Higher pay to civil servants is one possible positive outcome from improved funding for the civil service, as highlighted above. But the need for better pay for civil servants bears particular emphasis. As the World Bank has rightly observed in discussing the East Asian experience in building their civil service, "in bureaucracies, as in nearly everything else, you get what you pay for…in general the more favorably the total public sector package, the better the quality of the bureaucracy" (World Bank 1993:175). Low pay in the African civil service has been a major factor in the loss of bright professional staff to the private sector, research institutions, and international organizations. Low pay, together with the lack of security of tenure, has been a key motivation for civil servants in engaging in corrupt practices. The latter point is replete with ironies: corrupt public officials are often indicted for embezzling sums of money that are in excess of what could be adequate remuneration, and the cost of prosecuting them adds more financial burden to the government. Embezzling public funds tends to serve more than compensation for low pay; it is also an insurance policy against poor retirement benefits. It would be wrong to conclude that high pay would serve as insurance policy against fraud. However, good pay and carefully crafted sanctions have proven to be major deterrents to the frequency and magnitude of incidences of fraud, bribery, and corruption.

A higher salary to all public servants is both unattainable and undesirable. What is important and feasible is to put in place reforms that ensure that the civil services pay comparable wages to what incumbents would receive in private sector or comparable organizational systems. Given the high levels of wage decompression it would mean higher pay for top flight professionals and managers, all of whom should be given clear contracts for improving performance over their contract term periods. But it would also mean taking out of the service a number of cadres and also imposition of substantial wage freezes for groups that are not in as much demand in the civil service—low level officials and those with low market opportunities (Adamolekun 2002; Kiragu and Mukandala 2003).

Recruitment to the Civil Service

The first essential step to building a competent civil service is to rearticulate meritocracy in hiring and managing civil services in the region. Indeed, there may be a need to blend the concern for meritocracy with representativeness on the basis of race, ethnicity, and gender, but this must never be at the expense of merit, in terms of demonstrable ability to contribute to the mission of each ministry or department.

Sound and effective recruitment policies and practices have been hindered by several "demand and supply" factors in Africa. On the demand side, the combination of political considerations and inconsistent application of merit criteria has compromised the quality of appointees into the civil service. On the supply side, the crisis in higher education, reflected in the decline in the quality of teaching and research in tertiary institutions and the persistent strikes and closures of universities, has adversely affected the quality of the professionals graduating from the institutions of higher learning. Improving the quality of civil servants will depend as much on changes on the supply as on policies and practices in the demand side. On the supply side, both governments and donors must appreciate the increasing emergence of charitable and private sponsored universities by encouraging them with support—scholarships, bursaries, research grants, and effective regulatory frameworks.

Some changes on the demand side can be initiated now. One approach drawn from the experience of the East Asian countries points to the need to recruit future high-level cadres from the ranks of the best and the brightest graduates from the tertiary institutions in their countries (World Bank 1997:94). Another approach is to open the higher civil service especially to lateral entry though direct contractual recruitment and periodic secondment from the private and non-governmental sector, academia at home or in the diaspora, to the civil service. Thirdly, independent professional groups should be represented in the recruitment of senior people into the higher civil service.

Public Service Capacity Building

Until now, the capacity building component of public service reform has adopted one of two approaches: a comprehensive approach adopted in the immediate post independence years or, more recently, the selective "enclaving" of few departments, mainly the financial institutions dealing with monetary, exchange rate, and fiscal policies, i.e., central banks, ministries of finance, and the revenue collection agencies (Ghana, Zambia, Uganda, RSA). The comprehensive model was suitable for such early concerns as Africanization. When it came to other issues, the comprehensive approach was difficult to manage. On the other hand, the selective "enclaving of departments" in the financial sector reflected the preoccupation with promoting macroeconomic stability as an important element of the economic reform program. As a public policy goal in a time of economic crisis, this was an admirable stance. Indeed, reflecting this consideration, the initial focus of the African Capacity Building Fund (ACBF)'s capacity building effort was on macroeconomic policy analysis (World Bank 1991). It is only recently that ACBF has broadened the focus of its capacity building effort to encompass other areas.

A public service reform effort designed in response to NEPAD should, instead, build capacities in the priority areas of that initiative. This means capacity building must adopt a sectoral approach, with a focus on what constitutes the strategic sectors of NEPAD, namely: infrastructure, agriculture, health and education, science and technology. This approach has many advantages. It would restore focus on the other priority areas of development that have been neglected. It will imbue the public service with technical competencies that are needed to perform functions related to regulatory policy and management and provide technical advice to political leaders. Above all, it will direct the effort of African governments to the sectors that are viewed increasingly as vital to Africa's growth and development.

African states have been largely relieved of their role in the productive sector of the economy. As such, the role of the public sector in the priority areas of NEPAD cannot be that of a direct provider of good or services. Instead, its roles would be as facilitator and regulator. These roles demand no less sophistication and technical expertise on the part of civil service than when it had an operational role (Otobo 1997). The idea that the civil service would require high technical expertise for its role as facilitator and as regulator in the post privatization setting may appear counterintuitive. Yet, these tasks not only require a shift in the orientation of the civil service, but also a shift in the skills of the civil servants. For example, an enhanced regulatory role would demand that the civil service or the relevant autonomous agencies take the lead in identifying, designing, and monitoring regulatory policies that strike a balance between the public's need for safe and healthy food and consumer products, social and environmental sustainability, and protection of labor and human rights and the private sector's demand for sound macroeconomic and market-friendly policies. The civil service's facilitatory role would encompass several aspects, including brokering public-private partnerships for project execution, strategic planning and policy coordination, mobilization of resources for program implementation, and promoting research and development. Building a critical mass of expertise in these areas must take center stage as part of the strengthening of the public service capacity.

Enhancing the Process of Policy Making and Coordination

Current efforts to address coordination problems have centered on merging the ministries of finance and ministries of economic planning into a ministry of finance and development and investing it with authority to serve as a central capacity for economic policy formulation. While this may have improved economic coordination in those countries that have adopted the merger approach, it has done little to improve information sharing among the ministries outside the economic sectors. This requires overcoming a weak capacity for policy analysis, a lack of coherence among departments/ministries within sectors, and a weak exchange of information. These remain the central challenges for reform.

Improving policy coherence in the public service requires a new approach with three crucial elements. First, the policy process should be opened up to citizens and especially to civil society through the parliament, the media, and research and policy think tanks. The latter have grown in the continent mostly through donors and international NGO funding. African governments should now cultivate the actors that bring innovation into the policy discourse. Secondly, there should be a substantial decentralization and devolution of responsibilities to local/regional entities and private and non-governmental actors. The adoption of principles of subsidiarity, community solidarity, and separation of production from provisioning responsibilities should increasingly lead to a situation in which the role of national governments is to focus more on providing strategic policy and legal frameworks, interlocuting globalization, and producing only those residual services that are best organized nationally.

A third element of the new capacity building approach is that it should be organized around major clusters, with the following ministerial/departmental composition: political and security (Defence, Foreign Affairs, Internal Affairs, Police Affairs, and Attorney-General); infrastructure cluster (Telecommunications, Power, Water Resources, Public Works and Housing, Transport and Aviation); social policy cluster (Education, Health, Housing, Environment, Youth and Sports, and Women Affairs); and economic policy cluster (Economic Planning and Development, Finance, Agriculture, Trade and Industry, Science and Technology, and Mineral Resources). Besides strengthening coordination with government departments, the clustering approach leads to a vastly improved information exchange among departments of government working in the same sector. This cluster approach would be particularly suitable to NEPAD's sector-based orientation. By contributing to a better flow of information among departments of government, the cluster approach also enhances the role of the civil service in policy development. Just as the civil service's role in policy development has traditionally complemented decision making by ministers, so would the clustering arrangement. In Ghana, where the clustering arrangement has been adopted at the cabinet level under the Rawlings regime, it has facilitated cabinet policy decisions because it allowed controversial issues to be worked out (Ayee 2002:178).

The clustering approach can serve as more than a tool of policy coordination: it can be an important instrument for public budgetary management. For example, by organizing national budgetary expenditures along the four proposed clusters, African governments can better shine the spotlight on where national budgetary priorities lay. Given that NEPAD has identified specific policy priorities, organizing budgetary expenditures on the cluster basis would help make governments allocate budgetary resources to NEPAD's priorities.

Redesigning External Support for Public Service Reforms

Donors can be partners in this effort but only on terms articulated by the host governments. This may, indeed, be the only way under present circumstances to bring about a convergence of donor and recipient interests—as the focus is on the contribution of reforms to improved service delivery, poverty reduction, economic growth, and reduction of systemic waste and corruption. To advance these proposals it would be necessary for Africa's critical regional institutions—especially the African Development Bank, African Capacity Building Fund, under the auspices of

NEPAD—to consider creating a Civil Service Leadership Fund, to which countries determined to rebuild their civil services can turn for development finance. The conditionalities for the disbursement of such a fund would be improvements in revenue mobilization, progress in the identified strategic sectors, and the installation of the strategic governance structures articulated above.

Critical to these efforts is the need for African leaders to provide a governance framework that enables them and their people to take advantage of the opportunities of globalization while limiting its negative tendencies. A recent study showed that African countries are the least prepared to take advantage of globalization (Kiggundu 2002). This needs to change. An apt place to begin is to institute dialogue on what constitutes the core values and aspirations of a country. This should be articulated in an indicative plan around which national efforts concentrate, irrespective of the political party in power. The public service or, more specifically, the civil service will play a key role in that effort. Hence, we have suggested that a merit based, performance oriented public service should constitute one of those core values.

Conclusion

African countries stand at different points on the spectrum in public sector reforms. The lessons from their experiences, as from other parts of the world, is that the state and especially the higher civil service **have** a crucial role in assisting political leaders to actualize their developmental and democratic goals. Furthermore, the experience shows that those countries that invest more in their higher civil services are able to manage the twin challenges of democratization and globalization more successfully. Hence, current tactical responses to change are not adequate. The issues outlined here should be the basis for launching an approach that is strategic, rather than tactical, in responding to these challenges.

We have argued in this paper that the launching of the NEPAD initiative provides an opportunity to realize the approaches articulated here. This is based on the understanding that recent governance reforms and globalization offer opportunities that can be seized only if national political leaders work closely with their internal and external development partners to realize their own visions of a better tomorrow. NEPAD as a supra-regional initiative can only be as strong as the national territorial units it represents.

NOTES

1   At the United Nations, two major programs framed as compacts between Africa and the international community had been adopted: the United Nations Program of Action for Africa's Economic Recovery and Development, 1986; and the United Nations New Agenda for the Development of Africa in the 1990s (UN-NADAF) 1991.

2   It was renamed the African Union in July 2002.

3   This description of the African Peer Review Mechanism draws on the following NEPAD documents: "Memorandum of Understanding on the African Peer Review Mechanism," 9 March 2003; "African Peer Review Mechanism organization and processes," 24 February 2003; "Objectives, standards, criteria and indicators for the African Peer Review Mechanism," 24 February 2003 (http://www.nepad.org/en.html).

4   This recommendation was made in report of the United Nations Secretary-General entitled "Independent evaluation of the United Nations New Agenda for the Development of Africa in the 1990s" A/57/156 of 2 July 2002.

REFERENCES

Adamolekun, L. 2002. "Africa's Evolving Career Civil Service Systems: Three Challenges—State Continuity, Efficient Service Delivery and Accountability." *International Review of Administrative Sciences* 67(3):373-388.

Adamolekun, L and K. Kiragu. 1999. "Pulic Administration Reforms." Pp. 159-174 in *Public Administration in Africa: Main Issues and Selected Country Studies,* edited by L. Adamolekun. Boulder, CO: Westview Press.

African Association for Public Administration and Management. 1984. *African Public Services: Challenges and a Profile for the Future.* New Delhi: Vikas Publishing House.

African Development Bank. 2002. *Achieving the Millennium Development Goals in Africa: Progress, Prospects, and Policy Implications* Abidjan: African Development Bank.

Ayee, Joseph. 2002. "Governance, Institutional Reforms and Policy Outcomes in Ghana." In *Better Governance and Public Policy: Institutions for Democratic Renewal in Africa,* edited by D. Olowu and S. Sako. Bloomfield: Kumarian Press.

Berg, Elliot J. 1993. *Rethinking Technical Cooperation: Reforms for Capacity Building in Africa.* New York, NY: United Nations Development Program.

Court, J., P. Kristen, and B. Weder. 1999. *Bureaucratic Structure and Performance: First Africa Survey Results*. Tokyo: United Nations University.

Devas, N., S. Delay and M. Hubbard. 2001. "Revenue Authorities: Are They the Right Vehicle for Improved Tax Administration?" *Public Administration and Development* 21:211-222.

Elbadawi, I. and A. Gelb. 2003. "Financing Africa's Development: Toward a Business Plan?" Pp. 35-76 in *Beyond Structural Adjustment: The Institutional Context of African Development,* edited by N. van de Walle, N. Ball, and V. Ramachandran. London: McMillan.

Haque, N. U. and J. Aziz. 1999. "The Quality of Governance: 'Second Generation' Civil Service Reform in Africa." *Journal of African Economies* 8(1):68-106.

Kiggundu, Moses. 2002. "Restructuring the African State for More Effective Management of Globalization." Special Issue of *African Development.*

Kiragu, K and R. Mukandala. 2003. "Public Service Pay Reform: Tactics, Sequencing and Politics in Developing Countries: Lessons from Sub-Saharan Africa." Paper presented at World Bank Regional Workshop on Governance and Public Management, Johannesburg, RSA.

Lienert, I. 1998. "Civil Service Reform in Africa: Mixed Results After 10 Years." *Finance and Development* 35(2):1-7.

Lindauer, D and B. Numberg, eds. 1994. *Rehabilitating Government: Pay and Employment Reform in Africa.* Washington D.C.: The World Bank.

Moore, M. 1998. "Death Without Taxes: Democracy, State Capacity & Aid Dependence in the Fourth World." Pp. 84-121 in *The Democratic Developmental State,* edited by M. Robinson and G. White. Oxford: Oxford University Press.

Mosher, F. C. 1968. *Democracy and the Public Service.* New York: Oxford University Press.

Mutahaba, G and K. Kiragu. 2002. "Lessons of Administrative Reform From Some African Countries." Special Issue of *African Development.*

NEPAD. 2003. *African Peer Review Mechanism*, Base Document. Africa: NEPAD.

OECD. 2001. *Public Sector Leadership for the 21st Century.* Paris: OECD.

Olowu, D. 1999. "Redesigning African Civil Service Reforms." *Journal of Modern African Studies* 37(1):1-23.

———. 2001. "Pride and Performance in African Public Services: Analysis of Institutional Breakdown and Rebuilding Efforts in Nigeria and Uganda." *International Review of Administrative Sciences* 67(1): 117-134.

———. 2003a. "African Governments and Civil Service Reforms." Pp. 101-30 in *Beyond Structural Adjustment: The Institutional Context of African Development,* edited by N. van de Walle, N. Ball, and V. Ramachandran. London: McMillan.

———. 2003b. "The Crisis in African Public Administration." In *Handbook of Public Administration,* edited by P. Guys and P. Jon. London: Sage Books.

Olowu, D., and S. Sako, eds. 2002. *Better Governance and Public Policy: Institutions for Democratic Renewal in Africa.* Bloomfield: Kumarian Press.

Otobo, E. 1997. "The Civil Service and the Private Sector in Africa: From a Relationship of 'Conflict' to 'Complementarity.'" *Development Policy Management Network Bulletin* Vol. IV, Number 1, July 1997.

Peters, G. 1996. *The Future of Governing: Four Emerging Models.* Kansas: University of Kansas Press.

Phiri-Mundia, Brenda. 2003. "Agencification as Strategy for Performance Improvement in Tax Administration: A Case Study of the Zambian Revenue Authority." Master of Arts Research Paper, Institute of Social Studies, The Hague, Netherlands.

Rakner, L. and S. Golpen. 2003. "Tax Reform and Democratic Accountability in Sub-Saharan Africa." Pp. 77-100 in *Beyond Structural Adjustment: The Institutional Context of African Development,* edited by N. van de Walle, N. Ball, and V. Ramachandran. London: McMillan.

Rouban, L. 1995. *The French Civil Service.* Paris: Institute International d'Administration Publique.

Schiavo-Campo, S. and P. Sundaram. 2001. *Improving Public Administration in a Competitive World.* Manila, Philippines: Asian Development Bank.

Smoke, P. 2003. "Decentralization in Africa: Goals, Dimensions, Myths and Challenges." *Public Administration and Development.* Special Issue on African Decentralization and Local Governance 23(1):5-16.

Stevens, M and S. Teggenmann. 2003. "Comparative Experience with Administrative Reforms in Ghana, Tanzania, and Zambia." Paper delivered at World Bank Regional Workshop on Governance and Public Management, Johannesburg, June 9-13.

United Nations. 2001. *World Public Sector Report: Globalization and the State, Part 2, Executive Summary.* New York: United Nations.

United Nations. 2002. *World Economic and Social Survey.* New York: United Nations.

World Bank. 1991. *The African Capacity Building Initiative: Toward Improved Policy Analysis and Development Management.* Washington: World Bank.

_____. 1993. *The East Asia Miracle: Economic Growth and Public Policy.* New York: Oxford University Press.

_____. 1997. *World Development Report–The State in a Changing World.* New York: Oxford University Press.

_____. 2002. *World Development Indicators 2002* Washington D.C.: World Bank.

_____. 2003. "Administrative and Civil Service Reform—Strategies and Sequencing in Public Sector Reform." Washington D.C.: World Bank. Retrieved September 26 at (www.worldbank.org/publicsector/civilservice/strategies.htm).

Young, M. 1958. *The Rise of Meritocracy 1870-2033.* Baltimore, MD: Penguin Books.

Chapter 10

RECONSTRUCTING SOUTH AFRICAN ADMINISTRATIVE CULTURE: FROM APARTHEID TO UBUNTU ORIENTED ADMINISTRATIVE CULTURE

Londoloza L. Luvuno

Prior to the first democratic election in South Africa, 1994, structural and administrative culture adjustments were urgently needed to ensure effective and efficient public service institutions. The ideology of constitutional supremacy over parliamentary supremacy had to be introduced, emphasized, and learned by public officials in all existing spheres of government institutions and by community members. Because of the introduction of constitutional supremacy in South Africa, public officials invested with authority were prevented from using their authority as they pleased. They had to exercise their authority in a manner that advanced public interest while remaining faithful to the purpose of enabling interim legislation, Act 200 of 1994. This major change earmarked the move from an apartheid administrative culture, characterized by separate racial developments, blood feud, socioeconomic and political exclusion, political and administrative instability, and the dispossession of land, to an administrative culture that is *Ubuntu* oriented. In contrast to the idea of *Ubuntu* is the concept of *Apartheid*. Translated from Afrikaans, *Apartheid* means "apartness." The term is used to describe the legalized racist policy of the National Party between 1948 and 1994.

In brief, *Ubuntu* oriented administrative culture basically emphasizes the opposite of apartheid administrative culture. That is, an administrative approach based on acceptable administrative morality, lawful administrative processes, and procedurally fair administrative tasks. The concept of *Ubuntu* emphasizes supportiveness, cooperation, and communalism. It is the basis for developing a greater sense of oneness within the public service institutions and community. The concept is a philosophical term, which derives from the Xhosa/Zulu expression "*umntu ngumntu ngabantu*" and implies: "I am because you are, you are because we are" or "I care for you just because you are a living being." In the context of the *Ubuntu* oriented administrative culture, the concept promotes inclusive administration and development, racial unity and trust, cooperation, democracy, and the application of the Rule of Law. This is expressed succinctly in Section 1 of the Constitution and in *Just Administrative Action* (Act 108 of 1996). Thus, it opposes the apartheid administrative culture and introduces an administrative culture that generally promotes coexistence, humanitarianism, and a democratic and bureaucratic ethos.

The argument here is that South African administrative culture has evolved. It has moved from an exclusive style of political governance, separate development and administration, and parliamentary sovereignty—which led to gross violations of human dignity, inequality, destabilization, injustice, racism and sexism—to become an administrative culture that promotes oneness, a learning environment, and the use of social-political precepts to create standards by which the quality of public administration can be judged. The main standards are honesty, responsiveness, efficiency, effectiveness, competence, adherence to democratic procedure, and social equity.

In his international conference presentation, Dwivedi (2002:7) identified three main approaches to studying the administrative culture of a nation. Two approaches, in particular, are relevant to the present argument. The *deontological approach* stipulates that the sources of administrative practice in a particular country are present in its religious or philosophical beliefs. According to this approach, a secular administrative theology provides guidelines for administrative ethics. The *teleological approach* to administrative culture analyzes the success of a decision based on the effects it produces. Thus, the emphasis is the causal relationship between means and desired ends. In this regard, administrative processes and procedures ought to be determined by their ultimate purpose/end. Hence, Dwivedi (2002:7) concludes that the teleological approach to administrative culture emphasizes effects observed, results achieved, and ends met. This article mainly focuses on the teleological analysis of the South African administrative culture.

The discussion begins with the definition and classification of administrative culture derived from British rule followed by the sources and support for administrative culture. Next, the article examines the foundations of South African administrative culture focusing on the South African constitutions and conventions, rule of law, bureaucratic and democratic ethos, the *Ubuntu* principle, and the *Abantu Kuqala* principle. The investigation continues with an examination of the stabilization, changes, and threats to South African administrative culture. Concerns about the political style of governance in South Africa are based on the current South African macro-organizational structure and governance and indigenous/traditional governance. The final section suggests additional administrative culture necessities for promoting good governance in South Africa, emphasizing the new public management approach and the National Integrity System (NIS).

Definition and Classification of Administrative Culture

To analyze the reconstruction of South African administrative culture, we will have to define the concept of "administrative culture" along with concepts such as *Ubuntu* and the *Abantu Kuqala* principle. Managers in public organizations (as well as private) cannot afford to overlook relevant situations such as a White manager criticizing a Black employee's administrative process. Instead of getting an explanation, the manager is met with silence or a stern, uncompromising look. As it turns out, Kroeber and Kluckhon (2000:421) maintain that Blacks, as a group, act more deliberately, respectfully, and are inclined to study a person's behavioral cues more than White people. This type of cultural behavior, according to Kroeber and Kluckhon (2000:421), can be classified as *psychological culture*. The psychological culture emphasizes adjustment of the consciousness as a problem-solving device. This refers to the conditioning of a person's behavior or as well as unlearning wrongs and re-learning new ways of doing things and living in a uniform society. Apartheid describes the legalized racist policy of the then National Party between 1948 and 1994. Its roots can be found in South Africa's earlier policies of segregation. Apartheid went further than segregation in formally regulating racial classification, relations, and divisions. It saw Black people as backward and uncivilized and, thus, they should be kept apart from White people. The only relationship that Black people were allowed to have with White people was one in which they served them. Black people were discriminated against in almost every sphere of life. Racist laws dictated where and how they could live, travel, work, go to school, marry, and socialize.

Schein (2000:102) defines culture as a pattern of basic assumptions invented, discovered, or developed by a given group as it learns to cope with its problems of external and internal organization. Therefore, it is possible for culture to be passed to new members as the correct way to perceive, think, and feel in relation to those organizational problems. This type of culture can be classified as *historic culture* because it emphasizes the social heritage or tradition of an organization. Fox and Meyer (1995:30) define culture as the sum total of the learned behavior, traits, and characteristics of the members of a society, community, or group.

Further, culture can be the values, norms, artifacts, and accepted behavior patterns of a society, community or group. This is sometimes termed *normative culture*. Normative culture, according to Kroeber and Kluckhon (2000:421), places more emphasis on rules or ways of doing thing as well as ideals, values, and human behavior. The term *administrative* in administrative culture can mean the ways in which administrative tasks and administrative processes are undertaken. In this context, *task* refers to an activity carried out by public officials to assist in the execution of the public sector policies and objectives. Similarly, the term *processes* refers to the ways in which public authorities perform their tasks, reach decisions, and implement them. Law plays a fundamental role in initiating, facilitating, and regulating the administrative process.

Based on the analysis above, administrative culture is more effectively explained by Anechiarico (1998:4) as a transmissible pattern of beliefs, values, and behavior in a public service organization concerning the organization's role and relationship to the public. It is produced by a combination of historical, structural, and contemporaneous political factors that shape internal rules and customs and the predisposition to reform. The behavior that is influenced by administrative culture includes interactions within and among government organizations and between the public and public officials and political appointees. Understanding South African administrative culture, in its broadest sense, as the modal pattern of *Ubuntu* and *Abantu Kuqala* common core values and norms, connotes the way services are delivered in South Africa.

Because the term *government*, for many people, denotes inefficiency, ineffectiveness, and waste, the new administrative culture also pivots around the idea of *doing things right on the first attempt*, such as mending racial divisions and mistrust and building government spheres that are cooperative and developmental in nature. Therefore, this type of administrative culture is classified *as structural culture,* which lay emphasis on the way South African institutions and hierarchical structure are organized. Such administrative institutions, according to Kroeber and Kluckhon (2000:421), are usually identified through visible national logos, seals, flags, ideas, symbols, and artifacts. They classify this culture as *genetic culture* (Kroeber and Kluckhon 2000).

The term *Ubuntu* implies the oneness of the various ethnic groups who adhere to written and unwritten ways of living and interacting with fellow beings. For example, in South Africa, there is a Xhosa, Sotho, Zulu, Indian, Colored, Afrikaans, and English culture living and interacting with one another. Although there is no concise definition of *Ubuntu*, the term alludes to ideas such as humaneness, brotherly group care, social unity irrespective of racial differentiation, and solidarity. Since the concept of *Ubuntu* contrasts with the idea of individual selfishness, public managers are required to promote social equity by ensuring that they do not harm the interest of one race nor advance the interest of another race undeservedly to the detriment of other races. The term can also be associated with *Abantu Kuqala*, which is a Xhosa term literally translated as "people first." Here, public managers are required to be subservient to the public they serve. They are required to render goods and service in accordance to the principle of "people first" stipulated in *The White Paper on Transformation of Public Service*.

Sources and Support for Administrative Culture in South Africa

Currently, according to the South African statutory law, Rule of Law, Section 195 of the Constitution of the Republic of South Africa, the *Ubuntu* and *Abantu Kuqala* administrative principles are deemed to be the sources of South Africa's contemporary administrative culture. Administrative processes inherited from the apartheid epoch contained administrative laws that mandated White public officials to maintain segregatory administration and development based on ethnicity. Managerial posts were reserved for Whites, who were a minority, and shop-floor posts were given to Blacks who were the majority. Thus, the current administrative culture for Black and White executive, middle, and lower level officials are directed by written guidelines that safeguard individual rights and protect against the inequitable exercise of bureaucratic power. Attempts are being made to introduce a new administrative morality where public officials must be honest, responsive, efficient, effective, competent, and adhere to democratic and bureaucratic ethos and social equity.

Foundations of South African Administrative Culture

The South African administrative culture is founded on a set of basic political and administrative principles that evolved from apartheid culture to the practical application of fundamental theses expressed in the current constitution, rule of law, democratic and bureaucratic ethos, and the *Ubuntu* and *Abantu Kuqala* principles discussed below.

The Constitution of the Republic of South Africa (Act 108 of 1996)

The Constitution *(Act 108 of 1996)* lays the foundation for a democratic and open society in which the three spheres of governments are based on the will of the people and where every citizen is equally protected by law. Here, the improvement of the quality of life of all citizens is emphasized. The Constitution also enforces the building of a united democratic South Africa able to take its rightful place as a sovereign state in the family of nations. Hence, Section 1 of the Constitution states that South Africa is founded on the following values:

- Human dignity, the achievement of equality, and the advancement of human rights and freedoms
- Non-racialism and non-sexism
- Supremacy of the Constitution and the Rule of Law
- Universal adult suffrage, a national common voters roll, regular elections, and a multi-party system of democratic governance to ensure accountability, responsiveness, and openness

Thus, administrative processes and administrative institutions that violate section 1 of the Constitution are deemed to be deviating from the articulated administrative culture. In terms of the constitution, as stipulated in Section 195, administrative culture should be composed of the basic values and principles governing public administration and read as follows:

- A high standard of professional ethics is to be promoted and maintained
- Efficient, economic, and effective use of public resources is to be promoted
- Public Administration must be developmentally oriented
- Services must be provided impartially, fairly, equitably, and without bias.
- People's needs must be responded to and the public must be encouraged to participate in policy-making
- Public Administration must be accountable
- Transparency must be fostered by providing the public with timely, accessible, and accurate information
- Good human resource management and career development practices, to maximize human potential, must be cultivated
- Even so, public administration must be broadly representative of the South African people, with employment and personnel management practices based on ability, objectivity, fairness, and the need to redress the imbalance of the past to achieve broad representation

The administrative cultures instigated by *Just Administrative Action* (Section 33 of the Constitution) derive from the interim constitution, Act 200 of 1993. According to this section, public managers who address public affairs must always to do the following:

Be lawful: Any government institution intending to undertake public activity must do so in accordance to the laws and policies of the country. Unlike the government prior to the democratic election, decisions could be diverted whenever it suits the state president.

Be procedurally fair: Taft (1991:87) interprets this to mean safe from bias, deceit, and any unscrupulous or prejudiced act. Whenever the legitimate expectations or human rights are threatened, corrective action must be swift. In this regard, *Abantu Kuqala* requires public managers to give an explanation with an apology and redress the matter as soon as possible.

Furnish a level-headed raison d'être: Where administrative tasks or service delivery declines, a written reason for the decisions not to render or deliver services must be given to the bereaved person unless stated in government gazette, notice board, or somewhere else. In the context of the South African administrative culture, the courts interpret the word "reasons" to mean "proper adequate rationale." As such, reasons that are set out in public administration activities must be intelligible enough to men in urban and rural areas (Ninnian 1999:403).

Render or deliver administrative services: Public managers must render or deliver administrative services that are justifiable in relation to the reason given, if any of the individual members of the society's rights are affected or threatened.

The Rule of Law and Public Administration in South Africa

According to Gray (1998:69), the bill of rights stipulated in the constitution (chapter 2 of Act 108 of 1996) constitutes a set of values that captured the imagination of the international community. Basically, no common administrative culture in South Africa can be successfully reconstructed without first assuring an environment founded on the rule of law and submission to the principle of legality. The rule of law doctrine, according to Rautenbach and Malherbe (1994:231), contains principles that formed a part of English law since the thirteenth century, though it was used by Dicey for the first time in 1885.

Within the South African context, the bill of rights was only enjoyed by the White community members. The formation of the African National Congress (ANC), the Pan African Congress (PAC) in 1911, and other similar political parties exerted a catalytic force on the apartheid government, its public officials, and unofficial bodies to reduce its exercise of power and the progressive denial of fundamental freedoms and human rights for Blacks, Coloreds, and Asians in South Africa and promote an administrative culture advocating procedurally fair administrative tasks. Currently, all people in South Africa enjoy these rights equally. As a result of the rule of law and the Declaration of the International Bill of Rights, interprets such influence to mean the following:

- Public authorities, officials, and unofficial bodies should not be allowed to exercise discretionary power, decisions, and service deliveries that are too discriminatory, too wide and unrestrained, nor should they be allowed to act in an arbitrary manner
- All races in South Africa should be equal under public authority service delivery and the administration of such services. Thus, they should be treated fairly in terms of such public administration activities
- The judiciary authority should function independently of the national, provincial, and local public authorities. Judges (including tribunal, magistrates, and legitimate human rights instruments) should act as independent

guardians to ensure that the inherent freedom, equality, justice, and dignity of all individual members of South African communities are respected.

It is in the context of this heated discussion that the South African rule of law requires that the reconstruction of South African administrative culture be supported by the well-known tenets of true democracy so that all races in South Africa may achieve their greatest welfare and prosperity. Therefore, the next section examines the democratic and bureaucratic ethos governing South African administrative culture.

Bureaucratic and Democratic Ethos Governing South African Administrative Culture

Although there are problematic occurrences between the bureaucratic and democratic practice of public administration, it should be noted that these problems are rooted in the different approaches to administrative culture and the frameworks of bureaucracy and democracy. As such, the deontological definition of "ethos" would thus imply "the characteristic, spirit or attitude of a community, people or system," while the teleological definition of "ethos" can imply the intentional and purposive approach to administration driven by intervening realities (means) to achieve goals (ends).

Bureaucratic Ethos Governing South African Administrative Culture

Bureaucracy is considered a classic form of organization. It conjures up an image of massive red tape and endless details of service delivery. However, Weber, in contrast, recognized that bureaucracy stresses order and stability, systems of governance, rationality, and uniformity. The following observations relate to bureaucracy in the South African context.

Order and *stability:* In the context of South Africa, prior to the democratic elections in 1994, chaos, rioting, and destabilization were a daily occurrence.

Systems of governance: In South Africa, the system of governance prior to 1994 promoted apartheid values justifying racism as necessary, supporting this view with evidence of conflicts between races and cultures around the world. Currently, the system of governance promotes democratic values and principles.

Rationality: In this regard, the apartheid judiciary systems were biased and favored the White community. Currently, the judiciousness of South Africa is constitutionalized and based on the rule of law.

Uniformity: Prior to 1994, separate developments and segregatory policies were promoted by the apartheid government. The current government promotes unity and uniform, user-friendly administrative processes.

After apartheid, South Africa needed a bureaucracy designed to dispose of a large body of work in a routine manner. According to Squire, Mathews, and Meehan (1997:427) an ideal bureaucracy is characterized by the following distinctive elements:

- Specialization, signifying the well-defined division of labor
- Hierarchy, signifying a clear chain of command and rank of authority
- Formality, signifying a set of rules and procedures to be adhered to, to ensure consistency and fairness to all races and non-sexism
- Professionalism, indicating that the South African institutions should be staffed with an educated pool of human resources. (See also Republic of South Africa 1996:83)

Accordingly, Woller (1998:105) insists on hierarchical accountability, technical expertise, and scientific rationality emphasizing effectiveness, efficiency, and productivity.

Democratic Ethos Governing South African Administrative Culture

Based on the definition of democratic ethos in this article, South African public authorities, by virtue of the reconstructed South African administrative culture, are required to govern by democratic values and principles. According to Dahl (1999), "democracy, in the ideal sense, is a necessary condition for the best political order" (Dahl 1999:64). Consequently, the conditions (means) necessary for the attainment of that political order must be an administrative culture governed by a democratic ethos (see Section 195 of Act 108 of 1996).

These values and principles, according to Teffo and Shergold (2000:87-88), should serve as basic democratic tenets of public administration and constitute the following:

- Public decision making should always aim at the most *reasonable* and *equitable* way in which service delivery can be allocated, as well as the most *efficient* and *effective* way in which public administration service delivery can be applied in order to satisfy the collective needs of the South African community.
- The *utilization* of public resources (authoritative, informational, organizational, financial, natural, and human resources) must satisfy the collective public needs of all races in South Africa *optimally*.
- *Public participation* in administration processes by users of services,

consumers, and taxpayers, either directly or indirectly, is a primary condition for democratic decision making.
- Only the collective body of elected political representatives has the authority to introduce taxes, to collect them, and to decide how to use the collected funds.
- Even public officials must be held *responsible* and *accountable* for all public administration activities that have failed or succeed in the execution of public programs.
- Public administrators and managers must be *sensitive* and *responsive* to the collective needs of the South African community.
- The public's needs must not only be satisfied as efficiently as possible, but also as extensively as possible through the *effective, efficient, and economic* administration of public services.
- Emanating from the Magna Carta of 1215, the principle that no tax or other charges can be collected from taxpayers without their consent and that this tax burden must be distributed in a *reasonable* and *equitable* way has become a prominent democratic value to South African communities.
- The outstanding characteristic of the concept of *social equity* is maintaining high ethical and moral standards and it requires the South African government, public officials, and unofficial civil servants to act with integrity. Integrity, according to Argyris et al. (1996), amounts to fairness, moral values, piousness, dignity, reasonableness, and honesty. This, in turn, is an extended requirement of section 33 of *Just Administrative Action*. In terms of social equity, these public officials and unofficial civil servants are to ask themselves the following questions:
    - How can more (and better) public administration processes be instituted and delivered equally to all South African races?
    - How can quality services be delivered to the poorest of the poor communities at a low cost?
    - Do the new democratic government policies promote equity?

One of the cardinal values instigated by the rule of law is that all activities connected to public administration and management must take place in public and not under cover of secrecy or so called "confidentiality" (Fox and Wissink 1990:83).

As such, the bureaucratic and democratic commitment to the public interest should provide a concrete foundation for producing a strong sense of duty (deontology) in public officials of all races with behaviors and attitudes that encourage administrative outcomes (teleology) that will benefit all races living in South Africa.

The Ubuntu Administrative Approach as a Foundation of South African Administrative Culture

Verwoerd has acknowledged the incompetence that existed in South Africa:

> My department's policy is that Bantu (African Blacks) education should stand with both feet in the reserves and have its roots in the spirit and being of Bantu society. There is no place for the Bantu in the European community above the level of certain forms of labour... What is the use of teaching the Bantu child mathematics, when it cannot use it in practice? That is quite absurd. Education must train people in accordance with their opportunities in life, according to the sphere in which they live. (Verwoerd 1958:14)

This incompetence paralyzed the development of cooperation, competitiveness, paradigms, perspectives, practices, administrative processes, policies, procedures, values, and administrative institutions of South African Afrikaans, Coloreds, and Indians. To reverse this paralysis, South African administrative culture is tailored toward reframing the minds and issues of public managers and the community relevant to the restructuring of societies and subservient public institutions, renewing the spirit and morale of the citizen, and the re-engineering of administrative processes and practices. According to Mbingi and Maree (1995:11-15), the *Ubuntu* administrative culture in South African should have several outcomes.

The *Ubuntu* administrative culture should develop a cooperative and competitive citizen. To ensure the South African economy survives and thrives in the global economy, the problem of shop-floor workers must be addressed long before new generations enter the educational systems. Their collaborative spirit must be developed in order to address the development issues facing South Africa. This means that all administrators and community members are eligible for serious training and development no matter what age or skill level. Currently, the culture of training is aimed at both horizontal and vertical multi-tasking with senior managers evaluated periodically.

Another outcome should be the development of a cooperative and competitive perspective. The shifting of perceptions is the most difficult aspect to understanding transformation. This is also complicated by the inflexibility of attitudes created by illiteracy among Blacks and the feudal, aristocratic attitude of Whites. The temptation becomes greater for disadvantaged communities and individuals to blame others for their circumstances. As such, attempts are being made to develop a competitive spirit and attitude to rise above the unfortunate historical circumstances of apartheid. Hence, the attitudes and perspective of public officials in South Africa is governed by the *Abantu Kuqala* principles discussed below. Even so, South African public administrators are urged to broaden their perspectives on service delivery, cooperation, and their ability to compete with other organizations in the global family.

Further, the *Ubuntu* administrative culture should develop a cooperative and competitive administrative process. The administrative lesson for South Africans is that if the public sector intends to compete on a global scale, it needs to develop unique, competitive administrative processes suitable for its community, a community in which the majority is illiterate. Thus, South African public service organizations need to reconstruct their administrative cultures, transform their institutions, and ensure a total paradigm shift on the part of all public officials intended to address public affairs. Thus, Oakes (2001) states "the historical nation make it clear that they succeeded by adopting and developing administrative cultures and processes that create value" (p.32).

The *Ubuntu* administrative culture should develop cooperative and competitive policies and procedures. Oakes (2001) argues that the challenge for public service organizations operating in a chaotic environment characterized by separate racial developments, blood feuds, socioeconomic and political exclusion, political and administrative instability, dispossession of land, and rapid change is to remain focused on operational events. The reality is that emerging patterns and issues of administrative approaches and cultures are a result of past or future systems, policies, and procedures. Therefore, public managers must reflect on the past in order to manage upcoming opportunities.

In addition, *Ubuntu* administrative culture should develop cooperative and competitive institutions. The intention of the current Constitution, Act 108 of 1996, was to ensure prosperity for all and to ensure a democratic country and cooperative institutions. Thus, the State departments established by Act 108 of 1996 require public managers to democratize their institutions by developing inclusive and collaborative managerial practices as required by the principle of cooperative governance and intergovernmental relations (Section 41 of Act 108 of 1996). In order to avoid the transfer of administrative culture and democracy to the hands of a few symbolic and capable leaders, institutional innovation bolstered by a bottom-up process is a critical managerial issue in South Africa.

Another outcome of *Ubuntu* administrative culture should be the development of cooperative and competitive public services. It is important that South African public service organizations meet customer requirements by creating user-friendly public goods and services. The South African public sector must have the courage to create unique public goods and services. South Africa needs to generate respect through the way the administration addresses its national and international public affairs. The administration needs to create respect for goods and services made in South Africa rather than exclusively importing the goods, services, and administrative cultures of other countries. As stated by Kenneth Kaunda: "[South] Africa must consume what it produces and not consume what it does not produce" (cited by Mbingi and Maree 1995:11).

The Abantu Kuqala Principle as a Foundation of South African Administrative Culture

As mentioned earlier, the term *Abantu Kuqala* is a Xhosa translation for "people first." Through the Constitution of the Republic of South Africa, the common core values of democracy led to the refinement of the following eight *Abantu Kuqala* principles found in *The White Paper on Transformation of Public Service*.

Consulting Users of Services

Public officials and unofficial public servants are required to consult with citizens about the level and quality of public service the citizens will receive and, wherever possible, a choice should be given concerning the services that are offered. This, in the segregatory regime was not acceptable. Under this regime, there were three houses of parliament; the House of the Assembly serviced the Whites; the House of Representatives serviced the Coloreds while the House of Delegates, the Asians. Through these three houses, citizens were consulted and received their services. However, the black Africans had no consultative mechanism because they were deemed to have their own, albeit very small country, and were expected to handle their own service delivery activities.

Setting Service Standards

This principle requires that South African citizens are informed of what level and quality of public services they will receive so that they know what to expect. This includes the introduction of new services to those who have previously been denied access. Even so, every attempt must be made by public officials to exceed the basic requirements that are to be set by the national government service standards. These services standard are to be precise and measurable, so that users can judge for themselves whether or not they are receiving what was promised. In addition, these service standards must be relevant and meaningful to individual members of the community.

Increasing access

As stipulated in the Rule of Law principle, "equality before the law," public officials are to render goods and services to South African communities equally. Indeed, some South Africans enjoy public services and administration of first world quality while many others live in third world conditions. Within the parameters of the Growth, Economic, and Reconstruction (GEAR) strategy, earnest attempts are being made to avail and rectify the inequalities to those who have been denied access to existing services.

Ensuring Courtesy

The concept of courtesy goes beyond merely asking public servants to give a polite smile and say "please" and "thank you." The code of conduct for public servants as incorporated in the White paper on Transforming Public Service Delivery (1997) makes it clear that courtesy and regard for the public is one of the fundamental duties of public servants. The document also specifies that pubic servants treat all communities as customers entitled to receive the highest standards of service. Many public servants do this instinctively; they joined the public service precisely because they have a genuine desire to serve the public. These standards should cover, among other things, the following:

- Greeting and addressing customer
- The identification of staff by name when dealing with customers, whether in person, on the telephone or in writing
- The style and tone of written communication
- Simplifying and redesigning "customer-friendly" public institution forms for administrative purposes related to the community
- The maximum length of time within which responses must be made to enquiries
- Interview conduct
- How complaints are dealt with
- Dealing with people who have special needs such as the elderly or infirm
- Gender
- Language

Providing More and Better Information

The *Abantu Kuqala* strategy requires that people are provided with full, accurate, and up-to-date information about public administrative action, the services available, and who is entitled to receive information. Information, according to the *Abantu Kuqala* principle, is one of the most powerful tools at the disposal of the customers in exercising their rights to good public administrative action. The dissemination of information must be done actively in order to ensure that all those who need it, especially those who have previously been excluded from the provision of public administrative actions and services, receive timely and correct information. A consultation process must be undertaken to determine what customers, and potential customers, need to know, and then to work out how, where, and when the information can best be provided.

Increasing Openness and Transparency

As one of the cardinal values of democracy instigated by the Rule of Law, public administration and management activities regarding public service delivery must take place in public and not under cover of secrecy or so called "confidentiality" (Fox and Wissink 1990:87-88). This value indicates the hallmark of a democratic public administration and is fundamental to the public service transformation process. Increasing openness and transparency in terms of equitable public administration means building confidence and trust between the public sector and the public they serve. A key aspect of this principle is that the public should know more about the way South African national and provincial departments are publicly managed, how well they perform, the public resources consumed, and who is in charge.

Remedying Mistakes and Failure

The maxim "*ubi jus ibi remedium*" (where there is a right there is a remedy) indicates the capacity of public administration and the willingness to take action when administrative activities go wrong. Accordingly, it is an important constitutional principle safeguarded by the South African office of the Public Protector; the Human Rights Commission; the Commission for the Promotion and Protection of the Rights of Cultural, Religious, and linguistic communities; and the Electoral Commission and Broadcasting Authority. The *Abantu Kuqala* principle of redress, as a result of the Rule of Law, requires a completely new approach to managing citizen dissatisfaction and/or complaints. Even so, the complaint system should conform to the following principles:

- *Accessibility.* Complaint systems should be easy to use. Excessive and complicated formalities should be avoided. Complaints are made vis-à-vis public servants. Therefore, complaints made telephonically should also be welcomed.

- *Speed.* The longer it takes to respond to a complaint, the more dissatisfied customers will become. An immediate and genuine apology together with a full explanation will often satisfy South African citizens.
- *Fairness.* Complaints should be fully and impartially investigated. Because of some community members are not aware of the rights they have, they might feel nervous about complaining to a senior official about a member of their staff or about some aspect of the system for which the official is responsible.
- *Confidentiality.* Though it may appear to contradict the principle of openness and transparency, this particular sub-principle is necessary to protect the complainant's confidentiality so that they are not deterred from making complaints by feeling that they will be treated less sympathetically in the future.
- *Responsiveness.* The complaint process should take full account of the individual's concerns and feelings. When a mistake has been made, or if the service has fallen below the promised standard, the response should be immediate, starting with an apology and a full explanation. Customers should be assured that mistakes will not be repeated, and that necessary remedial action will be taken. Wherever possible, public officials and unofficial bodies who deal with the public directly should be empowered to take action themselves to put things right.
- *Review.* The complaint system should incorporate mechanisms for review and for suggestions for changes so mistakes and failures do not occur again.
- *Training.* Complaint handling procedures should be publicized throughout the public administration institutions and training given to all staff so that they know what action to take when a complaint is received.

Getting the Best Possible Value for Money

During the apartheid regime, administrative forms were more complicated and exclusive in terms of language. This made things difficult for the illiterate community members. The *Abantu Kuqala* principle requires that public administration forms be simplified. Inefficiency and waste should be eliminated as much as possible. Indeed, it can be said that there are three E's of administrative "value for money." These are *effectiveness*, where public officials administer specific public activities within a short period of time; *efficiency*, where public officials administer specific public activities according to set standards and according to what the service was intended to do; and *economy*, in which the administration and delivery of such services or activities is affordable.

When considering the *Abantu Kuqala* principles, the concept of the citizen as a "customer" may seem inappropriate. Nevertheless, *Customer,* rather then *client*, is a useful term in the context of not only improving service delivery but also the application of the Rule of Law and all the accompanying principles. To treat the citizen as a customer implies listening to their views and taking them into account when making decisions about what administrative actions should be undertaken in service delivery; treating them with consideration and respect; making sure that the professional level and quality public administration activities are always of the highest standard; and responding swiftly and sympathetically when these professional standards fall below public expectations.

Stabalization, Change, and Threats to South African Administrative Culture

The democratization of South Africa in 1994 brought about national stability. In contrast to racial divide, the violation of inherent human dignity, inequality, injustice, racism and sexism, the current administrative culture ensures national unity, public trust, equality, justice, non-racialism, non-sexism and the acknowledgement of human rights. Furthermore, the perceived stability in South Africa led to economic growth and development, recognition of multiculturalism, equal opportunities for all, as well as international community participation, the establishment of the New Partnership for Africa Development (NEPAD), and the emergence of the Africa Union (AU), the Pan African Parliament (PAP), the African Court, the Africa Central Bank, the Africa Monetary Fund, and the Africa Investment Bank. Moreover, a democratic South Africa can serve as a mediator to rival countries within the African continent.

It is with such integrity that South Africa intends to enter the international community and start paving the way to administrative culture change, the restructuring and transformation of state and other institutions, and the implementation of the Reconstruction and Development Program (RDP). The focus for South Africa is on meeting basic needs, the development of rural and urban areas, the development of human resources, building the South African economy, and the complete and effective democratization of the state and society and its institutions.

The Political System of Governance in South Africa

After 342 years of White domination, some of this domination under Dutch and British colonialism, and some under so-called indigenous Afrikaner-led apartism, South Africa triumphantly achieved its ultimate goal of being a democratic country free from domination and political oppression. This section briefly addresses the political system of governance in South Africa that was prominent in the apartheid and democratic epoch. It will also address, briefly, the indigenous/traditional governance as perceived by traditionalists at present.

South African Political Style of Governance in the Apartheid Epoch

Before the first European settlement in South Africa, the inhabitants of the territory were not organized constitutionally within a framework comparable to that of a modern state. Because of the occupation of the country by the Europeans, new government structures were gradually introduced and the original institutions started to forfeit their jurisdiction. However, the indigenous or traditional structures, and the authority exercised within that framework, never disappeared completely. When the Union of South Africa was established on 31 May 1910, in terms of the provision of South Africa Act, 1909, four provinces were mandated to develop and govern themselves. This administrative system catered to Whites, Indians, and Coloreds. On the other hand, black Africans, the majority community, were excluded when South Africa became a Republic in 1961. With the Act of 1961, the most prominent constitutional change was the substitution of a republic for a monarchic form of state originated from British rule.

The British queen was thus replaced as head of state by a ceremonial State President elected by an electoral college consisting of the members of the House of Assembly and the Senate. Otherwise, the existing institutions and the Westminster system were retained intact. The South African apartheid style of governance became more exclusive to Africans when constitutional Act 110 of 1983 was adopted in September 1983.

Based on Act 110 of 1983, the macro organogram of South African government, as shown in figure 1 above, indicates that the apartheid style of governance became more prominent and thus strengthened the apartheid administrative culture, which opted for parliamentary supremacy. In accordance with the schematic representation above, the State President (SP) was the head of the republic. When addressing the affairs for Whites, Coloreds, and Indians, the State President could act on the advice of the Minister's council for Whites, the Minister's council for Coloreds, and the Minister's Council for Indians, as well as members of the Cabinet. Matters concerning general affairs were dealt with by legislative authority, which consisted of the three Houses.

The House of Assembly consisted of the legislative authority for Whites' affairs with the State President where 166 members were elected directly, 4 members were nominated by the State President and 8 members elected indirectly, thus giving a total of 178 White members of the legislative authority. The House of

Representative consisted of the legislative authority for Coloreds' affairs with the State President, where 80 members were elected directly, 2 members were nominated by the State President, and 3 members elected indirectly, thus giving a total of 85 Colored members of the legislative authority. The House of Delegates consisted of the legislative authority for Indians' affairs with the State President, where 40 members were elected directly, 2 members were nominated by the State President and 3 members elected indirectly, thus giving a total of 45 Indian members of the legislative authority. Any complex administrative matters where consensus could not be reached, joint/standing committees were consulted to address the matters and present the findings to the respective Houses, then to the President, before presenting them to the legislative authority on general affairs. The legislative authority on General Affairs, comprised of the State President and 208 members, addressed the administrative matters of the minority white population. But the affairs of black South Africans were not given due consideration by this authority on the pretext that this group had been already given communal homelands for self-governance.

The South African Political Style of Governance in the Democratic Epoch

In 1990, previously prohibited political groups in South Africa were allowed to organize. This, combined with the release of African leaders, facilitated the process of constitutional change. In December 1991, during multi-party negotiations, the majority of South African political parties signed a declaration of intent in which they committed themselves to drawing up a new democratic constitution as soon as possible. During the first half of 1992, different representative working groups negotiated, *inter alia,* the principles that should be included in a new constitution, the composition and functioning of a constitutional assembly, the possible reincorporation of small former homelands (Transkei, Bophuthatswana, Venda, and Ciskei) into the Republic, interim government institutions, and various other preparatory and transitional arrangements.

During 1993, multi-party negotiations were resumed and agreement was reached on the particulars of a transitional constitution, the arrangements necessary to ensure free and fair elections, and the establishment of a transitional executive council to supervise the implementation of the transitional constitution. The transitional constitution and other laws necessary to facilitate the transitional process to a new dispensation were adopted by parliament at the end of 1993. It was also agreed that elections for the transitional parliament would take place from 26 to 28 April 1994, after which the transitional parliament, acting as a constitutional assembly, would immediately begin to draft and complete a final constitution within two years. The election led to the establishment of the new legislative, executive, and judicial institutions at the various levels; a process that continued for a considerable time. The new, first Black President, Dr. Nelson Rolihlahla Mandela, was elected by parliament and assumed office on 10 May 1994, after which two deputy presidents, ministers, deputy ministers, and other office-bearers were elected.

Thus, a new South African macro organogram was constructed. After the first democratic elections in 1994, the constitution of the Republic of South Africa became the supreme law. The supreme law governs the administrative culture of legislative (Parliament), judicial, and executive authority. This includes the administrative cultures of national state departments and institutions, provincial government, local government, and the complementary institutions at local spheres of government. The legislative authority at the national sphere of government consists of members of the National Councils of Provinces (NCOP). From each of the 9 Provinces, 10 members are elected. The National Assembly consists of 400 members of parliament, each elected in accordance to the proportional representative system.

Thus, the legislative authority consists of 490 members. The judicial authority is divided into five levels of courts: The Constitutional court, which deals with constitutional matters, the Supreme Court, the High Courts, the Magistrates Court, and the Tribunals. The executive authority consists of the President, the Vice President, and 27 Ministers who are political and administrative heads of their respective ministries.

At the provincial level of government, there are the Members of the Executive Council (MECs), each under the authority of the Premier in each of the 9 provinces. The number of MECs appointed by the Premier depends on the province's established portfolio. At each Province, there is a legislative authority to which the Premier and their team, the MECs, are accountable. The local sphere of government consists of a Mayor who teams up with Local Councilors and a City Manager who teams up with Executive Directors. The total number of Executive Directors appointed also depends on the number of portfolios in that municipality. The complementary institutions also perform the administrative functions prescribed by the constitution. It consists of Traditional leaders, discussed below, and the Volkestad council, which consisted of a few White rulers who wished to create their own homeland without the interference of the current governing political party. Because of the overwhelming democratization of South Africa, the Volkestad no longer exist.

To warrant a sustainable democracy, the Constitution also provides for the creation of the state department consisting of the security service, the public service and administration, institutions supporting democracy, and other institutions all under the control of the Supreme law of the Republic of South Africa. Thus, these institutions and the three spheres of governments comprise the administrative culture and are not inconsistent with the constitution of the Republic of South Africa.

Indigenous/Traditional Governance in a Democratic South Africa

Most of the debates around South African administrative culture focus almost exclusively on urban areas. This is because the political structures are better organized in the cities than in the country areas and because the centralized South African political system has a natural urban bias because of its physical location. The apartheid regime extradited the majority of Africans to small homelands denoted by ethnicity. Even today, the majority of Africans live in these rural areas where the only form of governance for them is that of indigenous authority.

According to Tapscott and Ismail (1995), these indigenous authorities were criticized for collaborating with former homeland leaders, the apartheid government, and for representing the interest of only a small section of the population, mostly elderly males. The controversial nature of the indigenous governance, particularly during the apartheid era, resulted in civil organizations calling for the abolition of the illegitimate indigenous governors who were undemocratic, inefficient, ineffective, and corrupt. In contrast, Lungu (1995:7) states that the root cause of the contemporary crisis of the African state and its indigenous governance was the complete implantation, onto African societies, of the political ideology and institutions of the colonial powers.

As such, if Britain could succeed in bringing about an interface between tradition (i.e., Monarchy) and contemporary governance, then surely something workable can be found in South Africa. The various monarchs of the Xhosas, Zulus, Sothos, Tswanas, XiTsonga, Ndebele, Sepedi, SeSwati, and the Tshivenda in South Africa are traditional authorities, recognized in Chapter 12 of the constitution (Section 221 of Act 108 of 1996). These traditional authorities are mandated to observe customary laws subject to the constitution. They may amend and repeal customary legislations. They may also hold Tribunal courts when addressing customary law and customs.

The administrative cultures of traditional authorities are recognized as long as they are not inconsistent with the constitution. Thus, a House of Traditional leaders and a Council of traditional leaders were established (Section 212 of Act 108 of 1996). The political system of traditional governance in South Africa reveals a number of administrative cultures that are pertinent to the modern governance structure:

- There is a decentralized hierarchy with administrative action and powers delegated to regional chiefs and sub-chiefs who have a certain amount of autonomy
- The public participates in decision-making processes through open forums
- There is a relatively stable and reliable system of communication, which is critical to the survival and efficiency of traditional authorities
- Africans in rural areas are staunch followers of their traditional leaders. Thus, the regional chiefs occupy a critical role in the security of the state. Traditional leaders keep on the rural South African citizen.

Additional Administrative Culture Necessary to Promote Good Governance in South Africa

Throughout the industrial world, the rigid, hierarchical, bureaucratic form of public administration, which has dominated since the twentieth century, is changing to a flexible, market-based form of public management. This "new managerialism" represents not just a change in organization or management style but also a transformation of administrative culture that promotes good governance. This new public management system offers, in place of the traditional version of administering public programmes, a vigorous transformation and reconstruction of the relationship between the government and society.

The New Public Management (NPM) approach to administration advocates a business-like approach to public service delivery emphasizing effectiveness, efficiency, and productivity. Hughes (1998:6) identifies seven characteristics related to the New Public Management (NPM) analysis of administrative culture:

- Hands on professional management in the public sector
- Explicit standards and measures of performance
- Greater emphasis on output control
- A shift to disaggregation of units in the public sector
- A shift to greater competition in the public sector
- A stress on private sector style of administrative culture
- A stress on greater discipline and parsimonious utilization of public resources identified earlier in

When considering the South African political style of governance in the democratic epoch, it is imperative that public managers establish a National Integrity System (NIS) that emphasizes the transformation of administrative cultures and systems rather than blaming individuals in order to prevent corruption, fraud, maladministration, and the repetition of apartheid legacy in South Africa. The concept of a National Integrity System refers to a conscious and holistic approach to good governance, generally, in any given country. The NIS seeks to ensure a quality of life for everyone in South Africa. It also focuses on sustainable development and the application of the Rule of Law wherever administrative tasks are performed. Due to the history and the nature of administrative culture in South Africa, the Ministry of Public Service and Administration suggest eight pillars of the NIS:

- Public sector anti-corruption strategies
- "Watchdog" agencies
- Public participation in democratic processes
- Public awareness of the role of the civil society
- Accountability of the executive
- Legislative and judicial authorities
- The media, private sector, and international business
- International co-operation

These NIS pillars are interdependent. If one pillar weakens, the others have to bear the load and responsibility.

Summary

The Republic of South Africa had a fragmentary, segregating system of public administration with the administrative culture geared to serve only a portion of the population at the detriment of its largest client; however, since the 1995 General Election, a bottom-up, participatory, democratic managerial style is emerging in the post-apartheid era. Efforts are being made to shift power to elected officials, loosening of bureaucratic rigidities, and the utilization of participatory management. Nevertheless, the development of the South African public service cannot be understood without taking into account the history of apartheid. The challenge is how to ensure a just, equitable and sustainable non-racial society which can be a model to other African nations.

REFERENCES

Anechairico, P. T. 1998. *Modern Anthropology*. 2d ed. London: Thomas Nelson.
Argyris, C., P. D. Baderacoo, and E. Gallivan. 1996. *Overcoming Organizational Defence*. 6th ed. Needham Heights, Mass.: Allyn and Bacon.

Dahl, M. K. 1999. *On Reading the Constitutions.* Swansea: Swansea University Press.

Dwivedi, O. P. 2002. "Approaches to Study Administrative Culture: Balancing Common Themes and National Differences." Paper presented at IASIA Conference, June 17-20, 2002, Public Administration between Globalization and Decentralization: Implication for Education and Training. Istanbul, Turkey.

Fox, W. and I. H. Meyer. 1995. *Public Administration Diction.* Kenwyn: Juta and Co.

Fox, W. and H. F. Wissink. 1990. *Macro Organization of Public Institutions.* Stellenbosch/Grahamstown: University Press.

Gray, J. 1998. *False Dawn, the Delusions of Global Capitalism.* London: Granta Books.

Hughes, K. B. 1998. "Corruption and Ethics." *Quarterly Journal of Economics* 12(1):1-31.

Kroeber, A. L. and A. Kluckhorn. 2000. *Culture: A Critical Review of Concepts of Schooling.* London: Farmer.

Lungu, G. F. 1995. "Administrative Decentralization in the Zambian Bureaucracy: An Analysis of Environmental Constraints." MPA Thesis, University of Massachusetts, Boston, MA.

Mbingi, L. and J. Maree. 1995. *Ubuntu: The Spirit of African Transformation Management.* Randburg: Knowledge Resources (Pty) Ltd.

Ninnian, P. P. 1999. "International Rule of Law: Discrimination in the Constitutions of World." *Law Journal* 27(3):391-412.

Oakes, D. 2001. *You and Your Rights: An A-Z Guide to 1000 South African Consumer, Legal and Money Problems.* Pleasantville, New York: Reader's Digest Association, Inc.

Rautenbach, I. M. and E. F. G. Malherbee. 1994. *Constitutional Law.* Johannesburg: Lex Patria Ltd.

Republic of South Africa. 1961. *The Constitution of the Republic of South Africa.* Pretoria: Government Press.

_____. 1994. *The Constitution of the Republic of South Africa.* Pretoria: Government Press.

_____. 1995. *The White Paper on the Transformation of Public Service.* Pretoria: Government Press.

_____. 1996. *The Constitution of the Republic of South Africa.* Pretoria: Government Press.

_____. 2003. *Welcome to the Boer Afrikaner Nation.* Available at (www./southafrica/crime1justice).

Schein, T. 2000. *Culture Sciences, Their Origin and Development.* Urbana: University of Illinois Press.

Squire, P. J., B. Mathews, and E. T. Meehan. 1997. *Dynamics of Democracy.* Madison: Brown and Beuchmark.

Taft, K. L. Z. 1991. "The Network of American Laws." *Alternative Views: Law Review Quarterly* 31(8):112-201.

Tapscott, C. P. J. and N. Ismael. 1995. "Rural Local Government." University of the Westerns Cape, Bellville. Unpublished training module.

Teffo, G. N. and Shergold. 2000. "The Other African Experience." *South African Journal of Philosophy* 15(3):88-89.

Urray, E. M. F. and G. R. Webb. 1996. *Public Productivity Handbook*. London: Marcel Dekker Inc.

Verwoerd, H. F. 1958. *Separate Development: The Positive Side*. Pretoria: Information Service, Government Press.

Woller, G. M. 1998. "Towards a Reconciliation of the Bureaucratic and Democratic Ethics." *Administration and Society* 7(11):213-222.

Chapter 11

THE CULTURE OF DISTRUST IN LATIN AMERICAN PUBLIC ADMINISTRATION[1]

Jorge Nef

The study of the administrative culture of Latin America presents two special problems. One is the great diversity among the twenty republics south of the Rio Grande. Yet, there are also sufficient commonalities in circumstances, institutions, and traditions (Burns 1998:71) to configure an identifiable region; especially by contrast to the developed countries of North America. A second problem is the definition of administrative culture (Smucker 1988). To build an attitudinal, axiological, or ideological matrix characteristic of Latin America as a whole or, more specifically, of its white-collar class, with rigor and precision is virtually impossible. Nevertheless, one may sketch an interpretative profile of the underlying structure of significance, including practices, shared views, and value systems, present among Latin American functionaries. These could be referred to as administrative culture, (Ban 1995:22) encompassing the entirety of the public sector: the central government, autonomous and functionally decentralized state corporations, and territorially decentralized units. Though the emphasis is on government bureaucracy, it is not easy to separate public and private spheres. Both sectors, and their role-orientations, tend to intersect, especially at the top of the power elite (Mills 1957).[2] Neither does an administrative culture, whether business or public, exist in isolation from the broader patterns of political, social, or economic culture. Rather, the administrative dimensions of a culture are heavily imbedded in the way societies address and interpret their problems, including the collective recollection and sharing of historical memories, myths and symbols, as well as past cleavages.

The Historical Legacy

Though the complex pre-columbian theocratic civilizations—the Aztecs, the Mayans and the Incas—had sophisticated economic, political, and administrative systems, little of their managerial traditions remain. Since the sixteenth and seventeenth centuries, colonialism laid the foundations of Latin America's economy, society, and culture, and of the dominant administrative mode. The institutional suprastructure of the New World was born as a dependency of Madrid and Lisbon (Jaguaribe 1964). In this hierarchical order, the absolute power of the King was at the centre of all legitimacy and wisdom, and authority emanated, in theory at least, directly from the Crown. But geographical and operational reality made this power distant, aloof, and often merely symbolic. Under legalistic trappings, formality and reality were worlds apart, as functionaries enjoyed a great deal of discretion in interpreting and applying norms to concrete situations. An imitative and ritualistic administrative culture emerged. Even, the cosmopolitan appearance of the "modern" administrative culture of today can be traced back to the colonial tradition of obedience with avoidance (Moreno 1969).[3] Three centuries of peninsular government entrenched a pattern of exogenous modernization. European social and political events, more than internal needs, over-determined the life cycle of colonial officials. Semi-feudal and patrimonial forms inherited from the Hapsburg dynasty, with their emphasis on town councils, sinecures, patrimonialism, the auctioning or selling of government offices, and limited home rule, were displaced in the middle of the eighteenth century by the enlightened despotism of the Bourbon reforms. The latter pursued greater fiscal responsibility and accountability, enhanced efficiency and probity in public office; but above all they aimed at more effective administrative and political centralization. They also set the stage for the transition from mercantilism to early capitalism.

Independence in the early 1800s was more the consequence of European conflicts and big-power politics, such as Napoleon's invasion of the Iberian Peninsula, than widespread nationalism among New World aristocrats (Keen 1992). The disintegration of Spanish and Portuguese colonialism was also a manifestation of a legitimacy crisis inside the monarchies, which until then had been the apex of the carefully crafted system of imperial domain. By-and-large, emancipation was not a consequence of bourgeois revolutions based upon ideas of liberty, equality, civil rights, or effective citizenship. Political liberation, though violent, maintained almost intact the property and privilege of the same landed oligarchy that profited from colonialism. In the midst of extreme centrifugalism, the key issues of governance in the early nineteenth century were state and nation building (Burns 1986). Centralization, order, and the preservation of property relations constituted the primary task of the new governments. Another important task was the reinsertion of the recently independent nations, with their structurally dependent economies, into the post-Congress of Vienna international division of labor. National unity meant the curbing of local loyalties and chieftains and the foundation of a credible pact among various national oligarchies. The very viability and legitimacy of the state became paramount. Constitutional experiments throughout the region ranged from utopian attempts at grafting Benthamite principles into constitutions, to efforts of re-instituting monarchies under republican guise, all under the spell of Bonapartist authoritarianism.

Most countries remained in the throes of civil strife; the public treasury and the state becoming the spoils of the victor, until unifying dictatorships under triumphant warlords managed to bring about a semblance of order. By the middle of the nineteenth century, with expanding demand for Latin American raw materials and greater surplus to split among the elites, more stable and institutionalized forms of power sharing began to take place (Burns 1986). Republican structures, formally resembling either the French or American models, increasingly replaced warlordism. But deeply ingrained practices, such as sinecures, nepotism, particularism, and patronage went hand-in-hand with universalistic discourse. The patrimonial tradition of the state was largely untouched (Keen 1992). As the states adopted seemingly modern patterns, civil society remained weak: rather than citizens with rights, political constituencies were mostly families, clients, and subjects. The growing discrepancy between norms and behavior, between discourse and reality, presented a widening double standard. Corruption, paternalism, and violence filled the gap.

The political systems that evolved in the region, even in the most institutionalized and stable countries were, for all intents and purposes, at best autocratic republics, not popular democracies by any standard of definition (Burns 1998). Responsible and constitutional government meant, in this context, abeyance to the formal rules of the game, not an entrenched view of rights and accountability. Constitutional and legal forms transplanted from the North were often a measuring rod of "modernity" by imitation, not a substantial rendering of a public service. Government jobs were mostly a recognition of loyalty to the powers that be, not the presence of a neutral, representative, and responsible bureaucracy (Gouldner 1954).[4] Even, when efforts at the professionalization of the civilian and military cadres of the state began in the 1880s, this seemingly neutral body of state employees was an elitist stratum, to which ordinary people had little access. Bureaucratic and authoritarian traditions intersected in a political and social order, which was patrimonial at its core and only superficially legal-rational.

Waves of migration (including foreign migration) into the expanding cities, combined by the transformation of peasants into blue-collar labor in the first decades of the twentieth century brought about a simultaneous process of state-expansion and professionalization. The export-driven growth mentioned here (1880s to 1920s) undermined the old patterns of paternalistic social relations.

Acute polarization pitched an ever more alienated labor force against a socioeconomic order based upon land ownership, money, and privilege. Further insertion into the international division of labor, accompanied by rapid urbanization, incipient industrialization, and the upsurge of the middle strata, made white-collar employment, especially public service, the venue of choice to attain limited social mobility (Burns 1998). A white and blue-collar alliance presented a threat to oligarchical interests. The professionalization of the civil service, the expansion of public education, and budding social security reforms initiated by the ruling elites were intended to mollify a volatile social environment. It was also a way to build a coalition between the aristocracy and the middle sectors. It configured a type of "butler" class: an employee class objectively proletarianized, while subjectively oligarchical and dependent upon the largesse of the aristocracy. In this sense, the expansion of the state sector was a way to prevent further mobilization and threats to social peace. Patronage politics under the guise of educational merit was instituted.

The administrative culture to emerge from this alliance reflected distinctively aristocratic values. Secondary, technical, normal, military, and post-secondary/professional education was geared not only to develop managerial, technical, and clerical skills, but also to socialize the new middle classes into "gentlemanly" values. As the state was becoming the single largest employer, it also prepared them for roles into an expanding public sector. Since industrial development lagged far behind the export-driven economy and the dramatic expansion of urbanization, the nascent white-collar ideology, nurtured by the public education system, was more clearly nested among public employees than in the non-state components of the service sector. Middle-class "respectability," a growing corporate identity, and rhetorical nationalism remained at the core of this emerging professional bureaucratic mentality. Yet equally imbedded and seemingly contradictory attitudes toward authoritarianism, formalism, patrimonialism, and venality coexisted as distinct cultural layers in this incipient state class (Graf 1988, 1996). This ideological amalgam was particularly noticeable among one of the most typical fractions of the Latin American middle classes: the officer corps (Nun 1968).

However, this modernization of sorts failed to enhance social integration and trust, and failed to configure a political community based upon commonly accepted values. The linkage between this status officialdom and the public was one of mutual distrust: "us" versus "them." On the one hand, officials looked at civil society with contempt as a potentially disruptive force. On the other, the public perception of the state functionaries was one of illegitimacy and suspicion. Only the combination of export-driven prosperity among elites and the forceful containment of popular demands gave this old republican system a semblance of order and cohesion.

The social contract resting upon the export economy collapsed with the Great Depression. The consequence of the catastrophe on bureaucratic culture was twofold. On the one hand, the role of the military as a conflict-manager and as an enforcement mechanism of last resort (i.e., protectors of elite privilege) was enhanced. On the other, it expanded the mediatory function of a now middle-class controlled and relatively autonomous state to arbitrate social conflict by means of economic management. Thus, to the early law and order, educational, and social tasks of the state, a new mission was added: economic development. A rational-productivity techno-bureaucracy grew alongside the more traditional patrimonial and legal-rational central administration. This meant the creation of a myriad of government corporations with broad functions in planning, financing, energy, industry, and marketing. It also meant a Keynesian policy orientation known as Import Substitution Industrialization (ISI) (Furtado 1976).

The specific effects of ISI varied with time and place, but, overall, it meant a corporatist arrangement: an enlarged state apparatus, with the white-collar classes playing broker between business and labor, while maintaining the status-quo. In the more developed countries (Argentina, Brazil, Uruguay, Chile, Costa Rica and Mexico), a combination of ISI policies and populism, helped to reduce social tensions by means of tactical alliances between the urban blue-collar unions and the state classes. In the less developed ones, the initial social and economic conditions for this project were absent and military rule ended up prevailing over economic management. In the first case, and for as long as fiscal resources (depending on export surpluses) were available, autonomous development occurred well into the 1950s, and further professionalization of some of the leading sectors of the bureaucracy took place. It also gave rise to an embryonic administrative state and a public service ethos. In the second case, the civil service remained ineffectual and patrimonial, while the commanding heights of the state continued in the hands of military rulers. As chronic deficit financing, inflation, and paralysis signalled the exhaustion of Import Substitution, tensions between labor and business increased, this time in the context of the Cold War. Lower class defiance grew in intensity. Populism of the kind espoused by ISI was simultaneously under attack by both ends of the social spectrum. Political and administrative immobilism, deadlock, and hyperinflation fed on each other. Legitimation crises affected the relatively more institutionalized administrative states, while those under protracted military rule faced crises of domination: the inability of the repressive apparatus to control by force.

Under the guise of the UN First Development Decade, the U.S.-sponsored Alliance for Progress (1961), a reaction to the Cuban revolution, constituted a belated attempt to stabilize the region by means of development assistance.

Development administration and administrative development were part of a strategy using development as counterinsurgency (Nef and Dwivedi 1981). Foreign aid, training, and development planning played an important role in a broad effort at refurbishing the administrative cadres of Latin America. Under USAID sponsorship, increasing numbers of Latin American students and trainees were exposed to "American ways." Money was also pouring in to carry on domestic programs in educational, agrarian, and tax reforms, and also for the training and rationalization of the civil service under the principles of Scientific Management, program budgeting, and the like. More important, however, were the modernization and retooling of the security apparatus along national security and counterinsurgency lines (Barber and Ronning 1966). While the reforms of the civil service, though extensive, remained largely unfocused and piecemeal, the transformation of the security apparatus had an enormous and long-term systemic impact.

The Alliance was a case of too little, too late; and subsequent U.S. administrations saw it as in effectual. As the Keynesian postulates of the program—the same ones underpinning ISI—were profoundly questioned by business and intellectual elites in the center, the very substance of the administrative reforms became objectionable. The dreams of a Marshall Plan for Latin America were finally scuttled by the Nixon administration in 1969. With the failure of the reformist project, the Latin American middle-class states were, once again, in crisis. The military bureaucracies[5] became the pivot of a new alliance of panicking oligarchs, U.S. military and business elites, and disgruntled segments of the professional sectors. These "reactionary coalitions"(Moore 1966; North 1978) managed to bring down much more than an illusive leftist threat; populism and constitutional democracy went down too, ushering in, instead, military rule.

In their beginnings, some national security regimes were associated with the so-called bureaucratic authoritarian state (O'Donnell 1977).[6] However, the main function of these regimes was not to provide an alternative path to industrialization, but rather to effect a transition between Keynesian structuralism to monetarist neoliberalism and from nationalism to transnational control. Even in the rare cases when the military regimes pursued protectionist industrial policies, as in Brazil, their net effect was both to reduce the role of the civilian techno-bureaucracy to that of a tool of the military and to further disarticulate whatever precarious civil society and citizenship existed from before intervention. The early neoliberal "shock treatments" (Garreton 1993)[7] of structural adjustment, privatization, denationalization, deregulation, and downsizing, started by the military regimes, deflated the status of the public sector. As the state became ever more associated with corruption, gross human rights violations, and sheer terror, the public service function as a whole lost prestige. Despite rhetorical chauvinism, the military regimes of the 1970s were objectively not only parasitic, but also instrumental in undermining the limited sovereignty of the Latin American nations. The "managers of violence" also had been incompetent conflict and development managers (Burns 1986). Yet, they succeeded in radically restructuring the nature of the Latin American state, as well as the latter's relations with both civil society and the interamerican system. The U.S.-sponsored transitions to democracy in the 1980s occurred in the context of these profound alterations (Black 1998).

While military rule floundered in the midst of a staggering debt-burdens and mismanagement, critics within the West began to perceive such regimes as a liability for the survival of their economic and strategic interests. A carefully orchestrated transition to restricted democracy, superintended by the regional superpower, ensued (Nef 1998). This "return" had strict limits and conditionalities. Generally, it maintained the socio-economic and political forces that had benefited from decades of military rule, while excluding radical and popular sectors. The retreating security establishment was to be both the warrantor of the process and the central authoritarian enclave of the new institutional arrangement. This "low-intensity" democracy (Gil, Rocamora, and Wilson 1993) also preserved the basic neoliberal economic agendas of the authoritarian era. Chief among these legacies was a "receiver state," whose prime goal was to manage the fiscal bankruptcies and facilitate IMF-inspired structural adjustment packages (Vilas 1995). Incomplete transition, restricted democracy, and the receiver state have had profound effects upon administrative values and attitudes. Privatization, budget cuts, downsizing, deregulation, and denationalization—especially in the social and developmental areas—have radically minimized the scope and function of the state. As profit and personal gain, on the one hand, and the national interest, on the other, become blurred, the notion of public service becomes increasingly redundant. Furthermore, as the status and income levels of civil servants sink, and with a thriving illegal economy such as the drug trade (Lee 1988), systemic corruption is on the rise and reaches the highest levels of government and administration.

The Cultural Matrix

The historical continuities and discontinuities discussed above have resulted in a complex cultural matrix (or "mind-set") in which there is not so much a synthesis as the coexistence of numerous, and often incongruous, elements or layers. These include foreign and domestic influences, attempted reforms, and persistent crises. The above mentioned "administrative mentality" reflects deep contradictions affecting Latin American societies, and is generally defined by three main parameters. The first is the opposition between growing social expectations and limited economic capabilities. The second tension is that between the "haves" and the "have-nots." The third tension is between the formality of sovereignty and the reality of dependence. The outcome of such contradictions is a zero-sum game, where politics, and administration, oscillate between stalemate and repression (Nef 1982). In order to systematize, we could sketch the content of these layers into an ideal-typical construct with five characteristics.

1. Particularism: In its outer layer, the administrative cultural mix of Latin America presents significant universalistic and achievement-oriented traits. Yet, the core component of Latin America's administrative culture is defined by the persistence of amoral familism. Primary groups, especially extended families, and friends play a fundamental role in social life, even in the allegedly "modern" confines of urban life. The endurance of patrimonialism, *"amiguismo"* and *"compadrazgo"* are manifestations of this built-in particularism. So is the over all level of inwardness, ascription, lack of transparency, and distrust of strangers surrounding the performance of public functions.

2. Formalism: The Latin American state classes have, since their origins, been a status officialdom (Morstein-Marx 1963:63), derived from their possessing official titles that enhance their social importance. A bureaucrat (even a white-collar employee in a private corporation) or an officer, irrespective of the discredit in which the service may find itself, is a "somebody." In a hierarchical social order, being middle class confers a degree of respectability and a semblance of propriety. Ritualism, hyper-legalism, and the profound incidence of Civil and Roman law make the behavior and expectations of officials depend upon deductive and detailed interpretations of norms. There is a fundamental double standard: a public "facade" for outsiders and a private zone of exceptionality for insiders (Riggs 1967). The same applies to the use of time: delays, waiting, and slowness are used selectively to define the importance of the relationship and delineate power and hierarchy.

3. Discretionality: Under the mantle of formalism, as described above, there is a perceived role expectation on the part of functionaries as having a surprisingly great degree of operational autonomy. Formalism and particularism ostensibly clash, with the former becoming a mechanism for avoiding responsibility or for justifying dynamic immobilism and aloofness. The flip side of this contradiction is that it transforms the role of the civil servant into one of dispensing personal favors as well as facilitating exceptions from existing norms. This exceptionalism gives rise to recurrent nepotism, corruption, patronage, and abuse.

4. Corporatism and authoritarianism (Malloy 1977): The official's understanding of the relations between state and society is influenced by the weak brokerage and associational representation for most of the public vis-à-vis the government. This means a very weak civil society. Moreover, the recognition of an

entrenched elitist socioeconomic structure enhances a self-perception of autocracy, where the bureaucracy acts as a mediator and arbiter of the social conflict (Heady 1984). There is a profound schism between "insiders" and "outsiders." Clientelism, patrimonialism, the ubiquitous use of "pull," and the persistence of episodes of military intervention, reinforce the aforementioned traits. Though the white-collar military and civilian state classes cannot be equated with the landed and commercial oligarchy, public officials are in the domain of the elites and some of them are able to make their way into the upper crust. Their connection with essentially undemocratic practices and governments makes the functionaries prone to assuming an attitude of arbitrariness and disregard for the public. This demeanor toward the outsiders, especially the lower strata, is pervasive not only in government but also in the private sector.

5. Centralism: Most administrative structures and processes are heavily centralized at the top. The administrator's values, behaviors, and expectations reflect a view of "the public" characterized by high levels of territorial and operational concentration. Decisions normally flow up to the "top," so does responsibility (Campos 1967). Though operational autonomy is not uncommon in practice, the propensity to delegate is rather infrequent.

Cultural Reproduction

The ideological "software" of the Latin American public sector is the result of an on-going process of immersion, acculturation, and socialization, whose structural drivers are both implicit and induced. The primary vehicles for the reproduction of the administrative culture are in their most basic levels the family, the educational system, peer groups, and direct experience with the public service. As indicated earlier, the fundamental class identification of civil servants is with the middle strata. There is a sort of circular causation here: the middle strata produces employees, while becoming a white-collar worker confers the attribute of "middle classness."

Class distinctions are very important in Latin America and social identity is a function of ancestry, neighborhood, education, tastes, gender, ethnicity, and language. The educational system, especially its secondary and tertiary levels, is quite exclusive and discriminating. High school and university educations are, in general, the points of entry for employee roles. More specific training may occur at the post-secondary levels either in public service schools or in university careers geared to administrative postings. These are connected to law, business and economics, but also the study of public administration. Few countries have developed an administrative class, in the sense understood in North America, the United Kingdom, and continental Europe (Heady 1984), and many point to Costa Rica,

Uruguay, and Chile as possible examples approaching the model of a "neutral," "effective," and relatively more transparent bureaucracy. But even these cases appear problematic when closely scrutinized.

In the case of the military, officers' academies at the secondary and post-secondary levels give specificity to a distinct body of doctrine and *esprit de corps*. National security and counterinsurgency doctrines define a predominantly antidemocratic and ultraconservative view of the world, heavily dependent upon ideological and material support from the United States. In fact, beyond the veneer of nationalism, most security forces act as occupying forces of their own countries. Civilian and military roles are sharply divided, with military professionalism being largely defined by the control over the instruments of force, institutional autonomy, verticality, rigidity, secrecy, high transnational integration, hubris, isolation, and corporate identity (Nef 1974). With the shrinkage of the developmental function of the state, by design and by defect, security management has evolved into the most ostensible function of the state (Nef and Bensabat 1992). With the Cold War over, the role of national security has been redefined to encompass "wars" on drugs, "terrorism," or whatever justifies the paramountcy of the institutional interests of the security forces. The key latent function of armed force in the region remains that of being an insurance policy for domestic and foreign elite interests.

Conclusions

The interpretative exploration undertaken, though tentative, may also allow us to hypothesize about the relationships between the modal pattern of administrative culture, sketched above, and the larger social and political order. As a general conclusion, six critical propositions can be derived from the preceding analysis.

1. The administrative culture (or, more properly, cultures) of Latin America reflects the distinctiveness and complexity of the various national realities. These include persistent dependence, the perpetuation of rigid and particularistic social structures, chronic economic vulnerability, weak and unstable growth, marginalization, low institutionalization, and acute social polarization. This translates into high levels of ambiguity, uncertainty, and human insecurity.

2. Historically, the administrative culture of Latin America has been molded by numerous failed attempts at modernization and cyclical crises. The end result of crises and failed modernizations is a continuing condition of underdevelopment. This situation also contributed to perpetuating a self-fulfilling prophecy of immobility (Adie and Poitras 1974).

3. Conjunctural circumstances and challenges directly affect the outer layers of the administrative culture of the region. The incomplete transition to

democracy of the 1980s, the debt crises, and structural adjustment policies are altering the very essence of public policy (Nef 1997). There is also a revolution of rising frustrations resulting from demographic pressures, urbanization, and the demonstration effect. The paradox is that while demands on the public sector to provide more services are growing, the state apparatus is shrinking.

4. Latin America's administrative ideology is part of a larger ideological matrix containing values, practices, and orientations toward the physical environment, the economy, the social system, the polity, and culture itself. A predatory attitude toward resource extraction (often fuelled by the foreign debt and a practice of resource-based development), possessive individualism, amoral familism, a weak civic consciousness, and a tendency to imitate "the modern" configures a conservative mind-set lacking the capacity, and the will, to anticipate and make strategic policy shifts.

5. The administrative culture of Latin America has been distinctively derivative. As a reflection of an entrenched center-periphery regional and global order, it has tended to follow the inclinations of developed societies. In this sense, it has been exogenous in its motivations, definition of problems, and prescriptions.

6. Any profound administrative reform entails significant attitudinal and value –that is, cultural— changes. Thus, efforts at administrative restructuring, "modernization," and the like must address first, either directly or indirectly, the question of administrative culture. This culture is heterogeneous and dynamic: syncretism, continuities, and discontinuities are a part of its fabric and texture. The socialization and training of the administrative cadres from a culture of distrust to an ethos of service and public accountability remains the crucial link for such attitudinal, axiological and behavioural change.

NOTES

1   This is a revised an updated version of an earlier article on "Administrative Culture in Latin America: Historical and Structural Outline," in *Africanus, Journal of Development Alternatives*, Special Issue on Administrative Culture, edited by O. P. Dwivedi and J. Nef. Pretoria: University of South Africa. Vol. 28, No 2, pp. 19-32.

2   The term is used to refer to the overlapping convergence of the highest circles of the economic, military, and political cliques.

3   Under this "authoritistic" system, the Crown had ultimate, but not immediate, power over decisions. A well-known formula to circumvent royal ordinances in Spanish America was for the local authority to assume that the king could not give

4   an inappropriate command. Often, colonial officials held a royal edict over their heads, as a sign of respect while stating in the presence of a notary public: "I obey, but do not comply."

4   He distinguishes among representative, punishment-centered, and mock bureaucracies. Accountability, responsibility, and oneness characterize the workings of the civil service in an industrial democracy.

5   The "new" military was proposed by the Nixon administration as the alternative to leftist tendencies, corruption, and mismanagement and was articulated in the Rockefeller Report. The ideas were largely the product of the Rand Corporation.

6   For O'Donnell, this type of state entails a "deepening" of ISI, under authoritarian government. Yet, with the exception of Brazil, all other bureaucratic authoritarian states—Argentina, Uruguay and Chile—followed a policy of de-nationalization, privatization, and de-industrialization.

7   Similar policies were pursued by the military regimes of Argentina and Uruguay following the coups of 1973 and 1976 and, to a certain extent, Brazil, after 1964.

REFERENCES

Adie, Robert and Guy Poitras. 1974. *Latin America. The Politics of Immobility.* Englewood Cliffs: Prentice-Hall.
Ban, Carolyn. 1995. *How Do Public Managers Manage? Bureaucratic Constraints, Organizational Culture and the Potential for Reform.* San Francisco: Jossey Bass.
Barber, William and Neale Ronning. 1966. *Internal Security and Military Power: Counterinsurgency and Civic Action in Latin America.* Columbus: Ohio State University Press.
Black, Jan. 1998. "Participation and the Political Process: The Collapsible Pyramid." In *Latin America. Its Problems and its Promise. A Multidisciplinary Introduction,* edited by Jan Black. Boulder: Westview Press.
Burns, E. Bradford. 1986. *Latin America. A Concise Interpretative History.* 4th ed. Englewood Cliffs: Prentice-Hall.
———. 1998. "The Continuity of the National Period." In *Latin America, Its Problems and its Promise. A Multidisciplinary Introduction,* edited by Jan Black. Boulder: Lynne Rienner.
Campos, Roberto de Oliveira. 1967. "Public Administration in Latin America." In *Readings in Comparative Public Administration,* edited by Nimrod Raphaeli. Boston: Alyn and Bacon.

Furtado, Celso. 1976. *Economic Development of Latin America*. 2d ed. Cambridge: Cambridge University Press.

Garreton, Manuel Antonio. 1993. "The Political Evolution of the Chilean Military Regime." Pp. 101-103 in *Transitions from Authoritarian Rule. Latin America,* edited by Guillermo O'Donnell, Philippe Schmitter, and Laurence Whitehead. Baltimore: The Johns Hopkins University Press.

Gil, Barry, Joel Rocamora, and Richard Wilson. 1993. *Low Intensity Democracy: Political Power in the New World Order.* London: Pluto Press.

Gouldner, Alvin. 1954. *Patterns of Industrial Bureaucracy.* Glencoe: The Free Press.

Graf, William D. 1988. *The Nigerian State. Political Economy, State Class and Political System in the Post-Colonial Era.* London: James Currey.

———. 1995. "The State in the Third World." Pp. 140-162 in *The Socialist Register 1995,* edited by Leo Panitch. London: Merlin Press.

———. 1996. "Democratization for the Third World. Critique of a Hegemonic Project." *Canadian Journal of Development Studies.* Special Issue on *Governance, Democracy and Human Rights* XVII:37-56.

Heady, Farrel. 1984. *Public Administration. A Comparative Perspective*. 3d ed. New York: Marcel Dekker.

Jaguaribe, Helio. 1964. *Desarrollo económico y desarrollo político* (Economic Development and Political Development). Buenos Aires: EUDEBA.

Keen, Benjamin. 1992. *A History of Latin America*. 4th ed. Boston, MA: Houghton-Mifflin Co.

Lee, Rensselaer W. 1988. "Dimensions of the South American Cocaine Industry." *Journal of Interamerican Studies* 30(3):87-104.

Malloy, James. 1977. "Authoritarianism and Corporatism in Latin America: the Modal Pattern." Pp. 3-19 in *Authoritarianism and Corporatism in Latin America,* edited by James Malloy. Pittsburgh: University of Pittsburgh Press.

Mills, C. Wright. 1957. *The Power Elite.* New York: Oxford University Press.

Moore, Barrington. 1966. *Social Origins of Dictatorship and Democracy. Lord and Peasant in the Making of the Modern World.* Boston: Beacon Press.

Moreno, Francisco José. 1969. *Legitimacy and Stability in Latin America. A Study of Chilean Political Culture.* New York: New York University Press.

Morstein-Marx, Fritz. 1963. "The Higher Civil Service as an Action Group in Western Political Development." In *Bureaucracy and Political Development,* edited by Joseph LaPalombara. Princeton: Princeton University Press.

Nef, Jorge. 1998. "The Politics of Insecurity." In *Latin America. Its Problems and its Promise. A Multidisciplinary Introduction,* edited by Jan Black. Boulder, CO: Lynne Rienner.

———. 1997. "Estado, Poder y Políticas Sociales: Una Visión Crítica." In *Cambios sociales y políticas públicas en América Latina,* edited by Raúl Urzúa. Santiago: Andros.

Nef, Jorge. 1982. "Empate Político, Inmobilismo e Inflación; Algunas Notas Preliminares (Political Deadlock, Immobilism, and Inflation: Preliminary Notes)." *Revista centroamericana de Administración Pública* Year 2, No. 3, July-December:141-155.

———. 1974. "The Politics of Repression: The Social Pathology of the Chilean Military." *Latin American Perspectives* 1(2):58-77.

Nef, J. and R. Bensabat. 1992. "'Governability' and the Receiver State in Latin America: Analysis and Prospects." Pp. 171-175 in *Latin America to the Year 200. Reactivating Growth, Improving Equity, Sustaining Democracy*, edited by Archibald Ritter, Maxwell Cameron, and David Pollock. New York: Praeger.

Nef, J. and O. P. Dwivedi. 1981. "Development Theory and Administration: A Fence Around an Empty Lot?" *The Indian Journal of Public Administration* 28(1):42-66.

North, Liisa. 1978. "Development and Underdevelopment in Latin America." Pp. 79-80 in *Canada and the Latin American Challenge*, edited by J. Nef. Toronto: OCPLACS.

Nun, José. 1968. "A Middle-Class Phenomenon: The Middle-Class Military Coup." Pp. 145-185 in *Latin America: Reform or Revolution? A Reader*, edited by James Petras and Maurice Zeitlin. Greenwhich: Fawcett.

O'Donnell, Guillermo. 1977. "Corporatism and the Question of the State." Pp. 47-84 in *Authoritarianism and Corporatism in Latin America*, edited by James Malloy. Pittsburgh: Pittsburgh University Press.

Riggs, Fred. 1967. "The Sala Model: An Ecological Approach to the Study of Comparative Administration." Pp. 415-416 in *Readings in Comparative Public Administration*, edited by Nimrod Raphaeli. Boston: Alyn and Bacon.

Rockefeller, Nelson. 1969. *The Rockefeller Report of a United States Presidential Mission for the Western Hemisphere*. Chicago: Quadrangle Books.

Smucker, J. 1988. "La Culture de l'Organisation comme Idéologie de Gestion: Une Analyse Critique (Organizational Culture as Management Ideology: A Critical Analysis)." Pp. 39-68 in *La culture des organisations*, edited by Gladys Symmons. Québec: Institut Québécois de Recherche sur la Culture.

Vilas, Carlos. 1995. "Economic Restructuring, Neoliberal Reforms, and the Working Class in Latin America." Pp. 137-163 in *Capital, Power, and Inequality in Latin America*, edited by Sandor Halebsky and Richard Harris. Boulder: Westview.

Chapter 12

ARE ADMINISTRATIVE CULTURES THAT DIFFERENT?

Gerald E. Caiden

Are administrative cultures that different? Some thirty or so years ago, the answer was obvious; it could only be "yes." Today, with globalization, the differences are narrowing but nonetheless the answer remains the same. While superficial resemblances can be and always have been observable, especially in the universal bureaucratic frameworks that have dominated governments for some five thousand years, the ways in which public administration has been carried out are as numerous as the stars above. None are identical. Administrative cultures may be similar, but they can never be exactly the same from one moment to another, from one administrative system to another, even in the same constellation of administrative units. Max Weber identified some basic underlying characteristics of an ideal model of bureaucracy, but even he added and subtracted characteristics and described different models during his long academic career. Although he abstracted common features from a wide array of historical governments, he recognized that they operated quite differently from one another, as history testified.

Several years ago, I copied Max Weber's example when I was asked to contribute to a volume entitled *Governing India* (Caiden 1998) commemorating the fiftieth anniversary of independent India. Such occasions are usually complimentary; it is considered bad form to voice any unpleasantness. Yet, I could not in good conscience repeat the customary platitudes, not when I knew the reality of public administration in India. Strange to many readers, I wrote about public administration or rather the changing administrative culture of the State of Israel, a country so different that my contribution seemed quite out of place. Closer reading revealed that much of what was being said was really about India not Israel. Herein could be found many criticisms of public administration in India that would have been impolite and certainly impolitic for one native to India to have written so about their own homeland. Several Indians told me that they had understood what I had done but several Israelis expressed surprise that I could have pulled off such a trick and raised the question whether administrative cultures had more in common than generally supposed.

In that essay, I had described my predicament in trying to deal with administrative systems unlike any I had previously encountered:

> While superficially they appeared just the same, they operated in quite different ways, ways which initially I was unable to fathom. To me, as a newcomer, they seemed totally oblivious to my needs, uncaring, insensitive and highly bureaupathologic, until gradually through trial and error, I began to understand how they operated and how to turn what previously I had considered their dysfunctions to my advantage. At the time, I considered all this part of my general cultural shock in confronting a new country, a new environment, a new language and a new people. (Caiden 1998:377)

I really was like a little lost boy again. I did not know how to operate. Yet, I was well educated, held a responsible academic position, and had many willing colleagues with all the right connections. I thought I knew my public administration. How wrong I was. It took time and patience (and much frustration) to learn the new ropes and readjust.

Perhaps the most difficult part of the transition was moving from English speaking countries to the State of Israel. The English speaking countries had all been prosperous democracies that shared a common heritage, held similar values, and operated more or less along similar lines. However, Israel, and the other countries I visited and studied in Europe, the Middle East, Latin America, Asia, and Africa, and later the ex-Soviet Union, did not. Many of the latter, especially those that belonged to the Commonwealth, claimed to mold themselves on the Westminster model or imitate the British administrative culture, by which they meant the Whitehall style. Although their elites spoke English and identified with Western liberal democracy, their circumstances were quite different and they ran their public administration on different lines. Superficially, there were many similarities, especially in form, structure, and legalities, but the spirit that flowed through their administrative veins contrasted one with another.

A Personal Odyssey

However, I must start at the beginning. I was born and bred in London, the heart of the United Kingdom and, at that time, the center of what was then proudly called the British Empire. I was a product of the English school system that tried to make us all good Englishmen, taught us civics, and expected us to be conforming, patriotic, respectable, responsible, participating, obedient, well-behaved citizens, good scouts, members of cadet corps, aping the mannerisms of our counterparts at public (i.e., private) schools (to which we were inferiorly compared), aspiring but knowing our proper place in the order of things. How we wanted to show how fit we were to join, contribute, and shine. But from the start, many of us came from minority cultures that religiously clashed with the dominant Anglican culture. We did not quite fit in as we were often reminded by our teachers when we failed to toe the line. We had not yet become one of them. Eventually, many did and they were absorbed into the mainstream. Others did not; they emigrated (although some of these later returned to their homeland) or they were radicalized and rebelled against the system (from criminals to sophisticated, scornful icons) or joined but worked from within to change the system with varying success. Thus, even before full maturity, this pattern was set and contrasted with the myths set out in Richard Sissons' classic *The Spirit of British Administration,* which portrayed the dominant administrative culture at that time.

At that time, too, the college I attended, the London School of Economics and Political Science (LSE), part of the University of London, was not Oxbridge, i.e., was not considered in the same class as Oxford and Cambridge. Founded by Fabian Socialists, it had the reputation of being iconoclastic or at least radical, although it was much more mainstream, politically central, and economically conservative than some notorious faculty would lead outsiders to believe. But in public policy and administration its Fabian tradition was being continued by Professors William Robson and Peter Self. Although they shared the Sisson view of public administration in the United Kingdom, they and others were critical of the British administrative system and its accompanying culture. While the LSE was but a short walking distance from Whitehall, it did not have the same entrée as Oxbridge. Between Whitehall and the LSE were the headquarters of the High Commissioners of the Dominions (Australia, Canada, New Zealand, and South Africa) which were considered a notch or two down in the administrative pecking order. To young graduate scholars, they proved much more helpful and encouraged research on their countries, countries that they claimed were more advanced than Whitehall. I chose two of these to study in depth and found that, indeed, the administrative systems and cultures of both contrasted with that of their Mother Country, and one with the other. To this outsider, it seemed that Australia was more egalitarian, open, economic, productive and effective, and that Canada had veered away from the British model and had become closer to the American model, a view that clearly reflected the Whitehall opinion that it was administratively superior to Washington.

The Canada Council provided me an opportunity for further study in Ottawa in association with faculty being attracted to the new Carleton University. Actual contact with federal civil servants proved an eye-opener. Though looked down on by their British counterparts, they were no less effective. They just operated differently, certainly less elitist, snobbish, privileged, and bureaucratic, and more down to earth, open, receptive, and friendly. They knew that Canada was overshadowed by the United States but they strove to be different, borrowing from their neighbor some of its most progressive ideas but opposing what they felt were improper practices. Unfortunately, they had often been overruled by their political overseers. Several proposals to update and modernize Canadian public administration had been ignored while their warnings against excessive politicization had been turned against them. Officially correct and proper, they harbored doubts about the state of drift within the country's administration. Their frustrations were reflected in the report written for the Canada Council that I hoped would be independently published. It was not published because by the time I had revised it and obtained official clearance, the Canadian government had acted and appointed what was to be known as the Glassco Commission, which was to substantiate many of the internal rumblings and begin a long process of administrative reform that was to move Canadian public administration even further away from Whitehall.

By then, I was getting a closer look at Australian public administration or more accurately the Commonwealth Public Service from the vantage point of the Australian National University in Canberra. Up close, it was not so progressive as it had appeared from afar. Indeed, in several respects, it was behind Canada and Whitehall with some absurd provisions, such as the ban on employing married women. Moreover, its administrative system was being manipulated from within with outcomes that were not so egalitarian, open, economic, productive, and effective. Furthermore, little research had been done and even Australian insiders were ignorant of their administrative past. As in Canada, there was little of that suspicious, standoffish attitude of Whitehall, although I was to learn Australian officials could also be touchy to outside criticism. Canada was forgotten as I researched a history that showed that Australia had well deserved its reputation for progress in public administration. The United Kingdom might learn a thing or two if it cared to look that far. Yet, Australia still looked up to the United Kingdom and followed the administrative reforms there. Nonetheless, journeying around Australia, public administration there was impressive and more to my liking if only certain changes could be made. It was to take another decade and rapid transformation of Australian society before complacent officialdom was prepared to question tradition and listen to radical overhauls of the public service that had, by then, become imperative.

Both Canada and Australia had retained a strong connection to the United Kingdom and the British influence remained strong. The State of Israel was something else. It too had been ruled by the British and even more recently, Whitehall had imposed its authority over Palestine from its capture from Turkey in 1917 until its departure in 1948 when the new state declared its independence. Israel took over what the British had left behind, that is much of its public administration and official administrative style. But the Jewish community had developed its parallel institutions, virtually a government within a government, and the two sets had to be integrated with the remnants of the British system being absorbed into a governance pattern far different from the Westminster model amid the chaos of war, post-war reconstruction, and the influx of Jewish refugees and immigrants, few of whom had ever experienced democracy. On the contrary, many were suspicious of all officialdom and brought with them cultures that greatly contrasted with that of the British. Still, some British characteristics lingered, and were even strengthened in some enclaves, but these faded in time as Israel struggled to evolve its own distinctive administrative culture.

So, when I went to settle in Israel in 1966, I was considered, by others, more British than I considered myself. Whether or not I was aware of the fact, I was steeped in British administrative culture with diminished elitism derived from Canada and Australia. But all three countries, like so many others, were bureaucratic cultures, that is, my generation was thoroughly bureaucratized. Most of us expected to be employed in bureaucracies and to be served by bureaucracies. In an assured, stable environment with a livable wage and opportunities to rise if competent and entrepreneurial, we expected to work with and through other people. We accepted authority and expected others to accept our authority. We would play by the rules and keep out of mischief. We would get on with the job at hand and distance ourselves from troublemakers, spoilers, and crooks. We would try to be objective, impartial, and loyal, especially those of us who welcomed public service and entered public administration.

Israelis, whether native born or immigrants, were not like this. They had different attitudes to authority, formality, procedure, style, politesse. They ranged all across the spectrum from the Middle European excessively formal and unbending bureaucrats who went solely by the book to the many pre-bureaucratic folks unused to following any rules but their own and who lived by their wits. These brought with them the baggage of administrative cultures that they had defied, evaded, or seduced. They were a mixture who could exploit both power and weakness, position and sabotage, connections and isolation. From their own points of view they personalized as much as they could and yet they could also be indifferent about strangers. In short, the Anglo-Saxons, as they dubbed the native English speakers, were a separate tribe, half admired for their British mannerisms but half scorned for their naïveté and unrealistic expectations. I was an Anglo-Saxon who was expected to adjust and learn how to get things done in an Israeli society that still harbored much ill will against the British.

The situation I found at that time in the mid-1960s I described in a short book entitled *Israel's Administrative Culture* (Caiden 1969). Several faculty members in Berkeley had been toying with the idea of redundancy as applied to social institutions and Israel seemed to present a good example. Israel had the traditional bureaucratic pattern of governance but it resembled more of a system of overlapping and competing administrative systems with rival education, health and welfare services, public enterprises, and development projects provided by public agencies, business corporations, and workers' cooperatives, and some essential public services run by nongovernmental organizations. The country was in such difficult straits that it could not afford any major disaster: it could not rely on monopolistic bureaucracies. Lest one fail, there had to be many back-ups capable of picking up any slack, filling vacuums, and catering for those left out elsewhere. The existence of so many competing units might be wasteful, duplicative, fractious, unmanageable, and invalidate many Western administrative precepts, but the whole network excluded nobody who wanted to be included, provided some minimum level of service to everybody, and kept all within (and identifying with) the system. To outsiders, it might look ugly, particularly to those from more advanced societies, but it worked and, more importantly, it worked well in a society confronted with frequent crises as Israel was in the mid-1960s. Looking from the inside out, it made greater sense. One had to live in it to understand it and see it from many different perspectives.

In Israel, there was not one predominant administrative culture, as in the United Kingdom, Canada, and Australia, but many—a profusion of administrative styles. Israel's administrative culture looked different according to where one stood. A member of a collective settlement (kibbutz) lived in a self-contained, isolated system without much need of outside contact other than through specially trained emissaries. That world was different from the world of a street pedler eking out a living on the margin of society or a highly prized professional pilot or a trader on the Tel Aviv stock market or a religious functionary supported by foreign donations. Some of these would be government officials in one capacity or another while others would not come into much contact with public administration. Some would have to deal with several different administrative styles and change their behavior accordingly while others would only know only one peculiar style and decide how active they would be. The contrasts were stark.

But, then, was this not also true of all countries? In the United Kingdom, Canada, and Australia, there were at least three different administrative styles in business: one for big business, another for very small businesses, and a third between them. There was one predominant style that operated in large anonymous towns and another for small rural hamlets. Within government and public administration, there was at least one that operated at national level, another at local government level, and perhaps a third at regional level. Within each of these official systems, there were distinct organizational cultures. Military and defense authorities acted differently than the police and local security agencies, which, in turn, contrasted with legal, regulatory, and finance bodies, which, in turn, were different from education, health, and welfare services. Was it not also true that citizens and subjects in different walks of life reacted differently to the organization cultures they encountered? They would deal differently with a teacher or a nurse or a police officer or a firefighter or a diplomat. There was more to the idea of administrative culture than first appeared. Much depended on where one stood, what position one held, how one had been bred, and with whom one came into contact.

This became quite obvious when I went to the United States in the late 1960s to visit and later in the mid 1970s to live. American society was in great turmoil. First, I was at the University of California, Berkeley. The campus was a microcosm of the major political and cultural movements of the time: students for the Free Speech movement were at odds with the university's administration, the Black Panthers were denouncing capitalism and White America, and the counterculture hippies were fighting the conservatism of the previous decades. The principles and practices of public administration concerned respectable, well-mannered, and dedicated professional public servants. However, outside there were mobs of young radicals trying to close down the campus, disrupt courses, and generally show contempt toward all authority in the way they dressed and lived. What was I supposed to teach? I had been given syllabi and texts used by fellow faculty members but little addressed the concerns of the people and none related to this new world. How could the old or traditional public administration be revised and rewritten into a new public administration that dealt with contemporary events that were a portent of a future quite different from the past? Actually, I rewrote my lessons and put the new versions together and published it as *The Dynamics of Public Administration: Guidelines to Current Transformations in Theory and Practice* (Caiden 1971) in which I attempted to place public administration in a much wider universal context than was customary in the United States.

Nonetheless, despite the disturbance, I could operate more effectively in Berkeley and the United States than I had been able to in Jerusalem and Israel. America seemed strange but was more familiar than Israel. I had comparatively few struggles with officialdom (except with the Immigration and Naturalization Service, a familiar experience to all aliens) as I had experienced in Israel. Things at the university worked smoothly as they did elsewhere. Things were done with little fuss, inconvenience, and trauma. Indeed, things were done perhaps even better than in Australia. However, then, America was richer and I was a White male who knew the ropes. I was also much troubled. Berkeley was not the place in which to bring up small children, at least not for my children. They had been better off in Israel. Intellectually, I was expected to teach American public administration. I never found it. There was a federal government superstructure from which one could generalize; but for every generalization, there were too many exceptions. The U.S. Government was uniform in name only. Seemingly, every federal agency was a law to itself; no two seemed to operate alike. The same could not be said so much about Canada or Australia. The more one studied them, the more the complexities grew. Berkeley was in the state of California and, again, the way that California and its agencies operated was often quite different from their counterparts in other states. Indeed, the United States consisted of some fifty separate and independent states or countries that went their own way, as became obvious when in my research I went around the country. Maybe, the differences were not so obvious as traveling in the 1950s around Western Europe, but the administrative contrasts were significant, especially between North and South, and East and West. Likewise, cities such as New York, Chicago, Washington, Seattle, Miami, and Boston, where academic meetings were held, could not be mistaken for one another. Each had its own distinctive flair. They were all in America, but which America?

By this time, my research and consulting had taken me to non-English speaking countries where I was supposed to confine myself largely to the same look-alike international hotels, organized conference sites, and specially selected government offices to which I was taken by official cars and accompanied by official guides. But I liked to explore, to walk the streets, travel on public transport, shop at local markets, and generally see what there was to see and mix with the local folk. I had been given official reports and pronouncements and had been shown the world of the official high and mighty. On one's own, one could see for one's self the reality, particularly the daily life, of the urban masses, which gave a different picture of terrible poverty, slums, illiteracy, disease, overcrowding, filth, sights that one could not block from one's mind and keep a civil tongue in the corridors of power. Much of what we foreigners were being told was for external consumption only, little more than public relations blurbs made up for the occasion. At the official meetings, few would dare to depart from their given script and say what they really wanted to say. Much was pretense; we outsiders pretended to believe the pretences of the insiders. Few were fooled but fewer still were prepared to admit they had not been. One had to play the game or never be re-invited.

Already by this time, too, this polite state of affairs had been shattered and was never to be the same again. It was shattered, of all things, by the Comparative Administration Group (CAG) of the American Society for Public Administration, formed by an august group of distinguished experts in comparative and development administration who had been employed at one time or another to help the U.S. Agency for International Development assist the many independent states in the Third World that were about to join the international community. Under the guidance of Professor Fred Riggs, CAG obtained a grant from the Ford Foundation to study their administrative systems and cultures, and out of the grant flowed a stream of original publications often at variance with official reports. The genie was now out of the bottle. With new freedom, the researchers trod on many official toes and took public issue with their own governments. But they were innovative and went where none had gone before, opening up avenues and topics that had once been taboo. Out went ideas about "one size fits all" and "the one best way" because it was so obvious that no administrative culture was identical with another; there were many similarities, but the differences turned out to be more important. Diversity ruled. One accepted the fact that no administrative system worked identically to another. Although, to an outsider, their structural features might appear alike, insiders knew they worked differently. Experts knew that any changes would have to be reshaped to fit the circumstances.

The Contrast between Public and Business Administration

All this was some thirty or so years ago. The world has moved on. Things have changed. Nowadays, the emphasis is different. Experts now want the circumstances reshaped to fit the changes they desire to impose. They do not have the patience to study all the details involved and to wait for circumstances to change until their proposals are more acceptable and practical. Time cannot wait. The needs are so desperate to avoid calamity that time has to be speeded up. Social engineering is back once again but with a different twist. Imposed national planning from above has been replaced by freeing people to choose their own destinies within a standardized international framework. Experts are now employed to aid countries in adopting this new global system, to reshape themselves to fit into it, and to master the painful transition. Diversity has to be smoothed out and quaint features retained only for show lest people forget their heritage altogether. There might be individual winners and losers, but overall it is believed more will win than lose.

So, the great divide between West and East has narrowed while that between North and South has widened. Globalization has brought all countries a lot closer and each has become more aware of common problems. Weak international authorities are strengthening themselves to provide and implement common solutions and they seek to impose greater uniformity, simplicity, and standardization. Strong regional alliances are moving in the same direction to iron out their differences, adopt mutual solutions, and simplify international relations. While acknowledging diversity and uniqueness, the pressure is on the other way, that is, to isolate and ignore countries that refuse to join in and to design workable compromises that all can live with. The outcome is a smoothing of the edges and the search once again for uniformities and generalities, common patterns and shared agendas. Many factors pull in this same globalized direction.

First, ideology is being de-emphasized. Pragmatism is preferred. Those who still insist on ideological imperatives are shunned. If they want to continue to go it alone, let them and let them forego the obvious advantages of globalization. Extremism is out; liberalism is in. What upsets this growing harmony among nations is the rise of religious fundamentalism and the embrace of reverse racism, opening up ethnic sores that fester into civil and regional wars that the international community tries to contain before they explode into global conflicts.

Second, world economic development is being pursued through increased trade and private investment. The state as *the* engine of development has been replaced by international business. The reduction and abolition of trade restrictions, the opening up of internal markets, the free flow of international capital and investment, greater competition for government contracts, downsizing the public sector, and the promotion of private enterprise are all components of the global package to reduce government interference and promote private and civic initiatives.

Third, international business is dictating a homogenized culture to world consumers. Children and teenagers are being made to demand identical products, best seen in what they wear. These days, they are much alike in dress. They are the first generation to be taught that they are global citizens, inhabitants of the same planet sharing a common destiny. Shopping malls and supermarkets resemble one another and they too look alike with their identical logos, shop layouts, and contents. In short, business influence goes beyond purely business concerns and is creating a more uniform world.

Fourth, the success of business or rather business methods has encouraged other types of organizations to emulate them. Business management has created its own international consulting business and is busy spreading its universal message. Other kinds of organizations have begun to copy business practices in the expectation that they will be as successful in what they do. In public administration, this approach is best represented by the New Public Management movement that has become so influential in the past decade and has been helping to strengthen conformity in management thinking and practice.

Above all else, and continually fueling globalization, is the technological imperative. Amazing inventions in the past thirty years alone have been imposing identical life styles, identical work styles, identical health styles, and identical travel styles that have been narrowing cultural differences. They are bureaucratizing everyone. They are strengthening the power of large-scale bureaucracies, and one bureaucracy appears much like another. The bane of most people's lives these days is having to deal with bureaucracies, public and private, their rules, their redtape, their mistakes, their delays, their anonymity. Max Weber pointed out their advantages over other types of organizations, but he also warned about their disadvantages; disadvantages are borne out in the inconveniences of every day living as more and more people come to depend on bureaucracies for almost everything and more countries and economies become globalized. More have become standardized as they opt for the conditions set by the World Trade Organization or have them imposed by the International Monetary Fund and other international agencies of which they are members. Computer technology, once rare and unaffordable, is now commonplace, although poor countries still lag far behind. All these trends are dulling differences between cultures. Most adults watch the same programs on television, which influences how they think, choose, act, and react. More people than ever before travel farther and more frequently. Fewer countries isolate their inhabitants from outside contacts. The current generation is the first truly global society that is more aware of how others live and behave and how an event in one part of the world affects everything else. The contrasts are not so wide as they used to be while the intelligentsia complains about the loss of local color, individuality, and the conformity of mass culture.

The best example of this growing sameness is found in the emergence of international business. Multi-national corporations operate or try to operate identically whenever and wherever possible. While there are local variations, they conduct themselves very much in the same fashion, using the same logos and operating methods drawn from centralized manuals. Headquarters expects and demands conformity. Much management training is identical and managers are swapped around. The end product is more or less the same. No departures, please. Just follow directions. Every locality has to copy the same formulas and implement the same universal models. This way business administration is simplified. Everybody studies and practices the same things. Thus, the same case studies, courses, and degrees can be offered everywhere to anyone qualified to enroll and able to pay the fees. Sponsors know exactly what to expect. Consequently, the business administration passport, the MBA degree, provides much the same preparation and experience. Business schools adopt a similar international outlook, have multi-cultural (or rather multi-national) student (and increasingly faculty) bodies and enjoy cross-border partnerships. More now compete for funds, reputation, and academic rigor more in consortia in which they seek international accreditation, join international networks, share facilities, and offer their students courses abroad. In them, multi-culturalism, through international programs, teamwork, collaborative projects, and bilingualism is currently all the rage.

Compare all this with public administration. The multiplication of international non-business organizations over the same period has not internationalized the study and practice of public management to anywhere near the same extent. Far from integrating their models and procedures, international non-business organizations keep their internal affairs much to themselves. Indeed, little is revealed; they are rarely transparent and they rarely share information. It may have been the fervent hope of the founders of the United Nations that a uniform international civil service would eventually evolve, providing exemplary public administration, a model for member states to emulate. Alas, little of the sort has occurred. Instead, most international organizations have gone their own way, heedless and inattentive to the inclinations of others. While business administration has been globalizing and standardizing, public administration seems to have gone in the other direction. Consequently, public administration has not matched the developments in business administration. The global bodies that may have taken the lead have been too often politicized, beset with internal rivalries and unable to speak with one voice. Member states protect their own national interests and avoid appearing as agents of some international or foreign body. The globalization of public administration is as far away as it has ever been and although there are growing signs of emerging universalism, the field remains fragmented and parochial.

This means that few people know how international organizations recruit and fewer still know how to prepare themselves for a career in international public administration. There is precious little information to guide them and little more to educate them. What is available is ample training and education for national public administration, some of which might contain comparative materials. Mostly it is highly selective and generalized, expecting students to pick up local organizational cultures for themselves. Students often complain that the materials they study do not adequately prepare them for the reality of working in their national public sector. Much of what they encounter reads like a parody or a wish list of how things should be rather than how they are (of course, the same could be said about business administration, that is, an idealization of how administrators and managers would like to portray themselves to the world and how they should behave rather than how they actually do behave). The images of foreign administrators again resemble caricatures rather than the complex portraits that exist. For instance, German public administrators were supposed to be obsessed by rules and to be more concerned that the rules were followed than justice was done. Swedish administrators were supposed to be more consensual, sensitive, human, approachable. Nigerian public administrators were supposed to be self-serving, untrustworthy, unreliable, and corrupt. To prevent such characterizations, most comparative studies avoided the behavioral element and concentrated on the legal formalities, formal structures, and public documents, with little indication of how they actually operated. The only way that outsiders could get an inclination of reality was actually to go see for themselves and to overcome their initial culture shock before trying to make sense of their experience. Otherwise, they had to rely on filtered materials that put a gloss on things. Who really was telling the truth about what was going on? Again, the same criticism could be voiced about business administration, which is far superior at public relations.

Nonetheless, clearly public administration and national administrative cultures do differ from country to country. Sometimes, the differences are not at all obvious, as, for instance, between Australia and New Zealand or between Canada and the United States. In other places, the differences are profound and obvious to all, as between North and South Korea or between Singapore and Malaysia. So, what makes their administrative and governance systems so different and keeps them apart? Why do public officials in some administrative cultures feel obliged to entertain their clients who feel obligated to show their respects by showering gifts as a matter of form while, in other administrative cultures, public officials would not dream of entertaining their clients or accepting personal gifts while their clients would never expect that they would have to offer gifts just to be heard? Why, in some administrative cultures, are family members expected to use their positions to help other family members by employing them and opening doors of opportunity for them, while in other cultures public officials are expected and even legally prohibited from behaving that way? Outwardly, all these public officials may dress alike, occupy almost identical work places, follow the same calendar, work the same hours, and even share similar life styles, but they think and operate quite differently. Why is this so?

The answer, as every student of culture would reply, is simple. Culture, that complex bundle of context, history, ideology, religion, regime, economy, politics, and values, is not the same from one place to another, in the same way that no two persons of all the billions who have lived are exactly the same, not even so-called identical twins. Their beliefs are different. Their priorities are different. Their attitudes to identification, loyalty, cooperation, trust, work (labor), thrift, education, equity, justice, social capital, and civic culture are different. It is these differences, in combination, that separate peoples and make for distinctive administrative styles. Many of these factors do not count so much in business, but they cannot be discounted in public life, community affairs, and public administration. The many reasons as to why various peoples distance themselves from one another may never be articulated or confessed, but the reasons exist, and that is sufficient, just as it is enough to distinguish organizational cultures, public and private, let alone whole national administrative cultures, if, indeed, these could be defined and analyzed without becoming caricatures.

What further complicates matters is that just as culture shapes administration, so, too, does administration, particularly public administration, shape culture. Public administration represents collective authority and exercises legitimate communal power. Its staff personalizes the imperial that shapes society and determines its dominant cultural patterns. Its foremost raison d'etre to protect and enhance public safety and security remains crucial. Should public administration fall down on that task, society is imperiled and may become victim to acculturation by another society or lost to history. So to survive and ensure continuity, every society has to garner or command sufficient resources and lay down common behavior patterns to deter invading outsiders and rebellious insiders. To this extent, it has to dictate how people behave toward each other, what they must individually sacrifice to preserve the group, and how the next generation should be socialized. Add all the other functions that governance and public administration have acquired over history, then their influence over culture only mounts. Business administration also shapes culture but nowhere to the same extent, not with the same degree of legitimacy and not with the same kind of authority. Business must first capture public opinion and public policy.

The Key is How Authority is Exercised

Among the many factors that differentiate administrative cultures, possibly the most important is how authority is exercised. In this, Max Weber was right. Look at how authority is exercised and one has the best clue how a society runs its affairs. Where *tradition* rules, things stay much the same. Most things are cut and dried, settled for the duration. Everyone knows his or her place and what to do. Everyone conforms. Anybody who steps out of line knows the unpleasant consequences ranging from a mere slap on the wrist to excommunication and execution. All is regular if not routine. Few question the system. But then few create, innovate, or change. The administrative culture, as such, is predictable. Skip a few generations, little will have altered. People might not be too happy with the system but there would be little movement to upset things beyond a little patching up here and there, nothing profound, merely cosmetic alterations to reassure complainants that their fears are groundless. Even in the twenty-first century, there are parts of the world where tradition still rules, where things stay much the same, irrespective of appearances to the contrary, where not much really changes regardless of leaders, elites, outsiders, and revoluntionaries who scheme otherwise.

In contrast is the *charismatic* authority that gets things done, often remarkable things, transformations that permanently change societies, with wholesale support. These venerated leaders succeed in moving societies in different directions than otherwise would have been the case. Their devoted followers revere them and enshrine their memory. Such enlightened and attractive leaders cannot be held back by tradition. They burst through. Their genius is readily acknowledged and they are given what they request. They are given the benefit of any doubt. Even the suspicious let down their guard and convince themselves that the new way is better and worth the sacrifice demanded. In such circumstances, administrative systems can be transformed virtually overnight with the reversal of public policies, amendments of laws, the abandonment and substitution of institutions, the reallocation of resources, the replacement of staff, and dramatic exhibitions of different outcomes. Taboos disappear. Nothing is sacred. All may be in flux, but little is left to chance; it is orchestrated to avoid chaos and anarchy so that people can feel secure, comfortable, even excited and enthused about the changes being made. All goes well until the inevitable happens: the charisma disappears. The charismatic leaders lose their skills and charm, run out of steam, lose interest or lose their way, or just die before completing their task. The momentum dies.

Hence, Max Weber, the intellectual, advocated *legal-rational* or bureaucratic authority that overcame the conservatism of tradition and avoided the erratic nature of charisma. Legal-rational authority ideally permits innovation and change. His analysis of the ideal characteristics of this legal-rational authority has since become standard fare. Nobody has attempted to replace his life-long research. However, Max Weber, the politician, had his reservations. By concentrating power in the hands of relatively few at the apex of bureaucratic organizations, legal-rational authority would deprive the masses of any effective say in their personal destiny, restrict choice to predetermined outcomes, and transform workers into anonymous practitioners of rote. Should the organizational elites collude, they could impose their iron rule over society and dictate from above. Should they be so mindful, they could use their absolute authority for human ill not human good. He feared such totalitarianism and supported social democracy as its antidote.

Alas, the world did not heed Max Weber and learned the hard way what happens when legal-rational authority is usurped by evil leaders unchecked by constitutional democracy, universal human rights, and the intelligent rule of law. The forms of bureaucratism appear the same everywhere but the purposes to which they are put and the ways bureaucracy operates differ from one political extreme to another, from cruel dictatorship to liberal democracy, from brutal police states to humanitarian welfare states, from kleptocracies to honest, transparent governance. Forget the formalities, what are the actual practices? Never mind how leaders describe themselves and their rule, how do they behave? Are people treated as subjects or as citizens? Are they treated with respect or disdain? Are they protected or abused? Are the laws appropriate, sensible, and fair? Is law enforcement independent, impartial, universal, just? Does justice go to the highest bidder? Is public administration an administration *of* the public or administration *for* (on behalf of) the public? Who is sovereign?

However, the exercise of authority is only one side of the equation. The other side is how people respond to its exercise. Even under totalitarianism, not all respond alike. Some peoples are so fiercely independent and proud of their own tradition that they go their own way regardless of authority. They just do not conform and nobody can make them. To force them to obey is too costly and not worth the bother. The solution is either to ignore them as if they did not exist and pretend that nobody else would be influenced by them or exterminate them altogether depending on what kind of fight they could put up and the support they receive from others. In short, much depends on how the population is composed and located, how mobile people are, how identified people are, how much resistance is likely, and how much support they have from others. The world has not yet done away with genocide. But it is coming more to terms with diversity, autonomy, and tolerance. As long as nobody else is harmed, authorities are more prepared to live and let live. Unfortunately, some of the peoples under their jurisdiction do not see things that way and the authorities are forced to intervene in bitter local rivalries. Whatever they do, they are seen by one of the sides as being prejudiced and biased. This dilemma is often expressed by public administrators in the phrase "damned if you do, damned if you don't."

The virtue of homogeneity is that, in time, peoples merge, adopt the same cultural patterns, and eventually identify with the authorities set over them. Countries that pride themselves on their homogeneity forget what bloody histories they experienced and the heavy price that they paid to achieve cultural harmony. They tend to dissociate themselves from countries that have failed to achieve such conformity. But globalization and major population shifts have begun to upset things again. There is a growing dislike in settled cultures of newcomers, aliens, and foreigners who still do not fit in, hang on to their former traditions, and do not yet fully embrace their new milieu. Instead of genocide and slavery, the nonconformity has to be overcome in more gentle ways, largely through education, demonstration, and reassuring assimilation. Are countries with diversity more accepting and tolerant than those with homogeneous cultures? As usual, in public administration, the answer begins with "it all depends." Large countries usually have no option but to turn a blind eye to local variations. But even small countries like Belgium and New Zealand still have not united into one happy family. This applies wherever the British notion of "not being one of us" influences administrative behavior.

The administrative culture of a country is influenced significantly by economics. Wealthy countries are cushioned. They offer gainful employment to most, share or redistribute their resources to provide a safety net, and can afford ample public amenities to all. In the poorest countries, most people live on the edge wondering where their next meal is coming from. Competition is fierce. Winners take all; losers become desperate. Position is everything. The powerful are often free from restrictions while the powerless are at the mercy of authority, grateful for any crumb that comes their way and obedient as long as they remain hopeful, but defiant and reckless when disappointed. These circumstances make for quite different modes of the exercise of authority and quite different administrative cultures. Although corruption may be a fact of life in all countries, it is more likely to be an inescapable way of life in poor countries, especially the poorest where power tends to be more absolute. Public accountability and responsibility tend to be diminished and the masses tend to be willing to do virtually anything to survive so that corrupt practices are cruder and more open than in richer, more sophisticated countries. Indeed, in wealthier countries the public tends to be less tolerant of official corruption although people are possibly quite tolerant of what they mistakenly believe to be victimless crime. But, again, "it all depends" simply because generalizations are almost impossible given the extent of cultural diversity.

Change is in the Offing

This situation is unlikely to continue. Public administration and governance, like business administration, cannot avoid the implications of globalization. Just as globalization has produced the growing universalization of business practices and probably business ethics too, so it will probably bring about the growing universalization of public administration practices and ethics, if it has not already begun to do so. Unfair business practices are not tolerated by multi-national corporations, which play by what they consider international rules. They are using their power and influence to bring pressure on public bureaucracies to go after the business rascals and their allies in governance. In so doing, they are forced to respect the written rules of international business associations and treaties and to have such rules standardized internally and taught in the business schools. In turn, sooner or later, public bureaucracies, particularly those who supervise, regulate, or run business enterprises and administer public monopolies, will have to enforce such standardized practices and they will seek to enforce universal norms through some kind of international agency capable of ensuring effective compliance. This will tend to draw administrative cultures closer and reduce the different ways in which they operate.

The continuing standardization of business practices will affect all other organizations. Their cultures and behaviors will probably also draw closer. Similarly, different national administrative cultures will narrow. Those with known bad habits will be increasingly isolated and universally condemned. They will lose out in international competitions until they clean up their act. As access to computers increases around the world, people will come to know how they fare and compare with others. Grassroots pressure emanating from civic action will be exerted to improve the performance and treatment of public organizations and increased agitation and upheaval can be expected where the public is unwilling to put up with what it gets. On the other hand, as long as there are advantages in indulging in corruption and little disadvantage in being exposed, attempts to bring these bureaucracies into line will likely fail.

Contrary to popular impression, history illustrates the extent to which societies, irrespective of cultural differences, acknowledge similar moral precepts to guide them, if the obvious extremes are ignored. There seems to be a common core of norms that most societies follow, sometimes committed to formal codes, other times pretty much taken for granted, part instinct, part common sense, part self-preservation, part logic, part good manners. Extremists and moralists invariably stress the differences among cultures and justify their position in defence of their superior "good" as opposed to others' supposed "bad." Actually, there is more convergence than first meets the eye. The very basis of the democratic ethos is that diversity is a given, that people of good will can live together amicably with their differences, and that the test of leadership is to resolve disputes to the satisfaction of those involved. In short, there will come a time when the many parts of world will be similar ethically and cultural differences will eventually succumb to a democratic administrative ethos.

Fifty years ago, distinctions could be made between public and private organizations and between distinctive national administrative/bureaucratic systems and international entities. This is not true today. Clear divisions between cultures and organizations are now harder to recognize. Today, with globalization and governance, these categories are falling apart. The range of organizations now found in public administration extends from traditional government bureaucracies through a host of mixed partnerships to private corporations that perform contracted government services. Similarly, once centralized government functions have been decentralized, privatized, delegated, and otherwise localized, it makes less and less sense to compare national administrative cultures and systems. Modern technology is transforming administrative practices, smoothing out their rough edges and eliminating many idiosyncrasies identified with so-called national profiles. Besides, more and more countries are copying one another, adopting similar "best practices," standardizing laws and regulations, conforming to common administrative arrangements, and following the same expert prescriptions. The focus in public administration has been shifting away from national entities to things both larger and smaller. The international arena is larger. Local administrative arrangements are smaller. At both levels, international and local, there continues to be a proliferation of nongovernmental organizations.

The abundance of organizations suggests diversity and richness in operations. But, it is predominantly bureaucratic irrespective of ownership, size, function, legal status, and composition. Many organizations appear to behave in much the same way, irrespective of circumstances. From the viewpoint of the global citizen, they seem more or less the same, some more polite or efficient or client friendly than others but all have their rules and procedures. There are identifiable cultural differences but they make little difference to outsiders and what seems of more importance is their professionalism, performance, integrity, and responsiveness. Organizational culture seems more important than national administrative culture and as accountability, transparency, and effectiveness become more significant, differences attributable to culture fade. However, they cannot be eradicated or even discounted. So are administrative cultures that different? Yes, but they will probably be less so in the future unless regional variations are exaggerated—as, for instance, between fundamentalist Islamic administrative systems and secular democratic administrative systems—and deliberately widened as international alliances shift.

REFERENCES

Caiden, Gerald E. 1969. *Israel's Administrative Culture.* Berkeley, CA: Institute of Governmental Studies, University of California.

———. 1971. *The Dynamics of Public Administration: Guidelines to Current Transformations in Theory and Practice.* New York: Holt, Rinehart and Winston.

———. 1998. "Are Administrative Cultures That Different?" Pp. 377-389 in *Governing India,* edited by O. P. Dwivedi, R. B. Jain, and D. K. Vajpayi. Delhi: B. R. Publishing Corporation.

Chapter 13

GOOD GOVERNANCE IN A MULTICULTURAL WORLD: OCEANS APART, YET WORLD TOGETHER

O. P. Dwivedi

Governance: An Introduction

Governance emerged, during the 1980s as a new paradigm denoting something more than "government," replacing the traditional meaning of the term "government." The emphasis of this new paradigm was on reforming the management structures and processes of most Western nations. At the time, such reforms were considered to be part of a revolutionary change in the management of governmental affairs that involved a "paradigm shift" from the Weberian model of bureaucracy (a dominant model of the twentieth century) to the New Public Management (NPM), or the "new managerialism" (Saint-Martin 1998). The rise of the NPM was closely related to the election of right-of-center politicians like Thatcher of Britain, Regan of the United States, Chirac of France, Mulroney of Canada, and Fraser of Australia. These leaders wanted to restrain or cut back public service spending and employment, and roll back the boundaries of the welfare state. These leaders also thought that over the years, the exercise of political power to control and allocate state resources had created imbalances causing poverty and bad governance. For them, and those academics that were converted in their thinking, the term government was seen as too restrictive. A new emphasis was given to the term "governance," which essentially meant a minimal state with emphasis on less government through privatization of government operations (whereever possible), ensuring debureaucratization, treating citizens as clients, and using private sector techniques in achieving results (Dwivedi and Gow 1999). Soon, the ideas imported from business management dominated the governmental reform policy agenda of OECD countries.

That strange reform agenda, which started in the 1980s and was ushered in by certain politicians of the West, changed the traditional meaning of government as a set of instruments through which people living in a state and believing and sharing a common core of values, govern themselves by the means of rule of law.

State has been defined as "an association for securing the common interests and promoting the common purposes of the individuals who are its members" (Corry and Hodgetts 1957:41). A democratic government does not mean governing by majority alone. Rather, it is a system in which individuals have the freedom to express themselves, where the rule by law prevails, and where the liberation of, and respect for, individuals is protected. But, government as an entity was seen as pitted against the private sector, and did not include civil society and the claims of other stakeholders who saw themselves as an integral part of governing the nation. Soon, the importation of business management ideas and techniques into the public sector became a key factor in re-structuring the governmental machinery and the dispersal of state authority. A broader meaning to the term governance was offered:

> Governance includes a full range of activities involving all stakeholders in a country such as: all governmental institutions (legislative, executive and administrative, judicial, para-statals), political parties, interest groups, non-governmental organizations (including civil society), private sector, and the public at large. (Frederickson 1997:86)

In essence, the term governance implies a high complexity of activities, pluralistic in nature, inclusive in decision-making, set in a multi-institutional organizational context, empowering the weaker sections of the society, and geared to achieve the generally accepted common good. It was also claimed that good governance was founded on the pillars of legitimacy, transparency, accountability, and morality (Dwivedi 2002). Later, the World Bank jumped on the NPM bandwagon during the early 1990s and started insisting on the use of NPM as a conditionality of further aid and loan. It defined the term governance as "the exercise of political power to manage nation's affairs" (World Bank 1992) and that the exercise of political power entails steering and control, or, as Laswell has put it, "who controls what, when and how" (Lasswell 1956). In 1994, the World Bank refined this definition: "the manner in which power is exercised in the management of a country's economic and social development" (World Bank 1994:vii). Thus, politics, government, and governance are intimately related to each other. Politics deals with the allocation of state resources, government is concerned with mechanisms of control, while governance encompasses the first two and goes beyond to include other stakeholders in the society. Well-governed countries, then, are those where the rule of law, accountability, transparency, and the freedom to enjoy human and civil rights exist, and where state institutions protect these rights. A sharper definition of the concept of governance is provided by Hyden and Court: "Governance refers to the formation and stewardship of the formal and informal rules that regulate the public realm, the arena in which state as well as economic and societal actors interact to make decisions" (Hyden and Court 2002:19). However, Amartya Sen suggests the following five attributes crucial for nurturing good governance: political freedoms, economic facilities, social opportunities, transparency guarantees, and protective security (Sen 1999:10). To these, one may also include the sharing of power between the public and private sectors, civil society, and with religious as well as social organizations. It is a kind of governance where the societal needs and issues are not left entirely with the state apparatus. Rather, there is explicit collaboration to jointly manage such issues.

In addition, there are certain elements of governance essential for establishing a good governance regime. Hyden has suggested four basic elements: degree of trust, reciprocity of relationship between government and civil society, degree of accountability, and nature of authority wielded (Hyden 1992:7). A degree of trust is essential among elites about the nature and purposes of the state, including rules and practices of socio-political behavior. Without trust in the political system, individuals and other interest groups will have no reason to engage in active political life. Public trust helps to create an environment where multiple stakeholders are able to interact across the public, private, and community sectors to form alliances and seek change in the governing process. Reciprocity is necessary within a civil society because it permits associations, political parties, and other interest groups to promote their interests through competition, negotiations, and conflict resolution. A degree of accountability forces those who govern to be held accountable and act transparently through institutionalized processes such as fair elections, public oversight of governmental operations, and referenda. Finally, it is also important to understand the nature of authority and power wielded by political leaders with respect to policy-making and implementation of programs. In other words, the capacity to govern depends on the political legitimacy that is obtained by creating conditions in the polity that sustains the first three criteria. Of course, it should be noted that public confidence and trust in the process of governance is maintained only when it demonstrates a higher moral tone drawing on the spirituality of action and, most importantly, when it tries to sustain the public good.

Is good government/governance possible? This question has been asked in all cultures. Politicians, academics, ideologues, judges, and anyone unhappy with governmental bureaucracy stress its importance. And, as the expectation about what constitutes "good" differs among people, groups, cultures, religions, and nations, the term acquires a prescriptive tone, and is therfore seen as a subjective matter that can not be applied universally in all circumstances, all places, and with all cultures. Moreover, the term "good" is prescriptive in scope, and hence it is seen by some academics as being subjective, and lacking or escaping a rigorous analysis. Nevertheless, the importance of a normative analysis cannot be dismissed simply because it escapes a deductionist approach as some political scientists continue to argue.

Bad Governance and Developing Nations

It is a paradox of history that the empire builders of Europe who started their business in Asia and Africa with naked corruption ended up by handing over a relatively clean administration to the leaders of those newly independent colonies. Without doubt, during the British, French, Dutch, and Belgian rule there was corruption, but compared to the situation nowadays, colonial corruption paled. Although the leaders of those independent colonies began with a higher standard of probity and accountability, there exists in many nations a cesspool of corruption and bad governance (Dwivedi 2002:40). On the other hand, the major difference between corruption in the industrialized world and in the developing world is that the public office in an industrialized country does not sanctify the corrupt or immoral behavior of the office-holder. For example, the office of the Presidency could not protect Richard Nixon and he had to resign, nor could it shield Bill Clinton from the charges of moral lassitude. In contrast, it is evident that several developing nations protect their office holders against criminal prosecution, and from being held accountable while in power. Great cynicism exists among members of the public concerning the sustenance of public good and good governance.

Sustenance of public good through governmental institutions has been an enduring concern in all cultures and political systems around the globe as leaders continue to stress the importance of good administration. While this was the case among many industrialized nations until the first half of the twentieth century, the need for good government is much more emphasized in the developing nations, not only by its citizens but also (and perhaps more vigorously) by the donors and various international agencies. Our social science literature is full of information about *bad* government in developing nations. We all know that stories about corrupt politicians, bribe-taking government officials, badly conceived and mismanaged public programs, bloated bureaucracies and their disdainful attitude toward citizens, and galloping wage bill of government employees are plentiful. This worries neo-liberals and the *Washington consensus* or *public choice* theorists who advocate the retreat of the state, the increased uses of private sector concepts in government, and the privatization of many governmental functions to the private sector or NGOs (Tendler 1997). Of course, when one is specifically looking for faults and bad performance, they will be found. Let me explain:

(1) The mainstream development assistance community in the West is eager to label a whole country as bad or ungovernable. Of course, many developing nations have performed badly and there is sufficient literature that tells us why such governments do so badly. However, it is important to analyze the local culture and customs of poor countries to determine why, within the same country, some functions are performed well. No government in any part of the world, if it serves to some extent the needs of its people, can be totally and altogether bad. Is it possible that those who brand such countries as totally bad do not realize that their advice for improvement may be based on a consistently flawed body of information? Would it not be better if these advisors prescribed a cure based on some examples of good performance at the local level rather than trying to transplant a system from a different culture and tradition?

(2) When Western advisors to international development organizations analyze the behavior of poorer nations, they give advice based on the experience of how a remedy has worked in their own country. Thus, they do not hesitate in pressuring developing countries (often by influencing the donor agencies to place conditionalities with loans granted) to import recent reform ideas from their own industrialized countries. One example of how the West imposes its ideas on the developing nations is the New Public Management movement. On the other hand, alternative ideas emerging from the poorer nations are either discarded or rarely given any credit!

(3) The international development community has looked at the style of governance in developing nations from the biased eyes of their market mechanism for solving governmental problems. Thus, the reforms ushered in by Thatcher of Britain, Regan of the United States, Chirac of France, Mulroney of Canada, and Fraser of Australia appear to be the panacea of all ills, not realizing that the poorer nations do not have such developed market mechanisms, civil societies, and alert citizenry that can fill the vacuum left by the retreat of the state. Their blind faith in the role of civil society or consumer behavior that may monitor governmental performance or seek accountability is badly placed because such groups are either non-existent or controlled by a few elites.

(4) Finally, the industrialized nations should not forget that their own system of good governance went through large-scale corruption, patronage, and bad government during the nineteenth century and continuing up to the twentieth century. For example, the first Constitution of Canada (1867) has in its preamble three terms: "peace, order, and good government." It was not until the end of World War I that patronage appointments and corruption were controlled (although in some provinces, such as Quebec, it continued until the 1950s). There are similar examples in the United States, Australia, Italy (known for corruption until the 1970s), and many other Western nations. It will take time to establish good govern-

ment in developing countries although it seems that the mainstream development community has lost patience and is in a hurry to change the world in its own image here and now. One should not also forget that the desire for good government in developing nations exists but the means and political will are in short supply.

The above discussion is presented as a prologue to the next section, which is concerned with approaches to, and various models of, good government/governance.

A Framework of Good Government/Governance

Can there be a single approach or model of good governance? There is no general agreement among nations and cultures as to what constitutes good administration. As cultures differ among nations, the ways in which things are done also differ from country to country (or even within the same country if the country is large with many languages such as India, Canada, Russia, etc.). Thus, it is folly to suggest that anyone model of good governance is applicable in all circumstances. Instead, I am suggesting a framework of approaches and different models of governance.

A Framework

The term "good" is a value-laden term that involves a comparison between two things or systems using some standard of measure. A government or a system of governance is considered good if it exhibits certain fundamental characteristics. Perhaps the United Nations Development Program (UNDP) offers the most comprehensive definition and an idealistic model of good governance:

> Good governance is, among other things, participatory, transparent and accountable. It is also effective and equitable. And it promotes the rule of law. Good governance ensures that political, social and economic priorities are based on broad consensus in society and that the voices of the poorest and the vulnerable are heard in decision-making over the allocation of development resources. (UNDP 1998:3)

From the above, the following can be considered the prerequisites of good governance: (a) *democratic pluralism* - a cornerstone of liberal democracy based on three implicit values: equality, empathy, and tolerance for cultural and religious diversity. It also consists of three basic ideals: fundamental freedoms for all, equality of all, and the rule of law; (b) *public participation* in decision-making; (c) *transparency* for access to governing institutions and state information sources; (d) *responsiveness* of institutions to the needs of all stakeholders; (e) *consensus* among different and differing interests in the society; (f) *equity* assured to all individuals so that they may improve their well-being; (g) *effective and efficient responsibility and accountability* of institutions and statecraft, which meet the basic needs of all by using state-controlled resources to their optimum accountability; (h) *strategic vision* of the leaders for broad-range, long-term perspectives on sustainable human development; and (i) *moral governance* that reflects such values as the common good, cultural diversity, public service ethics and control of corruption, and governing elites who dedicate their lives to serving the public. Good governance and sustainable human development, especially for developing nations, also requires conscientious attempts at eliminating poverty, sustaining livelihoods, fulfilling basic needs, and offering an administrative system that is clean, accountable, and moral.

It is important to emphasize that the framework provides an indication of the nature and extent of good governance and points to some of the difficulties that are of greatest relevance for developing nations in their effort to fight bad governance. The framework consists of two major parts: specific approaches to the study of the culture of governance (including administrative culture), and various models that may be used to create conditions for good governance. The three approaches are: teleological, deontological, and spiritual (these approaches have been discussed in detail in an earlier essay by this author in this book). A brief summary of each approach is provided here.

The Three Approaches

The term "approach" denotes convictions or assumptions concerning what is important, where a particular emphasis ought to be placed, and what criteria is to be applied when deciding upon the relevance of methods used for explaining a particular situation. The focus could be descriptive, prescriptive, or explanatory.

The Deontological Approach

The deontological approach focuses on the ethics and morality of administration and governance, and includes the sense of duty a public servant ought to have toward the common good. This approach is based on the ideal of service to the community. It requires a demonstration of social conscience and caring behavior by public officials. Such behavior may lead to good governance.

The Teleological Approach

The teleological approach, based on the doctrine of final causes, asserts that processes and procedures in government administration are to be subordinated to their ultimate objectives/ends. The teleological approach toward good government involves ongoing modifications of institutions, changes in the formal or informal rules by which the behavior and roles of public officials are clarified, the introduction of new constraints, and the tightening of rules and regulations so that instances of mismanagement and bad governance are controlled.

The Spirituality-Based Approach

Spirituality can lead to mastery over our baser impulses such as greed, exploitation, abuse of power, and mistreatment of people. It requires self-discipline, humility, and, above all, the absence of arrogance when holding public office. Furthermore, it enables people to center their values on the notion that there is a cosmic ordinance and divine law that must be maintained. Spirituality serves as both a model and an operative strategy for the transformation of human character by strengthening the genuine, substantive will to serve the common people. A spiritually oriented public official knows that her duty enables her to serve others. In so doing, she will be fulfilling two duties: one to the self, whereby one seeks inner strength through spiritual action; and the other to the community-at-large, whereby one works for the common good. As such, personal spirituality can regulate human conduct by inculcating spiritual, social, and moral virtues and thereby strengthen the ethos that holds the social and moral fabric of a society together. Spirituality can help maintain order in society, build individual and group character, and create harmony and understanding (Dwivedi 2002:48).

Models of Good Government/Governance

Proponents and critics of the approaches outlined above often debate about various methods of how to attain good governance. Diana Woodhouse has suggested three models: the public service model of good government, the judicial model, and the New Public Management model of good governance (Woodhouse 1997). However, the present author believes that the essence and basis of good governance is a moral State that draws its strength from societal values, ethics, and spirituality. Thus, a fourth model is introduced here: the deontological/morality-driven model of good government. These models, individually, do not represent a comprehensive and an accurate description of creating better governance. Rather, they provide a useful means to consider various options for further analysis. Together, they comprise a holistic approach in analyzing the process for good governance.

The Public Service Reform Model of Good Government

This model reflects the traditional approach to eliminating patronage, corruption, etc. in government and strengthening the characteristics of good government upon which the modern civil service system was established. These characteristics are impartiality and objectivity in serving the public; integrity; appointment and promotion based on merit; political neutrality; and accountability through elected ministers to the legislature. Through these principles, which govern the administrative process and reinforce the constitutional position of civil servants, the requirements of good administration can be realized (Woodhouse 1997). In recognition of its importance, this model is examined in depth in a subsequent section of this essay.

The Judicial Model of Forcing Government to be Responsible and Accountable

Keeping the government honest and fair is the responsibility of a country's judicial system. However, this responsibility is rather reactive because the constitutional primacy for accountability rests with the legislature and other institutions, such as the office of auditor general, Ombudsman or Parliamentary Commissioner, Ethics Commissioner, Parliamentary Accounts Committee, and other bodies. Thus, traditionally, the courts do not intervene unless citizens with grievances against the government seek redress through the courts. Judicial review of government administration has been very limited and is restricted, by the executive, in order to maintain the separation of powers. For example, grievances can be brought before the courts about the principles of fairness and equity, about a delay in rendering or implementing a decision, about the excessive use of administrative powers, etc. Though some public officials view judicial activism as overly individualistic (instead of safeguarding the common good and community rights), the public, and especially the legal profession, think of the judiciary as the last bastion of liberal-democractic values. They believe the courts play a crucial role in fostering the principles of good administration. It is through the courts that principles such as reasonability, the proper use of power, judicious decision-making, procedural propriety, and the duty to act fairly can be upheld. For the judiciary, the administrative inconvenience or administrative chaos caused by its action is not important. Instead, from the judicial perspective, a good administration has to be based on the fair application of the rule-of-law. Thus, a tension has developed between the two branches of government. Can this tension be minimized? Some would suggest that it is going to grow unless a statutory code is created that articulates the principles of good government or creates a code of good administrative practice. Of course, some may argue that such a code might be desirable but it could not be comprehensive enough to include all situations and all possibilities. Irrespective of these matters, judicial activism is going to remain a bulwark for good governance.

The New Public Management Model of Good Governance

As mentioned earlier, the New Public Management (NPM) is overtly goal oriented. When analyzed closely, the NPM approach presents the following inherent problems:

- The managerial revolution has created the "hollow state," in which the state contracts out everything except planning and controlling functions. This corresponds with the "hollow corporation." The state delivers nothing itself, it only plans, coordinates, and seeks to exert control in the manner of the "hollow corporation."
- The metaphorical language of management seems to have been already adapted to the world of government with the wide use of such terms as "corporate culture," "corporate management," "management by results," and "value for money."
- A doctrine that is based on private interest professes to meet the requirements of the public good.

Thus, one side of the dilemma raised by the New Public Management's view of managerial work is its naiveté. In this respect, bringing the notion of entrepreneurship into government service would certainly be a "recipe for disasters by advocating measures that encourage information distortion and public risk taking, stifling voices of caution, experience and independence" (Hood and Jackson 1994:478). The trouble, then, with New Public Management from the point of view of ushering in an era of good governance is that it is "all technique" (Dwivedi and Gow 1999:177). Of course, much of the public management movement did evolve as a response to the rigidities and excessive entitlements that came from the excesses of bureaucracy that were introduced in the industrialized nations during the period of growth of government services from 1945 to 1980. We also note that New Public Management proponents usually say that they are aware that the state is not a business, but we have also seen how the classic values of accountability and respect for the law appear to have been eclipsed by it. In practice, very few public administration experts actually believe that government ought to be run as a corporation. To many, the greatest charge against managerialism is its reductionism and its lack of imagination. It tries to reduce complex phenomena to a single model drawn from business. It has been mentioned earlier that the appropriate image for the public administrator is the steward, not the entrepreneur.

The paradox of the New Public Management is that while its language is full of references to a proactive stance, where strategic planning, innovation, change, and growth are promoted, NPM is profoundly deterministic. Its message is that there really are no choices; that deficits, structural economic change, and world trade competition are forcing governments of all developed countries to adopt the same policies. In sum, if the teleological model of administrative analysis is carried to the extreme, an excessive reliance on techniques will drive out what is desirable to ensure good governance. The NPM sees good administration as befitting customer relations, efficiency, and cost effectiveness.

The Deontological/ Morality-Driven Model of Good Governance

The first three models seem to emphasize that ends are more important than the process employed to secure such results. Perhaps, to some people, means are seen as amoral entities. However, it is this author's view that both ends and means belong to the domain of ethics and moral choices; without a solid interconnection between the two, good governance is not feasible. A morality-driven model strengthens those broad principles that ought to rule our governmental conduct because they mark the direction toward which those who govern must channel their acts if they are to serve humanity. These broad principles include the call for individual spirituality, sacrifice, compassion, justice, a striving for the highest good, and, specifically, for public servants to consider their jobs a vocation. While the emphasis on secular government and liberal democracy assigns the place of morality to the individual's conduct and behavior, it has, nevertheless, acknowledged a continuing tension between the requisites of good governance (through its public policy and programs) and the spiritual and moral standards by which they can be measured. This tension needs to be reduced if justice, equality, equity, and freedom are to be maintained. It is crucial that proximate political and administrative actions be taken to strengthen the moral and spiritual foundations of governance. Spirituality, deriving from such foundations, thus provides an important base to the governing process. Confidence and trust in liberal democracy can be safeguarded only when the governing process exhibits a higher moral tone, deriving from the breadth of ethical and spiritual sensitivity. It is this expectation on the part of the public that requires public servants to exhibit additional virtues such as prudence in the use of taxpayers' money and commitment to the collective welfare of people in their society. Any predisposition to not honor such a commitment among public officials is certainly not going to serve the citizens of any country very well.

The Public Service Model of Good Government

One of the fundamental concerns of the modern state is the manner in which those who govern in the name of pursuing societal goals and objectives wield power and authority. The complexity and diversity of the modern state have resulted in a large increase in the power available to government. Governments continue to acquire more functions as the public keeps calling for governmental intervention to cure social ills and to promote common endeavor. This results in more power for the state as it attempts to satisfy the collective needs of the society, while the pervasiveness of governmental interference in nearly all aspects of life continues to increase. In order to fulfill these societal demands, there has been a corresponding growth in the number of government officials. This expansion, both in the scope of activity assigned to them and in quantity, has given the state a very wide power base. It is obvious that the more society is administered, the more power is concentrated in the hands of ministers and public servants. Thus, an administrative state has emerged in which public servants play the roles of crusaders, policy makers, social change agents, crisis managers, program managers, humanitarian employers, interest brokers, public relations experts, regulators of economy, bankers, and spokesmen for various interest groups including their own associations (Dwivedi and Jain 1985). These roles are in addition to the traditional functions of government, functions such as maintaining law and order, providing education and social welfare, managing health programs, operating transportation and communication facilities, and organizing various cultural and recreational events. Thus, through the performance of these several and various roles, public servants and their ministers have acquired enormous power.

This exercise of power by public officials has created a feeling that these officials, having become so powerful, are in need of restraint. Instances of the misuse of power are on the rise. As cases relating to the misuse of power and authority are brought to public attention, the more the public becomes worried. It now views the state as too big and too powerful and demands an honest administration with public officials exhibiting a higher moral standards compared to the people in business world, the responsible use of power and authority, and administrative accountability. The major concern is how to ensure that those who have power exercise it responsibly so that they are accountable for their actions. It should be clear that those who exercise the power of the state are obligated to answer for their actions whether those actions are taken individually or collectively, even when the legality of such actions is not in doubt. There are instances where ministers and senior officers have tried to evade responsibility for their actions by stating that such acts were performed to safeguard the interest of the state or by shifting the blame on to their juniors. Therefore, it is essential that we examine the nature of political responsibility before we discuss public service accountability (Jabbra and Dwivedi 1987).

Political Context of Accountability

The discussion so far has been general without applying the analysis to any particular region or a country. Let us now pay attention to the developing nations. We know that the machinery of government in developing countries was shaped primarily by colonial powers during their rule. Though many of these countries have made extensive reforms in their inherited systems of government since achieving independence, the basic foundation and main tenets of the administrative process have remained in place. While these developing countries often professed faith in such administrative values as ministerial responsibility, political neutrality, anonymity of public servants, and the merit principle in recruitment and promotion, many of their political leaders considered such public administration values significant challenges to their hold on the state and its machinery. A conflict ensued between two values: the expediency of results demanded by political leaders, and the inherent administrative and professional values supported by public servants. However, within a few years of independence, it became evident that in this conflict politics would emerge as the most important value in the governing of a nation. Ministers claiming the right to shape the destiny of the nation told public servants that the nation would not necessarily uphold the inherited colonial values of professionalism, neutrality, and objectivity if they were not in the public interest. Of course, no one could question the politicians who fought for the nation's freedom and who ostensibly made heavy sacrifices while the public servants continued to work for the colonial masters.

It was not surprising, therefore, to see power shifting from administrators to ministers as the latter acquired supremacy in decision-making matters, including control of public servants. When the power center moved from career administrators to politicians, the foundation and basic values of administration were under great strain. With this shift in the power base, particularly in civil service appointments, promotions, and the use of discretionary decision-making authority, certain side effects were inevitable. Some examples include politicians acting as brokers between a business concern and government departments; the politicizing of the interpretation and enforcement of laws; the censoring of the mass media so that anti-regime views are not circulated; interference in the normal functioning of administration to secure appointments for friends or supporters including loyal civil servants; the influencing of the sale of government property and the issuing of contracts and licenses; the improper use of police, para-military and military forces in the peacetime activities of citizens; the manipulation of and intervention in the purchase of machinery, property, equipment, and services for government departments; the misuse of official and confidential information for private gain; and the concentration of extra-constitutional and legal authority (and permitting the use of it) in the hands of individuals who may not hold any elected position (Caiden and Dwivedi 2001). Politicians have become an easy conduit for achieving such ends. Naturally, such an environment has influenced the behavior and attitudes of public servants who, by and large, have seen the benefit of adjusting to the situation. Consequently, the bureaucracy in many of these countries has become a pawn in the use and abuse of power and authority. The ascendancy of politics over administration has meant that political leaders are now capable of using their power and the state machinery to foster a growing personalization of their authority. However, the myth of political neutrality, non-interference in day-to-day operations, and the merit system continues while politicians seek legitimization of their actions by using the machinery of administration unchecked by any legislative body. Thus, a specific administrative culture has emerged which does not appear to be conducive to responsible and accountable administration.

Accountability in the Public Service

Accountability is the foundation of any governing process. The effectiveness of that process depends upon how those in authority account for the manner in which they have fulfilled their responsibilities, both constitutional and legal:

> Accountability is the fundamental prerequisite for preventing the abuse of delegated power and for ensuring instead that power is directed toward the achievement of broadly accepted national goals with the greatest possible degree of efficiency, effectiveness, probity, and prudence. (Canada 1979:21)

Consequently, at the very root of democracy lies the requirement for responsibility and accountability of ministers and public servants. Accountability means being answerable for one's actions or behavior. Generally, public officials and their organizations are considered accountable only to the extent that they are legally required to answer for their actions. However, the public does not perceive that the accountability of public officials and their agencies is limited only to the legality of their actions. From the public's perspective, other aspects such as professional conduct, fair play, justice, equity, and morality of administrative actions are equally important factors in the accountability domain. But let us examine the scope and definition of the term public service accountability. Public service accountability involves the methods by which a government department, a public agency, or a public servant fulfils its duties and legal as well as moral obligations, and the process by which that agency or the public official is required to account for such actions. Thus, it appears that all governmental actions are moral actions as enshrined in constitutional and legal documents. It is normal for the public to demand and expect moral conduct from its politicians and appointed public officials. Only when the administrative and political system of a nation exhibits moral accountability (a term that subsumes administrative, legal, political, and professional dimensions of an administrator's actions) can one hope to see a moral government and good governance.

At the same time, one must note that no amount of laws, codes of conduct, and threats of punishment can force public officials to behave ethically and to promote just government. Unless the public officials are guided by a sense of vocation, serving unto others, and accountability, it is impossible to expect a moral government. I have commented on this matter elsewhere:

> This belief holds that government is a public trust and public service is a vocation for persons who should know how to behave morally. Behaviour emanating from ideals associated with service as the highest calling includes possessing and exhibiting such virtues as honesty, impartiality, sincerity, and justice. Further, it is equally desirable that the conduct of public administrators should be beyond reproach; and that they should perform their duties loyally, efficiently, and economically. (Dwivedi 1995:297)

Moral lassitude is as undesirable in public life as it is in family life. This is why there is a constant need for spiritual guidance in secular affairs so that basic ethical ideals are sustained.

In the classical view of good governance, public service has always been an ideal. That classical view also includes such values as: probity, applying objective standards universally, willingness to speak the truth to Ministers (but also having readiness to carry out instructions to the contrary if overridden), and an appreciation of the wider common good, which is over and above the public interest, equity, and a constant concern for democratic ideals. Such is the duty of those who wish to be involved in the difficult and complex world of governance. This is the essence and basis of good governance.

Good Governance in the Multicultural World?

Sometimes, one will hear comments such as "what's wrong with the Third world," and "why do various efforts fail to modernize them?" Perhaps, five major reasons can be identified, if we consider the history of developing nations and Western efforts to "modernize" them. One is that development could only be attained by *modernization* (i.e., Westernization); that is to say, by the diffusion of Western values and technology. The second is that the predominant feature of development is *economic development*; the latter defined in terms of growth (i.e., the expansion of GNP per capita over a period of time). The third is that quantitative change (economic change) would produce a *critical mass* leading to qualitative changes. Sequentially, economic growth would bring about social changes that, in turn, would bring about political development. Structurally, an expansion of wealth in the hands of investor elites would trickle down, bringing generalized prosperity and a higher standard of living. The fourth theme is that once a region becomes developed, capital, technology, and ideas would bring development to other areas. The fifth developmental underpinning is the continuous pressure on developing nations to accept and implement various reforms (both institutional and socioeconomic) proposed by the West.

Despite such pressures, and much rhetoric, the style of governance has tended to be imitative and ritualistic. Practices, styles, and structures of administration generally unrelated to local traditions, needs, and realities succeeded in reproducing the symbolism, but not the substance, of a British, French, or American administrative system. Even where a relatively large contingent of trained functionaries existed, such as in India, Pakistan, Kenya, Nigeria, and Ghana, a continuation of colonial administrative culture prevailed. At the same time, a massive dose of political interference stifled developmental initiative. Confronted with an ineffectual developmental bureaucracy, the Western solution was to call for even more administrative development. This was also the preferred option of the local elites. Technical solutions were more palatable than the substantive political decisions needed to bring about real socioeconomic change. Administrative reorganizations and rationalizations for the sake of abstract principles soon became the ends rather than the means of development and administration.

However, something went wrong. An interpretative exploration as well as some general propositions can be offered:

(1) For years, Western scholars have been unable to include the alternatives in the form of non-Western contributions to developmental studies. Instead, it was expected that institutional imitation would easily produce similar results to those obtained in the West. Ethnocentrism and ignorance in the West have continued to overshadow the need to appreciate the importance of local culture, traditions, and the local style of accomplishing objectives. It is their style of governance and the

administrative culture that reflect the distinctiveness and complexity of their various national identities, realities, and cultural diversities. These factors should be taken into consideration when imposing conditionality. For example, we do know that the public expectations of government in the Third World are different from those prevailing in the West.

(2) The current circumstances and various global challenges directly affect the style of governance in these nations. The paradox has been that while demands on the public sector to provide more services are growing, the state apparatus in developing nations is being forced to shrink and retreat. It is also clear that in the name of globalization, certain dependence and continued reliance on the theory and methodology of the Western-style governance is being fostered on the developing nations with the emphasis on transplanting and replicating ideas and institutions of the West. As more and more Western values and practices predominate, with standards of performance based on the indicators developed in the West, an imitative and replicative system of public management is emerging in the rest of the world and public servants everywhere become a mirror image of the bureaucratic structures in Washington D.C., London, Paris, Bonn, and Ottawa.

(3) The Western-imposed public sector reform has created, in its wake, skewed management styles and structures that are unrelated to the prevailing cultural norms, needs, and realities, reproducing the symbolism but not the substance of Western administration. Thus, it is not surprising that the culture of governance in the Third World has tended to follow or, more precisely, has been forced to replicate the costly fads in the industrialized nations. We also know that any profound administrative reform entails significant attitudinal and value changes. Thus, efforts at administrative restructuring and "modernization" must first address, either directly or indirectly, the question of indigenous styles, values, and cultures of governance (Nef 1998). A lack of public morality leads to a proliferation of corruption, dishonesty, sleaziness, deception, and selfish individualism. As a result, good governance is difficult to attain. That is why the core values and moral principles of these nations must be reaffirmed. It is a truism that no nation or society, irrespective of its political system and religious orientation, can live in a moral vacuum.

The above discussion should not lead us to conclude that good governance is not possible in the Third World. Good govenance is attainable, but only if the holders of public offices are willing to acknowledge the moral responsibility for their actions as well as to accept accountability for such actions. Deflecting responsibility will not make action and its consequences disappear. Nothing is more damaging to public trust than justifying fraud and deception in the name of national security, government needs, or nation building. Problems are more pervasive at the top simply because it is there where more benefits can accrue or great loss is likely. Moral leadership must start at the top. The absence of such leadership breeds cynicism and generates tolerance of hypocrisy, greed, and self-indulgence. The state and society become the victims of those individuals holding public office who are unable to put the public business above their selfish inclinations.

For these countries, a persistent obstacle to good governance is the absence of moral leadership in general. Moral decay and double standards are reportedly pervasive both in the public place and in primary groups. "Righteousness" in public office is, of course, extremely difficult to define, just as it is hard to draw a line between public morality and private sin, or between public ethics and private conscience. In some cases, ethical lassitude in public offices may result partly from the absence of deterrence, but also partly from the increasing tendency to moral relativism resulting from rapid change and cultural disintegration. Political leaders frequently justify fraud and deception in the name of the self-serving principles of national security, government needs, economic rationality, or community demands. The absence of moral leadership at the top affects the entire state apparatus. Increasing moral disarray will affect the governing process of any developing country when people feel that dishonesty and corruption in the public life are endemic. In these countries, poverty, failed states, authoritarianism, turmoil, disintegration, and growing human insecurity provide the context for the collapse of moral standards and quality of public service. Of course, the developing world will have to set its house in order by controlling corruption, discontinuing unproductive public enterprises, and reforming the inefficient administrative system. Developing countries have a lot to change, and so does the West.

Concluding Observations

In the light of preceding analysis, one should ask a number of questions: Are the Western theories and practice of governance (the basic concepts, assumptions, and values) relevant for the entire world? How can various indigenously-developed alternatives more suited to tackling the satisfaction of people's basic needs, the eradication of poverty, and the protection of human dignity be implemented? Is it true that the current crisis of governance faced by many developing nations is precisely a consequence of the inability of the West to incorporate the substance of other non-Western developmental experiences into the prevailing conceptual mold? Finally, before another paradigm gets manufactured in the West (along with the notion that any problem can be solved by providing a detailed blueprint, promising some foreign aid, and insisting on changing the existing political equation on the part of a recipient nation), isn't it time to focus on results instead of continuing to create grand visions? Such grand visions continue to multiply as each international institution tries to broaden its idealism and scope of activities in the field of human development (Einhorn 2001). My view is that the new century demands new thinking in facing the greatest dilemma before humanity: Why do a small group of nations continually "progress," while the majority remains poor and deprived? Rather than theorize about how to install good governance (exported from the West), let the most basic and fundamental requisite be taken care of by the concerted efforts of the rich nations and the leaders of poor nations: stamp out starvation, destitution, inequality, and oppression. The framework suggested earlier, if applied with care and local support, might help to usher in an era of good governance.

REFERENCES

Caiden, Gerald E. and O. P. Dwivedi. 2001. "Official Ethics and Corruption." Pp. 245-255 in *Where Corruption Lives,* edited by Gerald Caiden, O. P. Dwivedi, and Joseph Jabbra. Bloomfield, CT: Kumarian Press.

Canada. 1979. *Royal Commission on Financial Management and Accountability*. Final Report. Ottawa: Government of Canada, Supply and Services.

Corry, J. A. and J. E. Hodgetts. 1957. *Democratic Government and Politics*. Toronto, Canada: University of Toronto Press.

Dwivedi, O. P. 1987. Moral Dimensions of Statecraft: A Plea for an Administrative Theology." *Canadian Journal of Political Science* 20(4):699-709.

———. 1995. "Reflections on Moral Government and Public Service as a Vocation." *Indian Journal of Public Administration* 41(3):296-306.

———. 2002. "On Common Good and Good Governance: An Alternative Approach." Pp.35-51 in *Better Governance and Public Policy: Capacity Building and Democratic Renewal in Africa,* edited by Dele Olowu and Soumana Sako. Bloomfield, CT, USA: Kumarian Press.

Dwivedi, O. P. and James Ian Gow. 1999. *From Bureaucracy to Public Management: The Administrative Culture of the Federal Government of Canada*. Peterborough, Canada: Broadview Press.

Dwivedi, O. P. and R. B. Jain. 1985. *India's Administrative State*. New Delhi, India: Gitanjali Publishing House.

Einhorn, Jessica. 2001. "The World Bank's Mission Creep." *Foreign Affairs* 80(5):22-35.

Frederickson, H. George. 1997. *The Spirit of Public Administration*. San Francisco, CA: Jossey-Bass Publishers.

Hood, Christopher and Michael Jackson. 1994. "Keys For Locks in Administrative Argument." *Administration and Society* 25(4):467-488.

Hyden, G. 1992. "The Study of Governance." Pp. 1-26 in *Governance and Politics in Africa,* edited by G. Hyden and M. Bratton. Boulder, CO, USA: Lynne Rienner.

Hyden, Goran and Julius Court. 2002. "Comparing Governance Across Countries and Over time: Conceptual Challenges." Pp. 13-34 in *Better Governance and Public Policy: Capacity Building and Democratic Renewal in Africa,* edited by Dele Olowu and Soumana Sako. Bloomfield, CT, USA: Kumarian Press.

Jabbra, Joseph G. and O. P. Dwivedi, eds. 1987. *Public Service Accountability: Comparative Perspectives.* West Hartford, CT, USA: Kumarian Press.

Lasswell, Harold D. 1956. *Politics: Who Gets What, When, How.* New York: Meridian Books.

Nef, Jorge. 1998. "Administrative Culture in Latin America: Historical and Structural Outline." *Africanus* 28(2):19-32.

Saint-Martin, Denis. 1998. "The New Managerialism and the Policy Influence of Consultants in Government: A Historical-Institutionalist Analysis of Britain, Canada and France." *Governance: An International Journal of Policy and Administration* 11(3):319-356.

Sen, Amartya. 1999. *Development as Freedom.* New York, NY: Alfred A. Knopf.

Tendler, Judith. 1997. *Good Government in the Tropics.* Baltimore, USA: Johns Hopkins University Press.

UNDP. 1998. *Good Governance and Sustainable Human Development*, New York, NY: UNDP (http://www.undp.org//docs/un98-1.pdf).

Woodhouse, Diana. 1997. *In Pursuit of Good Administration.* New York, NY: Oxford University Press.

World Bank. 1992. *Governance and Development: The World Development Report.* Washington DC: The World Bank.

———. 1994. *The World Development Report.* Washington, DC: The World Bank.

———. 1997. *The World Development Report.* Washington, DC: The World Bank.

INDEX

A

Abdo-Khalil, Z., 140, 150
Abussuud, A.N., 144, 148, 150
Adamolekun, L., 191, 195, 199, 204
Adie, R., 241, 243
Africa, 49, 189-192, 194-200, 202, 204-206, 247-248, 268, 283-284
African Development, 189, 202, 204-206
African National Congress, 213
Ahmed, M., 168, 172-173
Akhiezer, A., 132
Akhund, I., 162, 172
Al-Ahram, 142, 150-151
Al-Awaji, I.M., 138, 140, 142, 145-146, 148, 150
Al-Bilani, B., 140, 147, 150
Al-Farsi, F., 136, 151
Al-Ghamdi, A.A., 139, 142-143, 151
Al-Haj, L., 146, 151
Al-Hegelan, A., 141, 143, 149, 151
Ali, A.H., 156, 173
Al-Khaldi, A.M., 141-142, 146, 148, 151
Al-Mazrua, S.A., 138, 151
Almond, G., 39, 55
Alnimir, S., 142-143, 146, 148, 151
Al-Sadhan, A., 142, 151
Al-Salami, A., 143, 151
Al-Tawail, M.A., 147, 151
Altman, Y., 155, 172
Americans with Disabilities Act, 46
Anechiarico, F., 37, 55
An-Nahar, 143, 145, 151-152
Anthropology, 37
Apartheid, 207-209, 211, 213-215, 217, 222, 224, 227, 229
Appleby, P., 43, 55
Argentina, 236, 243
Argyris, C., 216, 229
Arrighi, G., 4, 17
Ashkanasy, 39, 55, 57
Asia, 49, 115, 125, 194, 206, 247, 268
Astley, W.G., 31, 34
Attrabi, H.A., 143, 151
Australia, 15, 55, 248-253, 258, 265, 269
Ayee, J., 202, 204
Ayubi, N., 137, 140-143, 146-148, 150-151
Aziz, J., 190-191, 205
Azrael, J., 121, 123, 132

INDEX

B

Bailey, S., 43, 55
Baldwin, R., 1, 17
Ban, C., 232, 243
Barber, W., 237, 243
Bashir, I., 140, 148, 150-151
Beech, H., 185-187
Beijing, 184-185, 187-188
Belgian Council of State, 84
Belgium, 13, 75-79, 81, 84-85, 87, 89, 91, 96-98, 100-101, 103, 106-108
Bensabat, R., 241, 245
Berg, E.J., 195, 204
Bergeron, G., 22, 34
Bernard, C.I., 29, 34
Bhutto, Z.A., 157, 162, 168-170, 172-173
Binsaleh, A.M., 141-142, 152
Black, J., 238, 243-244
Blair, T., 61, 65-71, 73
Bollens, J., 179, 187
Bolshevik Revolution, 109, 114
Bouvier, P., 80-81, 85, 107
Bozeman, B., 38, 55
Braibanti, R., 156, 159, 163-164, 172
Brazil, 121, 236-237, 243
Bribery, 174, 183
Bribosia, H., 82, 107
British Civil Service, 58, 59, 61, 63, 66, 71, 72, 73
Brokgauz, F.A., 109, 132
Bruce, W., 27
Bureaucracy, 246, 256, 260, 265, 267, 274, 278, 280, 283
Burger King, 6
Burns, E., 232-235, 238, 243
Butcher, T., 65, 73

C

Caiden, G., 15, 19, 34, 37, 55-56, 176-177, 184, 187, 246-247, 251-252, 264, 278, 283
Cambridge, 158, 172
Campos, R., 240, 243
Canada, 3, 15, 17, 32, 34-35, 37, 56, 248-253, 258, 265, 269-270, 278, 283-284
Catherine II the Great, 113
Chackerian, R., 140, 149, 152
Chan, C., 8, 17
Chapman, R.A., 61, 73
Charlick-Paley, T., 125, 133

INDEX

Chechnya, 122
Cheema, S., 5, 17
Chidiac, M., 13, 75, 103, 106-107
Chile, 236, 241, 243
China, 129, 174-179, 181-188
CIA, 46, 113, 116, 118, 120-121, 124, 131-132
Civil Service Reform Act, 47
Civil War, 41, 45, 143, 145
Clark, D., 93, 94, 107
Clinton, W., 52, 56, 268
CNN, 122
Cold War, 41, 236, 241
Columbia, 163
Conant, E., 130, 132
Corruption, 135, 140, 143-144, 146-147, 152, 154, 168-174, 176-184, 187, 193-194, 199, 202, 234, 237-239, 243, 268-269, 271-272, 281-283
Corry, J.A., 266, 283
Costa Rica, 163, 236, 240
Council of Europe, 82, 84
Court, J., 194, 205, 266-267, 284
Cray, D., 155, 172
Cuban Revolution, 236

D

D'Orville, H., 3, 17
Dahl, M.K., 215, 230
Deal, T.E., 155-156, 159-160, 163, 165, 170, 172
Democracy, 39, 43, 45, 56, 75-78, 89-90, 97, 103, 208, 214-215, 218-219, 221, 226, 230, 237-238, 242-245, 247, 250, 260-261, 270, 275, 278
Denationalization, 237, 238
Denhardt, A., 55-56
Denhardt, R., 55-56
Denmark, 97, 114, 160
Deontology, 25
Department of Defense, 42
Deregulation, 237-238
Deresky, H., 154, 172
Devas, N., 195, 205
Djilas, M., 183, 187
Dresang, D., 44, 56
Drewry, G., 8, 17
Dunsire, A., 30, 34
Dwivedi, O.P., 1, 7, 9, 12, 16-17, 19-20, 23, 25-27, 30-31, 34-35, 37, 55-56, 208, 230, 237, 242, 245, 265-266, 268, 272, 274, 276, 278-279, 283-284

INDEX

E

Eagles, M., 39, 56
Economic Development, 236, 244
Economic Growth, 202, 206
Ecuador, 163
Efron, I.A., 109, 132
Egypt, 137, 140-141, 150-151, 153
Einhorn, J., 283
Elazar, D., 40, 56
Elbadawi, I., 205
El-Fathali, O., 149, 152
Engelbert, E.A., 35
Equality, 26
Equity, 26-27, 30
Europe, 41, 45, 54, 146, 240, 247, 253, 268
European Parliament, 84, 95, 98
European Union, 54, 82, 84, 98, 104-105, 107

F

Farazmand, A., 139, 152
Farsoun, S.K., 139, 152
Favoritism, 144
FBI, 46
Federalism, 43, 56
Finland, 97, 160
Fox, W., 209, 216, 221, 230
Fradkov, M., 118
France, 13, 75-78, 81, 88, 91, 93-94, 96-99, 101-103, 107-108, 125, 265, 269, 284
Frederickson, H.G., 266, 283
Friedman, T.L., 2, 4, 17
Fulton Report, 59-60, 74
Furtado, C., 236, 244

G

Gable, R.W., 158, 172
Gaebler, T., 52, 57
Garreton, M.A., 237, 244
Gatley, S., 155, 172
George Washington, 44
Germany, 23, 121, 178
Germany, C., 45
Ghana, 194-195, 200, 202, 204, 206, 280
Gibson, P.A., 186-187

INDEX

Gil, B., 238, 244
Gilpin, R., 2, 17
Golden, M.M., 52, 56
Golpen, S., 198, 206
Goodnow, F.W., 23
Goodsell, C., 49, 51, 56
Gouldner, A., 234, 244
Governance, 265
Gow, J.I., 7, 17, 23, 31, 34-35, 37, 56, 265, 274, 283
Graf, W.D., 235, 244
Grassmuck, G., 136, 140, 142, 152
Gratchev, M., 112, 132
Gray, J., 213, 230
Greece, 165
Greenwood, J., 12, 58, 73-74
Greider, W., 4, 17
Grey, S., 169, 172
Grosenick, L.E., 186-187
Guatemala, 160, 163
Guillen, M., 35

H

Hampden-Turner, C., 155
Haque, N.U., 190-191, 205
Hauriou, M., 75, 107
Heady, F., 240, 244
Helliwell, J.F., 5, 17
Henderson, K.M., 12, 37, 53, 56
Hennessy, P., 27, 35
Hodgetts, J.E., 266, 283
Hofstede, G., 23, 35, 38, 56, 109, 132, 154-156, 160, 162-163, 165, 166, 172-173
Homeland Security, 42, 47, 51, 53
Hong Kong, 129
Hood, C., 274, 283
Horner, C., 41, 56
Huang, B., 181, 187
Huddleston, M.W., 54, 56
Hughes, K.B., 228, 230
Human Rights, 75-76, 83-84, 104, 108
Hummel, R., 49, 56
Hussain, A., 157, 169, 172
Hyden, G., 266-267, 284

INDEX

I

India, 1, 7-8, 37, 57, 158, 246, 264, 270, 280, 283
Indonesia, 4
Industrialization, 235-237, 243
Ingraham, P.W., 40-41, 56
Internal Revenue Service, 38
International Monetary Fund, 54, 256
Iran, 139, 152
Iraq, 49, 53-54
Iskandar, A., 148, 151-152
Islam, N., 14, 154, 157-158, 172-173
Israel, 15, 37, 55, 139, 153, 246-247, 250-253, 264
Italy, 178
Ivan IV the Terrible, 113

J

Jabbra, J.G., 1, 13, 55-56, 135, 145-147, 150, 152, 276, 283-284
Jabbra, N.W., 13, 135, 145-147, 150, 152
Jackson, M., 274, 283
Jacoby, D., 90, 107
Jaguaribe, H., 233, 244
Jain, R.B., 276, 283
Japan, 3, 166
Javidan, M., 132
Jiabao, W., 186
Jintao, H., 186-187
Jizhou, L., 174
Johnston, L., 39, 56
Jreisat, J.E., 135, 152
Justice, 26, 28-31

K

Kalb, D., 5, 17, 18
Karatnycky, A., 131, 133
Kasyanov, M., 118
Kaunda, K., 219
Keen, B., 233-234, 244
Kejie, C., 174, 183
Kennedy, C.H., 155, 157, 160, 172-173
Kenya, 190, 194, 280
Keraudren, P., 37, 56
Kettl, D., 41, 56
Khan, A.H., 160, 173

INDEX

Kievan Rus, 113, 115
Kiggundu, M.N., 2, 3, 5, 6, 18, 203, 205
Kiragu, K., 191, 194, 196, 199, 204-205
Kisirwani, M.Y., 136, 145, 147, 152
Kluckhohn, C., 154, 173
Kluckhorn, A., 209, 210
Klyuchevskiy, V., 112, 133
Kochanek, S.A., 163, 164, 173
Korchagina, V., 133
Korea, 37, 57
Korninghauer, L.G., 145, 152
Kravchuk, R., 55, 57
Krislov, S., 47, 56
Kristen, P., 194, 205
Kroeber, A.L., 154, 173, 209-210, 230
Kryshtanovskaya, O., 131, 133
Kuhn, A., 174, 187

L

Lasswell, H.D., 266, 284
Latin America, 15, 49, 53, 194, 198, 232-233, 237, 239-245, 247
Laveissière, J., 75-76, 88, 107
Law Enforcement, 174, 178, 184
Lawrence, P., 112, 133
Le Rendu, J., 88, 107
Lebanon, 136-137, 141-147, 151-153
Lee, R.W., 238, 244
Leila, A., 140, 148, 153
Lessem, R., 155, 172
Lewis, R., 112, 133
Li, Z., 174, 177-179, 183, 187
Liaoning Province, 177, 183
Liberalization, 11, 16
Lienert, I., 194, 205
Lindauer, D., 190, 205
Lipsky, G.A., 145-146, 152
Lungu, G.F., 227, 230
Luo, B., 178, 187
Luvuno, L., 15, 207

M

Ma, S.K., 14, 174-175, 183, 187
Magna Carta, 216
Major, J., 60, 62, 65-67, 69, 70-72

INDEX

Malaysia, 121, 258
Mallory, G.R., 155, 172
Malloy, J., 239, 244-245
Mandela, N., 226
Manzer, R., 31, 35
Maree, J., 217, 219, 230
Martin, J., 38, 39, 56
Martin, P., 1, 17
Masculinity-Femininity Dimension, 166
Mathews, B., 215, 230
Mauritius, 194
Mazari, S.K., 162, 173
Mbingi, L., 217, 219, 230
McDonald's, 6
McFaul, M., 117, 133
Meehan, E.T., 215, 230
Mexico, 4, 17, 236
Meyer, H., 209, 230
Middle East, 1, 49, 125, 135, 247
Mikhail Gorbachev, 3
Milanovic, B., 1, 18
Mills, C.W., 232, 244
Milvain, J.V., 99, 107
Mite, V., 132-133
Moore, B., 237, 244
Moore, M., 198, 205
Morality, 25-30
Moreno, F.J., 233, 244
Morstein-Marx, F., 239, 244
Mosher, F.C., 35, 196, 205
MSNBC, 122
Mukandala, R., 191, 196, 199, 205
Munla, H., 140, 152
Murad, M.W., 143, 153
Mutahaba, G., 194, 205

N

Nadel, M., 185, 187
Nakib, K.A., 140, 142-144, 148, 153
Nationalism, 233, 235, 237, 241
Nef, J., 15, 20, 33, 35, 232, 237-239, 241-242, 244-245, 281, 284
Nepotism, 144-145
Nevitte, N., 35
New Public Management, 19, 25, 32, 40, 42, 52, 54-55, 265, 269, 272, 274
New Zealand, 55, 97, 248, 258, 262

INDEX

Nigeria, 190, 192, 194, 205, 280
Ninnian, P.P., 213, 230
Nisbett, R.E., 41, 57
Nixon, R., 268
North America, 146, 232, 240
North Korea, 258
North, L., 237, 245
Northcote-Trevelyan, 58-60, 64, 67, 72-74
Norway, 97, 160
Novinson, J., 27, 36
Numberg, B., 190, 205
Nun, J., 235, 245

O

O'Donnell, G., 237, 243-244
Oakes, D., 218, 230
Oliker, O., 125, 133
Olowu, B., 14, 189-191, 194-196, 204-206
Orthodox Church, 112-113, 117
Osbourne, D., 52, 57
Otobo, E.E., 14, 189, 201, 206
Ott, J.S., 178, 187
Oxford, 158, 172-173

P

Paik, W., 37, 57
Pakistan, 14, 154-158, 160-173, 280
Palestine, 250
Palmer, M., 140, 143, 148, 151, 153
Pan African Congress, 213
Panama, 160
Paquet, A., 108
Paul, S., 150, 153
Pentagon, 42
People's Republic of China, 174-175
Perfilev, Y., 120, 133
Peter I the Great, 113
Peters, G., 176, 187
Peterson, D., 121, 123, 132
Peterson, M., 39, 55, 57
Pettigrew, A., 38, 57
Philosophy, 26, 32
Phiri-Mundia, B., 194, 206
Pinay, A., 90, 108

INDEX

Plant, J.F., 179, 187
Poitras, G., 241, 243
Pomfret, J., 177-178, 183, 186-187
Pope John Paul II, 3
Poverty, 3, 4, 6-7, 11, 17, 192, 202
Privatization, 237-238, 243
Prussia, 114
Public Management, 19, 24-25, 30-35
Public Servants, 24-27, 29-30, 32, 33
Putin, V., 116, 119-128, 130-133
Pye, L.W., 175, 187

Q

Qinglian, H., 174

R

Rakitski, B., 112, 132
Rakner, L., 198, 206
Ratnesar, R., 185, 187
Rautenbach, I., 213, 230
Reagan, R., 7
Redding, S.G., 155, 173
Religion, 26, 45
Revolutionary War, 43
Riccucci, N., 51, 57
Riggs, F., 239, 245
Riley, R., 44, 57
Rio Grande, 232
Robbins, S.P., 186, 188
Robertson, I., 154, 173
Robins, L., 12, 58
Rocamora, J., 238, 244
Rogovsky, N., 112, 132
Rohr, J., 31, 35
Roman Empire, 1
Ronning, N., 237, 243
Rosenbloom, D., 55, 57
Rouban, L., 196, 206
Rourke, F., 185, 187
Russia, 4, 13, 109-110, 112-134, 270

S

Sadik, M.T., 142, 153
Saint-Martin, D., 265, 284

INDEX

Sako, S., 194, 204, 206
Salem, E.A., 137, 141, 144, 147, 153
Salibi, K., 136, 140, 142, 152
Sanders, R., 41, 56
SARS, 185-187
Saudi Arabia, 125, 137, 141-142, 146-147, 149-153, 170
Sayre, W., 35
Schaeffer, R.K., 2-4, 18
Schein, E., 38, 57
Schein, T., 209, 230
Schiavo-Campo, S., 194-195, 206
Schmandt, H.J., 179, 187
Scotland, 61, 68
Sen, A., 267, 284
Serbinenko, D., 129
Shackleton, V.J., 156, 173
Shadukhi, S., 140, 152
Shah, S., 170, 173
Sharma, R.D., 37, 57
Shein, V., 13, 109
Shengyang, 177-178, 183
Singapore, 125, 129, 258
Singer, M., 21, 36
Sissons, R., 248
Smoke, P., 196, 206
Smucker, J., 232, 245
Social Equity, 208, 210-211, 216
Soloviev, S., 112
Sondargaard, M., 155, 173
Soros, G., 4-5, 18
South Africa, 15, 192, 194, 207-211, 213-219, 223-230, 248
South Korea, 125, 129, 258
Soviet Union, 1, 247
Spain, 97
Spirituality, 26-30, 33, 36
Squire, P.J., 215, 230
Stalin, J., 113-115, 130
Stenmans, A., 76-80, 85, 91, 107-108
Stevens, M., 191, 195, 206
Sundaram, P., 194-195, 206
Sweden, 76, 84, 97, 160, 166
Syal, R., 169, 172

T

Taft, K., 212, 230
Taiwan, 129

INDEX

Tanzania, 190, 194, 206
Tapscott, C., 227, 230
Tawati, A.M., 138, 142, 144, 149, 153
Taylor, C., 131, 134
Teffo, G.N., 215, 231
Teggenmann, S., 191, 195, 206
Tendler, J., 268, 284
Terrorism, 123, 241
Thailand, 4
Thatcher, M., 7, 61-71, 74
Theakston, K., 74
Thibault, A., 95, 108
Tobback, L., 91, 108
Tomlin Report, 59, 74
Trompenaar, A., 155, 172
Trosa, S., 94, 108
Turkey, 139, 250

U

U.S. Department of State, 114, 118, 134
Ubuntu, 207-211, 217-218, 230
Uganda, 194-195, 200, 205
United Kingdom, 23, 32, 91, 94, 96-97, 125, 159, 179, 240, 247-252
United Nations Development Program, 3, 270
United Nations, 3, 18, 76, 83, 104, 108, 193, 204-206, 257
United States, 1, 3, 6-7, 12, 23, 32, 37, 39-42, 45, 49-50, 53-55, 57, 59-61, 113, 120-121, 123, 125, 127, 129, 131, 133-134, 147, 159, 163, 181, 249, 252-253, 258, 265, 269
Urbanization, 235, 242
Uruguay, 236, 241, 243

V

Van de Ven, A., 31, 34
Van Riper, P., 43, 57
Vartanova, E., 132
Venezuela, 163
Verba, S., 39, 55
Verwoerd, H.F., 217, 231
Vilas, C., 238, 245
Violence, 234, 238
Vlachoutsicos, C., 112, 133

W

Waldo, D., 26, 36, 41, 57, 179, 188
Wales, 61, 68

INDEX

War on Terror, 42
Warner, S.E., 142, 153
Washington Post, 42, 57
Weber, M., 246, 256, 259-260
Weder, B., 194, 205
Western Europe, 3, 7
Wiener, C., 108
Wiess, A.M., 163-164, 167, 173
Wilderom, C., 39, 55, 57
Willa, B., 27, 36
Wilson Report, 68-69, 71
Wilson, J.Q., 175, 188
Wilson, R., 62, 68-69, 71, 73-74, 238, 244
Wilson, W., 23, 36
Wissink, H.F., 216, 221, 230
Woller, G.M., 215, 231
Woodhouse, D., 272-273, 284
World Bank, 54, 160-161, 170-171, 173, 190-191, 198, 200, 205-206, 266, 283-284
World Trade Center, 42
World Trade Organization, 3, 127, 256
World War I, 1, 41
World War II, 1, 19, 41, 48, 54, 76, 97, 139, 141

X

Xiaoping, D., 175, 186

Y

Yahoo, 122
Yassin, E., 140, 148, 153
Young, M., 196, 206

Z

Zaidi, M., 169, 173
Zambia, 194, 200, 206
Zhuplev, A., 13, 109
Ziring, L., 160, 168, 173

Printed in the United States
40190LVS00002B/5-34